American Business Values

With International Perspectives

FOURTH EDITION

American Business Values

With International Perspectives

Gerald F. Cavanagh, S.J.

*Charles T. Fisher III Chair of Business Ethics,
Professor of Management, and Chancellor
University of Detroit Mercy*

PRENTICE HALL, UPPER SADDLE RIVER, NJ   07458

Executive Editor: *Natalie Anderson*
Associate Editor: *Lisamarie Brassini*
Editorial Assistant: *Dawn-Marie Reisner*
Editor-in-Chief: *James Boyd*
Marketing Manager: *Stephanie Johnson*
Production Editor: *Maureen Wilson*
Managing Editor: *Dee Josephson*
Manufacturing Buyer: *Diane Peirano*
Manufacturing Supervisor: *Arnold Vila*
Manufacturing Manager: *Vincent Scelta*
Composition: *Rainbow Graphics, Inc.*
Copyeditor: *Joan Pokorny*

Copyright © 1998, 1990, 1984, 1976 by Prentice-Hall, Inc.
A Simon & Schuster Company
Upper Saddle River, New Jersey 07458

Library of Congress Cataloging-in-Publication Data
Cavanagh, Gerald F.
    American business values : with international perspectives / by
Gerald F. Cavanagh. — 4th ed.
        p.   cm.
    Includes bibliographical references.
    ISBN 0-13-518234-4
    1. Business ethics—United States.   2. Industries—Social aspects—
United States.   3. Social responsibility of business.   4. Free
enterprise—United States.   5. United States—Commerce.   I. Title.
HF5387.C379   1998
174′.4′0973—dc21   97-2915
                                                                          CIP

Prentice-Hall International (UK) Limited, *London*
Prentice-Hall of Australia Pty. Limited, *Sydney*
Prentice-Hall Canada Inc., *Toronto*
Prentice-Hall Hispanoamericana, S.A., *Mexico*
Prentice-Hall of India Private Limited, *New Delhi*
Prentice-Hall of Japan, Inc., *Tokyo*
Simon & Schuster Asia Pte. Ltd., *Singapore*
Editora Prentice-Hall do Brasil, Ltda., *Rio de Janeiro*

Printed in the United States of America

10 9 8 7 6 5 4 3 2

Contents

CHAPTER 4   Historical Roots of Business Values   106

Preface

American Business Values, with International Perspectives, 4th ed., probes the values and ethics of business and businesspeople. Values and ethics have a profound impact on the effectiveness of leadership, new products, product quality, productivity, work-place design, on-the-job relationships, and government regulations. Values thus have a pivotal influence on all people and on all firms. Moreover, business and work are so important in our lives that they in turn heavily influence our personal values, goals, and life styles. Our primary focus will be on American business values, but we will also examine how those values are influencing people throughout the world, and how American values are in turn being influenced by other peoples.

The purpose of this book is:

1. To help each person articulate his or her own personal values and goals;
2. To study ethical behavior within the firm, as it influences people, products, and the work environment;
3. To provide language, tools, and practice for doing ethical analysis, and to suggest how good moral habits can be developed;
4. To better understand the values, ethics, and beliefs upon which the free market system of production and exchange is built;
5. To help all men and women clarify their own role as well as the appropriate role of business and government in society.

Most agree that both business and government must take a long-range view in order to meet the demands of the global marketplace. Effective long-range planning demands ethics and values that respect the needs of all stakeholders.

Policies and plans that benefit a firm in the long-term require a consensus of people within that organization. That consensus can be built when they understand the mission of the firm and traditional business values, such that those values can be nurtured and also altered to meet new challenges. Creativity gives business its energy and success, but we also recognize the power of historical traditions, values, and beliefs. Hence, both traditional business values and the challenges to these values will be presented here.

I have great respect and affection for the free market system. Energetic and creative entrepreneurs, managers, and workers with a long-term perspective are required in order for business to be effective. I confess another bias: the central importance of *each* individual person. Every business decision, action, and policy should be made considering the best interests of *all* who are touched by that decision: customers, employees, suppliers, shareholders, neighbors, and the larger community. Shareholders are but one of many stakeholders of the firm. Not to be neglected are the unemployed, unskilled, and the poor; they are clearly stakeholders of society, but they are also stakeholders of the firm.

On a personal note, I was academic vice president and provost of University of Detroit when in 1990 it merged with Mercy College of Detroit to become the University of Detroit Mercy. I helped to develop a new mission statement, select new deans and vice presidents, and oversee 250 volunteer faculty and staff who worked on 30 committees to design the curriculum, standards, processes, and structure of the new university. I saw how a clear and compelling mission, talented leaders, wide consultation, and good communication brought energy to the university. I also witnessed the importance of shared values and ethics, which brought energy, consensus, and success to this new university.

This fourth edition of *American Business Values: with International Perspectives* retains the best elements of the third edition, yet adds important new features. Chapter 1 surveys current business problems, such as downsizing, takeovers, advertising, sexual harassment, pollution, and global operations. Chapter 2 examines how personal moral development takes place, as well as the stress that many face at work. Chapter 3 shows how ethical behavior benefits the firm, and how virtue can be encouraged. Chapters 2 and 3 have both been moved forward in the book so they can be used in analyzing cases. Chapters 4 and 5 probe the historical roots of American business. Chapter 6 critiques the free market system from traditional and more recent perspectives. Chapter 7 examines the influence of the organization on the values and beliefs of the individual. Chapter 8 describes how values and ethics affect the performance of the firm. Chapter 9 investigates mission statements and business planning, and projects some changes in future business values and beliefs. At the end of each chapter are questions for discussion, brief cases, and exercises.

This book is the result of research and enriching dialogue with many colleagues: businesspeople, scholars, students, and brother Jesuits. Gene Donahue, Allen Gray, and Tracy White provided very helpful comments on this fourth edition. It has also benefited from the insights of faculty who provided comments on earlier editions: Martin Calkins, Philip Cochran, Otto Bremmer, Kirk Hanson, Manuel Velasquez, Kristin Aronson, and John Fleming. Graduate assistants Romero Tavares from Brazil and Bernadette Kakooza from Uganda helped with research; Bernadette also prepared the index. Thanks to Deans Gregory

Ulferts and Bahman Mirshab and the College of Business Administration of the University of Detroit Mercy for their support for this project, and to the following for their helpful reviews: Susan Fox-Wolfgram, San Francisco State University; Don Huffman, Cedar Crest College; and James Wanek, University of Minnesota, Minneapolis. Thanks to Maureen Wilson, who edited the manuscript, and special thanks to Natalie Anderson, Senior Executive Editor at Prentice Hall, who from the very beginning has been a great help and encouragement for this fourth edition.

Gerald F. Cavanagh, S.J.
Charles T. Fisher III Chair of Business Ethics
Professor of Management and Chancellor
University of Detroit Mercy
Detroit, Michigan

American Business Values

With International Perspectives

CHAPTER

1

A Free Market
for Ethical Values

*Is it enough for Harvard to attract the brightest students, if we do not excel
in making them caring, active, enlightened citizens and civic leaders?*
—Derek Bok, President, Farewell Address

Entrepreneurs and business managers set the tone of our society. They provide the products, services, and jobs that we need. Bill Gates and Michael Jordan are extremely successful and highly rewarded businesspeople. Though different, they both heavily influence our values. A businessperson's values influence treatment of colleagues and customers and ultimately determine one's success or failure. Businesspeople in most nations today are models for behavior, both good and bad. Values in the United States have been heavily influenced by business; these same influences are now common in other nations, also. Because free enterprise is now dominant all over the world, many other peoples are being pulled, sometimes reluctantly, toward these same values.

American business is considered the archetype of business by people from other continents. English has become the language of business. Americans have the largest markets and, for better or worse, have an extraordinary influence on business and personal values. We recognize that values vary from one country to another. So we will focus here on American business values, so that American and other businesspeople may better understand their own values and goals.

In this book we will examine the values, ethics, and beliefs of American business and businesspeople. Whether one can trust an unwritten promise, or how one will be treated as a worker, depends on managers' values and ethics.

Business values and ethics have a profound impact on our lives, including new products, product quality, productivity, workplace design, relationships among colleagues at work, and government regulations. People's values and their ethics hold together the fabric of a firm's culture, and that culture ultimately determines a firm's success or failure. Moreover, work and the business firm are so central to our lives that they in turn strongly influence our personal goals and life-styles.

This first chapter will explore ways in which values and ethics affect our lives and businesses. Later chapters will go into detail on how we develop moral maturity, make ethical choices, and the history behind our business values. For a definition of some important terms, see Figure 1–1.

Values govern actions and personality. They undergird and direct the important decisions that an individual makes. Whether acknowledged or not, values profoundly influence our choices and our lives. To know one's values allows one to possess greater control over one's own actions and future.

A value system is at the foundation of personal and business decisions. Yet values become so much a part of us that we are generally unaware of their content and impact. An analogy might help. Consider the way we drive an automobile. As we learn to drive, the procedure becomes increasingly habitual or automatic. Gradually, driving becomes so much a part of us that we become explicitly aware of it only when we take time to reflect on our actions. Yet without our knowing that procedure, it would be impossible to drive. Similarly, without a value system or ideology, it is impossible to make consistent and reasonable decisions. To not grasp the importance of values prevents one from fully understanding one's own actions and the actions of others. This chapter will examine some business firms and current business practices, focusing on the values that undergird them.

FIGURE 1–1 Values and Ethics Terms

Ethics: The principles of conduct governing an individual or a group, and the methods for applying them.

Goal: The result toward which effort is directed; the end to be pursued.

Ideal: An ultimate aim that an individual or a society holds for itself; a standard of perfection.

Ideology: A cluster of values integrated into a comprehensive, coherent, motivating statement of purpose.

Moral: Dealing with or capable of distinguishing right from wrong.

Norm: Criterion for distinguishing what is right from what is wrong, and what is correct from what is incorrect.

Morality: The rightness or wrongness of principles, practices, and activities, along with the values and rules that govern them.

Value: A lasting belief that a certain goal or mode of conduct is better than the opposite goal or conduct.

FREEDOM AND MARKETS

Free enterprise values are familiar to each of us. Freedom is a foundation value of the economy: free markets, free movement of people, free entry into new businesses, freedom to take or leave a job. This freedom parallels the freedom that we cherish in political democracy. The free enterprise system, stimulated by freedom, provides many benefits to Americans:

1. An immense output of goods and services.
2. High standards of living available to the majority.
3. The 37 million new jobs that have been created in the United States in the last 15 years.[1]
4. The considerable rewards that come from the skill, new ideas, and initiative of entrepreneurs.
5. Encouragement of flexibility and innovation among people.
6. The reinforcement of personal freedom.

Yet in spite of these many successes of free enterprise, there are difficulties. It is vital to acknowledge and honestly address these difficulties, if we expect to improve our businesses and our lives. The values and goals that undergird our actions will be our focus. A better understanding of our values will enable us to improve ourselves and our performance.

LIVING FOR TODAY

Americans consume much and save little. We purchase cars and VCRs and go into debt to pay for them. Many prefer to purchase using their credit card, then cannot fully pay at the monthly billing time, and then pay 18 percent interest. Average credit card debt now is over $3,000, and at the present rate credit card debt doubles every 5 years.

Advertising encourages our need to possess things and thus to demonstrate to others our success. Success and a better life is measured in more goods: a bigger house, more expensive car, and club memberships. Consumer debt has surged to an average of 21 percent of total annual income (not including mortgages and equity loans on homes). Personal debt and personal bankruptcies are also currently at very high levels. Over one million Americans filed for personal bankruptcy in 1996, and the average amount that they owed at bankruptcies also skyrocketed to $135,000.[2]

---

[1] The U.S. Bureau of Labor Statistics arrived at this figure by subtracting the 43 million jobs eliminated from the 70 million new jobs created. Quoted in "Economic Change: Separating Fact from Fiction," *Workforce Economics*, June 1996, p. 3.

[2] "Personal Bankruptcies Surging as Economy Hums," *New York Times*, August 25, 1996, pp. 1, 15.

Our high rate of consumption and high debt means that our savings rate is too low. Since we save so little, we have too little capital for investment in critically needed new plants, equipment, and research. This forces interest rates up, making new investment expensive and thus more difficult. We are very far behind other developed countries in our rate of saving. Japanese save five times what Americans save, yet they have only one-half the number of people. Italians, French, and Germans all save more than three times the proportion of their personal income as do Americans.[3] We are a "buy now, pay later" culture, handing the bill for our purchases to future generations. Excessive consumption, little saving, and increasing debt result from short-sighted values.

Debt and Consumption

We demand more capital in the United States than we are able to provide ourselves. The national debt that accumulated from 1981 to 1995 is twice the total debt accumulated during the previous 200 years. Interest costs make up an immense portion of the annual federal budget. The fiscal year 1996 U.S. federal budget would be in surplus if it were not for the interest costs due to past overspending. Our children undoubtedly will resent paying the interest on that debt as well as the debt itself, from which they will gain no benefit. From 1982 to the present, the United States went from being the world's largest creditor to the world's largest debtor nation. Now people from other nations lend us larger sums so we can buy their goods, consume more than we produce and invest more than we save. Not only the federal government but also corporations and individuals have accumulated immense debt to foreign interests. This evidence might indicate that we Americans care more about our own comfort than about the future of our country or our children. Our priorities appear to be centered on ourselves.

In the United States we witness the very rich becoming richer and most people becoming poorer. During the last 15 years, the wealthiest are the only ones who have increased their real income. The share of total personal income earned by the richest 1 percent of American families more than doubled, while the real income of the bottom 60 percent of families declined.[4] Some think that this gap increased only during the 1980s, but the gap between the rich and the poor continues to widen. In contrast, in Britain and Sweden in the last 50 years the share of net worth of the top 1 percent of households has dropped by one-half. However, in the United States the share of net worth of the wealthiest 1 percent of households declined from 1930 to 1978, but now is higher than any time in the last 50

---

[3] *Statistical Abstract of the United States—1994* (Washington, D.C.: U.S. Department of Commerce, 1994), p. 522 for credit card debt; p. 863 for rates of saving. The figures on Japanese savings are from James Fallows, National Public Radio, October 11, 1995.

[4] "Inequality: Still on the Rise," *U.S. News & World Report*, July 1, 1996, p. 15; also "Why the Income Gap Won't Go Away," *Fortune*, December 11, 1995, pp. 65–70; Jim Hightower, "Where Greed, Unofficially Blessed by Reagan, Has Led," *New York Times*, June 21, 1987, p. E25.

years.[5] Some complain that they cannot maintain their life-styles on $400,000 per year. At the same time, two out of five Hispanic children and three out of five African American children live in poverty in families with total incomes of less than $20,000. The exorbitant incomes of Bill Gates, Michael Jordan, chief executive officers, professional athletes, and other successful entertainers contribute to this inequity. We will discuss compensation in more detail in Chapter 8.

The goal of an economy is to efficiently provide goods, services, and family incomes. Without those incomes, people will not be able to purchase the goods and services that we produce. The increasing disparity in income that we see above is a cause for social unrest. Dissatisfaction is generally expressed through the ballot box, but it also contributes to alienation, anger and sometimes violence, such as we witnessed in April, 1992 in the Los Angeles riots.

Examples of our focus on personal convenience, comfort, and short-term prosperity abound. In the 1970s after the Arab oil embargo, Americans realized that they had a voracious appetite for the finite supply of petroleum that exists in the world. Among the variety of strategies we used to make our use of petroleum more efficient was legislation of higher mileage standards for autos and a lower speed limit. But these efforts were undermined by raising the speed limits and by the popularity of pickup trucks and vans that are not subject to the fuel efficiency standards. This results in our using more petroleum, adding to our dependence upon foreign supplies, increasing air pollution, and also swelling considerably our imbalance of payments.[6] In addition, experiences show that higher speeds result in thousands more highway deaths each year.

Restructuring the Firm

American business has been restructured in the last decade. Firms have reduced costs and become "lean and mean" to better meet global competition. More than 3,000,000 jobs have been lost in each year since 1990, many of these to "restructuring and downsizing." From 1992–95, AT&T announced the elimination of 123,000 jobs; IBM: 122,000 jobs; General Motors: 99,400 jobs; Boeing: 61,000 jobs; Sears: 50,000 jobs; and so on.[7] Since 1978, 22 percent of the workers in the 100 largest companies in the United States, a total of 3 million workers, have been laid off.[8] Layers of line management and many staff people have been cut with the aim of better communication and greater efficiencies. Executives now say that their firm does not have responsibility for employment, but only for the "employability" of each worker. Maintaining employability is a

---

[5] "Workers Take It on the Chin," *U.S. News & World Report*, January 22, 1996, pp. 44–50.

[6] *Statistical Abstract of the United States—1994.* Washington, D.C.: U.S. Department of Commerce, 1994, pp. 584–85.

[7] "On the Battlefields of Business, Millions of Casualties," *New York Times*, March 3, 1996, Part 1 of 7 articles, pp. 1A, 14A–17.

[8] "Economic Anxiety," *Business Week*, March 11, 1996, pp. 50–57.

responsibility of both the employer and worker themselves to continually keep their skills updated through training, so that they can readily change jobs. However, other executives point out that layoffs are a mask for poor management decisions in the first place.[9] At best, restructuring has the effect of cutting costs, and perhaps increasing quality and customer satisfaction. However, such restructuring also has long-term negative effects.[10]

First, lost jobs brings loss of family income, and increased anxiety and health problems. In a national poll, 20 percent of Americans say that they have been laid off at least once since 1980, and 58 percent know a relative, neighbor, or good friend who has been laid off. When asked if they are at least as well-off financially as they expected to be at this point in their life, 53 percent of people in general and 71 percent of those who have been laid off say they are not as well-off. Moreover, when asked if they have been getting ahead financially, of all respondents, only 20 percent say they are getting ahead, and only 15 percent of those who have been laid off say they are. Nancy Bishop of Wheeling, West Virginia, says, "I take care of townhouses, and every day I see how layoffs affect tenants. I see marriages break up because of layoffs. I've seen husbands and wives just take off and leave their kids behind because they can't take the pressure. It's very sad."[11] Adding to the anxiety of both those laid off and survivors is evidence that the pressure of layoffs both encourages a few bosses to be brutal, while desensitizing others. Surveys indicate that 90 percent of American workers have at some point been subjected to some abusive behavior. The abuse results in anxiety, depression, heart problems, insomnia, gastrointestinal disorders, skin rashes, headaches, and sexual disfunction.[12] However, people must have incomes if they are to live decently and if they are to be purchasers of the goods and services produced.

A second negative effect is that layoffs reduce loyalty to the firm. From the first layoff, there is less security for all, and less long-term commitment. People begin to look over their shoulder asking who is going to be next. Two key executives left AT&T after the large scale layoffs. David Hunt, president of AT&T's Universal Card Services, and Alex Mandl, president, and heir apparent to chair Robert Allen.[13] AT&T was depending upon these men in the firm's future plans. In a national poll, 77 percent of Americans rated large corporations

---

[9] "The Issue Is Employment, Not Employability," *Business Week*, June 10, 1996, p. 643.

[10] The handbook for reengineering is Michael Hammer and James Champy, *Reengineering the Corporation* (New York: Harper, 1994). The cost to people of reengineering is well treated in "Voices of Survivors: Words that Downsizing CEOs Should Hear," Hugh M. O'Neill and D. Jeffrey Lenn, *Academy of Management Executive* (November 1995): 23–34; also "The Pain of Downsizing," *Business Week* (May 9, 1994), pp. 60–69, 102; the issue also will be treated in Chapter 7.

[11] "Big Holes Where Dignity Used to Be," *New York Times*, March 5, 1996, p. A8; also "In the Class of 1970, Wounded Winners," *New York Times*, March 7, 1996, p. 12A.

[12] Harvey Hornstein, *Brutal Bosses and Their Prey* (New York: Riverhead Books, 1996).

[13] "A Big Loss for AT&T," *Business Week*, September 16, 1996, p. 54.

only fair or poor at providing job security for workers, and 78 percent felt that the companies had no loyalty to employees.[14]

Third, the people who survive a layoff are expected to pick up the extra work. They are given "stretch goals" and are asked to "work smarter" with no new resources; often they are forced to use their own free time to accomplish the new goals. GE chief training officer Steve Kerr calls such demands on the part of managers immoral. His point: if more is expected of workers, they must be provided the tools they need.[15]

A fourth effect of cost-cutting has been a decline in research and development (R&D). Overall investment in corporate R&D declined from almost 7 percent of sales between 1975 and 1985 to 1.5 percent between 1985 and 1990.[16] When firms are restructured, R&D is streamlined and generally reduced. In other cases, R&D is often cut to help pay the outstanding debt resulting from the acquisition. Even when managers succeed in defending their firms from a hostile takeover attempt, they generally must cut costs, sell off assets and take on additional debt. This also results in decreasing the R&D budget. Decreasing R&D is like eating your seed corn. While it is a way to meet current problems, it steals from the future. Investment in R&D benefits the firm in the long-term. American R&D expenditures increased slightly in 1993 and 1994, but the United States still lags behind Japan and European countries.[17]

The low priority given to technology and innovation by American society and business is reflected in the proportion of scientists and engineers in the United States compared with Japan. For every 10,000 citizens, the United States has 70 scientists and engineers, whereas Japan has 400. On the other hand, for every 10,000 citizens, the United States has 20 lawyers and 40 accountants whereas Japan has but 1 lawyer and 3 accountants.[18]

A fifth negative effect of restructuring is that many firms have also cut other internal investments in balanced long-term growth because of the pressure to keep impatient shareholders happy.[19] An executive's own priorities might call for long-term investment, yet institutional shareholders, portfolio managers, and corporate raiders often pressure managers to neglect the long-term.

Finally, we find that cost-cutting and layoffs often result in not only no

---

[14] "Economic Anxiety," *Business Week*, March 11, 1996, pp. 50–58; also, "Two Cheers for Loyalty," *The Economist*, January 6, 1996, p. 49.

[15] Interview with Steve Kerr, "Stretch Goals: The Dark Side of Asking for Miracles," *Fortune*, November 13, 1995, pp. 231–32.

[16] Elizabeth Corcoran, "Redesigning Research," *Scientific American*, June, 1992, p. 103. Figures are from the National Science Foundation.

[17] "Blue-sky Research Comes Down to Earth," *Business Week*, July 3, 1995, pp. 78–80; and "In the Labs, the Fight to Spend Less, Get More," *Business Week*, June 28, 1993, pp. 102–104.

[18] James Fallows, "American Industry—What Ails It, How to Save It," *Atlantic*, September 1980, pp. 35–50.

[19] See Jeff Madrick, *Taking America* (New York: Bantam, 1987); "Trying to Streamline, Some Firms May Hurt Long-Term Prospects," *Wall Street Journal*, January 8, 1987, p. 1.

savings, but in increased costs for the firm. For example, Eastman Kodak laid off Mary Ellen Ford who made $15 an hour plus benefits. Then, because they needed the expertise she possessed, they hired her back on contract, and paid the contractor $60 an hour. Other examples of similar cost increases from Digital Equipment, RJR Nabisco, Continental Airlines, Nynex, and Peoples Natural Gas lead the *Wall Street Journal* to conclude "Despite warnings about downsizing becoming dumbsizing, many companies continue to make flawed decisions—hasty, across-the-board cuts—that come back to haunt them, on the bottom line, in public relations, in strained relationships with customers and suppliers, and in demoralized employees."[20]

Compare the above cases of firms that laid off employees to that of Malden Mills. Just before Christmas, 1995, fire destroyed the textile mill that employed 3,200 people in Lawrence, Massachusetts. Aaron Feuerstein, who owns Malden Mills, immediately promised to rebuild, to ensure the jobs of all 3,200 people, and even to pay their salaries for a while, as the new plant was being built. Feuerstein, an observant orthodox Jew, could have taken the hundreds of millions of dollars in fire insurance and called it quits. Or he could have built more modestly, and not promised to continue to pay idle workers.

Feuerstein's sense of responsibility to his workers is costing him tens of millions of dollars in the short-run. But Feuerstein knows that the textiles that have made Malden Mills a success have come from the ingenuity of Malden employees. Polartec is a very popular fabric for outdoor clothes that is sold to L.L. Bean, Lands' End, and Patagonia. Interim production takes place in warehouses, and the new plant is going up very rapidly. Feuerstein has been lionized across the United States for his protection of his workers. In response he says, "In my eyes, I did no more than just the simple right thing to do. . . . If we really believe man is created in the image of God, we've got to be sensitive to those creations who are made in that image. . . . You must recognize that labor is not merely an expense but also an asset."[21] Let us now turn our attention to the mergers, acquisitions, and takeovers that have been in the headlines for two decades.

MERGERS AND SPECULATION

The total volume of mergers and acquisitions in the United States in 1996 was the highest in history, $659 billion. This is up from $342 billion in 1994 and $150 billion in 1992.[22] Time Warner's merger with Turner Broadcasting, Walt

---

[20] "Call It Dumbsizing: Why Some Companies Regret Cost-Cutting," *Wall Street Journal*, May 14, 1996, pp. 1, 16.

[21] "The Risks of Keeping a Promise," *New York Times*, July 4, 1996, pp. C1, C3; also "When the Decent Thing Becomes Exceptional," *Responsive Community*, Spring 1996, p. 71.

[22] "Conditions Are Right for a Takeover Frenzy," *New York Times*, January 2, 1997, p. C3.

Disney's merger with Capital Cities ABC, and Chase Manhattan Bank's merger with Chemical Bank were all driven by an attempt to gain market dominance. In 1991 AT&T purchased NCR for $7.4 billion in another ill-fated attempt to break into personal computers. Only 5 years later, AT&T split itself into three separate firms with NCR again becoming a separate company.[23] Both the mergers and the splits are motivated by a desire to market globally and to lower costs by shedding jobs. But, as the AT&T split indicates, a larger firm is most often not more efficient. Moreover, when AT&T acquired NCR many jobs were lost; and Dayton, Ohio lost a major corporate headquarters. Yet the number of mergers continue to increase and are now again running at record levels.[24] Recent research indicates that a primary motivation for mergers is the desire of the CEO for more power, hardly a motive that gives one confidence that a decision to merge is well founded.[25]

The failed $20.5 billion bid of Las Vegas gambler and dealmaker Kirk Kerkorian and Lee Iacocca for Chrysler was an attempt at a hostile takeover (for terms, see Fig. 1–2). In an editorial comment on the bid, *Business Week* said that in the 1980s "in their drive for the quick buck . . . takeover artists forced companies to shake off years of bureaucratic lethargy, cut expensive layers of management and dispose of marginal operations." After pointing out that Chrysler is already efficient and listing its major innovations, they say that this bid would not be good for either Chrysler or the country. They conclude, "Corporate America does not need the lash of the 'greed-is-good' guys. This time around, greed is just greed."[26]

One of the largest leveraged buyouts in history, Kohlberg Kravis Roberts & Co.'s purchase of RJR Nabisco resulted in no significant profit for investors. But as a result of it, RJR Nabisco was forced to lay off 46,000 employees and sold $6.2 billion of its businesses to pay its debt.[27] On the other hand, KKR & Co.'s partners personally pocketed $500 million on transaction and other fees.

Raiders Kerkorian, Kravis, T. Boone Pickens, and many financial economists maintain that hostile takeovers occur only when a target firm's stock price is too low. This happens when the market judges that the firm is not using its

---

[23] "Land of the Giants," *Business Week*, September 11, 1995, pp. 34–39, 134; "Disney's Kingdom," *Business Week*, August 14, 1995, pp. 30–35, 114; "AT&T, Reversing Strategy, Announces a Plan to Split into 3 Separate Companies," *New York Times*, September 21, 1995, pp. A1, C1, C4.

[24] "Late Nights in the M&A Lab: Big Wall Street Firms are Helping to Concoct a Record Number of Mergers and Acquisitions. They Are Thriving on It," *The Economist*, November 11, 1995, pp. 73–74.

[25] Matthew L. Hayward and Donald C. Hambrick of Colombia University Business School are quoted in "An Argument That Big Ego Is Behind a Lot of Mergers," *New York Times*, September 28, 1995, C2.

[26] "A Greedy Grab for Chrysler," *Business Week,* May 1, 1995, p. 166. See also "Chrysler: Sandbagged by Its Biggest Shareholder," *Fortune*, May 15, 1995, pp. 44–48; and "Chrysler: The Inside Story," *Business Week*, May 15, 1995, pp. 39–42.

[27] Bryan Burrough and John Helyar, *Barbarians at the Gate: the Fall of RJR Nabisco* (New York: Harper, 1991); "Barbarians Revisited: KKR's Buyout of RJR Nabisco Was a Major Fizzle—for Investors," *Business Week*, April 3, 1995, pp. 46–47, 138.

FIGURE 1–2 Investor and Takeover Terms

Acquisition: The acquiring of one firm by another.

Friendly takeover: A takeover that occurs with the cooperation of the management and board of both firms.

Golden parachute: Guaranteed payment to top executives enacted as a disincentive to a hostile takeover.

Greenmail: When a raider requires a target firm to purchase the raider's stock at more than market value so that the raider will cease attempting a takeover.

Hostile takeover: A takeover that occurs in spite of the opposition of the target firm's management and board.

Insider trading: Purchase of stock based upon confidential information received from an officer or employee of that company.

Institutional investor: Institutions (e.g., pension funds, university endowments, trust funds, insurance firms) that hold common stock. Most have portfolio managers.

Junk bonds: High-yield, high-risk bonds sold to finance a leveraged buyout or the activities of a corporate raider.

Leveraged buyout: Purchase of outstanding shares with borrowed capital, sometimes by the firm's own management or workers.

Merger: The joining of two firms, either financially, operationally, or both.

Poison pill (also shark repellant):   An action that makes the target firm a less attractive target for a takeover.

Portfolio manager: A financial manager who oversees a portfolio of investments and tries to obtain the highest yield for an investor (usually an institution).

Put into play: Signaling that a firm is undervalued and ripe for a takeover.

Raider: The person or firm that initiates a hostile takeover.

Stakeholder: One who holds a stake in the firm; a constituency of the firm (e.g., customers, employees, the local community, shareholders, suppliers, the local government).

Stockholder: One who holds stock in a company; an investor who is considered an owner of the firm.

Takeover: The taking of ownership of another firm.

Target firm: The company being considered for a takeover.

capital resources efficiently. The external takeover market protects shareholders when the corporation's internal controls and board-level control mechanisms are slow or break down completely.[28] Note that the greatest benefits of

---

[28] Michael C. Jensen, "The Takeover Controversy," *Vital Speeches*, May 1, 1987, p. 427. See also Robert F. Bruner and Lynn Sharp Paine, "Management Buyouts and Managerial Ethics," *California Management Review* 30 (Winter 1988): 89–106.

takeovers accrue to the lawyers and analysts who plan it and to shareholders. Other stakeholders—terminated employees, affected local neighborhoods, and suppliers—generally bear the costs. As we have seen, long-term planning, new investment, and R&D also suffer.[29]

Mergers and acquisitions continued to occur at a rapid rate through the 1990s. On the one hand, some fostered the breakup of conglomerates that were not performing well financially. When they allow a firm to focus on its core business, mergers are more likely to be successful. On the other hand, many mergers, such as Time Warner and Turner Broadcasting, seem to stem from a motivation simply to grow. Such mergers are not as likely to yield efficiencies. They result in a larger organization, which makes management distant and the firm more difficult to manage. The merger movement may just be a risk averse strategy for growth that thereby neglects long-range planning, R&D, and a commitment to quality.[30]

Golden Parachutes and Greenmail

To defend themselves against hostile takeovers, executives sometimes resort to short-term strategies to make their firms less attractive to raiders. Executives may dispose of assets, sell a division, take on a large amount of debt, and generate golden parachutes and poison pills. Since golden parachutes guarantee large compensation for top executives even if the firm is taken over, top management benefits greatly. Even though their firm may be chopped up and many employees fired, top executives are not hurt, but benefited. These defensive strategies are as questionable as those used by the raiders themselves. They are a conflict of interest for top managers.

When a raider has already purchased a substantial portion of a target company's stock, the raider threatens to seize control of the firm and to then "restructure the company." The raider will then sell less profitable operations and fire current management and many staff people. Management may protect itself and the firm by offering to purchase back the raider's stock at a price greater than the price the raider paid for it. Thus the raider in a few weeks makes a large profit. Other shareholders most often are not able to sell their stock at this higher price. In addition, the firm generally must liquidate some of its assets or borrow large sums in order to purchase these shares from the raider. This leaves the company in much greater debt, and the rest of the shareholders and other stakeholders pay the bill. Greenmail is ransom paid to the raider at the expense of other stakeholders.

---

[29] Michael A. Hitt, et. al., "Are Acquisitions a Poison Pill for Innovation?" *Academy of Management Executive* (November 1991): 22–34.

[30] "The Case Against Mergers," *Business Week*, October 30, 1995, pp. 122–38; on the futility of bank mergers, see "Clueless Bankers," *Fortune*, November 27, 1995, pp. 150–58.

Institutional Investors

Institutional investors own most of the outstanding common stock of firms in the United States.[31] The larger of these institutions hire professional portfolio managers whose success is judged by the amount the total portfolio of stocks increases in a given quarter. An institution may switch from one portfolio manager to another if the rate of return is not what they think it should be. Hence the portfolio manager acts to insure that the stock continues to increase in value. Corporate raiders and downsizers usually bring about increases in share value, so portfolio managers normally support their actions.

A generation ago, when most common shares were in the hands of individuals and before computers, markets were more stable. Few individuals had the time or inclination to watch the market daily. Investors looked on their investments as long-term ownership and thus were concerned about the future of the firm.

A portfolio manager is interested in a firm's profitability and the rate of return generated by dividends and capital gains. With the aid of computers, their full-time occupation is to watch the market. They can thus buy and sell a block of stock many times a day to make incremental gains, sometimes large gains.

This, in turn, puts considerable pressure on top managers of firms to keep their stock price up.[32] Indeed, that is the only sure way to keep the raiders away. When the stock is undervalued, a firm becomes a ripe target for a raider. However, keeping the stock price up can lead paradoxically to sacrificing long-term health for short-term returns, as we saw earlier. This can have negative effects on jobs, new products, and long-term prospects for the firm. In addition, the stock price reflects the perceptions of Wall Street; it is not always an accurate indicator of the current health and future value of a firm.

Insider Trading

Ivan Boesky, David Levine, and Martin Siegel acknowledged using confidential information obtained from clients to amass personal fortunes. Michael R. Milken, head of junk bonds at Drexel Burnham Lambert, in 1990 pleaded guilty to six felony charges of securities fraud and conspiracy. He spent 2 years in prison, and paid $1.1 billion in fines. His firm had filed for bankruptcy the year before.[33] But the old and respected houses of Kidder, Peabody & Co., and

---

[31] James E. Heard, "Pension Funds and Contests for Corporate Control," *California Management Review*, Winter 1987, pp. 89–100; see also "Evening Odds in Proxy Fights," *Business Week*, July 4, 1988, p. 37.

[32] Samuel B. Graves and Sandra A. Waddock detail short-term perspective of portfolio managers and the resulting pressures on corporate executives in "Institutional Ownership and Control: Implications for Long-term Corporate Strategy," *Academy of Management Executive* 4 (January 1990): 75–83.

[33] "We Meet Again, Mr. Milken," *Business Week*, October 16, 1995, p. 6; "Milken Gets 10 Years for Wall St. Crimes," *New York Times*, November 22, 1990, pp. 1, C4–6; For a more complete view, see Connie Bruck, *The Preditor's Ball* (New York: The American Lawyer and Simon & Schuster, 1988).

Goldman, Sachs & Company were also involved.[34] Financial bankers and others know that without trust a Wall Street firm cannot successfully operate, and trust cannot exist without confidentiality.

The ethics of insider trading is clear: It is a breach of confidentiality. It is unfair to shareholders to use information to which even they as owners do not have access. Those with inside information gain personally by purchasing their shares at artificially low prices.

The insider trading scandals grew with increased merger and acquisition activities. When a merger is planned, information on it becomes valuable because the stock of the target company increases in value when the news becomes public. So, if one has early notice of a merger, one can make large profits quickly, at little risk, and no effort. It is a free enterprise dream: to become rich without effort or risk.

Although illegal, insider trading does take place on Wall Street. Many careers of bright, capable, but greedy, people have come to an end because of insider trading. In spite of the many convictions, insider trading is difficult to police. Even though every purchase of stock leaves a record of who buys, at what price and at what time, it is still hard to prove that a purchaser had information from a confidential source. Wall Street brokers, financial bankers, and risk arbitragers live on recent, accurate, sometimes gossipy information. Nevertheless, communicating inside information is both illegal and unethical. Greenmail and poison pills are legal, but in most cases they abuse the system and are unjust.

Proponents of takeovers say it turns capitalism loose to eliminate the inefficiencies of business. The free operation of capital markets has and will continue to force firms to restructure and become more efficient. Because of the need to compete in the global marketplace, it is essential that firms be efficient and productive.

On the other hand, critics of takeovers and mergers acknowledge the necessity of achieving efficiencies through restructuring, but hold that restructuring should be for the *long-term benefit* of the firm and its *many stakeholders*. Critics maintain that raiders are often merely seeking a quick financial killing and are not interested in the firm they take over; nor do they usually make a firm more efficient in the long term.

MANAGEMENT SELF-INTEREST

In a large firm, top managers find it more difficult to know specific products, markets, or employees. Given the greater distance from consumers, new product ideas, production, and the public, executives turn to what they *can* under-

---

[34] "The Wall Street Career of Martin Siegel Was a Dream Gone Wrong," *Wall Street Journal*, February 17, 1987, pp. 1, 30; "Suddenly the Fish Get Bigger," *Business Week*, March 2, 1987, pp. 28–35.

stand—the control mechanism at their fingertips—"the numbers." Managers then rely on return on equity, market share, and other numerical indices of success. Focusing on short-term measurable results can lead managers to reduce research, risk taking, and eventually productivity.

In sum, the principal cause of a lack of loyalty, lack of innovation, and generally poor management is an emphasis on short-term goals. Managers, like others, sometimes take the easy way out; they prefer measurable, short-term results so that their personal record looks good. This same underlying motive often leads to unethical behavior, also. Thus, it is fair to conclude that short-sighted values lead to a host of problems, among them a lack of ethical behavior within the firm.

Public Confidence in Corporations and Executives

Americans do not have confidence in either big business or big government, or their respective leaders. Attitudes toward business and business leaders have been probed in opinion surveys. Most Americans, 58 percent, feel that the ethics of business executives are fair or poor; only 40 percent think that their ethics are good. This same survey found that 90 percent thought that white-collar crime is a common phenomenon.[35]

Some additional survey items are shown in Table 1–1. Among graduate business students currently 69 percent feel that "business is overly concerned with profits and not concerned enough with public responsibilities." This is not surprising, given the lack of job security and company loyalty that we have seen above. These students average 28 years old and have experienced several full-time jobs. Supporting this, 88 percent feel that the real power in the United States rests with the "giant corporations and financial institutions." That is, they feel that there is a locus of power, and that it is being exercised by corporations for their own interests. In these cases the level of cynicism is close to the earlier high levels of the 1970s and early 1980s.

Sexual Harassment

Sexual harassment, at best, consists in unthinking, insensitive, unwanted words and/or actions of one worker toward a coworker. At worst, it stems from egoistic, brutal and self-centered attitudes. Two examples of sexual harassment that affected many women at each firm were revealed at Astra USA pharmaceutical and a Mitsubishi Motor Manufacturing factory at Normal, Illinois. In the Astra case investigations found that young women sales trainees were expected to attend company drinking parties. Several women charged that the CEO, Lars Bildman, would run his hands down their backs while dancing close. Other women charged executives with touching and grabbing them during company

---

[35] "Is an Antibusiness Backlash Building?" *Business Week*, July 20, 1987, p. 71.

TABLE 1–1   Attitudes of Graduate Business Students on Issues Underlying the Business System

	Percentage Agreeing[*]				
	1974	1981	1983	1988	1996
1. Business is overly concerned with profits and not concerned enough with public responsibilities	75%	70%	51%	66%	69%
2. Our foreign policy is based on narrow economic and power interests	70	75	54	53	38
3. Economic well-being is unjustly and unfairly distributed	80	34	34	42	38
4. The real power in the United States rests with					
a. the Congress	52	61	69	61	66
b. the giant corporations and financial institutions	81	88	87	89	88
c. the public	43	45	56	50	50

[*]Graduate business students from author's classes at Wayne State University (1974), at the University of Detroit (1981, 1983, 1988), and at the University of Detroit Mercy (1996).

drinking parties. A few were asked to accompany senior executives to their hotel room after the parties; these women were referred to as "the chosen." Astra's own investigations confirmed many of the allegations, and found financial improprieties, also. Astra, a Swedish-owned firm, fired Bildman and two other executives from its U.S. subsidiary.[36]

While sexual harassment has existed since men and women have worked together, sensitivity to it in the United States has increased dramatically over the last two decades. Investigations normally reveal varying stories. What one woman or man will describe as harmless fun, another will find grossly offensive. Much of what was accepted by women in the United States two decades ago, and is still endured in many cultures, is now no longer acceptable in the United States. This change in expectations puts special demands on operations in the United States of foreign-owned firms. In the above cases of Astra and Mitsubishi, neither had a clear and detailed sexual harassment policy statement that was given to all, and neither did an even-handed investigation of the early complaints.[37]

[36] Mark Maremont, "Abuse of Power: The Astonishing Tale of Sexual Harassment at Astra USA," *Business Week*, May 13, 1996, pp. 86–98, 166; "Day of Reckoning at Astra," *Business Week*, July 8, 1996, p. 36.

[37] "Sexual-Harassment Cases Trip Up Foreign Companies," *Wall Street Journal*, May 9, 1996, p. B4.

Pollutants and Police

Focusing exclusively on profits provides both theoretical and psychological support to those businesspeople who "look out for number one first." Two instances of this occurred with Royal Dutch Shell Oil Company in 1995. Shell announced that it would dump in the North Sea the Brent Spar, a worn-out oil rig that contained toxic chemicals. Angry citizens in the Netherlands and Germany boycotted Shell gasoline, and political leaders pleaded with Shell not to do so. Shell finally agreed to dispose of the rig more safely on land, but not before its reputation had been severely damaged.[38]

In an even more serious case Shell relied on the military dictatorship in Nigeria to protect its petroleum drilling there. Shell has extracted $30 billion in petroleum from the Niger delta, which is the homeland of the ethnic minority Ogoni people. Some of the profits left in Nigeria from this project go to selected development projects, but most goes into the pockets of the military dictators. Because their land is being ruined by oil spills and they shared little of the benefits, Ogoni protested. To quiet protests, Nigerian soldiers tortured and killed many members of the group.

Ken Saro Wiwa, an author and playwright, took up the cause of his Ogoni people and organized the minority in an attempt to obtain a hearing. He was arrested for these activities in 1994. In November, 1995, Saro Wiwa, along with eight others, were executed by the Nigerian military dictatorship, after a staged trial. Protests from around the world failed to halt the executions. The military regime remains in power, but Shell now acknowledges that it caused environmental damage to the area, and promises to clean up its practices.[39] Although Shell denies it asked for the crackdown, they benefited mightily.

When a firm emphasizes profits exclusively, it then attempts to place some of its own costs of production on innocent third parties. Pollution, whether from production facilities or moving vehicles, is a classic example. Others who may or may not benefit from the product pay the cost by ingesting disease-causing pollutants. There are many other examples. A large-scale dump for toxic chemicals was established by Hooker Chemical (now a division of Occidental Chemical) in the old Love Canal near Niagara Falls, New York. Homes and a school were built over the dump, and various physical ailments began appearing among the residents—miscarriages, birth defects, and mental retardation. Hundreds of people were forced to leave their homes.

In another case, the pesticide Kepone was manufactured by a firm under license from Allied Chemical (now Allied Signal) in Hopewell, Virginia. The highly toxic chemical was handled casually, and waste was flushed into the

---

[38] Christopher Flavin, "Oil Production Rises," in Lester Brown et. al., *Vital Signs–1996* (New York: W. W. Norton, 1996), p. 48.

[39] "A State's Well-Oiled Injustice," *World Press Review*, January, 1996, p. 14 quoted from *The Observer;* also "The Latest Shell Shock," *Business Week*, November 27, 1995, p. 48.

river. Serious illnesses among employees and the contamination of the entire James River and the Chesapeake Bay resulted.[40] The World Health Organization and The National Cancer Institute estimate that over two-thirds of all cancer in humans is caused by substances we ourselves have introduced into our environment.

The central point is that the desire to cut costs can lead a firm to dump its toxic waste and thereby hurt innocent third parties. It is cheaper to do so. Users of pesticides, rubber, autos, and plastic products thus do not pay their full cost. Those who ingest the toxic substances pay by suffering ill health with the danger of having months or years taken off their lives. People who live in smog filled areas like Los Angeles and Denver are examples. An efficient and just system requires manufacturers to "internalize" these costs of production (reduce pollution), so that those who use the products pay the costs, rather than innocent bystanders.

The Environmental Protection Agency (EPA) was set up to help accomplish this. While the EPA is not always efficient, it is clear that the unrestrained free market has no mechanism for controlling pollution. In fact, the market encourages firms to pollute as long as they are not penalized. With regard to pollution, the question for government is not whether to regulate but how to regulate efficiently and equitably.

ADVERTISING, MEDIA, AND GLOBAL FIRMS SHAPE VALUES

Advertising is the communication link between producer and consumer. Without advertising, the prospective purchaser is not aware of the price and qualities of goods and services to be sold. A free market demands a free flow of information, and advertising provides a major portion of the information that is so essential to consumers.

From the standpoint of the consumer, the purpose of advertising is to obtain information that will help make a purchasing decision. From the standpoint of the seller, the purpose of advertising is to convince people to purchase products or services. The success of advertising is demonstrated by the fact that sellers in the United States spend more than $120 billion on it each year.[41]

Advertisers use a variety of approaches to influence the purchasing decisions of consumers. Some advertising is informative, tasteful, and supports the values of individual responsibility, family, and community. Recall the Gallo TV

---

[40] For an account of the Love Canal, Kepone, and other cases, see "The Chemicals Around us," *Newsweek*, August 21, 1978, pp. 25–28; see also "Who Pays? Cleaning up the Love Canals," *New York Times*, June 8, 1980, sec. F, pp. 1–5.

[41] *Statistical Abstract of the United States—1994* (Washington, D.C.: U.S. Department of Commerce, 1994), p. 543.

ads, which feature birthdays, weddings, baptisms, and a variety of family-oriented activities. On the other hand, some advertising is sexist and self-oriented. Note cigarette and beer ads in college newspapers—targeted at individuals who are susceptible to peer group pressure and most of whom cannot purchase beer legally. A minority of ads are even deceptive, crude, and demeaning. Not surprisingly, people become suspicious and cynical about the messages they see and hear in advertising.[42]

Young children constitute one group not yet suspicious of advertising. They have not had the experiences necessary to build critical judgment. Up to age seven, children tend to take at face value what they see in ads and on television; they often cannot distinguish the ad from the program. As children grow older and begin to distinguish, advertising and television implicitly tell children that "grownups tell lies for money quite well."[43]

Nike dominates athletic footwear worldwide, largely because of its advertising. It has shoe revenues of more than $4 billion annually, and its earnings were up 38 percent to $553 million in 1996. Nike subcontracts the making of its shoes to six manufacturing plants in Indonesia. Girls and young women workers are housed in barracks, and overtime is compulsory. The minimum wage in Indonesia is $2.59 per day; Nike workers' base wage is $2.23 per day.[44] Workers are not allowed to organize for better wages or working conditions, and the government guarantees that there will be no strikes. Yet the government acknowledges that even the minimum wage is not sufficient to pay family expenses. Total labor cost for a pair of shoes that sells in the United States or Europe for up to $150 is $2.50. Advertising and endorsements are much greater costs.[45] In contrast, another footwear manufacturer, New Balance, pays U.S. wages, and spends very little on endorsements and advertising.

Nike spends hundreds of millions on brand advertising. Most of their advertising money goes to endorsements of high profile professional athletes who are already making millions of dollars. Michael Jordan has an annual salary of $25 million. The $20 million that Michael Jordan reportedly receives each year for promoting Nike shoes is greater than the entire annual payroll of the Indonesian factories that make the shoes.[46] Nike is reportedly bidding to sponsor the Brazilian soccer team for 10 years for $200 million.[47]

---

[42] For a fuller treatment of these ethical issues in advertising, see Chapter 5, "Advertising and Television," in Gerald F. Cavanagh and Arthur F. McGovern, *Ethical Dilemmas in the Modern Corporation* (Englewood Cliffs, N.J.: Prentice Hall, 1988).

[43] Robert Heilbroner, "Realities and Appearances in Capitalism," in *Corporations and the Common Good*, ed. Robert B. Dickie and Leroy S. Rouner (Notre Dame: University of Notre Dame Press, 1986), p. 38.

[44] "Pangs of Conscience: Sweatshops Haunt U.S. Consumers," *Business Week*, July 29, 1996, pp. 46–47.

[45] "An Indonesian Asset Is Also a Liability," *New York Times*, March 16, 1996, p. C17.

[46] David C. Korten, *When Corporations Rule the World* (San Francisco: Berrett-Koehler, 1995), pp. 110–11.

[47] "Run, Jump and Sell: Commercial Exploitation of Sports Explodes," *Business Week*, July 29, 1996, pp. 36–37.

Nike's advertising theme is, "Just Do It." Or, in another version, "We are all hedonists and we want what feels good. That's what makes us human." Or to paraphrase the theme: "Do what you feel like, act on impulse, don't analyze or inhibit yourself." Nike is an example of a mature market that shifts rewards away from those who produce real value toward those who create image and illusion in order to convince consumers to purchase a product that they do not need at inflated prices.

Nike is not alone with its self-oriented advertising theme. Burger King has, "Sometimes, you gotta break the rules." Neiman Marcus says, "Relax, no rules here." Bacardi Black Rum promises to take the drinker to a tipsy night where anything goes: "Some people embrace the night because rules of the day do not apply." Nike, Burger King and firms with similar advertising themes are promoting, "self-obsession, narcissism, and contempt for all rules, they strike at the sense of connectedness that any society needs to cohere and to care about its common problems and least fortunate members."[48] Thus they make it far more difficult for us to develop common values in order to face our common problems.

In spite of their goal of global dominance in sports equipment, and their immense advertising budget, Nike was *not* one of the official sponsors to the 1996 Summer Olympic Games in Atlanta. It cost up to $40 million to become an official sponsor. Nevertheless, Nike did run a series of ads in Olympic looking surroundings on the athletes it had under contract. Before the Olympics they also announced a "sports-oriented Web site cunningly called @lanta." IBM sponsored the official Web site. The Atlanta Committee for the Olympic games considered suing Nike for their attempt to get free exposure at the expense of the Olympic games and legitimate sponsors.[49] Nike's sweatshop wages, its advertising themes and its cheap antics with regard to the Olympic Games tell us much about the values of Nike, and the values that it tries to communicate to us.

Calvin Klein has a series of ads on buses and magazines with young teens posing in "what looks like opening scenes in a porn movie." In one ad, a girl is shown lying down with her skirt up, exposing her panties. In another shot from the crotch of a young curly headed boy, he gazes out sadly, as if looking for his next sexual relationship.[50] Sex is offered casually and as a commodity, but this is normal advertising copy for Calvin Klein.

Selling cigarettes to the growing new markets in Asia, Latin America, and Africa is very profitable. Because of aggressive advertising, smoking is fashionable. Hundreds of millions of Asians have begun to smoke. Physicians say that Asia's smoking problem is terrifying, but it is being largely ignored. Health experts expect worldwide tobacco-related deaths to more than triple over the next two or three decades from 3 million to 10 million a year, largely because of

---

[48] John Leo, "Not Too Calvinist," *The Responsive Community*, Fall 1995, pp. 12–14.

[49] "Is Nike Playing Olympic Games?," *Business Week*, July 1, 1996, p. 4.

[50] "Not Too Calvinist," *op. cit.*, p. 12.

Asia. One expert calculates that 50 million Chinese children alive today will eventually die from diseases linked to cigarette smoking.[51]

Advertising Affects Values

Given the volume and the pervasiveness of advertising, and its effect on our values and the values of our children, it should be of great concern to all—both as citizens and as consumers. However, it is difficult to show a clear causal connection between advertising and values. Advertisers do try to convince us that if we feel unattractive, ill, or unhappy, they have just the right product for us. Something we can purchase can solve our problems. In order to sell, advertisers often intentionally appeal to materialism, lack of self-esteem, social status and fear of ridicule.

Advertisers have been accused of being "creators of dissatisfaction." They present the handsome, immaculately dressed woman or man as an ideal to strive for; yet the ideal inaccurately reflects the actual world. Moreover, it can create unattainable expectations and hence frustration, especially for the impressionable. To judge a person by the style of his or her clothes is shallow and dehumanizing. Moreover, such an attitude sets one up to be disappointed later in life when one discovers that money, possessions, and power do not bring happiness.

Advertising encourages consumption. Advertising, in its promotion of an affluent life-style, also presents an image of Americans as materialistic, superficial, and self-centered. Nevertheless, some argue that developed nations are less materialistic than other societies:

> The more affluent a society is the less materialistic it tends to be, not because affluence makes for virtue but mainly because people have less to worry about to survive from one day to another, and therefore there is a somewhat greater chance for altruism.[52]

Hence, a paradox: People in wealthier nations, because of their affluence, have the opportunity to be less materialistic and self-centered. At the same time they are pressured by advertising and each other to be more dependent upon consumer goods and status.

Advertising firms sell not only products but political candidates as well. For the past generation, advertising firms have provided idealized images of political candidates in order to influence our voting decisions. Instead of being shown a real person giving statesmanlike explanations of complex issues, we are subjected to a carefully crafted thirty-second image—complete with film footage, sound overlays, and other trappings of advertising. We are not introduced to a person but rather presented with an idealized image. In an election

---

[51] For much detail on advertising and selling cigarettes in Asia, "Asia's Having One Huge Nicotine Fit," Philip Shenon. *New York Times*, Sunday, May 15, 1994, Sec. 4, pp. 1, 16.

[52] Peter Berger, "The Moral Crisis of Capitalism," in Dickie and Rouner, *Corporations and the Common Good*, p. 24.

campaign, we are thus asked to make a choice between two unreal images. A thirty-second ad does not provide the time to discuss difficult issues. Even worse, it often communicates that complex issues are simple and easy to resolve, given a certain ideology. Of course, this is not only false but it can undermine democracy.

People in advertising often tell us that they do not promote values. A national business magazine, *Fortune*, ran an ad in *Advertising Week*[53] encouraging advertisers to take out ad space with it. The text of the ad ran, "I'd say we have a mature, responsible attitude toward our major competitors. We'd like to *see them dead.*" The ad text went on: ". . . For some marketers, *stalking those fractions* (of a share point) *is a blood sport.* In issue after issue *Fortune takes dead aim on the strategies, tactics and technologies of the hunt.* Unlike other business publications that simply report the who and the what, Fortune *cuts it closer to the bone.* That's called journalism." The emphasis, which is ours, emphasizes violent, antisocial behavior. Presuming that the expensive two-page spread is not a joke, this ad exploits violent language to gain our attention. Does this language encourage distrust, playing rough with stakeholders, and even violence? One wonders what sort of person would thus choose to advertise in *Fortune.*

In making the case that they do not influence our values, advertisers say they are professionals, and they offer their skills and knowledge without regard to the merits of a particular product or firm. Morally, however, this is an unacceptable position. Products, firms, and advertising strategies differ widely. Some products are more worthwhile than others. Some firms treat customers and employees well; others do not. Some advertising campaigns are informative and uplifting, whereas others are manipulative, trivial, and even deceptive.

Advertisers also tell us that they do not create values; they merely build on the values that they find already present. Successful advertising does appeal to our existing values. Nevertheless, advertising can reinforce and solidify childish, self-centered, and materialistic values latent in all people. It does this especially among the young and less mature. Moreover, advertising promotes national brands, so it encourages people to value Coke more than juices, Fritos more than vegetables, Porsches more than people, fashionable clothes more than art, and soap operas more than reading. Along with its positive contributions to the free market, advertising can also promote shallowness, acquisitiveness, and egoism.

Global Firms: Corporate Citizens of the World

Global corporations such as IBM (U.S.), Toyota (Japan), and Shell (Netherlands) not only sell their products but also have operations in most of the countries in the world. These firms are but examples of the hundreds of businesses that affect our lives every day. They and the countries they represent are members of the

---

[53] *Advertising Week*, November 17, 1986.

"interlinked economy." Further binding countries together economically, the North Atlantic Free Trade Agreement (NAFTA) links Canada, Mexico and the United States. The European Union (EU) does much the same for European countries. We have become a world without economic borders with capital, products, services, and managers moving easily from one country to another. The very idea of a significant product produced entirely by people of any one country is becoming obsolete.[54]

The global corporations provide many benefits to people. They provide jobs, goods, and income to hundreds of millions of people around the world. Global firms hire local people to manage, and provide them with training and sometimes education. Moreover, they have a vested interest in stability. Wars and revolutions disrupt business as well as bring anguish and death to people.

The global firm bridges nations, cultures, and peoples. While political institutions—individual nations and even the United Nations—are burdened by nationalism and bureaucracy, the global corporation is able to cross boundaries and deal with people where they live. From the standpoint of values, the global firm brings the immense advantage of jobs, person-to-person contact of people of different cultures, and the *necessity* that one understand and work with people of varying cultures.

If a global firm tries to export its own national values, it will not be successful. If "headquarters" tries to direct attitudes and business practices without great attention to local needs, the operation will fail. Kenichi Ohmae, after years of consulting with global firms at McKinsey & Company, outlines five stages of development of the global firm. In the fifth and final stage, the firm must "create a system of values shared by company managers around the globe to replace the glue of nation-based orientation once provided."[55] This system of building trust and shared values is difficult and takes time. However, whether a firm's shared values are an adequate substitute for the values of family, neighborhood, and nation is indeed doubtful.

In any case, building shared values can best be done when one understands one's own starting point and one's own values. Moreover, it is aided when one is aware of the processes that reinforce or undermine values. In this book we attempt to clarify the values of industrialized peoples, especially Americans. Moreover, the book also spotlights the way that the values of an organization influence one's personal values, and the way that the values of the individual can influence the group and the organization (Chapters 2, 7, and 8).

New Horizons for Global Business

Doing business globally involves using electronic mail (e-mail) and the Internet, and it also demands that one understands the culture of other nations. The

---

[54] Evidence for this is presented by Kenichi Ohmae, *The Borderless World: Power and Strategy in the Interlinked Economy* (New York: Harper, 1990).
[55] *Ibid.*, p. 91.

Internet system provides a unique ease of communication between peoples and nations. The number using Internet went from 1 million in 1988 to 20 million in 1996 and continues to grow at a very rapid rate. Internet communication is cheap, accurate, direct, and can span continents in moments. It is used by firms for billing, ordering from suppliers, planning, and for advertising on the World Wide Web.

At present there is very little law that applies to the Internet. Net purists maintain that there should be no regulation at all. It is true that whatever law there is will probably be easy to circumvent. For example, it is simple to copy copyrighted work. A person who would never break a car window to steal a stereo thinks little of punching the enter key to copy $300 worth of software. And it is hard to detect the theft. Scam artists can obtain credit card numbers under false pretenses from unsuspecting customers, and operate offshore to avoid the law. And pornographic material can be brought into the home by a 5-year-old.[56] The Internet and the World Wide Web are powerful tools, and we have not yet determined the ethical and legal boundaries for their use.

Businesspeople who are dealing regularly with people of other cultures and nations must understand the values of those other cultures if they are to operate successfully there. Some cultures have elements that make them less attractive for business. It impedes development when government officials demand large payments just to obtain permission to operate. Not only do the dollars not go to those who deserve them, suppliers, workers, or local investors, but it makes business planning difficult, since one does not know when an arbitrary new demand may be made.

Indonesia, a country of 190 million people, 19,000 islands and 350 languages, has made considerable progress in climbing from abject poverty to a middle income level in three decades. The economy has been growing at a 7.8 percent rate in recent years. But corruption there is now impeding growth. Doing significant business in Indonesia is impossible without obtaining the approval of 75-year-old President Suharto or a member of his family. That approval can generally be gained by paying that relative millions of dollars per year, and appointing the relative as an agent, a consultant, or a part owner. Prior to the death of Suharto's wife Tien, she had been called "Tien Percent," referring to her cut on business deals early in his term.

The Suharto family either owns or is involved in almost every aspect of Indonesia's economic life. The net worth of the Suharto family cartel is estimated at $30 billion. However, the first family's business interests cannot be discussed openly in Indonesia, because Suharto tightly controls the content of

---

[56] "Ethical Issues Surrounding the Use of Electronic Mail," Bonnie Glassberg, William Kettinger, and John E. Logan. Paper presented at the Social Issues Division, Academy of Management, August, 1995; also "Law Creeps Onto the Lawless Net," *Business Week*, May 6, 1996, pp. 58–62.

the press and television. Moreover, "there is virtually no functioning legal system in which to resolve commercial disputes."[57]

Ford, Toyota, Chrysler, and General Motors all canceled plans to invest in Indonesia, when they learned of the favored treatment given to a local firm. The joint venture with Korean Kia Motors is controlled by Hutomo Mandala Putra, youngest son of President Suharto and known as "race car Tommy" because of his favorite sport.[58] That firm was given 3 years of tax breaks (which generally add as much as 35 percent to the cost of a vehicle).

At a recent meeting of the World Trade Association, the United States suggested that there be a rule outlawing bribery on government projects. However, the Association of Southeast Asian Nations issued a statement condemning the idea. Malaysian officials called the proposal a tool for Western protectionism. And Indonesian Trade Minister Tunky Ariwibowo said, "We do not have common standards on issues like corruption. . . . Any effort to relate them to trade will be detrimental to the functioning of the WTO in the future."[59]

When one attempts to understand varying cultural values, it is important to live with and speak to nationals other than those who benefit from bribes. Most Indonesians are as outraged at the injustice of the powerful taking huge cuts as anyone else. Nevertheless, developed nations share the blame, since bribery is explicitly allowed in about half the countries in the developed world. In Germany one can charge a bribe off as a cost of business for tax purposes. In contrast, U.S. law outlaws overseas bribery, as we will see in more detail in Chapter 8, but U.S. firms can be ingenious in circumventing the letter of the law.

With popular support Korean courts in 1996 sentenced four corporation presidents, including the Chairman of giant Daewoo, and a former president of Korea to jail for corruption. His predecessor as president of Korea, Chun Doo Hwan, received a death sentence for his role in the massacre of pro-democracy demonstrators in 1980.[60] A ranking of 41 nations on corruption placed Korea in the middle and Indonesia last. For the full rank order, see Table 1–2. Berlin-based Transparency International used seven separate surveys of businesspeople, journalists, and others to compile the list: 3 from Switzerland, 3 from Hong Kong, and 1 from New York.[61] The list is comprehensive on Asia, but lacks the

---

[57] "Suharto's Family Value: $30 Billion," *World Press Review*, July, 1996, p. 17. Originally from *Wirtschaftswoche*, Duseldorf, March 28, 1996; also Edward A. Gargan, "Family Ties that Bind Growth: Corrupt Leaders in Indonesia Threaten Its Future," *New York Times*, April 9, 1996, pp. C1, C2.

[58] "Irate at Subsidy Program, GM Halts Investment in Indonesia," *Wall Street Journal*, June 12, 1996, p. C6; about this boondoggle and another to build a subsidized jet aircraft, see "Flights of Folly," *The Economist*, March 2, 1996, pp. 60–61.

[59] "Is Corruption an Asian Value? " *Wall Street Journal*, May 6, 1996, p. A14.

[60] "Unfinished Business: Kim Sends the Chaebol a Message," *Business Week*, September 9, 1996, pp. 56–57.

[61] See the list as reported in "A Global Gauge of Greased Palms," *New York Times*, August 20, 1995, p. E3, and also in daily newspapers. A listing with parallel results for Asian nations was done by Political & Economic Risk Consultancy, Ltd. from Hong Kong.

TABLE 1–2   Global Index of Integrity and Corruption

Country	Index (10 = good; 0 = bad)[*]
New Zealand	9.55
Denmark	9.32
Singapore	9.26
Finland	9.12
Sweden	8.87
Canada	8.87
Australia	8.80
Switzerland	8.76
The Netherlands	8.69
Norway	8.61
Ireland	8.57
Britain	8.57
Germany	8.14
Chile	7.94
United States	**7.79**
Austria	7.13
Hong Kong	7.12
France	7.00
Belgium/Luxembourg	6.85
Japan	6.72
South Africa	5.62
Portugal	5.56
Malaysia	5.28
Argentina	5.24
Taiwan	5.08
Spain	4.35
South Korea	4.29
Hungary	4.12
Turkey	4.10
Greece	4.04
Colombia	3.44
Mexico	3.18
Italy	2.99
Thailand	2.79
India	2.78
Philippines	2.77
Brazil	2.70
Venezuela	2.66
Pakistan	2.25
China	2.16
Indonesia	1.94

[*] 10 = no corruption; 0 = corruption is everywhere

Source: Transparency International. Quoted from *New York Times*, August 20, 1995, p. E3. Quoted with permission.

former Soviet countries and most of Africa. The mediocre ranking of the United States may partially be due to "political action committees"; they provide contributions to political candidates in order to obtain their votes on legislation, and this could be considered bribery. It is illegal for a firm to contribute to political candidates in the United States, but corporate PACs legally and publicly do so.

Crony capitalism, rampant in many Asian countries, such as Indonesia, China, India, Thailand, and Malaysia means that who you know and the connections you have are far more important than price or quality. Military, political, and ruling family groups require cash payments for permission to invest.[62]

In sum, where there is widespread bribery of officials, it is difficult to do business in that nation, since costs are increased often by 10 to 30 percent, and one can never be certain if that is the end of the demands. Moreover, the bribe dollars do not go to legitimate costs such as workers or suppliers, but to people who are already wealthy—those who have power.

Influence of Global Firms

With its global operations, the business firm generates jobs and wealth and also transfers technology. Less widely acknowledged are the values that are communicated. The global firm brings the values of industrialized societies to developing ones. Values of individual responsibility, discipline, a regulated workday, and rewards for work under direction of another often conflict with local values of responsibilities to extended family, tribe, and village. Global managers are confronted with a variety of cultural values and are thus challenged to understand and build on these values.

People in developing countries seek a better life. This normally is translated by them to mean jobs, increased income, and more goods and services. The global company is a major factor in aiding the economic development of poorer countries. Since 1960 real gross domestic product per person in the developing world has gone from $950 to $2,730 per year life expectancy has gone from 46.2 years to 63.0 years; the adult literacy rate from 46 percent to 69 percent.[63] Aiding in this development, the global firm:

1. Brings jobs, capital, technology, and managers to a people.
2. Develops leadership and provides training for local people.
3. Reinvests at least some of its profits in the local economy.
4. Provides business for local firms and hence creates jobs, both through purchasing from local suppliers and through workers' purchases.
5. Provides mechanization, fertilizers, and other aids to local agriculture.
6. Produces foreign exchange by exporting goods.

---

[62] See, for example, "The Suharto Empire: Can the Family's Big-Business Deals Survive After the President Is Gone?" *Business Week*, August 19, 1996, pp. 46–50.

[63] Data from "A World in Balance," *Business Week*, March 6, 1995, p. 68.

7. Aids the host nation's development plans.
8. Encourages the development of engineering and other professional skills among local people.
9. Contributes to local and shared ownership projects.

However, there is a negative side to the foreign-owned global corporation and its role in development. Disparity of incomes between the richest and the poorest peoples of the world have increased dramatically in recent years (see Table 1–3). The richest 20 percent of the world's peoples receive 84.7 percent of world's Gross National Product (GNP) while the poorest 20 percent of the world's people receive but 1.4 percent of GNP.[64] Many claim that the global corporation contributes to making the disparity worse. Specifically, the global firm:

1. Widens the gap between the few rich and the many poor in the host country.
2. Encourages urbanization and the resulting uprooting of families and villages.
3. Finances the injustice of government officials' luxurious living in countries in which bribery is common (e.g. Indonesia, Nigeria, Malaysia, Thailand, China).
4. Closes plants abruptly when wage rates rise, workers organize, or regulations become burdensome.
5. Advertises and sells many expensive, unnecessary, and sometimes dangerous consumer goods (e.g., cigarettes, alcohol, weapons).
6. Purchases from suppliers who run sweat shops—low wages, long hours, and unsafe working conditions (e.g., Nike, Fruit of the Loom, Wal-Mart, Gap).
7. Sends profits from operations in poor countries back to richer home nation.
8. Favors and supports a dictatorship over democracy when it is a stable, predictable, probusiness regime (e.g., Singapore, China, Indonesia, Saudi Arabia).

TABLE 1–3   Global Income Distribution, 1960–1989

Year	Share of Global Income Going to Richest 20%	Poorest 20%	Ratio of Richest to Poorest
1960	70.2%	2.3%	30/1
1970	73.9	2.3	32/1
1980	76.3	1.7	45/1
1989	82.7	1.4	59/1

Source: United Nations Development Programme, *Human Development Report—1992* (New York: Oxford University Press, 1992). Quoted with permission.

---

[64] *Ibid.*

VALUES OF FREE ENTERPRISE

Let us return to the values of free enterprise. We have sketched above the flexibility, initiative, and creativity, and also the short-term, materialistic, self-interested attitudes that free enterprise encourages. The intrusion of government and the growth of a sense of entitlement are blamed by many for a new frame of mind according to which one should try to do the least amount of work for the best possible pay.

A distinguishing feature of democratic capitalism and the entrepreneurial spirit is that they encourage individuals to be the main source of social and economic energy.[65] In fact, the past success of democratic capitalism in the United States puts it in a vulnerable position: It is envied by poorer peoples and criticized as exploitative. Moreover, parents who grew up in poverty do not know how to bring up their children under affluence, and those children can become pampered and lazy. Both of these factors blunt the spirit of innovation and the attitudes that encourage the entrepreneur.

Self-Interest as a Goal

The predominant business ideology in the United States holds that when firms and individuals pursue their own self-interest, market forces and the "invisible hand" bring about the most efficient use of resources and result in the greatest satisfaction of people's needs. According to this ideology of self-interest, the best that IBM can do for society is to provide quality computers at a reasonable price and, in so doing, provide a good return to shareholders. This is IBM's contribution to society. If IBM fails in this, it is a failure as a business firm.

The ideology of self-interest has worked well for generations in the United States. It is justified by economic theory and blessed by the Protestant ethic. (The Protestant ethic will be discussed in Chapter 5.) Individuals and businesses pursuing their own self-interest have brought economic development to Western Europe, Japan, and the United States. Acquisitiveness, coupled with creativity, has made our economies successful. The ideology of self-interest acknowledges that people tend to be selfish. Capitalism (or free enterprise) builds on this and directs it to work for the benefit of the entire society. Nobel prize-winning economist Milton Friedman is the intellectual spokesperson for the ideology of self-interest, and we will consider his views in greater detail in Chapter 6.[66]

Economic goals—increasing productivity, personal income, gross national product, and the availability of more and better goods—are even said to be the

---

[65] Michael Novak, "Toward a Theology of the Corporation," in *Business and Society: Dimensions of Conflict and Cooperation*, ed. P. Sethi and C. Falbe (Lexington: Lexington Books, 1987), pp. 1–20; idem., *The Spirit of Capitalism* (New York: Simon & Schuster, 1982).

[66] Milton Friedman and Rose Friedman, *Free to Choose: A Personal Statement* (New York: Harcourt Brace Jovanovich, 1980); see also Milton Friedman's earlier and better reasoned *Capitalism and Freedom* (Chicago: University of Chicago Press, 1962).

most important goals of our society. As President Calvin Coolidge put it, "The business of America is business." One of the most favorable features of free markets is the potential for the creation of jobs. Most jobs are created by entrepreneurs, or managers who are creative, plan for the long-term, and take risks. Yet Raymond Ketchledge, president of Sandy Corporation, finds it necessary to chastise managers of organizations for *risk avoidance.* He goes on:

> Entrepreneurship by definition carries the willingness to take risks. Yet today we can look throughout American industry and . . . find organizations dominated by the idea of being risk averse. It shows up in succumbing to the pressures for short term financial results, and accepting the dilution of responsibility into faceless committees.[67]

Other challenges to self-interest ideology arise early in industrialization, when there are sweatshops employing 10-year-olds for seventy-hour work weeks. Similar challenges arise with respect to pollution. Although it is in the interest of firms—because it maximizes profits—to use cheap child labor and not to pay for safe disposal of toxic waste, it is not good for the rest of society. The pursuit of self-interest causes these problems in the first instance, and one could hardly expect that same motive to bring a solution.

To narrow the purpose of firms to the making of profit for shareholders is shortsighted. Kenneth Mason, when president of Quaker Oats, said, "Making a profit is no more the purpose of a corporation than getting enough to eat is the purpose of life. Getting enough to eat is a requirement of life; life's purpose, one would hope, is somewhat broader and more challenging. Likewise with business and profit."[68]

Moreover, an exclusive focus on self-interest can breed a self-righteousness in pursuing narrow goals that result in indifference to consequences. These attitudes are described flippantly as "creative greed." Consider the values and tactics of gamblers and raiders Kirk Kerkorian, Charles Hurwitz, and T. Boone Pickens. Critics note that the system thus honors those who are most aggressive in their greed; it rewards them with money, power, and status; and thus it reinforces selfishness and narrowness of vision.

The successes and failures of Master of Business Administration (MBA) graduates indicate their values and ethics. As one executive graphically puts it, "In my business I'd as soon take a python to bed with me as hire [a Harvard MBA]. He'd suck my brains, memorize my Rolodex, and use my telephone to find some other guy who'd pay him twice the money."[69]

James Burke, a Harvard MBA himself and who was CEO of Johnson & Johnson, explains why his firm rarely hires such graduates:

---

[67] Raymond A. Ketchledge, "Challenges to the Entrepreneurial Spirit." A lecture at University of Detroit Mercy, April 8, 1992, p. 4.

[68] Kenneth W. Mason, "Responsibility for What's on the Tube," *Business Week*, August 13, 1979, p. 14.

[69] Laurence Shames, *The Big Time: The Harvard Business School's Most Successful Class and How It Shaped America* (New York: Mentor, 1986), pp. 181–82.

The problem begins with the selection process. If you lean heavily on test scores, you necessarily end up with people who are very adept at quantification. And human nature being what it is, people who are good at numbers tend to put a lot of faith in numbers. Which means that kids are coming out of business schools with less and less language skills, less and less people skills, and more and more to unlearn. The really important decisions don't have anything to do with quantification, as everyone figures out—eventually.[70]

Defenders of the ideology of self-interest have responded by maintaining that they speak of "enlightened" self-interest, that is, self-interest taken over the long-term. It is in the long-term self-interest of a manager and a firm to produce high-quality goods in order to maintain the loyalty of customers. So, too, with safe and healthy working conditions that help to hold able employees. Contributions to universities are justified because graduates will benefit the firm and the firm's community. Indeed, some research indicates that a firm that obeys the law, is more socially responsible, and contributes more to charities does have a better financial performance.[71]

Most who reflect on the purpose of the economy and society conclude that money and wealth are instruments of bringing work and goods to people and are not ends in themselves.[72] When money and wealth become ends in themselves, values, priorities, and ethics are altered. Spelling out the cost of this skewing of purpose, Oliver Williams says, "Capitalism without a context in a humane community would seem to inevitably shape people into greedy and insensitive human beings."[73]

Individualism, Commitment, and Community

The emphasis on self-interest and freedom of the individual can run counter to cooperation, commitment, and community. One of the most basic human needs is to share joys, problems, and aspirations with others. Our deep-rooted values of individualism and self-interest, which support a free enterprise system, can nevertheless fracture community and turn the individual in on oneself. The business firm values the person who is mobile, energetic, creative, and ambitious. People like this were attracted to the New World and have thrived here in succeeding generations. However, we have rarely acknowledged the negative qualities of people of this type. Granted, the New World gained the energetic and the daring; but it also drew more than its share of the rootless, the unscrupulous, those who value money over people, and those who put self-interest before love and loyalty. More critically, we gained and encouraged people who, when faced

---

[70] *Ibid.*, p. 182.

[71] Richard E. Wokutch and Barbara A. Spencer, "Corporate Saints and Sinners: Philanthropy, Crime and Organizational Performance," *California Management Review* 29 (Winter 1987): 62–77.

[72] Amitai Etzioni, *The Moral Dimension: Toward A New Economics* (New York: The Free Press, 1988).

[73] Oliver F. Williams, "To Enhance the Common Good: An Introduction," in *The Common Good and U.S. Capitalism*, ed. Oliver F. Williams and John W. Houck (Lanham, Md.: University Press of America, 1987), p. 5.

with a difficult situation, tended to abandon it all and flee to a new environment. The same qualities that we value so highly—mobility and willingness to take risks—encourage us to flee the difficult situation in the hope of leaving our problems behind when we begin again. We have all seen lives and careers that have been shattered when a person walks out, whether it be on a firm, a group of friends, or a family. It is not difficult to escape long-term responsibility in the tolerant, freedom-loving United States, if one has a mind to do so.

Two current trends in political life accelerate the loss of a sense of the common good in the Unites States: Narrow special interests are now stronger and more vocal, and there is a paralyzing lack of consensus regarding national priorities and direction. The confrontational mode of dealing with others has long been a part of the American way. Not only do we use the adversary system in the law courts, but we have institutionalized much conflict (e.g., labor versus management, business versus government). The rhetoric is one of "battle" and "struggle," "win or lose," as if a loss for one group is a win for another. Special interest groups have gathered in the political arena to push for their narrow objectives. These include the American Medical Association (physicians), National Rifle Association, National Educational Association (public school teachers), auto dealers, antiabortionists, and the New Right, who all target members of Congress who are not to their liking. In their turn, the media focus on conflicts and scandal; consensus building and successes do not make the headlines. Cynicism, and a lack of communication and trust, grows at a time when cooperation is badly needed.

When Americans agree on an issue, the agreement often is about being against something: taxes, censorship, big government, bureaucrats. But we Americans find it hard to tell others what we stand *for*—what kind of a society we favor. We find it difficult to express social ideals and we lack the vocabulary to do so. We are not helped by our national political discussions, which appeal to simplistic ideologies and fail to aid us in sorting out priorities and balancing the resulting tradeoffs. Yet it is essential to discuss our priorities, both personal and national, if we are to decide what kind of society we want. These failures of the political forum tend to encourage Americans to be deaf to others' views and distrustful of one another. Finding a common bond and developing a sense of community become both more important and more difficult.

Summary and Conclusions

The U.S. economy has been successful in providing jobs, goods, and services for hundreds of millions of people. Free markets, competition, flexibility, and innovation are all strongly held values of U.S. society. On the other hand, increasing debt, hostile takeovers and mergers, and trivial advertising also stem from those same values.

Capital markets are designed to provide funds for new projects, which in turn provide jobs, products, and services. Speculation is secondary, and unnecessarily injuring stakeholders is unethical. Global business has broadened our horizons. We must understand other peoples if we are to work with them and sell to them. Some global firms support other peoples; others operate sweatshops to produce their goods.

Self-interest motivates business and our society. Advertising and the media encourage self-interest. Yet excessive self-interest undermines loyalty, family, community, and being of help to others. The following chapters will examine personal moral development, ethical behavior, the historical roots of and additional effects of American business values.

Discussion Questions

1. What are the principal benefits to people of a healthy business system?
2. Why do Americans choose to consume more and save less than people in other countries? How does this affect (a) productivity and (b) values?
3. Are the rich becoming richer and the poor becoming poorer in developed countries? Why is this so?
4. List the negative effects of layoffs. When a firm finds it necessary to "downsize," what are its responsibilities to affected parties?
5. Compare AT&T and Malden Mills and their attitudes toward their workers when problems arose.
6. What role do institutional investors play in the U.S. economy? Describe the negative effects of the actions of portfolio managers.
7. Evaluate the morality of insider trading.
8. What is the evidence for a loss of confidence in American business?
9. What causes most of the cases of cancer in men and women? What are the implications of this for private sector planning? For public policy?
10. Comment on the advertising and business strategy of Nike. Evaluate the ethics of that strategy.
11. In what way does advertising and the media influence values? Do they present a false and deceptive image to people?
12. How do global firms benefit peoples? What are their negative contributions?
13. In a developing country, what environment encourages and what discourages business (e.g., Singapore vs. Indonesia and India)?
14. Is self-interest as a personal motivation a correct description of most business activities as you find them?
15. Is self-interest an adequate motivation for businesspeople? When is it most effective? When is it not adequate?
16. What analogy does Kenneth Mason, former president of Quaker Oats, use in rejecting Milton Friedman's position that the purpose of a corporation is to maximize returns to shareholders?
17. Does self-interest as a goal for businesspeople necessarily cast government in the role of a regulator? How so?

Exercise:
Personal Values and Life Goal Inventory

This exercise is designed to help you to better understand your own personal values, and to see how these values and personal experiences support or conflict with your life goals.

I. **Procedure:**
   A. Rank order the values on the value survey below (sixteen long-range values).
   B. Complete the life goal inventory. Write out your major goals for the next 1 to 2 years in each of the areas indicated.
   C. Write a paper (maximum of six double-spaced typed pages) examining and comparing your experiences, your most important values and your life and career goals. It is not necessary to turn in the completed order of personal values or the completed life goal inventory.

II. **Criterion** for evaluating the paper: demonstration of your ability to analyze and articulate your own values, goals, and experiences. Such demonstration includes the following.
   A. Clarity of analysis of experiences, goals, and values.
   B. Ability to recognize and deal with the implications of support and conflict among experiences, values, and goals, and their significance for future career and life-style decisions.

III. **Suggestions** for writing the paper:
   A. Write in the first, not the third, person.
   B. Include a paragraph or two of personal history to put your values and goals in context. What events in your life have affected your values and goals?
   C. Discuss at least briefly each of the five goals but deal only with the most important values or cluster of values.
      1. What do these values imply about personal goals? Do your values support your goals? Or do they conflict?
      2. To what extend have your life experiences followed your values and/or goals to date?
      3. Compare your present activities, job, and so on, with these values and goals.
      4. Is there any particular satisfaction or frustration that might be explained by support from or conflict between values and goals?
      5. Clarify points with specific personal experiences and examples.
   D. Write reflections honestly and straightforwardly. No one else will see your paper. It is confidential, and will be returned quickly.
   E. The values and goals sheets are to help you in your analysis. Use them to help you in writing your paper.
   F. Use clear language and good grammar. Choose directness and clarity over elaboration.

IV. I apologize for intruding into your personal values. However, experience indicates that most of us do not explicitly reflect on our goals and values unless (1) we are asked to do so, or (2) a crisis arises in our lives. The paper will enable you to gain a better understanding of yourself before a crisis arises.

Rank Ordering of Personal Values

Rank the following sixteen personal values in order of importance to you, that is, insofar as they are guiding principles in your life. Study the list of values carefully. Place a 1 in front of the value that is most important in your life, a 2 in front of the next most important, and so on. The least most important value for you should be ranked 16. If you change your mind, feel free to change the ranking.

When you are finished, the list should roughly indicate the importance of the various values in your life.

_____ Achievement (promotions at work)

_____ Beauty (natural and artistic beauty)

_____ Cooperation

_____ Dollar rewards (money and salary)

_____ Equality (equal opportunity for all; everyone as equal)

_____ Family security (taking care of and being with loved ones)

_____ Freedom (independence)

_____ Love, friendship, and intimacy

_____ Physical health and well-being

_____ Pleasure (sensually and sexually enjoyable personal life)

_____ Possessions (good car, clothes, home, many material goods)

_____ Recognition (respect, admiration from others)

_____ Self-respect (a good self-image, self-esteem)

_____ Sense of accomplishment (making a lasting contribution)

_____ Union with God (prayer, striving to be a good person)

_____ World at peace (lessening of war and conflict)

Life Goal Inventory

This inventory is designed to help you examine your life goals. Describe as fully as possible your aims and goals in all areas of your life. List all goals that are important to you, whether they are fairly easy or difficult to attain. Be honest in this assessment; only then will the inventory be useful to you. For example, if your major goal is to enjoy leisure satisfactions, indicate this, so as to better understand and assess yourself. In your own words, describe two to five goals in each of the following areas over the next year or two. The categories are a guide; feel free to change them to suit your own goals.

Career Satisfaction
Goals for future job or career; specific positions aimed for.

1.

2.

3.

Personal Relationships
With friends, parents, spouse, colleagues, others.

1.

2.

3.

Leisure Satisfactions
Vacations, sports, hobbies, other interests.

1.

2.

3.

Learning and Education
New skills you would like to learn or areas of knowledge you would like
to study.

1.

2.

3.

Spiritual Growth and Religion
Relation to God, prayer, giving self to others, larger questions.

1.

2.

3.

CASES
College Test

Kathy Blakenship and Joe Fontana are juniors in the business school at Lincoln University. Both are taking a basic finance course taught by Hugh Sikora. Kathy is a member of the Honors Program. Joe, a friendly young man, is an average student. On the first exam, Kathy scored the second highest grade in the class and Joe failed. The next exam, more heavily weighted, was given the following month. During the exam Hugh noticed Joe glancing in the direction of Kathy's paper several times. When grading the papers, Sikora noted all fifteen multiple choice items to be identical on Joe's and Kathy's papers, including two responses that were incorrect.

1. You are a student sitting behind Joe, and you see what he is doing. Do you have any responsibility to speak to Joe? To the instructor?
2. As the instructor, you noticed Joe's activities during the exam. What should you do? Why?
3. As you grade the papers, you note the identical items on the exam. What should (or would) you do?
4. What ethical issues are involved here?

Confidentiality of Electronic Mail

Alana Shoars, an e-mail administrator for Epson America in Los Angeles, arrived at work early one morning to find her supervisor reading e-mail messages between employees. She protested, and was fired. Although the company had no stated policy on the privacy of messages, they argued that the network was their property and was purchased for company business. Bank of Boston found one employee using e-mail to play the horses and another was running an Amway business from office e-mail.

1. Does a firm have the right to monitor employees' e-mail?
2. Does a firm have an obligation to inform employees of their policies on e-mail?
3. Comment on the ethics involved in the situation at Epson and Bank of Boston.

CHAPTER

Maturity
and Moral Development

Greed in business is healthy. You can be greedy
and still feel good about yourself.
—Ivan Boesky

Let us be concerned for each other, to stir a response in love and good
works. Do not stay away from the meetings of the community, as some do,
but encourage each other to go.
—Hebrews 10:24–25

We are not born with moral maturity. A sense of right and wrong is learned from parents, friends, churches, schools—and from experiences like those we examined in Chapter 1. In this chapter we will examine: (1) the moral development of the individual person, (2) the stress that stems from a lack of personal values and goals, (3) methods of making personal values explicit, and finally (4) the reasons for considering ethics when making all business decisions. First let us examine some examples of executives under stress.

Lee Iacocca was president of Ford and chairman of Chrysler, but he says himself that he flunked retirement. He says his life was so structured and isolated as CEO, that he was not able to deal with the flexibility of retirement. He participated in the hostile and ill-fated attempt to take over Chrysler. His third wife of three and one-half years led him to move to California, and then fought him in a nasty divorce six months later.[1]

---

[1] "How I Flunked Retirement," Interview with Lee Iacocca. *Fortune*, June 24, 1996, pp. 50–61.

James E. Olson, the last chairman and chief executive officer (CEO) of AT&T, died suddenly at age 63. He had just cut 1 billion dollars from AT&T's operating costs the year before and had overseen the largest corporate restructuring in American history—the breakup of the AT&T system into numerous operating systems.[2]

The space shuttle Challenger was launched on January 28, 1986. Roger Boisjoly, Senior Seal Specialist, and other Morton-Thiokol engineers were concerned that the seals on the rocket would fail because of the cold temperatures. In meetings the previous evening they urged that Challenger not be launched. But the launch had been postponed three times, and there was pressure to show Congress some success in the space program to assure future funding. The engineers were overruled by NASA and their own vice president. They watched the rocket launch; it failed 70 seconds into the flight and 7 crew members died.[3]

Eli Black, CEO of United Brands, broke the window of his forty-fourth floor office in Manhattan with his attaché case and jumped to his death in 1975. Two months later the Securities and Exchange Commission revealed that United Brands had paid a $1,250,000 bribe to a government official in Honduras for a reduction in the export tax on bananas. Black knew about the bribe.

Each of these executives faced stress, anxiety, and a conflict in values. They are particularly visible examples of the strains and anxieties that face businesspeople every day. This chapter will examine the sources of and some solutions to the conflicts that arise. Some of the data in this chapter are taken from psychology and sociology. The application to people in business is generally obvious.

LACK OF MATURITY BRINGS STRESS

People who are mature and morally developed (for definitions, see Fig. 2–1) are more relaxed, enjoy life more, are able to more fully utilize their talents, and are generally more liked and respected by their families and peers. Moreover, they are also considered wise and are more often consulted by others. On the other hand, crises, stress, and illness often plague the person who has failed to achieve maturity and moral development.

Midlife Crisis

A person who has not internalized his or her own values is often pressed into making important life and career decisions before clarifying goals or examining alternatives. This then often leads to a midlife crisis.

---

[2] *Business Week*, May 2, 1988, p. 34.

[3] *Report of the Presidential Commission on the Space Shuttle Accident* (Washington, D.C.: U.S. Government Printing Office, 1986).

FIGURE 2–1 Moral Development Terms

Character: A stable organized personality with a composite of good and bad moral habits within a person.
Common good: Good of the group as a whole; general welfare.
Community: Any group sharing goals, interests, work, and so on.
Maturity: State of being fully developed as a person.
Moral development: Increased ability of a person to distinguish right and wrong and to engage in good behavior.

Adrienne Glasgow was manager of international finance at Borden at the age of 35. She quit her job, because she was not fulfilled. She is now consulting.[4]

John Z. DeLorean was vice president in charge of General Motors car and truck divisions in North America. DeLorean quit because he felt that the GM committee system was too unwieldy. It dispersed authority and responsibility, and he felt that as a result no one could show initiative. Whether one agrees with DeLorean or not, his case is not unique. The *Wall Street Journal* and *Fortune* have run articles on scores of people who left well-paid corporate jobs to do something quite different at a fraction of their former pay. These people found their work in the corporation to be confining, and most turned to a simpler and less-structured life. Typical is Ross Drever, age 52, who quit as director of Amsted Industries' research division at a $100,000 salary. He now works a cranberry bog in Three Lakes, Wisconsin. He says, "I have a lot of suits and shoes I'll never use again."

These managers felt they were giving too much time to a job that gave them little satisfaction. They made a radical change; they left comfortable jobs, homes, and friends to carve out a new life. These women and men show us how some at midlife examine their own values and goals and act on what they find.

This reassessment often occurs in women and men around the age of 40. One looks around and asks if this is the way one would choose to lead the rest of one's life. Time is running out; there may be only 2 decades of healthy work life left.

A midlife crisis can be traumatic—to family, to fellow workers, and to the person experiencing it. On some occasions the person experiencing the midlife transition panics and seeks a dramatic change. The individual sometimes breaks all connections with the past, leaves spouse and children behind, and goes off with different friends. This sort of radical break can cause much hurt and disruption to families, neighbors and coworkers. Such a reaction to the midlife reassessment is desperate and immature. However, the frequency of these sharp midlife breaks show that too few of us have sufficiently probed our own goals

---

[4] Betsy Morris, "Executive Women Confront Midlife Crisis," *Fortune* September 18, 1995, pp. 60–86. This article chronicles a dozen such cases, and gives an overview of the midlife crisis for women.

in order to take charge of our lives. Too often we allow salaries and status to determine our career and our goals for us.

The midlife journey can be a gradual, life-giving reassessment, especially if the person has internalized his or her own goals and values. The journey can become a crisis if one's goals and values have not been examined and if one's life has been determined by "opportunities" (salaries and the lead of others) instead of by enlightened choices. The objective is to consciously take possession of your own values and goals. The more clearly you recognize what your heart-felt goals are and what brings you real happiness, the greater the chance that your midlife reassessment will be a peaceful one.

Stress and Illness

Self-esteem depends on the positive and negative feedback a person receives from others. In the American culture, those who gain the esteem of their peers are considered successful. Such people are typically competent, goal-oriented, conscientious, ambitious, and hard working, qualities which will be identified with the Protestant ethic in Chapters 4 and 5.

The culture, through families, schools, churches, business, and government, communicates its values to the individual. A culture thus gives people direction and integrity. Without this socialization process, it is not possible to know what one person may expect of another in everyday dealings. We will examine the socialization process within the firm in Chapter 7.

Although some cultural expectations are not now as strong as they were a generation ago, there is more consensus as to the importance of success in business. People who are not successful are often judged inferior by others. Such lack of success is an added source of stress. Further job-related stress is caused by conflict and confusion over a person's responsibilities[5] or when the job calls for actions that conflict with an individual's ethics. In these cases, either a compromise is reached or something is sacrificed. The result is anxiety and frustration.

Those who are judged successful according to the prevailing norms (i.e., viewed as competent, ambitious, and hardworking) may by that very fact suffer anxieties. Successful corporate managers are mobile. They are able to leave their present jobs and homes in order to move on to "better" positions. Psychologists tell us that anxiety is caused by moving from the known to the unknown. Having mastered one environment, it is unsettling to be asked to move to a new one. It is true that in order to mature, one must take risks and

---

[5] See "Stress: The Test Americans Are Failing—It's Taking a Greater Toll on CEOs, Managers, Factory Workers," *Business Week*, April 18, 1988, pp. 74–76. Among the top items CEOs worry about are (in descending order) their own health and fitness, their company's future, the lack of time for family or leisure pursuits, their children's problems, job-related stress, keeping up with technology, product quality, and personal investments; from John H. Sheridan, "What Worries Today's Executives," *Industry Week*, November 30, 1987, pp. 27–32.

change. Yet being uprooted every few years—leaving behind not just the confidence built in mastering a job but also friends, relatives, and knowledge of the community—can undermine the willingness to commit oneself to a new job or neighborhood. People in such situations may be forced in upon themselves and may come to depend more on their aggressiveness than on the help and cooperation of coworkers, friends, and neighbors. When they choose to grow in this fashion, they demand their spouses and children undergo the same cyclic trauma of arriving and departing, along with the pain and anxiety it involves.

The unknown, even more the uncontrollable, produces anxieties. Ulcers and stress are often manifestations of anxiety; they usually result when there are conflicting demands on the individual. Neuroses have been experimentally induced in animals exposed to ambiguous stimuli. After the same or very similar stimuli, the animals were sometimes rewarded and sometimes not (or sometimes rewarded and sometimes punished). Gastric ulcers developed in caged laboratory rats who spent 1 month subjected to ambiguous stimuli. During 47 hours of every 48-hour period, they had to endure an electric shock every time they went to the food box or the water cup. They needed the food, but also feared the shock. Furthermore, since they were not shocked during the remaining hour, they were never sure whether they would get a shock along with their food. The conflict of wanting the food and yet being afraid of the pain, plus a lack of control over the situation, produced the ulcers. Control rats, which were simply deprived of food and water for 47 of the 48 hours, did not develop ulcers.[6]

Cats that were first fed and then shocked following the same buzzer exhibited a wide variety of aberrant physical activities, such as restless roving, clawing at wire cages, butting the roof with their heads, and ceaseless vocalizing—all indicating a high degree of anxiety. These cats were then given the opportunity to drink milk that had been laced with alcohol. Half the animals quickly learned that the alcohol relieved the symptoms of their anxiety, and they invariably chose the 5 percent alcohol mixture served in a distinctive cocktail glass. The cats preferred the alcohol as long as their tensions persisted and they remained neurotic. When the animals experienced psychic pain because of lack of control, they sought relief in withdrawal, and their neurotic symptoms disappeared under the influence of the alcohol.

People, too, attempt to escape from the pain that arises from uncertainty and the inability to control their immediate environment. That escape can be healthy or can result in a refusal to face the issues that are causing the problem. The stress that ensues can bring on ulcers, high blood pressure, a heart attack, or even cancer.

---

[6] Bernard Berelson and Gary A. Steiner, *Human Behavior: An Inventory of Scientific Findings* (New York: Harcourt, Brace & World, 1964), pp. 276–79; see also "The Crippling Ills That Stress Can Trigger," *Business Week*, April 18, 1988, pp. 77–78.

Large amounts of stress cause poor job performance. Therefore, job re-lated stress has taken on new importance for businesspeople.[7] Stress and the ill-ness, absenteeism, and health care costs that are related to it have become im-mense expenses for firms. Making the problem worse, the United States ties Japan for having the fewest average annual vacation days (10), a possible time of renewal. Most European countries have two to three times as many vacation days.[8] In addition, in a few notable court cases, firms have been held responsi-ble for work-related stress. However, not all stress is bad for the individual or for job performance. In fact a moderate amount of stress correlates with better job performance; the "fight or flight" response releases a moderate amount of stimulants and thus enables a person to better achieve the objective. Greater so-cial support results in less stress, even in the face of the same challenges. Exercise and relaxation will reduce stress. Firms such as Bank of America, IBM, General Motors, Xerox, and Johnson & Johnson provide wellness pro-grams for their people.[9]

Stress can also lead people to seek quiet places in order to reflect on themselves and their goals, thus enabling them to emerge from the stressful sit-uation healthier and in better control of their lives. Quiet time, reflection, medi-tation, and prayer are being rediscovered. They are effective in dealing with normal stress and in helping people to grow in maturity. The need for business-people to take charge of their own lives and to pursue moral development is un-derscored by the fact that Steven Covey's books emphasize this and have been best sellers for several years.[10] Stress and anxiety are lessened when people are explicitly aware of their own values. In the process, people become more ma-ture and morally developed.

MORAL DEVELOPMENT

We know and have read about people who are willing to work unselfishly for the benefit of others, even when it demands personal sacrifice. Some people in every community spend their lives providing the sick and homeless with food

---

[7] Michael Manning, et al., Occupational Stress, Social Support, and the Costs of Health Care," *Academy of Management Journal* 39:3 (1996), pp. 738–750; Victoria Doby and Robert Caplan, "Organizational Stress as Threat to Reputation: Effects on Anxiety at Work and at Home," *Academy of Management Journal* 38:4 (1995), pp. 1105–23.

[8] "Yankees: Nose to the Grindstone," *Business Week* (September 4, 1995), p. 28; Kevin Williams and George Alliger, "Role Stressors, Mood Spillover, and Perceptions of Work-Family Conflict in Employed Parents," *Academy of Management Journal* 37:4 (1994), pp. 837–68; Wayne F. Cascio, *Costing Human Resources: The Financial Impact of Behavior in Organizations* (Boston: Kent, 1982).

[9] For an excellent overview of how these firms and others have introduced wellness programs and how they deal with these issues, see William M. Kizer, *The Healthy Workplace: A Blueprint for Corporate Action* (New York: Wiley, 1987).

[10] Steven Covey, *The 7 Habits of Highly Successful People: Powerful Lessons in Personal Change* (New York: Fireside, 1990); also Covey's *Principle-Centered Leadership* (New York: Fireside, 1991).

and shelter. Some executives habitually take into account the effect of their decisions "on the little guy." Some leaders take the blame for the blunders of subordinates. We consider such people to be morally good; they have a high level of moral development.

On the other hand, we also know others who consider only themselves. They may be well educated and articulate, but they are also manipulative and often skillful in hiding their self-centeredness. Some, of course, are straightforward in their greediness.

Let us examine some data on the moral development of graduate business students. Business students often display conventional thought and lack a clear personal vision. At Harvard Business School, a study of students' values found that:

> Many students came in the door, as it were, repeatedly espousing such credos as "The important thing is to act—whether you are right or wrong." or "I must do my personal best." The implications of these credos tend to flow something like this:
>
> INTERVIEWER: When all is said and done, what would you like your life ultimately to be about?
> STUDENT: I would like to achieve my personal goals.
> INTERVIEWER: What might some of those be?
> STUDENT: I guess that would depend on what company I was with.
> INTERVIEWER: What kind of company would you like to work with?
> STUDENT: It wouldn't really matter.

The authors concluded that the graduate business students' "primary values are those of achieving success, however it is defined by the prevailing culture, with little self-reflective choice. And if this is the case, we must assume that such students are extremely vulnerable to becoming the victims of unconsidered and inadequate goals."[11] Is this troubling judgment too severe?

Moral development is somewhat like physical development. People grow physically, psychologically, and morally. As an infant's body develops, it must physically progress through the stages of creeping, crawling, toddling, walking, and finally running. Likewise, a person morally progresses through certain identifiable phases. As a result of moral development, the person has a growing ability to recognize moral issues and to distinguish right from wrong. This ability to make moral judgments and to engage in moral behavior increases with maturity. People are not born with moral abilities; they must be cultivated and developed, much like skills and abilities of other kinds.

Scholars have observed moral development for centuries and have classi-

---

[11] Sharon Daloz Parks, "Is It Too Late? Young Adults and the Formation of Professional Ethics," *Can Ethics Be Taught? Perspectives, Challenges and Approaches at Harvard Business School* (Boston: Harvard Business School Press, 1993), pp. 24–25; quoted with permission. See also Frederick P. Close, "The Case for Moral Education," *The Responsive Community* (Winter 1993/94), pp. 23–29.

fied the stages of development in various ways. Child psychologist Jean Piaget was the first to collect data from observing and interviewing children. Psychologist Lawrence Kohlberg was concerned with moral development over the life span.[12]

Stages of Moral Growth

Kohlberg considered moral development to proceed through three levels, with each level consisting of two stages. Let us now examine these levels and stages.

Level I: Preconventional

At this level a child is able to respond to rules and social expectations and can apply the labels *good, bad, right*, and *wrong*. The child sees rules (1) as something imposed from the outside and (2) largely in terms of the pleasant or painful consequences of actions or in terms of the power of those who set the rules. The child views situations from his or her own point of view. The child does not yet have the ability to identify with others, so the child's point of view is largely one of self-interest.

Stage 1: Punishment and obedience orientation. The child does the right thing to avoid punishment or to obtain approval. There is little awareness of the needs of others. The physical consequences of an act determine its goodness and badness regardless of the wider consequences.

Stage 2: Naively egoistic and instrumental orientation. The child is now aware that others also have needs and begins to defer to them in order to obtain what he or she wants. Right actions are those which satisfy the child's own interests. Right is what is fair, an equal exchange, a deal. Human relations are viewed as being like the relations of the marketplace.

Level II: Conventional

Maintaining the expectations of one's family, peer group, or nation is viewed as valuable in its own right regardless of the consequences. The person at this level does not merely conform to expectations but is loyal to those groups and attempts to maintain and justify that order. The person is now able to identify with another's point of view and assumes that everyone has a similar point of view. The person conforms to the group's norms and subordinates the needs of the individual to those of the group.

---

[12] John Dewey, "What Psychology Can Do for the Teacher," in *John Dewey on Education: Selected Writings*, ed. Reginald Archambault (New York: Random House, 1964); Jean Piaget, *The Moral Judgment of the Child* (Glencoe, Ill.: The Free Press, 1948); and Lawrence Kohlberg, "The Cognitive-Developmental Approach to Moral Education," in *Readings in Moral Education*, ed. Peter Scharf (Minneapolis: Winston Press, 1978), pp. 36–51.

Stage 3: Interpersonal concordance: "good boy—nice girl" orientation. Good behavior is conduct which pleases or helps close family and friends and is approved by them. Right action is conformity to what is expected; the person conforms to stereotypes of what is majority or "natural" behavior. Behavior is frequently judged by intention: "He means well." One earns approval by being a "good boy" or a "nice girl."

Stage 4: Law and order orientation. Right behavior consists in doing one's duty, showing respect for authority, and maintaining the social order for its own sake. Loyalty to the nation and its laws is paramount. The person now sees other people as individuals yet also as part of the larger social system which gives them their roles and obligations. The person enters this stage as a result of experiencing the inadequacies of Stage 3.

Level III: Postconventional, Autonomous, or Principled

The person no longer simply accepts the values and norms of the groups to which she or he belongs. There is a clear effort to find moral values and principles that impartially take everyone's interests into account. The person questions the norms and laws that society has adopted and redefines them so that they make sense to any rational individual. Proper laws and values are those to which any reasonable person would be committed whatever the society or the status held within that society.

Stage 5: Social contract orientation. The individual is aware that people hold a variety of conflicting views, but rules must be upheld in the interest of the social contract. Laws are agreed on and must be followed impartially, although they can be changed if need be. Some absolute values, such as life and liberty, are held regardless of differing individual values or even majority opinion. Utilitarianism ("the greatest good for the greatest number") is the characteristic ethical standard. The morality of this stage is the "official" morality of the U.S. government and the Constitution.

Stage 6: Conscience and principle orientation. Right action is defined by decisions of conscience in accord with universal ethical principles which are chosen by the person because of their comprehensiveness, universality, and consistency. These ethical principles are not specific, concrete moral codes like the Ten Commandments. Instead they are based on the belief that persons are ends in themselves and should not be used merely as means, and the universal moral principles dealing with respect for the dignity of individual human beings, justice, public welfare, and the equality of human rights. The person's motivation for doing right is built upon care for fellow human beings and a belief in the validity of universal moral principles and a personal commitment to these principles.

Reasoning and Caring in Moral Development

Observations of morally mature people show that *all* persons move through these stages. Individuals are not able to move to a higher stage until they have passed through the lower stages. Examples of people who have moved through the earlier stages to Level III would be Detroit Mayor Dennis Archer, Deputy Mayor Nettie Seabrooks, and Chief of Police Isaiah McKinnon. Each quit higher paying jobs (Michigan Supreme Court, vice president of General Motors and director of security for the Renaissance Center, respectively) in order to serve the city. Each is active in meeting with community groups, aiding boys' clubs, working with volunteers, and so on. As devoted to spouse and their children, they are highly visible role models for younger people in the city. Their motivation goes beyond pleasing others (State 3), or even obeying the "rules of the game" (Stage 4). They pursue the "greatest good for the greatest number" (Stage 5), and they seem to be seeking the overall welfare of *all the people* (Stage 6). They are willing to give their own talents and energy in order to try to help all—perhaps especially disadvantaged people in an urban area. U.S. Housing Secretary Henry Cisneros praised Detroit's progress: In 4 years new investment in the city totals $2.1 billion; unemployment has dropped from 16.2 percent to 9.3 percent; violent crime has fallen nearly 10 percent; property values have risen more than 10 percent; and the rate of home ownership has climbed to 71.6 percent.[13]

However, not all people reach the higher stages of moral development; most remain stuck at a lower stage for their entire lives. Kohlberg finds that most Americans never do reach the higher stages but remain at stage 3 or 4.[14] For example, Kohlberg believes that former President Richard Nixon never got beyond moral stage 3 or 4. Nixon never really understood the U.S. Constitution, which is a document built on a stage 5 foundation. Psychiatrist Karl Menninger, founder of the Menninger Institute, agrees with Kohlberg's assessment of Nixon but goes further and adds him to the list of what Menninger calls evil men, which includes Adolph Hitler, Lyndon Johnson, and James Watt (President Reagan's antienvironmental Secretary of the Interior, who served time in jail).[15]

A few still claim that schools should be value-free and not concerned with moral development. Kohlberg responds that this is nonsense. All teaching communicates values. Choosing to be value-free is itself taking a value position. The important question is: What are the values that *are* communicated? And what values *should be* communicated? Supporting Kolhberg is the finding that the level of education is positively related to moral development. However,

---

[13] "Cisneros Praises Detroit Revival," *Detroit Free Press*, September 12, 1996, pp. 1A and 9A.

[14] Kohlberg, *ibid.*, p. 38.

[15] "Famed Psychiatrist Karl Menninger Analyzes the World, Finds It Needs Help," *Wall Street Journal*, December 23, 1985, pp. 1, 8; see also Karl Menninger, *Whatever Became of Sin?* (New York: Hawthorn Books, 1972).

business students are more conventional, less reflective, and seem to be less ethical than other students.[16]

An empirical study of 37 manager's actual handling of moral dilemmas found that "managers typically reason at stages 3 or 4." Mid-level business managers were interviewed and asked what they would do with three moral dilemmas. The managers, 86.5 percent male, operated at Kohlberg's Stage 3 (46%) and Stage 4 (40%). Managers in smaller organizations, under 250 employees, were more likely (54%) to reason at Stage 4. Managers in larger organizations were more likely (again 54%) to reason at Stage 3.[17]

Kohlberg's research was done only with males. To complete the model, Carol Gilligan examined the moral development of women. She found that, especially in the later stages, women's moral development differs from that of men. Whereas men tend to judge good and bad on the basis of reasoning and principles, women more often consider relationships, caring, and solidarity. Women (and in many cases men) at the higher stages of moral development often decide right from wrong on the basis of what effect the proposed action would have on relationships, love, and caring.[18] These insights have enabled business ethicists to identify caring as an additional ethical norm for making ethical decisions; caring and other ethical norms will be discussed in the next chapter.

The above theories of moral development have been both supported and challenged, but most challengers agree that moral development generally takes place in the way described. Kohlberg has carefully studied moral development and has provided a useful model.[19]

The stages of moral development described by Kohlberg are similar to those described by Dewey and Piaget. Edward Stevens uses Kohlberg's levels of

---

[16] Anthony J. Daboub, Abdul M. A. Rasheed, Richard L. Priem, and David A. Gray, "Top Management Team Characteristics and Corporate Illegal Activity," *Academy of Management Review* 20 (January 1995): 155.

[17] James Weber, "Managers' Moral Reasoning: An Exploratory Look at Managers' Responses to Three Moral Dilemmas," *Academy of Management Best Paper Proceedings—1989*, ed. Frank Hoy (Academy of Management, 1989), pp. 333–37.

[18] Carol Gilligan, *In a Different Voice: Psychological Theory and Women's Development* (Cambridge, Mass.: Harvard University Press, 1982). Robbin Derry found justice and caring orientations in both men and women and so did not verify the sex split; see Robbin Derry, "Moral Reasoning in Work Related Conflicts," in *Research in Corporate Social Performance and Policy*, ed. William C. Frederick, vol. 9 (Greenwich, Conn.: JAI, 1987), pp. 25–49. See also Andrew Wicks, Daniel Gilbert, and Edward Freeman, "A Feminist Reinterpretation of the Stakeholder Concept," *Business Ethics Quarterly* 4 (October 1995): 475–97.

[19] See, for example, Gerald Baxter and Charles Rarick, "Education for the Moral Development of Managers: Kohlberg's Stages of Moral Development and Integrative Education," *Journal of Business Ethics* 6 (April 1987): 243–48; see also Thomas Lickona, "What Does Moral Psychology Have to Say to the Teacher of Ethics? " in *Ethics Teaching in Higher Education*, ed. Daniel Callahan and Sissela Bok (New York: Plenum Press, 1980), pp. 103–32; for a detailed description of maturity, including Kohlberg's moral development model, see Robert Kegan, *The Evolving Self: Problem and Process in Human Development* (Cambridge, Mass.: Harvard University Press, 1982), esp. pp. 50–71.

moral development as an outline, and proposes that some popular ethical theories can be explained by the fact that their originators were stuck at one of Kohlberg's lower levels. He finds that both social Darwinism (see Chapter 4) and Ayn Rand's objectivism flow from a primitive, preconventional view of moral development (see Table 2–1).

Kohlberg thinks that moral judgment is the single most important factor in moral behavior. It is impossible to be morally mature without the ability to confront various options and to make intelligent judgments on the rightness and wrongness of each. Moral judgment depends on moral reasoning, and we will discuss both moral judgment and moral reasoning in Chapter 3.

Individualism and the Common Good

Ethical acts and moral development presuppose that there is a moral good and that there is some agreement on what it is. Robert Bellah and his coauthors investigated the American view of a good society.[20] They interviewed a wide variety of Americans from coast to coast and found that society places obstacles in the path of determining the moral good and of achieving a national consensus on important issues. The principal value for most Americans is freedom as we saw in Chapter 1 and will see again in later chapters. Hear the authors:

> Freedom is perhaps the most resonant, deeply held American value. In some ways, it defines the good in both personal and political life. Yet freedom turns out to mean being left alone by others, not having other people's values, ideas, or styles of life forced upon one, being free of arbitrary authority in work, family, and political life. What it is that one might do with that freedom is much more difficult for Americans to define. And if the entire social world is made up of individuals, each endowed with the right to be free of others' demands, it becomes hard to forge bonds of attachment to, or cooperation with, other people, since such bonds would imply obligations that necessarily impinge on one's freedom.[21]

Making freedom such an important value has given Americans a respect for other individuals and has encouraged creativity and innovation. However, it also has its costs:

> It is an ideal freedom that leaves Americans with a stubborn fear of acknowledging structures of power and interdependence in a technologically complex society dominated by giant corporations and an increasingly powerful state. The ideal of freedom makes Americans nostalgic for their past, but provides few resources for talking about their collective future.[22]

Such a sense of freedom leaves both the person and society with little inclination or vocabulary to address common concerns. The traditional term *com-*

---

[20] Robert N. Bellah et al., *Habits of the Heart: Individualism and Commitment in American Life* (New York: Harper & Row, 1985).

[21] *Ibid.*, p. 23.

[22] *Ibid.*, p. 25.

TABLE 2–1 Moral Development and Ethical Theory: An Overview

Theories of Moral Development and Corresponding Stages[a]

Jean Piaget's Theory	John Dewey's Theory	Lawrence Kohlberg's Theory	Edward Stevens' Theory
0. Premoral		0. Premoral	Group A
	I. Preconventional	I. Preconventional	1. Social Darwinism
1. Heteronomous (age 4–8)		1. Punishment and obedience orientation	2. Machiavellianism
2. Autonomous (age 8–12)		2. Naively egoistic and instrumentalist orientation	3. Objectivism (Ayn Rand)
	II. Conventional	II. Conventional	Group B
		3. Interpersonal concordance: "good boy-nice girl" orientation	4. Conventional morality
			5. Legalistic ethics
		4. Law and order orientation	6. Accountability model of ethics
	III. Autonomous	III. Postconventional, autonomous, principled	Group C
		5. Social contract orientation	7. Pragmatism
			8. Marxism
		6. Conscience and principle orientation	9. "Economic humanism"

Ethical Theories Corresponding to Stages of Moral Development[b]

[a] Adapted from Lawrence Kohlberg, "The Cognitive-Development Approach to Moral Education," in *Readings in Moral Education*, ed. Peter Scharf (New York: Winston Press, 1978), pp. 36–37.

[b] Adapted from rough congruence presented by Edward Stevens, *Business Ethics* (New York: Paulist Press, 1979).

mon good refers to the good of society as a whole, that is, all people taken together. It has almost fallen out of use, because its meaning is difficult to understand for many people in western societies.

This emphasis on freedom is generally hostile to older ideas of the moral order. The center of our current moral order is the individual, who is given full freedom to choose careers, commitments, and a life, not on the basis of obligations to others or of truths outside the individual, but on the basis of self-satisfaction as the individual judges it. Commitments—from marriage and work to political and religious involvement—are made as a way to enhance individual well-being rather than out of obedience to moral imperatives. If it is satisfying to me, I will do it; if it is not satisfying, I will withdraw. In a word, what is good is what one finds personally rewarding. If preferences change, so does what is considered good. Even the most fundamental ethical virtues are treated as matters of personal preference. Hence, the basic ethical rule is that individuals be able to pursue whatever they find rewarding as long as they not interfere with the actions and values of others.[23] This is the childlike Level I of moral development.

Individuals often elevate their subjective view of themselves and their world and declare it reality. It is true that our personal values and goals are a bedrock and upon them we build our life, our friends and our future. We are responsible before God to the extent we have been true to our own conscience. Nevertheless, personal values are rarely the best for society to use as a foundation in order to construct our future together.

An individualistic value system makes it very difficult to discuss issues that face groups of people. It provides no "public philosophy," no means of addressing large value questions. If every person is "defined by their preferences, but those preferences are arbitrary, then each self constitutes its own moral universe, and there is finally no way to reconcile conflicting claims about what is good in itself."[24] We thus turn away from the moral norms of Lincoln, Ghandi, King, and the Protestant ethic. Utility displaces duty; self-expression uproots authority; "feeling good" supplants "being good."

The gap between our moral ideals and what we actually do is often large. In public opinion polls of Americans, 94 percent say that voting is an important obligation, yet only 39 percent voted in the 1994 election. Keeping fully informed about news and public affairs is important to 92 percent, yet only 52 percent read a newspaper daily. Three quarters of working people say that excessive emphasis on money in the United States is an "extremely serious" or "serious" problem, yet 47 percent say that making a lot of money is "absolutely essential" or "very important." Finally, 83 percent say tolerance is an important

---

[23] *Ibid.*, pp. 6, 47. For a discussion of the meaning of freedom in business, see Michael Keeley, "Freedom in Organizations," *Journal of Business Ethics* 6 (May 1987): 249–63.

[24] Bellah et al., *Habits of the Heart*, pp. 76–77.

personal guiding principle, yet 48 percent would not approve of an interracial marriage.[25] Our ideals do not much affect our actions, so it would seem that our moral development is stunted. Our goals tend to be personal, and thus actions for the sake of the community or the common good are more difficult.

Each person thus decides what is the moral good for him- or herself, and there is no common ground for judging moral issues. A person becomes his or her own private judge on the most important questions in life. Our individualistic notion of the moral good is thus isolated from the influence of religious values, family values, and the values of the Founding Fathers, the U.S. Constitution, and our own history (see Chapters 4 and 5). When these sources no longer provide us with values, it is more difficult to build personal or common goals for moral development. As a result, three out of four Americans think we are in moral and spiritual decline. However, there have been a few recent efforts to probe our shared values, common goals, and even the common good in U.S. business life.[26]

Leaders Build Shared Values

Shared values for colleagues who work together is one of the most important characteristics of successful firms. Leaders of organizations, business firms included, have a unique responsibility to formulate and articulate shared values.

It is essential that leaders understand explicitly what they stand for. Their values set the standards and affect the behavior of everyone in the organization. Moreover, great energy and initiative results when the values of leaders and those in the organization are in synch with each other. The most admired leaders easily and proudly speak of our ethical aspirations. They know that we want to live up to our highest moral aspirations. They do this with carefully chosen language, metaphors, and stories.

Research on leadership shows that shared values:

1. Foster strong feelings of personal effectiveness;
2. Promote high levels of company loyalty;
3. Facilitate consensus about key organizational goals and stakeholders;
4. Encourage ethical behavior;
5. Promote strong norms about working hard and caring; and
6. Reduce levels of job stress and tension.[27]

---

[25] "Moral State of the Union," *The Responsive Community* (Winter 1994–95): 76–77.

[26] See John W. Houck and Oliver F. Williams, eds. *Is the Good Corporation Dead? Social Responsibility in a Global Economy* (Lanham, Md.: Rowman & Littlefield, 1996); also "Where Have Our Values Gone" and "Appealing to the 'Better Angels,' " *U.S. News & World Report* (Aug. 8, 1994, p. 100; and Feb. 7, 1994, p. 88); and Robert B. Dickie and Leroy S. Rouner, *Corporations and the Common Good* (Notre Dame: University of Notre Dame Press, 1986).

[27] James M. Kouzes and Barry Z. Posner, *The Leadership Challenge: How to Get Extraordinary Things Done in Organizations* (San Francisco: Jossey-Bass, 1987), pp. 192–93.

In Chapter 8 we will see examples of successful organizations in which the leaders articulate clear and inspiring values for their colleagues within the organization.

President Abraham Lincoln was one of the most effective and inspiring leaders in U.S. history. Lincoln was faced with the potential end of the United States during its Civil War. Note how he combines his own values with a deep concern for others and for future generations:

> It is not merely for today, but for all time to come that we should perpetuate for our children's children this great and free government, which we have enjoyed all our lives. I beg you to remember this, not merely for my sake, but for yours. I happen temporarily to occupy this big White House. I am a living witness that any one of your children may look to come here as my father's child has. It is in order that each of you may have through this free government which we have enjoyed, an open field and a fair chance for your industry, enterprise, and intelligence; that you may all have equal privileges in the race of life, with all its desirable human aspirations. It is for this the struggle should be maintained. . . . That nation is worth fighting for.[28]

But even when a person possesses good values, it is still important for that person to develop character and virtue.

PERSONAL VALUES OF BUSINESSPEOPLE

The value profile of the business student has for generations been more pragmatic, materialistic, and self-centered than that of the other students. For at least a full generation, concern for people has been the value of least importance to business managers.[29]

The values of managers from five countries—Japan, Korea, India, Australia, and the United States—were measured and compared.[30] The value systems of these managers in widely varying cultures were more similar than different. Among the minor differences, the Japanese were more pragmatic and more homogeneous in their values and Indian managers were more moralistic.

There were significant differences between the values of younger and older managers. Compared with their senior peers, younger managers across all cultures tended to:

1. place less importance on organizational goals
2. place less importance on coworkers and more on themselves

---

[28] Donald T. Phillips, *Lincoln on Leadership: Executive Strategies for Tough Times* (New York: Warner, 1992), pp. 164–65.

[29] Gordon Allport, Philip Vernon, and Gardner Lindzey, *Study of Values* (Boston: Houghton Mifflin, 1931); for the values of business managers, see William D. Guth and Renato Tagiuri, "Personal Values and Corporate Strategy," *Harvard Business Review* 43 (September–October 1965): 126.

[30] George W. England, "Managers and Their Value Systems: A Five-Country Comparative Study," *Columbia Journal of World Business*, Summer 1978, p. 35.

3. place less importance on trust and honor
4. place more importance on money, ambition, and risk
5. be slightly more pragmatic

Another study of moral judgment and values revealed that business students in a developing country, Belize, showed a "higher stage of moral judgment" than U.S. business students.[31]

The picture that emerges is of the competitive gamesman, someone primarily concerned with his or her own life and career and less concerned with the organization, trust, honor, or other people. Since this survey, the values of businesspeople as a whole have shifted more in the same direction, most likely because the values of the then younger managers are now predominant.

Measuring Personal Values

Another examination of the values of working people found six distinct sets of values: conformist, manipulative, sociocentric, existential, tribalistic, and egocentric.[32] The first four of these value sets were most common among managers. The conformist set was common among older, lower-level, and less-educated managers. The manipulative set was found most often among the well-educated, high-income workers in large retail organizations in the northeastern United States. Those with sociocentric values tended to be well-paid, well-educated company presidents over 60 years old.

One paradox of this study is worth our attention. Company presidents tend to have sociocentric values: They encourage the development of friendly relationships between people. For them, "working with people toward a common goal is more important than getting caught up in a materialistic rat race."[33] Ironically, sociocentric managers are significantly underrepresented in jobs just two levels below the presidency. Upper level managers are concerned with long-term goals, while younger managers are more likely to have short-term goals of being recognized and getting ahead. Therefore, the values that get a person to within sight of the top job are not the same values that will push her or him along further. Those searching the organization for potential successors to the CEO will find *few* candidates among those in the best preparatory slots in the organization: division managers, directors, and similar positions.

In every examination of values, managers are shown to be pragmatic—very concerned with efficiency and productivity. Interestingly, female managers seem to be even more pragmatic than male managers. Furthermore, female managers are more career-oriented than their male counterparts: 60 percent of

---

[31] Richard Priem, et al, "Moral Judgment and Values in a Developed and a Developing Nation: A Comparative Analysis," *Best Paper Proceedings—'95*, Dorothy P. Moore, ed. (Vancouver: Academy of Management, 1995), pp. 401–5.

[32] Vincent S. Flowers, et al., *Managerial Values for Working* (New York: AMACOM, 1975).

[33] *Ibid.*, p. 2.

female managers say that they get more satisfaction out of their career than their home life, whereas only 37 percent of male managers feel this way.[34] Also important, 61 percent of all managers respond that an improvement in the quality of life in the United States will come by means of a return to basic values, especially commitment and integrity. Overall, 80 percent of managers believe that their company is guided by "highly ethical standards." However, this belief is stronger among top management, and more cynical views tend to be held by those of lower rank.[35] Clear, strong, engaging values are essential to good leadership. "A leader needs a philosophy, a set of high standards by which the organization is measured, a set of values about how employees, colleagues, and customers ought to be treated, a set of principles that make the organization unique and distinctive."[36] Indeed, where members of a firm share values, the members tend to be more ethical. Or, putting it the other way, where values are not shared, managers are more likely to take bribes, falsely report earnings, steal company secrets, and the like.[37]

The above value probes of younger managers show them to be more concerned about themselves and less about the organization or other people. Since most firms now encourage cooperation and concern for customers, fellow employees, and teamwork, these attitudes of younger managers present a significant problem for American business. Since young people coming into business are so self-centered, it will be a challenge to choose those who respect their peers and can work in teams, and to socialize them to have greater concern for other people.

The above variations also underscore the need not to stereotype the values of businesspeople. Problems develop when we make decisions based on stereotypes: (1) the biases often present an erroneous image of businesspeople; (2) they tend to steer people of differing values away from business as a career; and (3) the biases tend to perpetuate themselves, that is, they are self-fulfilling. It is even more important for each individual, whether business-oriented or not, to examine her or his own personal values. Note that the exercise at the end of Chapter 1 is intended to aid in doing just that.

Personal Experience Gives Direction

In earlier generations, children growing up in a family would witness their father and mother working in or near home, whether as a shoemaker, baker, or

---

[34] Warren H. Schmidt and Barry Z. Posner, *Managerial Values and Expectations: The Silent Power in Personal and Organizational Life* (New York: American Management Association, 1982), pp. 28–29, 52–53.

[35] Warren H. Schmidt and Barry Z. Posner, *Managerial Values in Perspective* (New York: American Management Association, 1983), pp. 29–41.

[36] James M. Kouzes and Barry Z. Posner, *The Leadership Challenge* (San Francisco: Jossey-Bass, 1987), p. 187.

[37] Barry Z. Posner, James M. Kouzes, and Warren H. Schmidt, "Shared Values Make a Difference: An Empirical Test of Corporate Culture," *Human Resources Management* 24 (Fall 1985): 299.

farmer. They saw not only the skill and effort required in work but also the joy of accomplishment. Since commercial work is now generally done away from home, children rarely have direct contact with it and only hear about it through comments, often complaints.

The attitudes of all people, especially the young, are influenced by the media. Consider business as it is presented in literature, on television, and in films. Most TV and film writers have no direct experience with business. As a result, their portrayal is often caricature. The businessperson is generally pictured as shallow, grasping, narrow, and petty, concerned only with status and wealth. When did you last see a TV program or film that presented the joy of work or useful accomplishments in business?

When it comes to developing good habits or virtue, which we will discuss in Chapter 2, TV is a major hindrance. It relentlessly presents materialism, sex, and violence. A task force of psychologists reported that the average child witnesses at least 8,000 murders on TV by the time she leaves *elementary* school. Another group estimates that in 1991 ABC, CBS, and NBC displayed more than 10,000 sexual incidents. For every scene depicting sexual intercourse of married partners, these networks showed 14 scenes of sex outside marriage. With FOX network added that number will probably double. TV pushes materialism and immediate gratification by means of its roughly 20,000 commercials a year.[38] Thus the shallow, greedy, and biased view of life as shown on TV form values of children and others.

In sum, while the value tests described above support some of the media stereotypes of businesspeople, these same tests show that older managers have strong religious and social values and that top executives have more balanced values. Yet these latter facts are rarely reflected in the media. Thus biased perceptions have a powerful influence on all of us, especially the young and impressionable.

Helping Behavior

It is not merely businesspeople and business students who hold social values in relatively low esteem; this reflects the values of much of American culture. As laboratory experiments have shown, individuals are heavily influenced by the values and activities of others. In any culture, norms of right and wrong are inculcated by the family, television, the neighborhood, and the environment, but the attitudes of bystanders in the immediate vicinity also have a large influence. Several laboratory experiments were prompted by the murder of a young woman in New York City. She was stabbed to death in full view of many apartment dwellers. Later investigation showed that at least 38 people saw or heard the attack but not one tried to help; no one even phoned the police. This story shocked the country, and some researchers decided to try to determine what elements influence helping behavior.

---

[38] "The War Over 'Family Values,' " *U.S. News & World Report*, June 8, 1992, p. 36.

In one experiment, each subject was led to believe that there were several other subjects placed in adjoining rooms connected by an intercom.[39] Sometimes the subject was told there was one other subject, sometimes that there were two other subjects, and sometimes that there were five. In reality, the subject was the only person involved. During a discussion over the intercom on a topic of current interest, one "participant" suffered what seemed to be an epileptic seizure; that person choked, stuttered, and called out for help. The greater the number of persons the subject thought were present, the less likely the subject would be to help and would be slower to help. Apparently, the subject felt the problem could be left to others. If the subject thought there was no other person to help, the subject was more likely to feel the responsibility to respond to the participant calling for help.

Similar results were obtained when individuals were placed in a room and asked to fill out a questionnaire. Subjects were either alone in the room, with two other subjects, or with two confederates who were instructed to remain impassive. After a few minutes, smoke began to pour into the room through a small wall vent. Results of this experiment again showed that when other individuals are present, someone is less likely to respond in a socially responsible way. When subjects were with passive confederates, they reported the apparent fire only 10 percent of the time.

It seems clear that individuals will act responsibly when they feel the responsibility directly. When another unknown person is present, they are not as apt to stick their necks out. Nevertheless, these and other studies show that people will help others, even if they don't expect anything in return. Furthermore, people respond more quickly and responsibly if they have been the recipients of help themselves or if they have previously been successful in helping others. Let us now examine the need for businesspeople to develop a greater ability to identify ethical issues and engage in moral behavior.

NEED FOR ETHICS IN BUSINESS

No society can long exist without some agreement on moral values. Without a level of trust and concern for others, it is impossible to deal with others. Nevertheless, more than three-quarters of Americans (78%) think that the state of moral values in the United States is now weak. They are even more concerned about moral values (53%) than about the economy (38%). Even more surprising, 60 percent think that the government ought to be involved in promoting moral values.[40]

---

[39] Leonard Berkowitz, *A Survey of Social Psychology* (New York: Holt, Rinehart & Winston, 1980), pp. 374–75.

[40] Data from a Gallup/CNN Poll quoted in *USA Today*, August 6, 1996, p. 4A.

Managers recognize the need for ethical norms to guide their everyday actions. Decisions made at every level of the firm are influenced by ethics, such as those regarding dealings with subordinates and peers, use of company property, quality of work, worker and product safety, truth in advertising, and use and disposal of toxic materials.

Managers understand that without ethics the only restraint is the law. Without ethics, business agreements not written in contract form cannot be trusted. Government regulation is constraining, but less regulation requires managers to exercise better ethics in their ordinary behavior. The alternative is more regulation. Without reasonable regulations, unethical firms would market unsafe drugs and dump toxic wastes in our rivers. When dealing with unethical managers, business agreements and operations must have even more detailed contracts, insurance, reports, and more lawyers. Shall we be honest and free or dishonest and policed?

Business managers do act ethically under the following conditions: (1) when they believe that a moral principle has a bearing on a situation, and (2) when they perceive themselves as having power to affect the situation.[41] And not only top managers but also middle managers act ethically, especially when they understand the ethical issues and see that they have some influence on the outcome. However, as a group, middle managers are almost twice as likely to be unethical as either top managers or lower-level managers.[42]

Fraud is stealing by concealment. Losses to business from fraud may be in the hundreds of billions of dollars annually. Fraud raises costs, lowers profits, and accounts for 30 percent of business failures. Fraud occurs more frequently if a person is under financial pressure, if there is an opportunity for it, and if the person can rationalize the crime as justified, harmless, or temporary.[43]

A large number of American firms have been involved in both unethical and illegal activities. During one 10-year period, 11 percent of the largest U.S. firms were convicted of bribery, criminal fraud, illegal campaign contributions, tax evasion, or some sort of price fixing. Firms with two or more convictions include Allied, American Airlines, Bethlehem Steel, Diamond International, Firestone, Goodyear, International Paper, J. Ray McDermott, National Distillers, Northrop, Occidental Petroleum, Pepsico, Phillips Petroleum, Rapid-American, R. J. Reynolds, Schlitz, Seagram, Tenneco, and United Brands. Leading the list with at least four convictions each are Braniff International, Gulf Oil, and Ashland Oil. Both corruption of government officials and smaller

---

[41] See the field research reported in the series of three articles by James A. Waters and Frederick Bird: "Everyday Moral Issues Experienced by Managers," *Journal of Business Ethics* 5 (October 1986): 373–84; "The Nature of Managerial Moral Standards," *ibid.,* 6 (January 1987): 1–13; "The Moral Dimension of Organizational Culture," *ibid.,* 6 (January 1987): 15–22.

[42] "Middle Managers Most Likely to Be Unethical," *Management Accounting*, December 1987, p. 3.

[43] W. Steve Albrecht, Gerald W. Wernz, and Timothy L. Williams, *Fraud: Bringing Light to the Dark Side of Business* (Burr Ridge, Ill.: Irwin, 1995).

"facilitating" payments divert resources, undermine competition, and hinder economic development.[44] But crime and immorality are punished when the market price of a firm's stock declines as the news of the criminal act is made known.[45] The ultimate punishment is to be taken over (as Gulf was by Chevron) or to go bankrupt (as did Braniff).

Most of the major petroleum firms illegally contributed to Richard Nixon's reelection campaign for president of the United States: Standard of California, Exxon, Sun, Ashland, Gulf, and Getty. The chairman of Phillips personally handed Nixon $50,000 in Nixon's own apartment. Many firms were also involved in multimillion-dollar foreign "irregular" payments: Exxon, Lockheed, McDonnell Douglas, United Brands, Mobil, Gulf, and Phillips. Knowledge of this resulted in the U.S. Foreign Corrupt Practices Act (see Chapter 8). The chief executives of Gulf, American Airlines, and Lockheed lost their jobs because of the unethical payments. Other CEOs, who were just as guilty—those heading Northrop, Phillips, and Exxon—were excused by their boards. United States firms are not alone in engaging in unethical behavior. The Japanese electronics firm Hitachi and its executives stole trade secrets from IBM. After being caught, the firm and executives pleaded guilty and agreed to pay damages to IBM.[46] Other Asian, along with German and French, firms have also been guilty of bribery and stealing trade secrets.

Corporate Pressure or Personal Greed

Embezzlement, fraud, and political back scratching benefit the individual and are most often done out of personal greed. Bribery, price fixing, and compromising product and worker safety are often responses to pressure for bottom-line results. In the minds of the perpetrators, they are done "for the sake of the firm." A study of the ethics of managers showed that 59 to 70 percent "feel pressured to compromise personal ethics to achieve corporate goals."[47] This perception increases among lower-level managers. A majority felt that most managers would not refuse to market below-standard and possibly dangerous products. However, on the more encouraging side, 90 percent supported a code of ethics for business and the teaching of ethics in business schools. They presumably sought a level playing field where they would not be pressured into un-

[44] "The Destructive Cost of Greasing Palms," *Business Week*, December 6, 1993, pp. 133–38; Irwin Ross, "How Lawless Are Big Companies?" *Fortune*, December 1, 1980, pp. 56–64; see also Robert K. Elliott and John J. Willingham, *Management Fraud: Detection and Deterrence* (New York: Petrocelli Books, 1980).

[45] Wallace Davidson and Dan Worrell, "The Impact of Announcements of Corporate Illegalities on Shareholder Returns," *Academy of Management Journal* 31 (March 1988): 195–200.

[46] "IBM Data Plot Tied to Hitachi and Mitsubishi," *Wall Street Journal*, June 23, 1982, p. 4; David B. Tinnin, "How IBM Stung Hitachi: Espionage," *Fortune*, March 7, 1983, pp. 50–56.

[47] Archie Carroll, "Managerial Ethics," *Business Horizons*, April 1975, pp. 75–80.

ethical acts. Pressures to act unethically occur in all firms, but especially in large firms that are operating in a dynamic and competitive environment.[48]

Pressure and organizational climate can influence the ethical judgments of managers. Behavior that the manager finds unethical at home or before taking a job is sometimes considered acceptable once the job is taken. Two studies that are considered below question whether some American executives have a sufficient sensitivity to ethical issues and whether their work environment hinders moral development.

Public affairs officers in firms have direct responsibility for dealing with many stakeholders: customers, suppliers, the local community, and shareholders. These managers constitute a principal conduit through which the firm is informed of new social concerns. Even though public affairs officers spend more time with various stakeholders than do other company officers, they tend to be poor listeners. Evidence shows that the more contact company officers have with various segments of the public, the less sensitive they become to their concerns.[49]

Another ethically sensitive area for a business is lobbying public officials. The more involved company officers were in lobbying, the more dulled their conscience became. Corporate lobbyists often engage in ethically dubious actions. For example, they may invite members of Congress and their families on company-paid vacations in return for votes on legislation. Evidence shows that company officers who are closest to such activities are less sensitive to the moral and ethical issues involved. The manager who is more involved is more likely to declare as acceptable an activity that fellow managers would say is unethical.[50]

Laboratory research has shown that unethical behavior increases as the climate becomes more competitive and that it increases even more if such behavior is rewarded. Conversely, a threat of punishment tends to deter unethical behavior. Whether a person acts ethically or unethically is also very strongly influenced by the individual's personal ethical values and by informal organizational policy.[51]

Instances of unethical behavior by managers point to the need for:

1. good character, along with a sensitive and informed conscience;
2. the ability to make ethical judgments;
3. a corporate climate that rewards ethical behavior and punishes unethical behavior.

---

[48] Melissa S. Baucus and Janet P. Near, "Can Illegal Corporate Behavior Be Predicted? An Event History Analysis," *Academy of Management Journal* 34 (February 1991): 9–36.

[49] Jeffery Sonnenfeld, "The Executive Differences in Public Affairs Information Gathering," in *Academy of Management Proceedings*, 1981, ed. Kae H. Chung (San Diego: Academy of Management, 1981), p. 353.

[50] Steven N. Brenner, "Corporate Political Actions and Attitudes," in Chung, *Academy of Management Proceedings*, 1981, pp. 361–62.

[51] W. Harvey Hegarty and Henry P. Sims, Jr., "Unethical Decision Behavior: An Overview of Three Experiments," in *Academy of Management Proceedings*, 1979, p. 9.

In simpler societies, people have daily contact with others whom they might be tempted to cheat, and this provides a built-in sanction. In large, complex organizations or when people are dealt with over the telephone or by means of Internet, developing ethical sensitivities and moral habits is far more important in preventing wrongful actions.

Enlightened Self-Interest and Ethics

Some advocates of free markets argue that if managers pursue enlightened self-interest (for definition, see Fig. 2–2), it results in greater honesty and better ethics among businesspeople. The argument is that high ethical standards are in the long-term interest of the firm. There is a good deal of plausibility in such a simple and straightforward position.

There are also serious problems with this view. *Enlightened* is an elastic term and does not have the same meaning for everyone. Also, even if there were agreement on the meaning of *enlightened*, self-interest in action can easily slip into selfishness. Our normal human selfish desires (many call it original sin) distort our perceptions of what is in our long-term interest. In addition, the resulting selfishness is given justification by free enterprise ideologies.

Experience shows that for a mature person to operate effectively in any environment, some altruism is necessary. That is, one must consider the benefits and harms that others will experience, and one must also be willing on occasion to sacrifice one's own benefits for the sake of others. Altruism engenders good habits and virtue within individuals, and it is a protection for society as a whole. In many instances, enlightened self-interest provides a shortcut method of solving problems effectively and efficiently but, as with all shortcuts, it cannot handle all cases. In addition, when one chooses enlightened self-interest as an ideology, one feels compelled to justify every action by pointing out how it will increase the profitability of the firm. Some financial analysts and shareholders may be pleased, but this subordinates people and ethics to economics and places managers in a rigid, simplistic mind-set.

FIGURE 2–2 Self-Interest Terms

Enlightened self-interest: Norm for assessing self-interest, used by a mature, enlightened person, viewing the long-term.

Individualism: A view that all values, rights, and duties originate in the individual and that the community has no value not derived from the individual constitutents.

Self-interest: Norm for thinking and acting that focuses on the benefits and advantages accruing to oneself and/or one's own personal interests.

Selfishness: Concern for one's self without regard for others.

Instances will arise when ethical treatment of others, perhaps people outside the firm, will be at a net cost to an individual or to the firm. Since many popular forms of free market ideology do not permit consideration of others for their own sake, businesspeople who hold such values are close to falling over the cliff into immorality. Moreover, many do fall, as we have seen, and they are more likely to fall if they hold that enlightened self-interest should always be the motivation for one's actions. Examples of both ethically good and poor behavior will be presented in Chapter 8. In sum, enlightened self-interest will take one a long way toward being more effective and even more ethical, but it will not take one the whole way.

When considering the ethics of a situation, each person takes a basic stance toward other people. There are five possible ways one can consider oneself in relation to others: [52]

1. self alone
2. self first
3. self equally with others
4. others first
5. others alone

People who only consider themselves alone are selfish egoists. People who consider themselves first but also consider others are more enlightened. Equitable consideration of oneself and others is suggested by the Golden Rule ("Do unto others as you would have them do unto you"). Considering others first or others alone are generous forms of altruism. Good parents generally consider their children first. Consideration only of others is the attitude of a selfless, generous, saintly person (for example, Mother Teresa). Such saintly people are rare, and are heros and models of behavior for many other people.

Taste, Bias, and Culture

Even though managers recognize the importance of ethics, in the popular uneducated mind ethics is hard to distinguish from culturally determined attitudes and taste. Then difficult ethical dilemmas are resolved arbitrarily, for there seems to be no objective values or norms that can be used to help judge the issues. We noted the effect of the predominant American value of freedom on this earlier in the chapter (see "Individualism and the Common Good"). If each person provides his or her own unique ethical norm, it is impossible to decide that one action is ethical and another is not. Moreover, even experts in ethics differ among themselves, thus encouraging the popular notion that ethics is not an objective discipline and no common norms exist.

---

[52] Adapted from Garth Hallett, *Reason and Right* (Notre Dame, Ind.: Notre Dame Press, 1984).

Almost everyone recognizes the need for some ethical norms for use by managers, yet it is also clear that developing these norms is no easy task. We are faced with different value systems, various perceptions of facts, and different judgments on tradeoffs. Moreover, even if we could develop adequate ethical decision-making norms, this would not automatically make decision making easy. Ethical issues are not easily framed in terms of measurable data, unlike financial (return on investment) or marketing (share of market) issues. Nevertheless, a developed sensitivity to others and an understanding of ethical principles provides a foundation for making good ethical judgments. Moreover, it is effective insurance against serious ethical blunders, such as ITT helping to overthrow the elected democratic government of Chile and Lockheed bribing top Japanese and Dutch government leaders. Bettering the ethical behavior of managers also can enable a firm to be a better producer, employer, and citizen and thus a more trusted and valued contributor to society.

From the above we can conclude the following:

1. A sense of what is right and wrong, plus ethical norms for making judgments, is essential for any person and any organization, including business enterprises.
2. However, ethical norms are not easily derived. Moreover, there is often disagreement on the facts of a given case, the relevant norms, and the various tradeoffs.

Both the importance of the task and the difficulty of accomplishing it is recognized.

Young People and Morals

Those who, like Rousseau and Emerson, believe that human beings are by nature good would hold that young people are thus good until tarnished by modern civilization. The data indicate otherwise. An earlier section of this chapter on moral development presents evidence that infants are born self-centered and that persons mature in their ethical sensitivities.

Moreover, studies show that many young people are involved in unethical acts. A large-scale study of more than 3,000 Illinois teenagers done over a 6-year period revealed some startling facts. One-third of all 14- to 18-year-olds had been involved in a serious crime. Thirteen percent admitted taking part in a robbery, 40 percent acknowledged keeping stolen goods, and 50 percent admitted shoplifting. Moreover, many of the conventional "predictors" for criminal behavior did not hold true. Except with respect to the most violent behavior, the delinquent was just as likely to be a girl as a boy, to be white as black, to come from a small town as from an inner city. Peers had the most influence on these young people, more so than parents. In fact, in 80 percent of the cases, parents did not know about the offenses their children had committed. One research team member spent 2 years with youths in a wealthy Chicago suburb and reported a "near vacuum of morality enclosed by the perimeter of the edict to

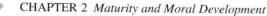

achieve. Anything that jeopardizes their occupational future is bad. The rest really doesn't matter." Peer pressure has a strong influence on adolescent attitudes and conduct.[53]

There is also considerable unethical behavior in colleges and universities. A recent study of 6,000 students in 31 colleges and universities around the United States indicated that over two-thirds admitted that they had cheated on a test or major assignment. The lowest percentage of admitted cheaters were in schools of education (57%); the highest percentage (76%) were in graduate business schools.[54] Once they got into the business world, 66 percent of all students in another survey said that "they would consider lying to achieve a business objective." Roughly the same proportion would "inflate their business expense report."[55] These attitudes present a problem for business schools and business firms.

Response of Business and Business Schools

Both business schools and business firms know that ethics and moral values are vital to any business enterprise. Harvard Business School studied the ethical needs of graduate business students as they considered introducing ethics into the curriculum. They found that:

> . . . these talented, highly motivated students have a strong sense of interpersonal accountability—of being trustworthy—in immediate face-to-face situations with colleagues and superiors. Yet perhaps because many of them have been insulated from diversity and failure, and have not heretofore been encouraged to critically reflect upon some of the important issues before them and their societies, they only have a limited sense of what is at stake. As a consequence, most do not yet articulate a vision by which they believe they could positively affect our collective life—signaling an absence of worthy myths and dreams. Unless they are effectively initiated into the public purposes and ethical norms of their profession, they will be ill-prepared to provide managerial leadership capable of engaging complex relationships among conflicting loyalties within a vision of the common good. They will not be able to provide ethical leadership in public life.[56]

---

[53] Donna R. Clasen and Sue Eicher, "Perceptions of Peer Pressure, Peer Conformity Dispositions, and Self-reported Behavior Among Adolescents," *Developmental Psychology* 22 (April 1986): 521–30; on earlier data, see "Kid Crime: Host of Juveniles Admit Serious Acts," *Detroit Free Press*, January 24, 1977, pp. 1, 2.

[54] Donald L. McCabe, "The Influence of Situational Ethics on Cheating Among College Students," *Journal of Sociological Inquiry* 63 (1992): 365–74.

[55] Rushworth M. Kidder, *How Good People Make Tough Choices: Resolving the Dilemmas of Ethical Living* (New York: William Morrow, 1995), pp. 48–50.

[56] Sharon Daloz Parks, "Is It Too Late? Young Adults and the Formation of Professional Ethics," *Can Ethics Be Taught: Perspectives, Challenges, and Approaches at Harvard Business School*, ed. by Thomas R. Piper, Mary C. Gentile and Sharon Daloz Parks (Boston: Harvard Business School Press, 1993), p. 19.

The required first-year ethics course that Harvard initiated, along with the efforts of other business schools to integrate ethics into the curriculum, will be discussed in Chapter 3.

Business executives and the actions of their firms also demonstrate the importance of ethics:

1. Almost two-thirds (63 percent) of executives are convinced that high ethical standards strengthen a firm's competitive position.[57]
2. Eighty-two percent of U.S. firms and 59 percent of non-U.S. firms have a code of ethics.[58]
3. More than 100 boards of directors of large firms have established an ethics, social responsibility, or public policy committee.
4. Speeches of chief executive officers and annual reports often allude to the importance of ethics in business decisions.

Additional information on the implementation of good business ethics will be discussed in Chapter 8.

In sum, the need for ethics in business is clear. The daily news stories of unethical activities remind us of the need for accepted ethical norms. Most business executives and managers are ethical. However, many business students and businesspeople have shallow personal goals and are not able to approach ethical problems intelligently. They do not possess the sensitivity, the concepts, or the models for effectively resolving ethical difficulties. The next chapter will provide some language, concepts, and models as an aid to managers in solving ethical dilemmas.

Summary and Conclusions

Emphasis on success and winning can cause stress and serious physical ailments. Particularly prone to heart attacks, ulcers, or other illnesses are the 60 percent of managers who are Type A: impatient, aggressive, restless, and pressured. Their ambition pushes them ahead rapidly in the organization. But it is ultimately a barrier to getting to the top. Chief executives generally are patient and have a greater ability to listen and weigh alternatives and to work with other people.

Maturity and moral development go hand in hand. In the same way as people grow emotionally and psychologically, so do they also grow morally. Without maturity and moral development, people risk traumatic challenges in middle age. On the other hand, people who have reflected on their values and

---

[57] *Ethics in American Business: An Opinion Survey of Key Business Leaders on Ethical Standards and Behavior* (New York: Touche Ross, 1988), p. 1; see also R. Edward Freeman and Daniel R. Gilbert, Jr., *Corporate Strategy and the Search for Ethics* (Englewood Cliffs, N.J.: Prentice-Hall, 1988).

[58] Ronald E. Berenbeim, "Corporate Ethics Practices: Corporate Ethics Codes," (New York: Conference Board Report, 1992).

goals do not face the same anxiety, stress, and the debilitating diseases that stem from stress; rather they deal with the changes that come with midlife reassessment with confidence and dignity. By being aware of their own personal values and goals and how these relate to the values and goals of others, they are in a better position to live, love, and enjoy life and work.

The morally developed person is better equipped to deal with ethical dilemmas. That person has the equilibrium necessary to gather the facts, search for the most appropriate ethical norms, and make a reasoned ethical judgment.

Much current evidence tells us that there is a need for ethics in business. The prevalence of corporate crime and of unethical and greedy acts by individuals, as well as the lack of ethical models within our American culture, argues for developing our ethical sensitivities and our ability to make ethical judgments. The next chapter presents some useful insights, methods and models that have proven to aid ethical development.

Discussion Questions

1. What are the symptoms of a midlife crisis? Under what conditions will the effects of the midlife transition be less traumatic?

2. Describe the differences between a person at Kohlberg's Level I and another at Level II. Describe the differences between one at Level II and another at Level III.

3. What causes anxieties and stress? What physical ailments do these lead to? What do the above described experiments with rats and cats tell us? What role does alcohol play?

4. What is the relation of moral development and maturity? What does moral development have to do with ethics?

5. What are the strengths and the weaknesses of the American view that freedom is the most important value? In what way is freedom a moral good?

6. How does this view of freedom affect moral development? Why is it an obstacle to discovering the "common good" or encouraging community values?

7. Business executives tend to have less social concern than others. What processes tend to perpetuate their lack of concern?

8. Under what circumstances is an individual more likely to come to the aid of another person? Describe the results of the experiments dealing with this issue.

9. What events of the last decade underscore the need for business ethics? List the ways that firms have responded positively to this need.

10. What did Harvard Business School find with regard to the need for ethics and a moral vision among its students? Are these values typical of other graduate business students?

11. What are the principal limitations of free enterprise or self-interest ideology? How do the limitations differ for self-interest that is "enlightened"? Does enlightened self-interest insure that a person will act ethically? Why? Give an example.

12. Is inflating costs or selling poor-quality goods less bad if the individual does not profit?
13. What do the surveys show about the ethics of young people compared with the ethics of their elders? What accounts for the difference?

Exercise:
Ethical Climate of an Organization

The goals, values, and ethics of an organization are vitally important yet often do not receive the attention they deserve. The purpose of this project is to enable you to examine and articulate the values, ethics, and commitments of an organization of your choice. To complete the project do the following:

1. Form teams of three people each by randomly counting off. Meet with your team and, through discussion, decide on the organization you wish to study (e.g., a firm about which you have access to information).

2. On a single sheet of paper indicate (a) your team members, (b) your choice of firm, (c) sources of information, and (d) plan for the division of labor. Turn this in at the beginning of the next class.

3. With your team, determine the *proclaimed* goals, values, and ethics of the organization and its proclaimed commitments to its key stakeholders—customers, employees, suppliers, the local community, the larger community (including the physical environment), and shareholders. For this purpose, study the mission or goal statement of the organization, its codes of ethics, the speeches of top managers, and relevant materials from annual reports or training manuals. Indicate any values missing from those proclaimed. Be explicit and comprehensive.

4. Determine the *real* goals, values, ethics, and commitments of the organization. Consult individuals who have direct contact (employees, customers, others), use personal observation, and study written materials evaluating the company.

5. Prepare a 12 to 20 page double-spaced typed report of your group's findings. This may include an appendix with supporting materials. Spell out the (a) *proclaimed* values and (b) *real* values of the firm. Determine if the organization is doing what it says it does. Specify what it is doing to meet obligations to stakeholders. Indicate if it is meeting these obligations very well, satisfactorily, or not well and give suggestions for improvement. Be explicit and specific.

6. Finally, evaluate your own and each team member's contributions to the project and give feedback to each team member. This written evaluation is due with the report.

CASES

Drug Test

Karen Matthews, 38, was working in her laboratory when her supervisor came by with a request. She handed her a small bottle and told her to produce a urine sample. Karen refused. The next day Karen was fired for her refusal. Was Karen correct to refuse? Does the company have the right to ask for a urine sample?

Bank Deposit Insurance

In an economic downturn investors worry about the safety and security of financial institutions. Perceptions that banks are unstable could cause investors to withdraw their money, and thus cause the failure. Hence, bank deposits up to $100,000 are insured by the Federal Deposit Insurance Corporation (FDIC).

Branch managers are responsible for maintaining deposit totals in their branch offices. You are an assistant branch manager and you have just heard your manager explaining the FDIC coverage to a customer who maintains over $300,000 in your bank. The customer was obviously very concerned about the safety of her funds. The bank manager misinterprets the FDIC guidelines and reassures the customer that her life savings are properly insured when they are not.

The manager's annual performance review and salary increase are partially based on the dollar amount of total deposits in that office. The manager knows that the customer will withdraw the funds that are not insured by the FDIC and that the branch will lose the deposits. You tell the manager that her assurance to the customer was in error.

The manager tells you not to be concerned, since the customer does not understand the financial soundness of the bank and is worried only because of a mistaken fear that banks will close as they did during the Great Depression. Discuss the ethics of the case. Since the customer does not understand the intricate workings of the banking system, is the manager justified in allowing the customer to believe her funds are safe? Is the bank manager's explanation acceptable?

CHAPTER

Ethical Behavior in Business

Business Ethics is about creating the right kind of community.
—Edwin M. Hartman

*The noble, many-storied mansion of democracy may be dismantled, leveled
to the dimensions of a flat majoritarianism, which is no mansion but a barn,
perhaps even a tool shed in which the weapons of tyranny may be forged.*
—John Courtney Murray, *We Hold These Truths*

To be an ethical adult requires moral maturity, the ability to make ethical judgments, and a developed habit of doing so. We examined moral development in the last chapter. In this chapter we will (1) provide the tools for making ethical judgments, and (2) describe how the individual person develops good moral habits, or virtue, within the organization.

In the first portion of the chapter we will ask: How does one make a judgment about what is morally right and wrong? What norms, models, techniques, and other aids are available for making ethical decisions?

Ethics is a system of moral principles and methods for applying them. Ethics thus provides the tools to make moral judgments. First a few examples of situations that call for ethical judgments:

> Beech-Nut, the second largest baby food manufacturer in the United States, sold what they called apple juice that was made of beet sugar, corn syrup, and other ingredients but contained little or no apple juice. The company, a division of Nestlé, made the adulterated apple juice for babies for 20 percent less than real apple juice and sold it for four years in twenty states.[1]

---

[1] "Two Former Executives of Beech-Nut Guilty in Phony Juice Case," *New York Times*, February 18, 1988, pp. 1, 27; "What Led Beech-Nut Down the Road to Disgrace," *Business Week*, February 22, 1988, pp. 124–28.

A Pennsylvania man advertised "Blank receipts, 100 restaurant receipts, 50 styles, $5.98. Satisfaction guaranteed." The blank receipts are attractively designed to look like the receipts of restaurants anywhere in America: Captain's Table, Trophy Room, Village Green, P.J.'s, and so on. The purchaser, after filling in the dates, number of diners, and total bill, can use them in reporting expenses. An IRS spokesperson says that selling blank receipts is not illegal.[2]

In a recent study of executive ethics, 47 percent of top executives, 41 percent of controllers and 76 percent of graduate business students were willing to commit fraud by understating write-offs that cut into their companies' profits.[3]

John Shad, former vice chairman of E. F. Hutton and former head of the Securities and Exchange Commission announced a contribution of $23,000,000 to support the teaching of ethics at the Harvard Business School. Shad was principally responsible for the insider trading prosecutions of Ivan Boesky and many others. Shad is a Harvard Business School alumnus, as were many of those involved in insider trading.[4]

Each of these cases raises ethical issues of concern to businesspeople today. They illustrate the central importance of ethics. Almost all important business decisions contain an ethical component. A purpose of this chapter is to better equip the businessperson to make effective ethical judgments.

FACTS, VALUES, AND ACTS

Ethics provides the tools, and helps develop habits for morally good behavior. Good behavior requires the ability to make moral decisions, so ethics presents concepts, norms, and models that enable an individual to make ethically good decisions. Making ethical judgments involves three steps: (1) gathering relevant factual information, (2) determining the moral norm that is most applicable, and (3) making the ethical judgment on the rightness or wrongness of the act or policy (see Fig. 3–1).

Nevertheless, ethical judgments are not always easy to make. The facts of the case are often not clear-cut, and the ethical criteria or principles to be used are not always agreed on, even by the experts themselves. Hence, to many businesspeople, ethics seems to be subjective, amorphous, ill-defined, and thus not very useful. Just as with politics and religion, there is often more heat than light generated by ethical discussions. This lack of confidence in ethics is unfortunate, since without some agreement on ethical principles, it is everyone for him-

---

[2] "Here's a New Way to Take the IRS Out to All the Finest Restaurants," *Wall Street Journal*, May 4, 1982, p. 27.

[3] "For Many Executives, Ethics Appear to Be a Write-Off," *Wall Street Journal*, March 26, 1996, pp. C1, C13.

[4] "Harvard's $30 Million Windfall for Ethics 101," *Business Week*, April 13, 1987, p. 40.

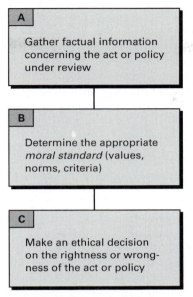

A

Gather factual information concerning the act or policy under review

B

Determine the appropriate *moral standard* (values, norms, criteria)

C

Make an ethical decision on the rightness or wrongness of the act or policy

FIGURE 3–1 Steps in Ethical Decision Making

or herself. In such a situation, trust, which is essential to any business transaction and to all commerce, is undermined.[5]

Dilemmas to Decisions

Let us begin our examination of ethical decision making by assessing a case that was first judged by 1,700 business executive readers of the *Harvard Business Review.* This case was part of a classical large-scale study of business ethics by Raymond C. Baumhart, S.J.[6]

> An executive earning $150,000 a year has been padding his or her expense account by about $7,500 a year.

---

[5] For a comprehensive overview of the importance of trust in organizations, see LaRue Tone Hosmer, "Trust: The Connecting Link Between Organizational Theory and Philosophical Ethics," *Academy of Management Review* 20 (April 1995): 379–403; see also Roger C. Mayer, James H. Davis, and F. David Schoorman, "An Integrative Model of Organizational Trust," *Academy of Management Review* 20 (July 1995): 709–734.

[6] Raymond C. Baumhart, S.J., *Ethics in Business* (New York: Holt, Rinehart & Winston, 1968), p. 21. For later views using the original instruments, see Steven Brenner and Earl Molander, "Is the Ethics of Business Changing?" *Harvard Business Review* 55 (January–February 1977): 57–71; S. T. Vitell and T. A. Festervand, "Business Ethics: Conflicts, Practices, and Beliefs of Industrial Executives," *Journal of Business Ethics* 5 (1987): 111–122; and Chiake Nakano, "A Survey Study on Japanese Managers' Views of Business Ethics," Paper presented at the Society for Business Ethics, Vancouver, B.C., 1995. The dollar figures in this case have been adjusted for inflation.

First some background: An expense account is available for expenses that are incurred in the course of one's work. It is not fair to ask an employee to use personal funds, without reimbursement, for legitimate business expenses.

To return to the case, how ethical is it to pad one's expense account? On numerous occasions over the years hundreds of other managers have been asked to judge this case, and the results have been substantially the same. Replying to an anonymous questionnaire and speaking for themselves, 85 percent of executives both in the United States and in Japan think that this sort of behavior is simply unacceptable. Perhaps more telling, almost two-thirds of them think their business colleagues would also see such behavior as unacceptable under any circumstances.

Why would padding an expense account be considered wrong by these executives? An expense account is not a simple addition to one's salary. It is designed to cover the actual expenses that are incurred by employees in the course of doing their work.

Pocketing a company pencil or making a personal long-distance phone call from the office may seem relatively trivial. Perhaps, but fabricating expenses up to 5 percent of one's salary is not trivial; it is a substantial violation of justice. The executive in the case is taking more compensation than he or she is entitled to. Presumably the executive's salary is ample compensation for the work, and the extra $7,500 is not intended as direct compensation, nor is it recognized by law as such.

Circumstances are often cited that might seem to mitigate the injustice. Some might say, "Many others are also doing it" or "My superior knows about it and says nothing." In the cited study, only about a quarter of the executives thought that their peers would justify such actions on these counts. A mere handful (about 10%) said that they themselves thought that it would be acceptable in such circumstances. An examination of these circumstances follows.

The Actions of Other People

The fact that many people are performing certain actions never in itself makes those actions ethically acceptable. For example, the fact that superiors ordered actions and others did them was no legal or moral defense for concentration camp officers at the post-World War II Nuremberg war crime trials. Even though these Nazi officers were under orders, and even though many of their peers felt that killing "undesirables" was alright, it was not accepted as a legal defense. Even less so is it a moral defense. Although ethics is influenced by conditions, a moral principle is not established by voting.

Let us go back to the case of the expense account. Assuming that the executive is a woman, we must acknowledge that it would be to her benefit if she could increase her salary by 5 percent. To have that extra $7,500 would be in her self-interest. Focusing primarily on her self-interest could easily lead her to be less objective in her search for the right action and would make her more prone to look for excuses to do that which would benefit her.

Justice calls for a fair distribution of the benefits and burdens of society. In this case, we are concerned with benefits. Is it ever ethical to take funds from an expense account? The executive's family is not starving because she has an abnormally low salary, so justice tells us that the expense account should be used for expenses, not as a salary supplement. Ignorance and coercion can lessen responsibility. However, in this case, the executive could hardly claim that she did not know what an expense account was or that she was forced into taking the money.

But if she can get away with it, why shouldn't she pad her expense account? A basic assumption that almost all businesspeople support is that a businessperson should be ethical. That is, individuals should try to do good and avoid evil, not only on the job but in all aspects of life. An essential foundation for business transactions is confidence that most businesspeople are trustworthy, truthful, and ethical. If most businesspeople were not ethical, it would be extremely difficult to purchase goods, sell property or securities, or do most of the buying and selling that we are accustomed to doing in modern society.

Admittedly there can be a short-term financial advantage for an embezzler or a supplier who takes 10 million dollars and delivers defective goods. It is because of individuals like this that we have laws, courts, and jails. Yet we also know that not all activities can be regulated, nor can all unethical acts be fully punished (in this life, anyway). If a large percentage of businesspeople did not pay their bills and took advantage of their business partners, the business system would collapse.

ETHICAL NORMS FOR BUSINESS DECISIONS

Ethical norms and models have been the subject of much reflection over the centuries. The theory of rights and duties focuses on the entitlements of individual persons. Immanuel Kant[7] (personal rights) and John Locke[8] (property rights) were the first to fully develop the theory of rights and duties. The theory of justice has a longer tradition, going back to Plato and Aristotle in the fourth century B.C.[9]

Of all ethical norms, businesspeople feel most at home with utilitarianism. This is not surprising, as the norm traces its origins to Adam Smith, the father of modern economics. The main proponents of utilitarianism are Jeremy Bentham[10] and John Stuart Mill,[11] both of whom helped to formulate the theory

---

[7] Immanuel Kant, *The Metaphysical Elements of Justice*, trans. J. Ladd (New York: Library of Liberal Arts, 1965).

[8] John Locke, *The Second Treatise of Government* (New York: Liberal Arts Press, 1952).

[9] Aristotle, *Ethics*, trans. J. A. K. Thomson (London: Penguin, 1953).

[10] Jeremy Bentham, *An Introduction to the Principles of Morals and Legislation* (New York: Hafner, 1948).

[11] John Stuart Mill, *Utilitarianism* (Indianapolis: Bobbs-Merrill, 1957).

more precisely. Utilitarianism evaluates actions in terms of their consequences. In any given situation, the one action which would result in the greatest net gain for all concerned parties is considered to be the right, or morally obligatory, action.

The ethical norm of caring has developed more recently from feminist ethics.[12] Theoretical work in each of these ethical norms continues to the present.[13] For an overview of these four ethical norms—their history, strengths, weaknesses, and areas of application—see Table 3–1 on pp. 76–77.

The Norm of Individual Rights and Duties

A moral right is an important, normative, justifiable claim or entitlement to something.[14] Moral rights and duties flow from one's human dignity and ultimately from the Creator, and are sometimes supported by law, such as our constitutional rights of freedom of conscience or freedom of speech. Moral rights have these characteristics: (1) They enable individuals to pursue their own interests, and (2) they impose duties or correlative requirements or prohibitions on others.[15]

Legal rights are stated in rules, laws, or a constitutional system. The U.S. Bill of Rights and the United Nations Universal Declaration of Human Rights are examples of documents that spell out individual rights in detail. Most legal rights stem from moral rights; but not all moral rights are enacted into law, and some bad law can even abrogate human rights (for example, rights of blacks in pre-1960s United States and Jews in Nazi Germany).

Every right has a corresponding obligation or duty. My right to freedom of conscience is supported by the prohibition of other individuals from unnecessarily limiting that freedom of conscience. With regard to business, my right to be paid for my work corresponds to my duty to perform "a fair day's work for a fair day's pay." In the latter case, both the right and duty stem from the right to private property, which is a traditional pillar of American life and law. However, the right to private property is not absolute. A factory owner may be forced by law, as well as by morality, to spend money on pollution control or safety equipment. For a listing of selected rights and other ethical norms, see Figure 3–2.

People also have the right not to be lied to or deceived, especially on matters about which they have a right to know. Hence, a supervisor has the duty to be truthful in giving feedback on work performance even if it is difficult for the

---

[12] See Carol Gilligan, *In a Different Voice* (Cambridge: Harvard University Press, 1982), and Nel Noddings, *Caring* (Berkeley: University of California Press, 1984).

[13] For example, John Rawls, *A Theory of Justice* (Cambridge, Mass.: Harvard University Press, 1971). See two books of readings: Thomas Donaldson and Patricia Werhane, *Ethical Issues in Business: A Philosophical Approach*, 5th ed. (Englewood Cliffs, N.J.: Prentice-Hall, 1996); Tom Beauchamp and Norman Bowie, *Ethical Theory and Business*, 4th ed. (Englewood Cliffs, N.J.: Prentice-Hall, 1993).

[14] Richard T. De George, *Business Ethics* (Englewood Cliffs, N.J.: Prentice-Hall, 1995), pp. 101–4.

[15] Manuel Velasquez, *Business Ethics: Concepts and Cases* (Englewood Cliffs, N.J.: Prentice-Hall, 1992), p. 73; see also Thomas Donaldson, *Corporations and Morality* (Englewood Cliffs, N.J.: Prentice-Hall, 1982).

FIGURE 3–2 Selected Ethical Norms

RIGHTS AND DUTIES

1. *Life and safety*: The individual has the right not to have her or his life or safety unknowingly and unnecessarily endangered.

2. *Truthfulness*: The individual has the right not to be intentionally deceived by another, especially on matters about which the individual has the right to know.

3. *Privacy*: The individual has the right to do whatever he or she chooses to do outside working hours and to control information about his or her private life.

4. *Freedom of conscience*: The individual has the right to refrain from carrying out any order that violates those commonly accepted moral or religious norms to which the person adheres.

5. *Free speech*: The individual has the right to criticize conscientiously and truthfully the ethics or legality of corporate actions so long as the criticism does not violate the rights of other individuals within the organization.

6. *Private property*: The individual has the right to hold private property, especially insofar as this right enables the individual and his or her family to be sheltered and to have the basic necessities of life.

JUSTICE

1. *Fair treatment*: Persons who are similar to each other in the relevant respects should be treated similarly; persons who differ in some respect relevant to the job they perform should be treated differently in proportion to the difference between them.

2. *Fair administration of rules*: Rules should be administered consistently, fairly, and impartially.

3. *Fair compensation*: Individuals should be compensated for the cost of their injuries by the party that is responsible for those injuries.

4. *Fair blame*: Individuals should not be held responsible for matters over which they have no control.

5. *Due process*: The individual has a right to a fair and impartial hearing when he or she believes that personal rights are being violated.

UTILITARIANISM

1. *Organizational goals* should aim at *maximizing the satisfactions* of the organization's constituencies.

2. The members of an organization should attempt to attain its goals as *efficiently* as possible by consuming as few inputs as possible and by minimizing external costs which organizational activities impose to others.

3. The employee should use every *effective* means to achieve the goals of the organization and should neither jeopardize those goals nor enter situations in which personal interests conflict significantly with the goals.

CARING

1. Each person has responsibility for the well-being of those people with whom one has a relation.

2. The responsibility to care increases as the dependency of the other person increases.

3. One cannot be obligated to provide care that one is incapable of providing.

TABLE 3–1 Ethical Models for Business Decisions

Definition and Origin	Strengths	Weaknesses	When Used		
			Example	Summary	

Definition and Origin	Strengths	Weaknesses	Example	Summary
1. Norm of Rights and Duties Individual's freedom is not to be violated: Locke (1635–1701)—property Kant (1724–1804)—personal rights	1. Ensures respect for individual's personal freedom and property 2. Parallels political "Bill of Rights"	1. Emphasis on rights can encourage individualistic, selfish behavior	1. Unsafe workplace 2. Flammable children's toys 3. Lying to superior or subordinate	1. Where individual's personal rights or property are in question 2. Use with, for example, employee privacy, job tenure, work dangerous to person's health
2. Norm of Justice Equitable distribution of society's benefits and burdens: Aristotle (384–322 B.C.) Rawls (1921–)	1. The "democratic" principle 2. Does not allow a society to become status- or class-dominated 3. Ensures that minorities, poor, handicapped receive opportunities and a fair share of the output	1. Can result in less risk, incentive and innovation 2. Encourages sense of entitlement	1. Bribes, kickbacks, fraud 2. Delivery of shoddy goods 3. Low wages to Hispanic, African-American, or women workers	1. Fairness, equal opportunity, for poor and unemployed 2. Setting salaries for workers vs. executives 3. Public policy decisions: to maintain a floor of living standards for all 4. Use with, for example, performance appraisal, due process, distribution of rewards and punishment

(continued on next page)

TABLE 3–1 Ethical Models for Business Decisions (*continued*)

Definition and Origin	Strengths	Weaknesses	When Used		
			Example	Summary	
3. Utilitarianism					
"The greatest good for the greatest number": Bentham (1748–1832) Adam Smith (1723–1790) David Ricardo (1772–1823)	1. Concepts, terminology, methods are easiest for businesspeople to use 2. Promotes view of entire system of exchange beyond "this firm" 3. Encourages entrepreneurship, innovation, productivity	1. Impossible to measure or quantify all important elements 2. "Greatest good" can degenerate into self-interest 3. Can result in abridging another's rights 4. Can result in neglecting less powerful segments of society	1. Plant closing 2. Pollution 3. Condemnation of land or buildings for "development"	1. Use in all business decisions, and will be dominant criteria in most 2. Version of model is implicitly used already, although scope is generally limited to "this firm"	
4. Caring					
Responsibility to a person because of relationship: Gilligan (1936–) Noddings (1929–)	1. Emphasizes care and responsibility for people 2. Builds trust, healthy communications and teamwork 3. Supports community and good for group	1. Poor at discriminating various responsibilities and equities 2. Without personal relationship there are no obligations	1. Mentoring colleagues and subordinates 2. Flexible hours and flexible leave policy for sake of family duties 3. At time of delivery of poor performance report or layoffs	1. Emphasizes interpersonal relationships 2. Care for employees and members of work group 3. Concern for those with personal or family needs	

supervisor to do so. Each of us has the right not to be lied to by salespeople or advertisements. Perjury under oath is a serious crime; lying on matters where another has a right to accurate information is also seriously unethical. Truthfulness and honesty are basic ethical norms.

Rights and duties express the requirements of morality from the standpoint of the individual. Rights and duties protect the individual from the encroachment and demands of society or the state. Utilitarian standards promote the group's interests and are relatively insensitive regarding a single individual except insofar as the individual's welfare affects the good of the group.

A business contract establishes rights and duties that did not exist before: The right of the purchaser to receive what was agreed and the right of the seller to be paid what was agreed. Formal written contracts and informal verbal agreements are essential to business transactions.

Immanuel Kant recognized that an emphasis on rights can lead people to focus largely on what is due them. Kant sought to broaden this perspective, so he emphasized what he called the "categorical imperative." The first formulation is: *I ought never to act except in such a way that I can also will that my principle should become a universal law.* An equivalent statement is this: *An action is morally right for a person in a certain situation if and only if the person's reason for carrying out the action is a reason that he or she would be willing to have every person act on, in any similar situation.*[16]

Kant's second formulation of the categorical imperative cautions us against using other people as a means to our own ends: *Never treat humanity simply as a means, but always also as an end.* In effect, an action is morally right for a person if and only if in performing the action the person does not use others merely as a means for advancing his or her own interests, but also both respects and develops their capacity to choose for themselves. The Golden Rule, "Do unto others as you would have them do unto you," reflects the earlier words of Leviticus (19:18) and Jesus (Matthew 22:19), "Love your neighbor as yourself."

Capital, computers, and business firms are means, and are thus to be used to serve the purposes of people. A person, on the other hand, is not to be used merely as an instrument for achieving another's goals. This rules out deception, manipulation, and exploitation in dealing with people.

The Norm of Justice

Justice requires all persons, and thus managers too, to be guided by fairness, equity, and impartiality. Justice calls for evenhanded treatment of groups and individuals (1) in the distribution of the benefits and burdens of society, (2) in the administration of laws and regulations, and (3) in the imposition of sanctions

---

[16] Immanuel Kant, *Groundwork of the Metaphysics of Morals*, trans. H. J. Paton (New York: Harper & Row, 1964), pp. 62–90.

and the awarding of compensation for wrongs suffered. An action or policy is just if it is comparable to the treatment accorded to others.

Standards of justice are generally considered to be more important than the utilitarian consideration of consequences. If a society is unjust to a group (e.g., segregation, job discrimination), we generally consider that society to be unjust and we condemn it, even if the results of the injustices bring about greater economic productivity. On the other hand, we are willing to trade off some equality if the results will bring about greater benefits for all. For example, differences in income and wealth are justified *only* if they bring greater benefits for *all*.

Standards of justice are not as often in conflict with individual rights as are utilitarian norms.[17] This is not surprising, since justice is largely based on the moral rights of individuals. The moral right to be treated as a free and equal person, for example, undergirds the notion that benefits and burdens should be distributed equitably. Personal moral rights (e.g., right to life, freedom of conscience, the right to free consent) are so basic that they generally may not be taken away to bring about a better distribution of benefits within a society. On the other hand, property rights may be abridged for the sake of a fairer distribution of benefits and burdens (e.g., graduated income tax, limits on pollution).

Distributive justice becomes important when a society has sufficient goods but not everyone's basic needs are satisfied. The question then becomes, What is a just distribution? The fundamental principle is that equals should be treated equally and that unequals should be treated in accord with their inequality. For example, few would argue that a new person hired for a job should receive the same pay as a senior worker with 20 years experience. People who perform work of greater responsibility or who work longer hours should receive greater pay. Hence, pay differentials should be based on the work itself, not on some arbitrary bias of the employer.

Even knowing all of the above, we still wouldn't be able to determine what is a fair distribution of society's benefits and burdens. In fact, quite different notions of equity are proposed. For example, the capitalist model (benefits based on contribution) is radically different from the socialist (from each according to abilities, to each according to needs). An important contribution to the theory of justice has been made by John Rawls.[18] Rawls would have us construct a system of rules and laws for society as if we did not know what roles we were to play in that society. We do not know if we would be rich or poor, female or male, African or European, manager or slave, handicapped or physically and mentally fit. Rawls calls this the "veil of ignorance." Constructing a system of rules under the veil of ignorance is intended to allow us to rid ourselves of the biases we have as a result of our status. In such circumstances,

---

[17] Jerald Greenberg, "A Taxonomy of Organizational Justice Theories," *Academy of Management Review* 12 (January 1987): 9–22.

[18] John Rawls, *A Theory of Justice* (Cambridge, Mass.: Harvard University Press, 1971).

each of us would try to construct a system that would be of the greatest benefit to all and that would not undermine the position of any group. Rawls proposes that people under the veil of ignorance would agree to two principles:

1. Each person is to have an equal right to the most extensive liberty compatible with similar liberty for others.
2. Social and economic inequalities are to be arranged so that they are both reasonably expected to be to everyone's advantage and attached to positions and offices open to all.

The first principle is consonant with the American sense of liberty and thus is not controversial in the United States. The second principle is more egalitarian and also more controversial. However, Rawls maintains that if people honestly choose as if they were under the veil of ignorance, they would opt for a system of justice that is most fair to all members of society.[19] We now turn to a norm that observes the *consequences* of actions on the entire group.

The Norm of Utilitarianism

Utilitarianism examines the consequences of an act. It judges that an action is right if it produces the greatest utility, "the greatest good for the greatest number." The decision process is very much like a cost-benefit analysis applied to all parties who would be touched by the decision. That action is right which produces the greatest net benefit when all the costs and benefits to all the affected parties are taken into account. Although it would be convenient if these costs and benefits could be measured in some comparable unit, this is rarely possible. Many important values (e.g., human life and liberty) cannot be quantified. Thus, the best we can do is to list the effects and estimate the magnitude of their costs and benefits as accurately as possible.

The utilitarian principle says that the right action is that which produces the greatest net benefit over any other possible action. This does not mean that the right action produces the greatest good for the person performing the action. Rather, it is the action that produces the greatest net good for all those who are affected by the action. The utilitarian norm is best for cases that are complex and affect many parties. Although the model and the methodology are clear in theory, carrying out the calculations is often difficult. Taking into account so many affected parties, along with the extent to which the action effects them, can be a tallying nightmare.

Hence several shortcuts have been proposed that can reduce the complexity of utilitarian calculations. Each shortcut involves a sacrifice of accuracy for ease of calculation. Among these shortcuts are (1) calculation of costs and bene-

---

[19] An organization that treats its employees justly reaps many rewards; see Blair H. Shepart, Roy J. Lewicki, and John W. Minton, *Organizational Justice: The Search for Fairness in the Workplace* (New York: Lexington, 1992).

fits in dollar terms for ease of comparison; (2) restriction of consideration to those directly affected by the action, putting aside indirect effects. In using these shortcuts, an individual should be aware that they result in simplification and that some interests may not be sufficiently taken into consideration.

In the popular mind, the term *utilitarianism* sometimes suggests selfishness and exploitation. For our purposes, the term should be considered not to have these connotations. However, a noteworthy weakness of utilitarianism as an ethical norm is that it can advocate, for example, abridging an individual's right to a job or even life for the sake of the greater good of a larger number of people. This and other difficulties are discussed elsewhere.[20] One additional caution in using utilitarian rules is in order: It is considered unethical to opt for narrower benefits (e.g., personal goals, career, or money) at the expense of the good of a larger number, such as a firm, neighborhood, or a nation. Utilitarian norms emphasize the good of the *group*; it is a large-scale ethical model. As a result, an individual and what is due that individual may be overlooked. Hence the norm of utilitarianism must be balanced by the use of the norms of justice, rights and duties, and the norm we will discuss next, caring.

The Norm of Caring

Over the centuries, ethicists, who were almost all male, developed the norms of rights and duties, justice and utilitarianism. These norms emphasize impartiality and abstract principles. A new norm of *caring* has been presented by scholars in the last few decades.[21] Caring is built upon relations between people and is an extension of family life. Rather than autonomous individuals making objective, impartial ethical judgments, in reality we experience numerous relationships, and each of these relationships influences our ethical obligations. We care for each other, and we have responsibilities to each other.

Ethicists who use caring as their norm demonstrate how womens' moral experience up to this time has been neglected. Carol Gilligan was among the first to point out that, when faced with moral dilemmas, women tend to focus on the relationships of people rather than on impartial, theoretical principles.[22] As we saw in Chapter 2, Gilligan amended the existing descriptions of the levels of moral development in the light of the experience of women. The male matures by developing autonomy and sees himself in opposition to the other, thus the insistence on personal rights. In the limiting case, a businessperson's values, if they are unduly influenced by rights, economics, and the market-

---

[20] Gerald F. Cavanagh, Dennis J. Moberg, and Manuel Velasquez, "The Ethics of Organizational Politics," *Academy of Management Review* 6 (July 1981): 363–74. For a more complete treatment, see Manuel Velasquez, *Business Ethics: Concepts and Cases* 3rd. ed. (Englewood Cliffs, N.J.: Prentice-Hall, 1992), pp. 58–72.

[21] See Rosemarie Tong, *Feminine and Feminist Ethics* (Belmont, Calif.: Wadsworth, 1993), esp. Chapters 3 and 4.

[22] Carol Gilligan, *In a Different Voice* (Cambridge, Mass.: Harvard University Press, 1982).

place, can result in paranoid tendencies which can cause him either not to relate to others or to relate to others only by contract.

The female matures by developing relationship-based morality. Although feminist ethicists are reluctant to analyze caring too exactly, we can note some qualifications of the norm of caring. First, the obligation to care is proportional to one's relationship. In extended relationships, caring does not require action if that action is very costly. Second, one's roles and obligations influence the responsibility to care. Caring for one's child has greater priority than caring for someone in one's work group. Third, one cannot be obligated to provide care that one is incapable of providing.[23] From the viewpoint of the organization and the manager, caring is a very relevant norm for many current business challenges. Trust, teamwork, good personal relationships, and communications build upon caring, and must be achieved, if the firm is to be competitive.[24]

Caring clearly engages our emotions, but in order to do *any* ethical reasoning, our emotions must be involved. While ethics is not to be equated with feeling, it is a sterile intellectual exercise if one's feelings are not engaged in the process. In making ethical judgments it is essential to consider the interests of others. In order to incorporate the interests of others into one's decision-making processes, one must be able to feel and to empathize with those that are affected by one's decisions. In Kohlberg's terms, one must at least have achieved Level 2 moral development (see Chapter 2). Ethical decision-makers must learn how to regularly and habitually put themselves in the position of other persons. They must learn how others perceive a situation and sense what others feel and suffer. Without this ability to care for others on a sensible level, it is impossible to examine the moral dimensions of life in any significant way.[25]

Ethical Norms for Global Business

Some business ethics scholars have examined the varying business customs and practices in various countries throughout the world, and they have concluded that new norms are needed in international business ethics. They have proposed a variety of different models, based upon rights, social contract, and negative and modified utilitarianism.[26] Other scholars, however, have found similar fundamental ethical values in business in different cultures.[27]

---

[23] Gerald F. Cavanagh, Dennis J. Moberg, and Manuel Velasquez, "Making Business Ethics Practical," *Business Ethics Quarterly* 5 (July 1995): 399–418.

[24] Jeanne M. Liedtka, "Feminist Morality and Competitive Reality: A Role for the Ethic of Care?," *Business Ethics Quarterly* 6 (April 1996): 179–200.

[25] On the importance of empathy in ethical decision making, I thank Manuel Velasquez.

[26] Thomas Donaldson, *The Ethics of International Business* (New York: Oxford University Press, 1989); Richard T. DeGeorge, *Competing with Integrity in International Business* (New York: Oxford University Press, 1993); Thomas Donaldson and Thomas Dunfee, "Toward a Unified Conception of Business Ethics: Integrative Social Contract Theory," *Academy of Management Review* 19 (April 1994): 252–84.

[27] For example, Japanese businesspeople have roughly the same values as do American, even though business ethics is not as institutionalized in Japan. See Chaiki Nakano, "A Survey on Japanese Managers' Views of Business ethics," *op. cit.*

Manuel Velasquez applied the new proposed models adapted to global issues to several important cases in international business ethics.[28] He demonstrates the limitations of each of those new proposals. On the other hand, he found that the comprehensive model and the norms of rights and duties, justice, utilitarianism, and caring as presented in this chapter are more flexible and are better suited to dealing with global ethical issues. Let us now use these norms and tools in solving ethical problems.

SOLVING ETHICAL PROBLEMS

Any human judgment is preceded by two steps: gathering the facts and determining the appropriate criteria (see Fig. 3–3). Before any ethically sensitive situation can be assessed, it is essential that all the relevant data be considered. As an aid to determining the appropriate criteria, we have presented the norms of rights and duties, justice, utility, and caring. Figure 3–3 is a schematic diagram of how ethical decision making should proceed. Although it contains greater detail than Figure 3–1, the same three steps, (A) data gathering, (B) analysis, and (C) judgment, are underscored. Even Figure 3–3 is simplified, but nevertheless it can aid in solving ethical problems.

Let us apply our scheme to the case presented earlier of the executive who padded her expense account. We will accept the limited data provided in the case. The rights norm is not so useful here: The executive has no right to the extra money, although we might make the case that the shareholders' and customers' right to private property is being violated. With regard to justice, salary and commissions constitute ordinary compensation for individuals. Expense accounts have a quite different purpose. In this instance, most managers responding to the case held that it was unethical for the executive to pad her expense account. John Rawls would maintain that all of us would set the rules to prohibit such padding of expenses if we did not know what roles we ourselves would have in society. Using the utility criterion, we judge that although padding her expense account is in the interest of the executive, it does not optimize benefits for others. Her actions hurt shareholders, customers, and more honest executives. Moreover, padding one's expense account adds to the expense of doing business and in this way also violates utility. Claiming nonexistent expenses does not indicate care for others in the firm. Hence, we conclude that padding one's expense account is judged unethical on all four ethical norms, and is therefore morally wrong. Note that 73 percent of the executives who were asked came to the same judgment.

---

[28] Manuel Velasquez, "International Business Ethics: The Aluminum Companies in Jamaica," *Business Ethics Quarterly* 5 (October 1995): 865–82.

FIGURE 3–3 Flow Diagram of Ethical Decision Making

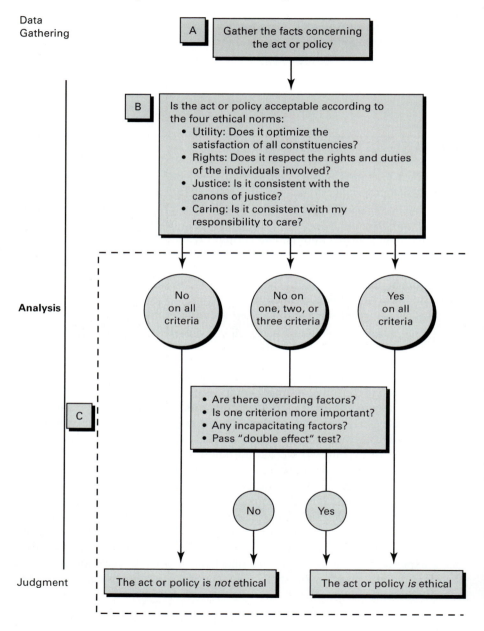

Source: Adapted from Gerald F. Cavanagh, Dennis J. Moberg, and Manuel Velasquez, "Making Business Ethics Practical," *Business Ethics Quarterly* (July 1995); and Manuel Velasquez, Gerald F. Cavanagh, and Dennis Moberg, "Organizational Statesmenship and Dirty Politics," *Organizational Dynamics* (Fall 1983).

Let us consider the Beech-Nut apple juice case given at the beginning of the chapter. The rights of parents to the truth were violated, since the product was not what it claimed to be. Perhaps the health of the babies was even endangered, for the mixture might have contained unhealthy chemicals (one former employee testified it did). Beech-Nut did not provide the product they had promised, so the sales contract was breached and justice also was violated. When we apply the utility criterion to the action of the executives at Beech-Nut who were responsible for selling pseudo-apple juice, we find there was a short-term gain to the firm and the executives from the added profitability. On the other hand, parents and babies were harmed, since the babies given the juice did not obtain the vitamins and nutrients that were expected. In the long run, the firm, the executives, and the shareholders also lost, because there was unfavorable publicity and a resulting loss of business. So the action does not pass the utility criterion. The act clearly does not demonstrate care for customers. The action was unethical according to all four norms. In fact, the two executives were sentenced to a year in jail and fined $100,000 each, and the company paid a $2,000,000 fine.[29]

What of the second case, in which an entrepreneur advertised official-looking blank receipts of fictitious restaurants? Salespeople and managers could fill out the receipts and submit them for reimbursement. The receipts would "prove" the purchase of meals that never existed. Using our model, what would we say of the ethics of the person selling such receipts? Or of the person purchasing them and using them? Respond to this case using the flowchart in Figure 3–3.

A short-cut test of oneself can be helpful in these and in other cases. Would I do it if I knew that the decision was going to be featured on this evening's TV news? Could my decision and behavior bear the sharp scrutiny of a probing reporter?

Decision Making Using the Model

Let us examine another case:

> Brian Curry, financial vice president of Digital Robotics Corporation, is about to retire and has been asked to recommend one of his two associates for promotion to vice president. Curry knows that his recommendations will be acted on. He also knows that since both associates are about the same age, the one not chosen will have difficulty getting future promotions. Debra Butler is bright, outgoing and has better leadership skills. She is the most qualified for the position. Moreover, her father is president of the largest customer of Digital, and Curry reasons that Digital will more likely keep this business if his daughter is made an officer. On the other hand, John McNichols has been with the company longer, has worked seventy-hour weeks, and has pulled the company through some very difficult situ-

---

[29] "Jail Terms for Two in Beech-Nut Case," *New York Times*, June 17, 1988, pp. 29, 31.

ations. He has continued putting in extra effort because he was told some time ago that he was in line for the vice presidency. Nevertheless, Curry recommends Butler for the job.

Let us again use our norms and Figure 3–3 to decide this case. Neither Butler nor McNichols has a right to the position. As for justice, we conclude that because the promotional decision was made on the basis of relevant abilities, it did constitute fair treatment. On the other hand, McNichols worked extra hours because of the promised promotion. Much of his work effort was based on a false promise. McNichols had a right to know the truth and to be treated fairly. Utility tells us that the selection of Debra Butler optimally benefits shareholders, customers, management, and most of the workers, because she is a better leader.[30] Since Butler and McNichols were both associates to Curry, caring would most likely extend to both equally.

Thus, according to the criteria of overall justice, utility, and caring, the appointment of Butler is morally acceptable. However, because of the promise made earlier to McNichols, which resulted in extended work weeks, he is being treated unjustly. We can then ask if there are any "overriding factors" that ought to be taken into consideration.

Overriding Factors

Overriding factors are factors which may, in a given case, justify overriding one or two of the four ethical norms: rights and duties, justice, utility, or caring (see Figure 3–3). Overriding factors can be examined when there is a conflict in the conclusions drawn from the ethical norms. For example, there might be incapacitating factors. If there are any elements that coerce an individual into doing a certain action, then that individual is not fully responsible. Let us take the example of Bausch and Lomb. CEO Daniel Gill expected division managers at Bausch and Lomb to show double digit earnings each quarter. Under this unrelenting pressure, the managers faked sales of sunglasses, forced distributors to accept unneeded products, and probably laundered drug money for drug dealers. This eventually resulted in a collapse of revenues and an SEC investigation. Even though what they did was unethical, these managers are not as guilty as they otherwise would be because they were pressured by their CEO.[31]

Also, someone might not be able to utilize the norm owing to a lack of information. A manager might suspect that another manager is embezzling from the firm. However, to report them to superiors might ruin that person's reputation. Therefore, even though stealing is a violation of justice, in this instance

---

[30] A manager can score him- or herself as being predominantly a user of the utility, justice, or rights norm by using a set of questions developed by Marshall Sashkin. See his *Managerial Values Profile* (Bryn Mawr, Pa.: Organizational Design and Development, 1986).

[31] "Blind Ambition: How Pursuit of Results Got Out of Hand at Bausch and Lomb," *Business Week,* October 23, 1995, pp. 78–92, 146.

there is not yet sufficient information to act. In addition, the manager may be sincerely uncertain of the norm or its applicability in this particular case.[32]

Consider again the case of appointing a financial vice president. Utility calls for recommending Debra Butler for the position. The right to full information and perhaps justice support McNichols' claim. McNichols has worked more hours and harder because of a promised reward. Since the position was promised to him, fair treatment requires giving him special consideration. On the basis of the importance of a verbal promise and of justice, we might conclude that McNichols should get the position.

Because there is now a conflict between these two norms, any overriding factors should be considered. Is one criteria more important? The effective operation of the firm is an important ethical goal, since many jobs and family incomes depend upon it. How much better a manager is Butler and how would her selection affect the firm's performance and the jobs of others at Digital?

With regard to incapacitating factors, there seems to be little coercion involved, certainly no physical coercion. That Debra Butler's father is president of Digital's largest customer might constitute psychological coercion. However, Curry seems to have made his decision freely.

Another important factor to consider is exactly what sort of promise was made to McNichols? Was it clear and unequivocal? If the "promise" was in fact a mere statement that McNichols had a good chance at the promotion or if Butler's performance in the VP job is expected to be significantly better than McNichols', then Curry could ethically recommend Butler. However, some sort of compensation should then be made to McNichols.

When different norms provide opposing conclusions in the same case, another kind of overriding factor helps us judge. It is the so-called principle of double effect. Let us take an example of firing a worker who is not a very good performer but who is the sole provider of a family. Using the utility norm, we would probably say the firing was ethical. But using the justice norm, we might call it unethical, because an entire family would be deprived of income. There is a conflict between the conclusions reached using the different norms, so the principle of the double effect is appropriate. The principle is applicable when an act has both a good effect (e.g., bringing greater efficiency to the firm and providing honest feedback to the worker) and a bad effect (e.g., eliminating the principal support for the family). One may ethically perform such an act under three conditions: (1) One does not directly intend the bad effect (e.g., depriving the family of income); (2) the bad effect is not a means to the good end but is simply a side effect (e.g., depriving the family of income is not a means of making the firm more efficient); and (3) the good effect sufficiently outweighs the

---

[32] For a detailed and insightful explanation of how incapacitating factors lessen a moral agent's moral and legal responsibility and hence guilt, see Oswald A. J. Mascarenhas, "Exonerating Unethical Marketing Executive Behaviors: A Diagnostic Framework," *Journal of Marketing* 59 (April 1995): 43–57.

bad (e.g., the benefits of greater firm efficiency are sufficiently greater than the difficulties the family will face). Going back to the preceding case, would the appointment of Butler pass the double effect test?

Case of Selling Cigarettes

Let us assess the ethics of the following case:

> Philip Morris and RJR Nabisco (formerly R. J. Reynolds) hold about two-thirds of the market for cigarettes in the United States. Approximately 430,000 Americans and 3,000,000 people world-wide die prematurely each year of tobacco related causes. Medical scientists estimate that 30 to 40 percent of all who smoke will die of cancer, cardiovascular disease, or chronic obstructive lung disease caused by their smoking. The number of people in the United States who smoke has declined to only 25%. Nevertheless, through successful strategic planning, the tobacco firms are still extraordinarily profitable.
>
> Tobacco executives initiated strategies to market cigarettes to: 1) teenagers and minorities, and 2) people in other countries. They employ "image" advertising and widespread distribution. Cigarette advertising shows members of the dominant social or racial group smoking cigarettes in attractive surroundings. Moreover, U.S. trade negotiators have pried open Asian markets for U.S. cigarettes. U.S. market share in four Asian countries rose 600% because of the opening of markets, and cigarette smoking was found to be about 10% higher than it would be if it were not for the U.S. cigarettes.[33]
>
> Smoking is thus increasing in Europe, Asia, South America and Africa. More than two-thirds of men in Korea, Cambodia, Indonesia, China and Japan now smoke. Advertising also focuses on women, whose use of tobacco is presently lower, but is rapidly rising. Experts predict the death rate due to tobacco world-wide will reach 10,000,000 annually by the year 2020. And total exports of American cigarettes have increased by more than 300% in the last decade.[34]

Let us apply our norms in deciding the ethics of the above case. Cigarette executives claim that they are not violating anyone's right to life in selling cigarettes to them, since information is available on the health hazards. However, many people, especially youth and overseas, may not be aware of the likelihood of serious disease and death that follows use of tobacco. Both justice and rights call for cigarette sellers to be truthful in advertising products with such dangerous consequences.

Utilitarians calculate that those who benefit are the cigarette companies and the user who in the short-term is able to address her or his nicotine addiction. On the other hand, the user's health is often seriously impaired. This can

---

[33] "Big Tobacco's Backlash in Asia: Health Critics Decry U.S. Invasion," *Business Week,* June 17, 1996, p. 30.

[34] "RJR's New Ad Campaign: It's Hip to Smoke," *Wall Street Journal,* April 16, 1996, pp. B1 and B6; see also two books, Philip Hilts, *Smokescreen: The Truth Behind the Tobacco Industry Cover-up* (Reading, Mass.: Addison Wesley, 1996); and Richard Kluber, *Ashes to Ashes: America's Hundred-Year Cigarette War, the Public Health, and the Unabashed Triumph of Philip Morris* (New York: Knopf, 1996).

result in large costs in health, dollars, and time to them, their dependents, their employers, and others. Society as a whole pays, since income is lost and costs rise, because of the many common tobacco related illnesses. Justice might call for tobacco firms, which reap large benefits in profits from cigarette sales, to share in the burdens of paying the additional health costs.

Genuine caring for people would lead tobacco executives to stop trying to sell to new users and possibly even to withdraw tobacco products from the market altogether. Do you agree with this analysis? Have we been too harsh on cigarette firm executives and their supporters?

The ethical model described in this chapter and used above is used in many basic management textbooks.[35] It enables the manager to integrate ethical analysis into business decisions, and to thus complement and correct traditional financial analyses.

Loyalty and Whistle-blowing

In addition to making ethical decisions, a member of an organization is sometimes faced with a situation where superiors seem to be blind to unethical acts. This presents a difficult dilemma. The following real case, where the stakes were high, demands careful analysis and additional criteria:

> An engineer in the design section of an airplane manufacturing firm is convinced that the latch mechanism on a plane's cargo door does not provide sufficient security and that the door has to be redesigned in order to insure against the possibility of a crash. He presents his supervisor with the information and is told that the Federal Aviation Administration (FAA) has given the required approval and that he should not "rock the boat." He goes to the president of the firm and gets the same answer.

Would that engineer be justified in taking this information to the news media? The answer to this question is extremely important. The danger to the lives of hundreds of passengers might argue for going to the news media. On the other hand, the reputation and perhaps the financial viability of the firm are also to be weighed. A mistake in either direction could be disastrous. Thus it is important to do the ethical analysis very carefully.

The right to life and safety is at issue. If indeed the designer is correct that the faulty latch mechanism puts the plane in danger of a crash, then the lives of the passengers would assume paramount importance in the calculations. While the designer owes loyalty to his employer, nevertheless justice requires that future passengers should not unknowingly be in danger of their lives due to the faulty design.

---

[35] See, for example, Heinz Weihrich and Harold Koontz, *Management: A Global Perspective*, 10th ed. (New York: McGraw-Hill, 1993), pp. 70–73; James Gibson, John Ivancevich, and James Donnelly, *Organizations*, 8th ed. (Burr Ridge, Ill.: Irwin, 1994), pp. 292–93; Stephen Robbins, *Organizational Behavior*, 6th ed. (Englewood Cliffs, N.J.: Prentice-Hall, 1993), p. 30.

Utilitarians would total up the costs and benefits to all parties affected. Redesigning the aircraft and recalling planes already in service would cost the firm tens of millions of dollars. More immediately, taking the issue to the scandal oriented and poorly educated media people would result in a serious erosion in reputation for the firm. On the other hand—assuming that 300 people would be aboard the first plane to crash—how much are 300 lives worth? Utilitarians, too, would conclude that the designer would be justified in taking the issue outside the firm. Caring would cause the engineer to opt for the safety of the passengers also. Even 69 percent of the corporate executives who examined the case thought that the designer was justified in breaching loyalty and taking the issue to the media.[36]

When to Blow the Whistle

Since opportunities for whistle-blowing are becoming more common and the stakes are higher, it is important to give some attention to the special conditions that would allow and sometimes require whistle-blowing. Whistle-blowing has been defined as "the disclosure by organization members (former or current) of illegal, immoral, or illegitimate practices under the control of their employers, to persons or organizations that may be able to effect action."[37] According to Sissela Bok, ethical whistle-blowing to external persons should meet several criteria:[38]

1. The purpose should be moral: to benefit the public interest.
2. What is protested should be of major importance and should be specific.
3. The facts of the case must be certain; they should be checked and rechecked.
4. All other avenues for change within the organization must be already exhausted.
5. The whistle-blower should be above reproach. In particular, the whistle-blower should not gain anything through revealing the information. Ideally the individual should openly accept responsibility for the whistle-blowing.

Let us examine these criteria. The first demands that the purpose of whistle-blowing should not be to attract attention, to seek revenge, or to achieve some personal goal. In many cases, whistle-blowers are trying to wreak vengeance on a supervisor or a company that they believe has been unfair to them. Perceptions regarding one's own grievances can be biased and do not provide a solid basis for whistle-blowing. Instead, the revelation of wrongdoing should be for the common good.

Second, whistle-blowing requires that the wrongdoing be a serious breach of ethics. Much is at stake, and the action should not be taken lightly. The unethical act protested should be a specific act, not a vague attitude which is hard to document.

---

[36] "Business Executives and Moral Dilemmas," *Business and Society Review* (Spring 1975): 52.

[37] Janet P. Near and Marcia P. Miceli, "Effective Whistle-Blowing," *Academy of Management Review* 20 (July 1995): 680.

[38] Sissela Bok, "Whistleblowing and Professional Responsibilities," in *Ethics Teaching in Higher Education*, ed. Daniel Callahan and Sissela Bok (New York: Plenum Press, 1980).

Third, the facts of the case must be ascertained, and the evidence must be double-checked.

The fourth criterion demands that superiors and other higher officials in the organization who might be able to rectify the situation have been informed and that they still refuse to do anything. This requires going to the president or even the board before going to an outside party. If a federal regulatory agency could be involved, then, assuming all internal avenues have been tried, the agency is to be preferred to the news media.

The fifth criterion is that the whistle-blower should not benefit from the revelation. If one's career is benefited or one makes money from exposing the situation (e.g., money made from writing a best-selling expose), one's motives are suspect. Considerations of self-interest can unconsciously enter into one's deliberations. To compensate for possible personal bias, a person should seek considerable objective advice so as not to blow the whistle on the basis of mis-information or partial information. The potential whistle-blower should also be aware of all the arguments for and against whistle-blowing before going to an outside party. Ideally, the whistle-blower should be willing to accept responsi-bility for providing the information. Granted, this takes courage, since the per-son's job may be on the line. It is also a test of one's motives. Moreover, anony-mous informers are justifiably not often trusted.

Let us apply the criteria to the case of the aircraft designer. His purpose in blowing the whistle is to serve the public interest by preventing an airplane crash and saving hundreds of lives. The facts of the situation should be checked. From the description of the case, we do not know that the designer is well-in-formed or even mentally stable. We also do not know whether he has checked his calculations with others who would be in a position to affirm or correct his estimates. The whistle-blower has already gone to his own supervisor and to the president. The FAA does not seem to have found the design problem. However, before going to the media, the designer should check to see if the FAA is aware of the problem. If not, apprising the FAA of the problem could achieve the safety goal without a public splash and thus prevent severe loss to the manufac-turer and to the airlines that would eventually be using the plane. Since the whistle-blower has not yet acted, we do not know whether he will identify him-self. In the same vein, we know nothing of his character. However, probably no personal advantage will be gained by the whistle-blowing.

In conclusion, the whistle-blower, assuming he has the correct facts, would be justified in going to an external agency. This case is not fictitious. Had someone noted and protested the cargo door latch problem on the DC-10, a Turkish airliner taking off from Paris would not have crashed with the loss of more than 300 lives.[39]

---

[39] Paul Eddy, Elaine Potter, and Bruce Page, *Destination Disaster* (New York: New York Times Book Co., 1976), esp. pp. 33–63.

Wrongdoing within the firm can "damage a company's profitability, tarnish its reputation, demoralize its employees, and result in substantial fines or costly lawsuits."[40] Hence, in order for management to obtain information on such potentially damaging actions or products, it should provide a vehicle for an employee to report wrongdoing internally.

A serious deterrent to whistle-blowing is the well-known fact that most whistle-blowers are penalized by being fired, demoted, or shunted off to an unimportant job. They are labeled as "stool pigeons" and "squealers."[41] Court decisions have provided some protection for whistle-blowers. Employees now cannot be fired for whistle-blowing, at least in certain restricted circumstances.

On the other hand, as any experienced manager knows, only when communications are not good and managers are not open to hearing bad news does whistle-blowing become necessary. The moral problem would not have arisen, for example, with better design of the product, clearer delegation of responsibilities, and better communications. Whistle-blowing becomes an option when supervisors do not listen to subordinates and their legitimate concerns. These concerns are often not well-founded, but it is essential that they be heard. Ambitious managers can blind themselves to shoddy products and practices while they attempt to show higher quarterly profits or to maintain the status quo. In short, whistle-blowing activity is a sign that the organization is not performing well, has poor management, or both.

GOOD HABITS CREATE VIRTUE

Executives and scholars are increasingly asking how good character can be developed within the organization. Character development includes good habits of integrity, trust and loyalty. Because of the greater cooperation and loyalty that is required in the global marketplace, many suggest that character development must be an important priority for a firm. Moreover, a firm cannot build "trust, commitment, and effort among the stakeholders of the firm" without giving attention to character development. From another perspective, because of fewer middle managers, greater personal responsibility is required today among members of organizations just in order to perform the ordinary tasks within the firm. This latter, which has been described and measured, is called "organizational citizenship."[42]

---

[40] Marcia P. Miceli and Janet P. Near, "Whistleblowing: Reaping the Benefits," *Academy of Management Executive* 8 (August 1994): 65–72.

[41] Linda Klebe Trevino and Bart Victor, "Peer Reporting of Unethical Behavior: A Social Context Perspective," *Academy of Management Journal* 35 (February 1992): 38–64.

[42] Rabindra N. Kanungo and Jay A. Conger, "Promoting Altruism as a Corporate Goal," *Academy of Management Executive* 3 (1993): 37–48; LaRue Tone Hosmer, "Why Be Moral? A Different Rationale for Managers," *Business Ethics Quarterly* 2 (1994): 191–204; Jill W. Graham, "Leadership, Moral Development and Citizen Behavior," *Business Ethics Quarterly* 1 (January 1993); and Linn Van Dyne, Jill Graham and Richard Dienesch, "Organizational Citizenship Behavior: Construct Redefinition, Measurement, and Validation," *Academy of Management Journal* 37 (1994): 765–802.

FIGURE 3–4 Moral Habits Terms

Character: A stable organized personality with a composite of good and bad moral habits within a person.

Ethics: The principles of conduct governing an individual or a group, and the methods for applying them.

Habit: An acquired behavior pattern followed until it becomes almost automatic.

Moral: Dealing with or capable of distinguishing right from wrong.

Moral habit: A morally good or bad behavior pattern.

Value: A lasting belief that a certain goal or mode of conduct is better than the opposite goal or conduct.

Vice: A bad moral habit.

Virtue: A good moral habit that has been acquired by choosing the good (that is, not mere innocence).

Some go further and argue that trust and a healthy community life is essential for prosperity. Francis Fukuyama maintains that some societies currently have low trust (China, Italy, and France), and others are high trust (Germany, the United States, and Japan). He warns that individualism is a threat to trust. And some nonrational factors, such as religion, tradition, honor, and loyalty, are essential in building trust.[43]

The development of character and virtue (for definitions, see Figure 3–4) is now receiving attention in business firms. We often speak of honesty, trust, justice, and integrity as if people are born with those virtues. This is not the case. Such virtues are achieved only with deliberate and specific effort. Ethical *behavior* does not necessarily flow from people who are intelligent. The example of intelligent and sophisticated people who supported Hitler (Martin Heidegger, Carl Jung, Ezra Pound), or the straight "A" student who sexually exploits others, demonstrate that intelligence and a good education does not result in good character.[44] Yet there has been little recent inquiry into what makes good character. For centuries the Aristotelian understanding of virtue has been helpful. Recently Robert Solomon applied Aristotelian ethics, and especially virtue, to business and the business firm. Solomon sets the tone when he says:

> There is no room in this picture for the false antagonism between "selfishness" on the one hand and what is called "altruism" on the other. For the properly constituted social self, the distinction between self-interest and social-mindedness is all

---

[43] Francis Fukuyama, *Trust: The Social Virtues and the Creation of Prosperity* (New York: Free Press, 1995).

[44] Robert Coles, "The Disparity Between Intellect and Character," *Chronicle of Higher Education* (September 22, 1995): A68.

but unintelligible, and what we call selfishness is guaranteed to be self-destructive as well.[45]

A morally mature person is able to and will develop good habits, commonly called virtues. As Solomon puts it, "the ultimate aim of the Aristotelian approach to business is to cultivate whole human beings, not jungle fighters, efficiency automatons, or 'good soldiers.' " Solomon goes on to describe in some detail a series of virtues that he sees as necessary for business: honesty, fairness, trust and toughness; friendliness, honor, loyalty, shame; competition, caring and compassion; and finally justice. He points out that envy and resentment are vices for business; they poison the business firm. Vices are bad habits that are also developed through repeated acts, in the same fashion as good habits are formed.

A person who wishes to develop good habits does so by consciously and repeatedly performing that act.[46] Developing a habit takes time and effort, but once a good habit is in place, through the active effort of the person, later similar actions come easily and naturally. That is, a person, by intentionally developing good habits through good acts, makes additional good acts easier to perform.[47] Moreover, people who possess those virtues will be more reliable colleagues and they will build a more effective firm in the long term.

Ethical decisions are generally the core of moral acts, and these good acts then provide the building blocks for good habits. Once a person has developed a good moral habit, say courage or prudence, that person is able to act with courage or prudence much more easily in each new instance. This ability we identify as *virtue*.

Before we proceed further, allow us to give two examples of good and bad moral habits:

> With the aid of junk bonds, Texas financier Charles Hurwitz took over Pacific Lumber. Pacific Lumber had provided steady employment for generations by means of selective logging and at the same time had protected many old growth California redwood groves. To pay off his junk bond debt, Hurwitz took $50 million from the Pacific Lumber employee retirement fund, and he clear-cut thousand-year-old redwood trees. Now the area around Scotia, California has lost many of its redwood trees and its jobs.[48]

---

[45] Robert C. Solomon, *Ethics and Excellence: Cooperation and Integrity in Business* (New York: Oxford University Press, 1993), p. 106; see also Solomon's "Business and the Humanities: An Aristotelian Approach to Business Ethics," in Thomas J. Donaldson and R. Edward Freeman, eds., *Business as a Humanity* (New York: Oxford University Press, 1994), pp. 45–75.

[46] Rushworth M. Kidder makes this same point in his chapter, "Ethical Fitness," in *How Good People Make Tough Choices* (New York: William Morrow, 1995). Kidder uses excellent examples throughout the book.

[47] George P. Klubertanz, S.J., *Habits and Virtues*, "How is Virtue Acquired," (New York: Appleton-Century-Crofts, 1965), pp. 171–77. For excellent references, see Klubertanz and Alasdair MacIntyre, *After Virtue* (Notre Dame: University of Notre Dame Press, 1981).

[48] David Harris, *The Last Stand: The War Between Wall Street and Main Street over California's Ancient Redwoods* (New York: Times, 1996).

When a demented individual laced Tylenol capsules with cyanide, and seven people in Chicago died, executives at manufacturer Johnson & Johnson were willing to spend hundreds of millions of dollars to recall all existing capsules rather than endanger additional lives. Although the FBI and consultants advised against it (it might encourage others), the recall decision was made quickly. By the account of the J&J executives themselves, this was because they based their decisions upon the mission and basic values of Johnson & Johnson, and the good moral habits that had been developed.[49]

Why did the above executives act so differently? Why did Johnson & Johnson executives almost instinctively look to the benefit of their customers, while Charles Hurwitz and executives at Bausch and Lomb sought primarily their own self-interest at the expense of employees, dealers, and others? We will show that moral habits, that is, virtue or vice, account for most of the difference. Moreover, we maintain that the presence or the absence of such moral habits are the foundation for and an accurate predictor of such good or bad behavior in the future. Let us go into more detail on these moral habits.

The Principal Virtues

A moral virtue indicates a development of character and personal excellence in that area of human activity. Virtue is a settled moral habit that moves one toward the middle ground or between extremes in acting.[50] Four basic moral virtues were identified by Aristotle and examined in detail by Thomas Aquinas. These four virtues are sometimes called the cardinal, principal, or chief virtues: fortitude (courage), temperance (self-discipline), justice (fairness), and prudence.[51]

Fortitude enables one to overcome obstacles to be or to do what is necessary to achieve a good goal. An entrepreneur must have fortitude in order to take the necessary risks to begin and maintain a business. Fortitude enables one to overcome the temptations to both cowardliness and foolhardiness. Patience and perseverance are integral parts of fortitude. For example, given the exploitative record of financier Charles Hurwitz, the members of Pacific Lumber's board of directors probably lacked fortitude when they gave up and sold the firm to him. In our everyday work, it is often easy to dodge difficult issues; we need fortitude to deal honestly with those challenges.

Temperance or self-discipline is the developed ability of not going too far toward a good. Whether with regard to our sensible appetites (e.g., eating, drinking, sex) or in wanting to possess or control things, we often experience a

---

[49] See Laura L. Nash, "Johnson & Johnson's Credo," in *Corporate Ethics: A Prime Business Asset* (New York: The Business Roundtable, 1988), pp. 80–82.

[50] Edwin M. Hartman has a superb discussion of virtue in the last section, "The Good Life and the Good Community," of his *Organizational Ethics and the Good Life* (New York: Oxford University Press, 1996), pp. 182–85.

[51] Thomas Aquinas, *Summa Theologia*, I-II, Questions 49–67; Aristotle, *Ethics, op. cit.* See also Robert G. Kennedy, "Virtue and Corporate Culture: The Ethical Formation of Baby Wolverines," *Review of Business* 17 (Winter 1995-96): 10–15.

temptation to obtain or consume too much of these goods. A temperate person is not avaricious or greedy. There is little in us that sensibly inclines us to be self-disciplined, yet we know that there is a need to stop at a suitable, harmonious mean before we destroy ourselves from gluttony, sclerosis of the liver, or sexually transmitted diseases. Charles Hurwitz appears to have lacked the virtues of temperance and justice when he took over Pacific Lumber. Rather he displayed the vice of greed. Unfortunately, we witness avarice and greed among many financial professionals. Many try to rationalize this vice by explaining that the market system directs them to make as much money as possible. Providing the necessary capital for business is important and generally demands virtue to achieve it. However, Aristotle maintains that to own and/or control significantly more than is required for oneself and one's family to live on or more than is ultimately a benefit to others is a vice. This limit on the possession of wealth conflicts with contemporary attitudes on the accumulation of goods and the inviolability of private property.

Justice is the regular and constant disposition to give another her or his due. One chooses to do the just thing *because it is just.* The virtue of justice would lead a manager to pay an equitable wage and to avoid race and gender discrimination. When Bausch and Lomb CEO Daniel Gill forced unrealistic sales goals on his division executives and distributors, he violated the virtue of justice. Rather than provide a corporate climate that supported justice, Gill's policies pushed his subordinates into vicious behavior.

Prudence is the concrete judgment that a person makes to recognize a good goal and to determine the means or strategy to be used in order to obtain that goal. The other virtues also require the judgment of prudence in order to be exercised. While the virtues are independent, they are nevertheless intertwined in each person. For example, without temperance or self-discipline, greed will lead us to unjust actions. In strategy classes business students learn the techniques of marketing *any* product, or financing *any* endeavor, and some might call this prudence. However, the ability to develop strategies to obtain goals that are not good is not prudence. For example, to develop strategies to sell a product that kills, such as tobacco, or to take over a firm in a hostile fashion, loot its retirement plan, and fire its employees as Hurwitz did to Pacific Lumber, we might call shrewdness, but not prudence.[52]

A manager cannot develop virtue in people by making them do things. They must *intend* the good act. So developing virtue is not easy. It requires a good intention and perseverance, and it is difficult because of our own inborn self-interest. As Philippa Foot puts it: "If people cared as much about the rights of others as they care about their own rights no virtue of justice would be needed to look after the matter, and rules about such things as contracts and

---

[52] George P. Klubertanz, *Habits and Virtues*. See also Charles M. Horvath, "Excellence v. Effectiveness: MacIntyre's Critique of Business," *Business Ethics Quarterly* 5 (July 1995): 499–532.

promises would only need to be made public, like the rules of a game that everyone was eager to play."[53]

Good moral behavior is influenced by mentoring, modeling, executive vision, and the particular corporate culture that this creates. Just as individuals must choose to be virtuous and must repeatedly act to bring that about, so too, managers must choose a specific way of managing if they seek to encourage a moral corporate culture. However, the contrary is also true. Managers who themselves engage in morally selfish acts thus model and encourage bad behavior and vicious habits among their colleagues and subordinates.

Founders and leaders of organizations normally would like their organizations to be successful over the long-term. To accomplish long-term results requires the moral habits of fairness, courage, and trust. Good moral habits, like moral principles, enable one to achieve moral goals. Most managers also would like to encourage ethically good behavior and good moral habits for the people in the work group they lead. Such basic ethical behavior as honesty, trust, respect for other people, and an ability to cooperate and work with others help make an effective organization.

A good moral habit arises from morally good actions that are repeated over a period of time. Hence, when a person regularly makes ethical decisions and performs ethical acts, it will develop that person's own good moral habits or virtues. Good moral acts performed by the members of the work group will also encourage good moral habits in other members of the work group.[54]

Choosing to Support Virtue in the Organization

To develop a habit of a particular good moral act requires that the individual *choose* that moral act. Virtue will grow to the extent that the person performs the act because she chooses the behavior for its own sake. Good moral acts that are motivated largely by fear, peer pressure, a control-oriented supervisor, or purely extrinsic rewards like compensation, will not develop virtue. Nevertheless, motives are seldom pure.

Leaders of organizations regularly attempt to communicate the values of the organization through socialization processes to new hires and to those who are already colleagues.[55] Leaders attempt to select people appropriate for the firm and for the job, and then socialize them to be persons who will work well within that organization. Formal and informal socialization are treated in more detail in Chapter 7. Nevertheless we here mention the importance of performing acts of, for example, courage, justice, trust, and integrity, because they are morally *good*

[53] Philippa Foot, *Virtues and Vices and Other Essays in Moral Philosophy* (Berkeley: University of California Press, 1978), p. 9.

[54] Klubertanz and MacIntyre, *After Virtue.*

[55] H. M. Trice and J. M. Beyer, *The Cultures of Work Organizations* (Englewood Cliffs, N.J.: Prentice Hall, 1993).

acts. When this is supported by the modeling behavior of leaders, it can be effective in forming good moral habits, which will then change behavior.

A leader must have a vision of how she wishes to operate, if she wishes to affect the behavior of members. Stories of managers who model the values that are described in the mission statement of the firm support that vision. The compensation system of the organization must also support the kind of behavior that is to be encouraged. While we tend to build reward systems around measurable standards of performance, acting out a moral habit is not always measurable. Nonetheless "colleague-of-the-week" programs and other rewards can be designed to identify a person who has done something of benefit for the firm or for others.

If the reward system narrowly insists on easily measurable financial returns, that may encourage vice rather than virtue. In the Bausch and Lomb case managers inflated profits, manhandled distributors and engaged in other vicious activities.

The development of good moral habits are diagrammed in Figure 3–5. Each person has their own unique package of good moral habits. Practice in making ethical decisions and performing good acts develop those moral habits. Ethical acts are the specific, identifiable action items. With regard to the diagram, for example, person #1 possesses greater, more developed moral habits or virtue, so the ethical issues that require judgment will be easier to identify, and easier to decide. Moreover, each specific act of that virtue will come more easily. Also note that each individual act strengthens the virtue, so that the act is easier to perform the next time. Person #2 has lesser development of good habits, so it will be harder for that person to identify the issues, and more difficult (i.e., a greater stretch) to make an ethical judgment. But notice that in this case, also, the level of virtue is increased, even if slightly, after each individual good moral act.

FIGURE 3–5 Development of Good Moral Habits

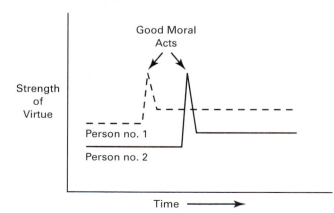

A person's *character* is formed by the constellation of such good moral habits. Every group or organization of which a person is a part influences that person's attitudes and actions, builds good and bad habits, and ultimately forms that person's character. Moreover, an organization made up of people of largely good habits and hence good character, will more likely be one which possesses a good ethical climate and thus a good corporate culture.

The *goal* of a business must be to increase the well-being of women and men, which includes supporting the development of virtue in working colleagues. We cannot assume that the development of virtue will take place if a business only meets its goals of profit and growth. Profit, along with return on investment and increasing market share, are important measurable *means* to achieve the *ultimate goals* of the firm.

A good manager generally has developed many good habits, many virtues, in the process of becoming a good manager. For example, a manager who regularly trusts subordinates develops the virtue of trust and eventually trusts almost automatically. A manager who makes little effort to develop the habit of trust will find each new case difficult and challenging. Such a manager will find that it takes far more time and energy to be a good manager—if indeed that person will ever become a good manager.

One method of affecting attitudes and behavior and thus developing several virtues, is to do some sort of service for the poor. Service projects are now popular in colleges and universities for this reason; one's motivation is generally positively affected by personal contact with those in need. Moreover, research by health care professionals show that helping other people even may be good for your heart, your immune system, and your overall vitality.[56]

ETHICS IN BUSINESS EDUCATION

Citizens and leaders alike agree that there is a need for ethics in business and in all schools. In a survey of corporate CEOs, business school deans, and members of Congress by a leading public accounting firm 94 percent said that the business community is troubled by ethical problems today. Further, 63 percent of these leaders believe that a business firm actually strengthens its competitive position by maintaining high ethical standards. These leaders also said that there was an observable difference in the quality of ethics in various parts of the United States. Areas of the country they ranked from most ethical to least are as follows: Midwest, Northwest, New England, South, Southwest, West, and East.[57]

---

[56] William Honan, "President of Harvard Cites Need for Commitment to Social Service," *New York Times* (Nov. 1, 1993), p. 16; Eileen Rockefeller Growald and Allan Luks, "Beyond Self: The Immunity of Samaritans," *American Health* (March 1988): 51–53.

[57] *Ethics in American Business: An Opinion Survey of Key Business Leaders on Ethical Standards and Behavior* (New York: Touche Ross, 1988), pp. 1, 10.

Difficulties in arriving at an ethical judgment on cases in our experience stem largely from our lack of familiarity with ethical norms and the classical ethical traditions. Most managers are not immoral, but many are amoral. They simply fail to adequately consider the morality of their actions.[58] They are hampered by the fact that ethics is not always taught in American grammar schools, high schools, and universities. On the contrary, the traditionally competitive, individualistic methods of learning and grading impedes the development of a sense of community and obligations to others. With regard to higher education, the environment of universities and professional schools also obstructs the development of an ethical sense. Former president of Johns Hopkins University, Steven Muller, maintains that this is the principal failing of universities today: "We fall short in exposing students to values. We don't really provide a value framework to young people who more and more are searching for it." He goes further:

> The failure to rally around a set of values means that universities are turning out potentially highly skilled barbarians: people who are very expert in the laboratory or at the computer or in surgery or in the law courts, but who have no real understanding of their own society.[59]

Ethics was not always so unknown. Ethics, or moral philosophy as it is often called, was the center of the curriculum of American universities throughout the nineteenth century. A general ethics course was required of all seniors and, because of its importance, was often taught by the college president himself.[60] This course integrated all that the students had learned, and prepared them for the working world. More specifically, this course sharpened the ethical sensitivity of students and enabled them to deal better with the ethical problems they were about to face.

Educators during this period judged that no nation could survive and prosper without common social and moral values. For a society such as ours, which was so fragmented because of differences in ethnic backgrounds, interests, expertise, and allegiances, it was very important to provide a structure whereby students could unify their learning: "The entire college experience was meant above all to be an experience in character development and the moral life, as epitomized, secured, and brought to focus in the moral philosophy course." [61]

Graduate business programs have been criticized as being too narrow, analytic, and technical by business executives and also by a committee set up by

---

[58] Archie B. Carroll, "In Search of the Moral Manager," *Business Horizons*, March–April 1987, pp. 7–15.

[59] Steven Muller, "Universities Are Turning out Highly Skilled Barbarians," *U.S. News and World Report*, November 10, 1980, p. 57.

[60] Douglas Sloan, "The Teaching of Ethics in American Undergraduate Curriculum, 1876–1976," in *Ethics Teaching in Higher Education*, ed. Daniel Callahan and Sissela Bok (New York: Plenum Press, 1980), p. 2. *Ethics Teaching* contains several other excellent essays on the teaching of ethics.

[61] *Ibid.*, p. 7.

the business school accrediting association.[62] This definitive report concluded that MBA curricula lacked vision and integration. There was insufficient attention given to leadership and communication skills, global business, ethics, and the legal, social, and political environment of business. In response to this, most MBA curricula have been drastically revised and the business accrediting association now requires more than half of an undergraduate curriculum be in the liberal arts. Some suggest that all graduate and undergraduate business students have a primarily humanistic education.[63]

Ethics is now a part of most undergraduate and graduate business curricula. Business ethics courses increased dramatically over the last two decades, such that at present there is at least "one course in two out of three undergraduate and graduate business programs, and almost half of them are required."[64] The $23 million gift to Harvard Business School for ethics that was mentioned at the beginning of the chapter is an example of this new concern. The donor, John Shad, underscored the need for ethics education when he noted the decline of ethical values in the United States:

> The erosion of ethical attitudes in America since the end of World War II can be attributed to the dispersion of families, rising divorce rates, the Vietnam War, the "permissive" and "me" generations, the drug culture, the affluent society and, most important, the substitution of television for the family, church, and school as the principal purveyor of social mores.
>
> We should redouble our efforts to induce television sponsors to increase the ethical content in interesting and amusing television cartoons and other programming. The business and financial communities also need to inspire and enforce higher ethical standards.[65]

Shad goes on to present his goals for business schools:

> It is not enough for these schools to certify that their graduates have mastered the fundamentals of their profession. The schools must hone their ability to certify that their graduates have the character and integrity to use the knowledge gained for the benefit—rather than the abuse—of society.[66]

In 1988 Harvard Business School introduced a required ethics course module that is taught at the very beginning of first year to all 600 first year graduate business students. The stated goals of that course include, "To emphasize the centrality of ethical values in the context of individual and organizational effectiveness; specifically, 'honesty, trust, respect, fairness.' "

---

[62] Lyman Porter and Lawrence McKibbin, *Management Education and Development: Drift or Thrust into the 21st Century?* (New York: McGraw-Hill, 1988).

[63] Richard T. De George, "Business as a Humanity: A Contradiction in Terms?," In Thomas J. Donaldson and R. Edward Freeman, eds., *Business as a Humanity* (New York: Oxford University Press, 1994), pp. 11–26.

[64] For a critical and perceptive review of business ethics and business and society courses and programs, see Dennis Collins and Steven L. Wartick, "Business and Society/Business Ethics Courses: Twenty Years at the Crossroads," *Business and Society* 34 (April 1995): 51–89.

[65] John S. R. Shad, "Business's Bottom Line: Ethics," *New York Times*, July 27, 1987, p. 19.

[66] *Ibid.*

The last dean of Wharton Business School, Russell Palmer, agrees with Shad on the role of business schools. He speaks for fellow deans when he said,

> We who run America's business schools are concerned about how people behave in business, and our responsibility to influence positive ethical behavior is considerable and urgent. We must teach not only the skills of management but also the principles of right and wrong.[67]

There are practical reasons for including ethics in the business program. One is that making ethical judgments before one is exposed to real business pressures to act unethically can result in behavior that is more ethical. In an experiment, college students were presented with a case involving an ethical dilemma and asked to judge a course of action. The experimenters then presented the actual situation to these same students two weeks later. The students acted more ethically than did a control group that had not earlier discussed the case. In an actual situation, the pressures of time and the job push one to compromise.[68]

When considering a dilemma away from the pressures of the actual situation, a person tends to consider the ethical issues in a more objective and balanced way. The conclusion: The informed discussion of ethical cases and the making of ethical judgments most likely have a significant effect in bringing about better ethical behavior.

Recognizing the importance of ethics education, between 30 and 40 percent of business firms now do it themselves. Their goals include building integrity and loyalty among colleagues and avoiding the penalties of illegal activities. Allied, General Electric, IBM, Johnson & Johnson, Merck, and McDonnell Douglas, for example, all have ethics education programs.[69]

Summary and Conclusions

We examined moral development in the last chapter and found that selfish (Kohlberg's Level I) behavior is more typical of adolescents and the immature than of mature women and men. Businesspeople want to be ethical; they have many good habits. Nevertheless, bribery, fraud, and stealing of trade secrets remain major problems for business. In many cases, managers say that they could not distinguish the right action from the wrong action. Generations now growing up have even fewer moral skills. The media and advertising teach us that ethics is relative, and many people have not learned the ability to make ethical judgments.

The cases and models presented in this chapter are intended to aid businesspeople in the development of their ethical skills. The decision models and

[67] Russell E. Palmer, "Let's Be Bullish on Ethics," *New York Times*, June 20, 1986, p. 23.

[68] Steven J. Sherman, "On the Self-erasing Nature of Errors of Prediction," *Journal of Personality and Social Psychology* 39 (March 1980): 211–19.

[69] Susan J. Harrington, "What Corporate America is Teaching About Ethics," *Academy of Management Executive* 5 (February 1991): 21–30.

norms are not perfect; they will not solve all ethical problems easily. But they are presented as a foundation for use, reflection, and improvement. In addition, decisions affect behavior, enabling people to be more honest and trustworthy, and ultimately possess greater integrity and virtue.

Businesspeople lament the lack of ethical skills among students and the lack of formal ethics in college curricula. In earlier centuries ethics had a central place in the lives of college students. It is a paradox that businesspeople have learned exact decision rules for inventory, finance, brand marketing, and other issues that face them, but have so few models for moral decisions and actions. If businesspeople are not moral, business will become a jungle, both hostile to people and highly inefficient.

These ethical norms and models can be learned and used, and thus become an aid to businesspeople. The decision rules can be expanded to handle more difficult cases, including cases in which the norms conflict. Moreover, there is evidence that making ethical judgments in the classroom helps to bring about more ethical behavior in business.

In addition, the intentional repetition of good moral acts develops moral habits or virtues. Good moral habits among colleagues can make a working environment more effective and also more humane. Given all the above, it is not surprising that in the better business schools ethics is well integrated into the curriculum and that business ethics is growing in importance.

Discussion Questions

1. What is the principal difference between rights and duties and utilitarian norms? Do an individual's intentions have any role in utilitarianism? Do intentions have a role in the theory of rights? Explain.

2. What does John Rawls add to the traditional theory of justice? Compare Rawls's theory and the traditional theory of justice with utilitarianism.

3. What is the norm of caring built upon? How does it compare with rights and duties, justice and utilitarianism?

4. Indicate the strengths and weaknesses of using the norms of (a) utility, (b) justice, (c) rights, and (d) caring.

5. Outline the criteria for whistle-blowing. If you were an insider and knew of payments by your firm to a manager in a competing firm for insider information, should you blow the whistle? Apply the criteria in deciding this question.

6. Do many college students take a course in ethics? What is the advantage of such a course? What is the disadvantage of ethics not being taught? Have you had such a course?

7. Do you agree with John Shad's assessment of the roots of the lack of ethics today? From your experience, which is the greatest contributing factor? Do you agree with his suggestions regarding television and business schools?

8. Is the purpose of studying ethics to develop ethical decision-making skills or to influence good behavior? Does the former affect the latter? How?

9. Describe how a person can develop good habits. What is the relation of virtue and character?

10. As an executive would you prefer that the members of your firm have good character? As a peer in a firm, would you prefer colleagues to have good character? Why?

Exercise:
Memo to the Chief Executive

You are assistant to the CEO of a firm in a very competitive industry. A competitor has made an important scientific discovery that could give it an advantage that would substantially reduce, but not eliminate, the profits of your company for about a year. A scientist who knows the details of the discovery applies for a job at your firm. There are no legal barriers to hiring the scientist.

The CEO knows that you had some ethics in your MBA program and so asks you to present your advice. In a single page memo to the CEO, indicate the major issues and ethical norms to be used, and make a recommendation.

Exercise:
Service-Learning in Community

Doing volunteer work for people in need in conjunction with agencies in the city provides an opportunity for experiential learning. Service-learning also enables you to gain insight into some of the issues that you will be studying in this course: personal values, moral development, workplace diversity, poverty, ecology, moral responsibilities of management, and corporate social policy. In addition, without healthy persons, families, and neighborhoods, businesses will have difficulty finding good employees. Moreover, if people do not have jobs and income, businesses will not have new customers. Service-learning is a part of more than two dozen graduate business programs in the United States.

In order to participate in the service-learning project, you are asked to:

1. *Volunteer* for at least 10 hours of service during the term in an agency that you and the instructor agree upon. This should be an agency that serves the poor, such as a homeless shelter, soup kitchen, tutoring inner city youth, or delivering food to disabled and elderly in the inner city.

2. *Write a journal* with at least several sentences of your own reflections after each hour of volunteer work.

3. *Attend a reflection session* that will help you to reflect on your experiences. Some questions to consider for the reflection session:
   a. What was the experience you had?
   b. What about the experience was most troubling?
   c. What was most inspiring or empowering?
   d. How were you affected or changed by the experience?

4. *Write a 3-page reflection paper* on your service-learning experiences.
5. *The reflection paper and journal* are due on the second-to-last class.

CASES

Double Expense Account

Frank Waldron is a second-year MBA student at Eastern State University. Although he has had many job offers, he continues to have the university placement office arrange interviews. He reasons that the interview experience is good for him and a better offer may even come along. Frank has also discovered a way to make money from job interviews.

Two firms invited Waldron to Los Angeles for visits to their home offices. He scheduled both visits on the same day and billed each for his full travel expenses. In this way he was able to pocket $1,000. When a friend objected that this was dishonest, Frank replied that each firm had told him to submit an expense account and that therefore he was not taking something to which he had no right. One firm had not asked for receipts, which he interpreted to mean that it intended to make him a gift of the money.

Is what he is doing unethical? Which norms help most in deciding the question? What advice would you give Frank?

Tax Assessment Kickback

You own a large building in a major city. The real estate assessor offers, for a fee, to underestimate the value of your property and save you a substantial amount in real estate taxes. Assume that this is a usual practice in this city. Do you pay the fee? Which norm is most helpful here?

CHAPTER

Historical Roots
of Business Values

4

Probe the earth and see where your main roots are.
—Henry David Thoreau

K nowing history benefits the businessperson and the business student.
The manager is thus able to recognize problems that were solved earlier
by others, and is better able to recognize situations that are new and
hence demand new solutions. History embraces such diverse elements as the
growth of business and cities and the energetic, entrepreneurial attitudes of earlier generations.[1]

We are products of our past. No matter how rapidly society changes, current attitudes have their roots in history. What we do and how we think are
much influenced by past values and attitudes.[2] Whether we view the present as
part of an organic development from earlier events or as breaking new ground,
the past has great influence. For example, a historical faith in progress undergirds the conviction of many that global competition is good for all. On the
other hand, concern for work satisfaction and for a clean environment stems

---

[1] "Why History Matters to Managers," a roundtable discussion with Alfred D. Chandler et al., ed. Alan
M. Kantrow, *Harvard Business Review* (January–February 1986), pp. 81–88.
[2] *Ibid.*, p. 84.

partly from a disenchantment with attitudes of earlier generations that were shortsighted and wasteful. It is impossible to understand current values and what the future will bring without knowing the path that has led us to where we are.

QUESTIONING THE PAST

People in both industrialized and developing societies need to assess their values for several reasons. First, the many more choices that people face in industrialized societies—choosing a career, a life-style, whether or not to marry and have children—require that they know their values in order to make better decisions.

Second, they have more education, and formal education encourages people to be more questioning and reflective.

Third, change takes place so rapidly that people need a new understanding for their activities and behavior. Some values are basic, provide a sense of stability, and endure through major changes; other values are no longer helpful. It is essential to examine our values so as to determine which remain relevant.

Fourth, an understanding of basic values and goals is necessary in industrialized societies because actions, goals, and rights often conflict. For example, the goal of loyalty within the firm conflicts with downsizing. The goal of producing at lowest cost conflicts with the goal of reducing pollution. The resolution of these conflicts requires clarification of goals and values. Moreover, this reflection can serve as the foundation for future business and public policy, and will affect individual lives and society as a whole.

Some ask the fundamental question: Why work? What is the value of work? Further, what is the value of business? Granted, if I want a car or a VCR, someone must design and manufacture it and I must have money to obtain it. But if I can obtain it in a lawful fashion without working, why not? If I can get rich gambling or speculating without working, why not place my efforts there? Does work have any other value to a person or to society than the financial compensation? Citizens around the world inquire about the intrinsic value of work and the goals of free enterprise. An intelligent response is essential for a mature people and a successful society.

These questions are not new; however, now they are asked by more people. In earlier societies, they were theoretical questions and were asked by educated people, but not by ordinary citizens. The ordinary worker's life was largely determined at birth. If a man's father was a shoemaker or a baker, he would become one also, and would use the tools, workshop, and home that had belonged to the family for generations. Rarely was there any question of whether a person *would* work, or at what occupation. There was little choice. There was also little regret or frustration, because there were no alternatives. Heredity, custom, and geography determined most of a person's life. To ask people in economically undeveloped, traditional societies why they work is like asking them why they try to stay alive. They have little reason to question the value of work.

Attitudes toward work are the foundation for business success or failure. The early American Puritan ethic supported tireless work and economic growth. However, this is but one strand of our history. Let us examine other strands.

LISTENING TO OUR FOREBEARS

Change took place rapidly in the United States from its beginning. Most of its people immigrated from other lands, largely from Europe. The Founding Fathers were influenced by European thinkers, such as John Locke, Jean-Jacques Rousseau, and Adam Smith, on such issues as the value of work, business, and private property. Although there were alternate strands of thought in the East, these values as yet have had less impact on American business values. Hence we will focus largely on Western history and philosophies as they affect business.

Throughout recorded history, work has been an integrating activity for most people. It was a binding cord for the fabric of the family, the city, and the social system. It gave stability and meaning to people and their relationships. A clear change, however, emerged with industrialization. Changes in work, such as division of labor, mass production, and "scientific management," were introduced. And the individual worker had increasing choice as to the type and location of the work he or she performed. It is ironic that just when individuals began to be able to choose work and thus expect greater satisfaction from their jobs, work became more fragmented, repetitive, and less able to provide pride of workmanship and accomplishment.

The Ancient Greek Attitude Toward Business and Work

The ancient Greeks thought of work and commerce as demeaning to a citizen. At best, it was a burden required for survival. The meager legitimacy and value accorded to work was given to it, not because it had any value in itself, but because it was a necessary evil. There are two limitations to our knowledge of ancient attitudes toward work. First, most of our information comes from written sources whose authors were generally the minority, those who were citizens and hence persons of leisure; they were not from the working class. Second, most of the work was done by slaves under dirty, grueling and often unsafe conditions. These slaves were uneducated and often prisoners of war from conquered nations.

Plato speaks of work as if it were a temptation to be avoided because it hinders a person's ability to live, to think, and to contemplate. In his *Laws*, Plato speaks also for his fellow citizens when he urges, "If a native stray from the pursuit of goodness into some trade or craft, they shall correct him by reproach and degradation until he be brought back again into the straight course."[3] Citizens of ancient Athens thought of work as something not worthy of a citizen. Plato, however, reveals the extent to which his contemporaries' attitudes were based on the conditions under which work was done, as he cuts to the heart of their disenchantment and even revulsion with work:

> Suppose the very best of men could be compelled—the fancy will sound ludicrous, I know, but I must give it utterance—suppose they could be compelled to take for a time to inn-keeping, or retail trade or some such calling; or suppose, for that matter, that some unavoidable destiny were to drive the best women into such professions: then we should discover that all are humane and beneficent occupations; if they were only conducted on the principles of strict integrity, we should respect them as we do the vocation of mother and nurse.[4]

Thus, Plato recognizes that most of the objections to work are not basic to work itself. In fact, these occupations are in themselves "humane and beneficent."

Plato's pupil Aristotle is more severe in his condemnation of the life of the worker or tradesperson. To him, such a life is irksome and beneath the dignity of a citizen:

> The citizens must not lead the life of mechanics or tradesmen, for such a life is ignoble, and inimical to virtue. Neither must they be husbandmen, since leisure is necessary both for the development of virtue and the performance of political duties.[5]

From his observations, Aristotle found crafts, trade, and business detrimental to health and character. Much of the work was done in cramped and unhealthy surroundings, and it was necessary to have daily dealings with rude, unprincipled, and unethical people. So industrial and commercial life was thought to rob the body of its health and to degrade the character. Moreover, whether those who followed a trade or craft should even be admitted to citizenship was a problem for Aristotle. This sort of work was generally done by slaves, and many contemporary states did not admit the laborer and the skilled worker to citizenship. "Even in states which admitted the industrial and commercial classes to power, popular sentiment held trade and industry cheap."[6]

Aristotle speaks of two types of business and trade activity, and his distinction goes to the root of a difficulty that perplexes many to the present day: the difference between the careful management of goods and what often appears to be a merely selfish profit orientation. He approves of the first but disapproves of the second. *Oeconomia*, from which our word economics derives, is literally "household management." It includes careful, prudent use not only of the household but of all one's property and resources. On the other hand,

---

[3] Plato, *The Laws of Plato*, trans. A. E. Taylor (London: Dent, 1934), p. 847B.

[4] *Ibid.*, pp. 918B–E.

[5] Aristotle, *Politics*, in *Basic Works of Aristotle*, ed. Richard McKeon (New York: Random House, 1941), p. 1141.

[6] W. L. Newman, *Politics of Aristotle*, vol. 1 (Oxford: Clarendon Press, 1887), p. 98.

chrematistike means the use of skill and goods to achieve a profit. This term described the city traders, who were few in number compared with the farmers and skilled workers. These traders often resorted to deceptive practices; and it seemed to Aristotle, and scores of generations that followed him, that they really contributed little or nothing to society. Aristotle's objections are not unlike those of Karl Marx: The trader's service as a middleman adds no value to the good. Hence, Aristotle approved of *oeconomia* but disapproved of *chrematistike*.

Plato and Aristotle generally agree in their objections to the pursuit of a career in trade or a craft, although Aristotle raises these objections more strongly: (1) The practice of business or a craft deprives a person of the leisure necessary to contemplate the good, the true, and the beautiful. (2) It hinders proper physical, intellectual, and moral development. (3) It is "illiberal" because it is done for pay. (4) It is less perfect because its end is outside of itself.

Work in Biblical Times

Unlike the Greeks, who had slaves, the ancient Hebrews could not remain aloof from work. They saw work as an essential part of their lives but also as a hardship. Even the painful aspect of work had its self-inflicted cause in original sin. This gave reason, integrity, and even verve to what for most other cultures was only something to be endured. On the positive side, the Jews pointed to the commands of God in Genesis that men and women were to cultivate the world and subdue it (Gen. 2:15). Craftsmen like Bezalel, who built the ark of the convenant, were honored in the Jewish tradition.[7] Thus work was integrated into their lives and had meaning for them. The God of the Hebrews is close to them. God is often pictured as one who labors: a vine dresser (Ezek. 15:6), a pottery maker (Gen. 2:7), a soldier (Is. 27:1).

Christianity built on the Jewish tradition with regard to work, trade, and commerce. The members of the new religion were from the working class. Jesus was a carpenter (Mark 6:3) and Paul, a tentmaker (Acts 18:2). The apostles were all working people; many were fishermen. They were not from the priestly class. Jesus in the Gospels cautions against an excessive concern with work and the things of this world (Matt. 6:24–34), but he also makes clear that work is a serious responsibility for the Christian (Luke 12:41–49). Furthermore, in the often-quoted parable of the talents (Matt. 25:14–30), the servant who has intelligently and profitably invested his money and his efforts is the one who is given additional rewards.

But the unique contribution of Christianity with regard to the value of work is its view that work is done also out of love and concern for one's broth-

---

[7] Rabbi Jeffery Salkin, *Being God's Partner: How to Find the Hidden Link Between Spirituality and Your Work* (Woodstock, Vt.: Jewish Lights Publishing, 1994).

ers and sisters. Work is necessary not only to earn one's living, asking alms of no one, but above all so that the goods of fortune may be shared with one's needy sisters and brothers.[8] The foundations of industrial civilization rest on a new concept of love preached by Jesus Christ and presented in the New Testament. It is "a peculiarly generous concept of charity, of the opportunity we have to give ourselves to others here and now, insofar as we love our neighbors for God."[9] Throughout the ages, including our own time, Christians most often have fallen short of these ideals. Nevertheless, as a foundation for work and business values, especially in its emphasis on love of neighbor, Christianity was an important step forward.

In the early centuries of the Christian era, the most important commentator was Augustine. He approved of handicraft, farming, and commerce on a small scale. But in any selling, no more than a "just price" can be asked; charging interest on the use of money is immoral. Those who have wealth should prize it as a trust from God. After their own modest needs are met, they should give the rest to the poor.[10] As early as the fifth century, Augustine held that work was obligatory for monks. During later centuries in the monasteries, especially among the Benedictines, a new work ethic developed.

Monks as Capitalists

Benedictine monasteries have been credited as being "perhaps the original founders of capitalism."[11] The Benedictine Rule, as embodied in tens of thousands of monasteries throughout Europe, brought a much more positive attitude toward production and work. For the monks, manual work was not a curse and a degradation. They looked on work as an opportunity to build, to grow and develop personally and as a community. They chose to work together, and they were among the first to cooperate voluntarily in all tasks. Since the monks often worked in groups and varied their occupations, they found it helpful to work by the clock. They would begin and end their work together. They standardized tasks so that anyone could handle the job.

Living and working as a cooperative community stimulated the use of various labor-saving devices. When, in 1115, Bernard of Clairvaux led a band of monks to found a new monastery, one of his prime requisites for a new site was that it have a rapidly moving stream that could be harnessed by the monks to help them do their work. Bernard himself provides us with a description of his famous

---

[8] Adriano Tilgher, "Work Through the Ages," in Sigmund Nosow and William Form, *Man, Work and Society*, (New York: Basic Books, 1962), p. 13.

[9] John U. Nef, *Cultural Foundations of Industrial Civilization* (Cambridge: Cambridge University Press, 1958), p. 89.

[10] Tilgher, "Work Through the Ages," pp. 14–15.

[11] Lewis Mumford, *Techniques and Civilizations* (New York: Harcourt, Brace, 1934), p. 14.

abbey at Clairvaux, and he provides considerable detail on the mechanical devices that are geared to waterwheels to make the work of the brothers easier.[12]

The monastery is built at the base of a mountain and extends over a fast-moving stream to make best use of the waterpower. The river is guided by "works laboriously constructed" by the monks so that the water may be of the greatest help to their efforts. The water thus "passes and repasses the many workshops of the abbey." The water is channeled so that it "passes on at once to drive the wheels of a mill." In moving these wheels, "it grinds the meal under the weight of the mill-stones, and separates the fine from the coarse by a sieve." The river's waters are also harnessed to raise and drop hammers for the fulling of cloth and to help the shoemaker in his chores. The waters are then split into smaller streams where they help "to cook the food, sift the grain, to drive the wheels and hammers, to damp, wash, soak and so to soften, objects; everywhere it stands ready to offer its help." The monks also constructed an elaborate irrigation apparatus to water the fields. Recall that all this happened in the 1100s, 6 centuries before the Industrial Revolution.

A century later the great Christian theologian of the Middle Ages, Thomas Aquinas, provided a rationale for work. He spelled out clearly and in some detail the reasons why it seemed to him that manual labor was necessary for all: to obtain food, to remove idleness, to curb concupiscence, and to provide for almsgiving.[13] Although Aquinas saw that work was not only necessary but also of great value, there was still a remnant of the view that work was a burden, something to endure for the sake of leisure.

Work, however, was not a burden for the monks; it was a vehicle of love and service. When setting up a new monastery, the monks would deliberately choose a site far from existing towns. They did this both because it would be a better locale for prayer and because they deliberately set out to communicate their new view of the value of work as rooted in charity. Benedict and Bernard expected their monks to work in the fields and the shops, whether they were sons of aristocrats or of serfs. According to Lynn White, Jr., historian of technology and industry, this provision

> marks a revolutionary reversal of the traditional attitude toward labor; it is a high peak along the watershed separating the modern from the ancient world. The Benedictine monks regarded manual labor not as a mere regrettable necessity of their corporate life but rather as an integral and spiritually valuable part of their discipline. During the Middle Ages the general reverence for the laboring monks did much to increase the prestige of labor and the self-respect of the laborer. Moreover, since the days of St. Benedict every major form of Western asceticism has held that "to labor is to pray," until in its final development under the Puritans,

---

[12] Bernard of Clairvaux, *Patrologiae Latinae*, ed. Migne, vol. 185 (Paris: Garnier, 1879), pp. 570–74. A translation of much of this is in Samuel J. Eales, *Life and Works of St. Bernard*, vol. 2 (London: Burns & Oakes, n.d.), pp. 460–67. The quoted words that follow are those of Bernard himself.

[13] Thomas Aquinas, *Summa Theologica*, II–II, qu. 87, art. 3.

work in one's "calling" became not only the prime moral necessity but also the chief means of serving and praising God.[14]

The monks lived together thriftily, and that enabled them to invest in productive machinery like that described above to aid them in their work. This is why some call the monks the first capitalists. Their resources and inventiveness combined and resulted in division of labor, interchangeable work, a clock-regulated work-day, and ingenious labor-saving equipment—all of which added up to considerably greater productivity. They used the additional time that was then available for their prayer and community life together. A few hundred years later, this same love-centered ethic was brought to the cities and marketplaces of seventeenth-century France by an eminent group of artists, poets, theologians, and saints. John Nef maintains that it was this unique emphasis on the centrality of love for one's brothers and sisters, especially as embodied in women, that made industrial society and its requirement of cooperation and hard work possible.[15] More specifically, he shows that the law of love and its vision as carried out by women were two of the greatest impetuses to the sort of civilization that makes industrialized society possible.

By 1700, Christianity, with its central love ethic, had helped to provide many of the elements necessary for the development of business and commerce. Work began to be looked on as something of value; it provided self-discipline and an integrating force in a person's life. Christianity helped the individual to focus on the value of the product of work; if the same thing could be produced more easily, this was good—especially when it enabled one to help one's family and neighbors. The importance of producing a greater quantity of goods and a new consciousness of time developed first in the monasteries and then spread to the larger society. Furthermore, the Catholic church urged all to attend mass side by side: rich and poor, worker and artisan, peasant, scholar, and duke. This fostered communication and cooperation.

In its otherworldly theology, however, Catholicism thwarted the coming of capitalism. Material goods, wealth, and success were not the measures of holiness. According to Jesus, the purpose of life on earth was not merely to build up material goods. This attitude led to suspicion of those who would lend money to others and charge them for the use of it. Even as late as the sixteenth century, theologians condemned the opening of state banks.[16] Lending money at interest in the Christian tradition was the sin of usury.

In Christian society, work and industry were much more respected than they had been in aristocratic Greece or Rome. The average citizen had many reasons to do tasks well, and there were no slaves to do them instead. In addi-

---

[14] Lynn White, Jr., "Dynamo and Virgin Reconsidered," *American Scholar* 27 (Spring 1958): 188. Quoted with permission.

[15] See Nef, *Cultural Foundations*; see also his briefer *Civilization, Industrial Society and Love* (Santa Barbara, Calif.: Fund for the Republic, 1961).

[16] Lewis Mumford, *The Myth of the Machine* (New York: Harcourt, Brace & World, 1966), p. 279.

tion, a person's trade or craft gave meaning and integrity to life. But it was the Protestant Reformation that provided the impetus for the development of attitudes that would propel Western society toward rapid economic growth.

From Luther and Calvin to the Protestant Ethic

It was Protestantism that eventually established hard work and the making of profits as central to a Christian life. Ironically, Martin Luther (1483–1546), the initiator of this new movement, intensely disliked the commerce and economic individualism of his day. Luther was appalled at the regal high living of local merchants, princes, and popes. The sharp contrast between the ideals of Christianity and what Luther actually found around him motivated him to push for reform. He called for a return to a simple, hardworking peasant life; this would bring sufficient prosperity for all. A person should earn a living and not make an excessive profit.

Luther thought a number of Christian customs encouraged idleness: the many religious holidays, the mendicant friars glorifying begging, and the monasteries' supporting some who did not work. Idleness is unnatural, according to Luther, and charity should be given only to those who cannot work. His original contribution was in emphasizing the importance of one's profession. The best way to serve God was to do the work of one's profession as well as one could. Thus Luther healed what had been a breach between worship and work. As long as work was done in obedience to God and in service to one's sisters and brothers, every type of work had equal value in God's eyes.

Luther held that a person's salvation is achieved solely through faith in God; good works do not affect salvation. Moreover, all legitimate human activities are acts of worship, no one more than another. Since formal prayer and worship, and especially the monastic life of prayer, are no more valuable than tilling the fields, Protestantism released all human energies for the world of work. The farmer, the smith, and the baker all do work that is quite as honorable as that of the monk or priest. Although the life of the simple worker is better, Luther concedes that:

> trade is permissible, provided that it is confined to the exchange of necessaries, and that the seller demands no more than will compensate him for his labor and risk. The unforgivable sins are idleness and covetousness, for they destroy the unity of the body of which Christians are members.[17]

Luther was vehement in preaching against lending at interest, yet paradoxically his denial of all religious authority eventually set economic life free from strictures on usury. This denial left business and commerce to develop their own life and laws independent of existing moral authorities. Capitalism thus set up its own norms of right and wrong, and capitalist activity was carried on beyond the influence of the church.

---

[17] R. H. Tawney, *Religion and the Rise of Capitalism* (New York: Mentor, 1947), p. 83.

Luther's insistence on investing everyday life with the same value as worship and on breaking the system of canon law and religious authority eventually resulted in profound changes in economic and social life. The elaborate prescribed relationships with neighbor, family, and church were swept away. Although they were encumbering and limiting, they also provided roots, personal relationships, and meaning for life. Secular interests, work, and business now formed another world, one little connected with the religious and moral values that had until this time governed all aspects of life.

The most important influence on what we now call the Protestant ethic was the theology of John Calvin (1509–1564), who followed Luther as a reformer of Christianity. Calvin and his followers did not idealize the peasant, as did Luther, but accepted urban life as they found it. As R. H. Tawney puts it, "Like early Christianity and modern socialism, Calvinism was largely an urban movement."[18] Calvin's central theological notion, which distinguishes his position from that of Luther and of Catholicism, is predestination. According to Calvin, God is infinite, absolute, supreme, and totally above and beyond human beings. There is no way of our fully understanding God and God's ways. Moreover, God because of infinite wisdom knows all people who were and *will be* saved in the world. In God's power and wisdom, God has determined that it is fitting for his glory if only a small number of men and women are saved. Moreover, Calvin maintains that there is absolutely nothing a person can do to influence his or her own salvation; from all eternity God has freely predetermined it. A person lives to glorify God, and the major way a person glorifies God is in his or her life. If a person bends every talent and expends every energy in work and achieves success, this may be an indication that he or she is one of the saved. Although these individual efforts cannot directly affect or ensure salvation, if successful they do glorify God and may thus be a sign that the person is numbered among the elect. Probably even more motivating was the conviction that if a person was idle, disliked work, or was not successful, these were most likely signs that that person was not among the saved.

Calvin taught that all must work and must never cease working. Profits earned must not be hoarded but must be invested in new works. Investment and the resulting profit and wealth were thus encouraged: "With the new creed comes a new man, strong-willed, active, austere, hard-working from religious conviction. Idleness, luxury, prodigality, everything which softens the soul, is shunned as a deadly sin."[19] Calvin proposed a unique paradox: Deny the world; live as an ascetic in the world, because it cannot guarantee your salvation. Yet remember that your one duty is to glorify God, and the best way of doing that is by being a success at your chosen work, your calling. It is a precarious balance, difficult to achieve and even more difficult to maintain.

---

[18] *Ibid.*, p. 92.
[19] Tilgher, "Work Through the Ages," p. 19.

The Protestant ethic, therefore, stems directly from Calvin's teachings. He stressed the importance of hard work and the necessity to reinvest one's earnings in new works. Moreover, Calvin did not condemn interest and urban trade, as did Luther and Catholic leaders. Calvin not only urged working hard at one's occupation but also held that successful trade and commerce was but another way of glorifying God.

Weber's Analysis of the Protestant Ethic

Before leaving the influence of the Reformation on business ideology, let us look at the summary of that influence drawn up some 200 years later by the sociologist Max Weber in *The Protestant Ethic and the Spirit of Capitalism*. It is ironic that Weber, a German, cites no other person more often as an example of the Protestant ethic than Benjamin Franklin, an American. We will examine Franklin's contributions later in this chapter.

Weber begins his analysis by noting that "business leaders and owners of Capital, as well as the higher grades of skilled labor, and even more the higher technically and commercially trained personnel of modern enterprises, are overwhelmingly Protestant." He goes on to compare the Catholic and the Protestant: "The Catholic is quieter, having less of the acquisitive impulse; he prefers a life of the greatest possible security, even with a smaller income, to a life of risk and excitement, even though it may bring the chance of gaining honor and riches." [20] In trying to determine the reason why Protestants seem to be more successful, Weber examines the roots of the theology of Luther and Calvin, as we have done above. He notes that Reformation theology encouraged individuals to look on their work more seriously. Life demanded sobriety, self-discipline, diligence, and, above all, planning ahead and saving. A person's attention to the life of this world was serious in the extreme. In addition to having its own rewards, success was a reflection of God's glory and hence a hint as to whether that person was saved or not. It was therefore incumbent on all to be successful. Moreover, they had the means to achieve that success: "In practice this means that God helps those who help themselves. Thus the Calvinist himself creates his own salvation, or, as would be more correct, the conviction of it."[21]

An asceticism adequate to achieve the goal flowed from the Calvinistic ethic: "Waste of time is thus the first and in principle the deadliest of sins." On the same theme, the Calvinist asceticism "turned with all its force against one thing: the spontaneous enjoyment of life and all it had to offer." On the positive side, in the Calvinist and Puritan churches Weber finds "the continually repeated, often almost passionate preaching of hard, continuous bodily or mental labor." But Weber observes that even in his day "the people filled with the spirit

---

[20] Max Weber, *The Protestant Ethic and the Spirit of Capitalism*, trans. Talcott Parsons (New York: Scribner, 1958), pp. 35–41. Quoted with permission.

[21] *Ibid.*, p. 145.

of capitalism today tend to be indifferent, if not hostile, to the Church." When that happens, the pursuit of business and a career often take on the vehemence and all-embracing aspects of active religion: "Business with its necessary work becomes a necessary part of their lives." But this is what is "so irrational about this sort of life, where a man exists for the sake of his business, instead of the reverse." The Protestant ethic changed history. Contrary to the ethical convictions of centuries, "money-making became an end in itself to which people were bound, as a calling."[22]

In his last chapter Weber quotes founding Protestants John Wesley and John Calvin when they point out a paradox. It is religion that makes people careful, hardworking, frugal; and this, in turn, enables them to build up wealth. "But as riches increase, so will pride, anger, and love of the world," in Wesley's words. Speaking of those on the lower end of that same economic ladder, Weber quotes Calvin: "Only when the people, i.e., the mass of laborers and craftsmen, were poor did they remain obedient to God."[23] Therein lies a paradox; the men who themselves are most responsible for the Protestant ethic foresee its collapse. Their religion demands hard work and saving, and this provides wealth. But wealth brings pride, luxury, and lack of will. It is therefore an unstable ethic, in part because its religious foundations tend to dissolve. As we will see with Benjamin Franklin and many others, the ethic can take on a secular life of its own. It may be able to continue with other, though less vital, sources of motivation. It remains for us to see what this new secular vision and motivation will be.

The Protestant ethic (see Fig. 4–1) derives from the Calvinist vision of how people should act in order to be successful in this life and also in the next. With the help of its tenets, many have achieved success and developed the values that will be described in the next chapter in the section "Values in Modern Life."

FIGURE 4–1 The Protestant Ethic

THE PROTESTANT ETHIC URGES:

- Hard work
- Self-control and sobriety (that is, humorlessness)
- Self-reliance
- Perseverance
- Saving and planning ahead
- Honesty and "observing the rules of the game"

---

[22] *Ibid.*, pp. 70–73, 157–66.

[23] *Ibid.*, pp. 175–77. Some reject the attempt to link economic success with religious faith. They maintain that there are more plausible explanations for commercial success, such as "special education, family relationships and alien status." See Kurt Samuelson, *Religion and Economic Action*, trans. E. G. French (New York: Basic Books, 1961), p. 154. Nevertheless, the fact that Weber's theses are so widely accepted makes it a theory to be reckoned with. Whatever the causal relationships, religious values and economic development are there to be observed, and they have had a marked influence on one another.

The Protestant ethic urges planning ahead, sobriety, diligence, and self-control for the individual. It promises a material reward and, in its religious strand, a good chance of salvation. Moreover, the Protestant ethic serves an additional and psychologically perhaps more important purpose. It assures the successful and wealthy that their wealth is deserved. They have property because they have worked for it and so have a right to it. As Weber himself observed, the wealthy man is not satisfied in knowing that he is fortunate:

> Beyond this, he needs to know that he has a right to his good fortune. He wants to be convinced that he "deserves" it, and above all, that he deserves it in comparison with others. He wishes to be allowed the belief that the less fortunate also merely experience their due.[24]

Thus the Protestant ethic not only provides a set of directions on how to succeed and a motivation for doing so but also attempts to legitimate the wealth that is acquired. The successful person says, "Anyone who was willing to work as hard as I did could have done as well, so it is clear that I deserve the wealth I have." This attitude was also in accord with social Darwinism and the survival of the fittest.

John Locke and the Right to Private Property

John Locke (1632–1704) had a considerable influence on the Founding Fathers and through them on the American Constitution. He and Jean-Jacques Rousseau also influenced the French Revolution and most of the subsequent efforts to move toward more democratic governments. The Oxford-educated Locke was both a philosopher and a politician. He was a practical man having served various government figures of his day, so in his philosophy he examined political and social questions.

Locke was concerned with various natural rights, but the right to which he devoted most of his energy was the right to private property.[25] Locke held that an individual has a right to self-preservation and so has a right to those things that are required for this purpose. Individuals require property so that they may feed and clothe their families and themselves. A person's labor is what confers primary title to property. If individuals settle on land and work it, they therefore deserve title to it. Locke's ideal was America, where there was unlimited property available for anyone who was willing to clear and work it.

Locke has been criticized for overemphasizing the rights of private property and thus catering to the interests of his landowning patrons, and this criti-

---

[24] Max Weber, "The Social Psychology of World Religions," in *Max Weber: Essays in Sociology*, ed. H. H. Gerth and C. Wright Mills (New York: Oxford University Press, 1946), p. 271.

[25] John Locke, *An Essay Concerning the True Original Extent and End of Civil Government*, especially Chap. 5, "Of Property," and Chap. 9, "Of the Ends of Political Society and Government." See also the summary in Frederick Copleston, *A History of Philosophy*, vol. 5 (London: Burns and Oates, 1964), pp. 129–31.

cism may be justified. But he did not allow for a person's amassing wealth without limit. Whatever is beyond what the individual can use is not by right his or hers; it belongs to others and should be allotted to them.

Rousseau's Social Contract

Jean-Jacques Rousseau (1712–1778) shared with other members of the French Enlightenment a distrust of contemporary society and its institutions. He believed that society, and even Enlightenment ideals such as reason, culture, and progress, had created unhealthy competition, self-interest, pseudosophistication, and a destruction of the "simple society" he valued. He believed society was unjust, effete, and dominated by the rich and by civil and church authorities. According to Rousseau, "Man was born free and everywhere he is in chains." Men and women's original state in nature is free, and although some form of society is necessary, freedom, reverence, family life, and the ordinary person must be central to it.

The *Social Contract* is an attempt to achieve the necessary activities, associations, and governments required in a civilized society without losing basic individual rights. A citizen's duty of obedience cannot be founded simply on the possession of power by those in authority. To be legitimate, it must rest on some sort of freely given consensus.[26] Rousseau's distrust of society's institutions also included private property. According to him, when private property is introduced into a society, equality disappears. Private property marks a departure from primitive simplicity and leads to numerous injustices and evils such as selfishness, domination, and servitude. In the state he proposes, Rousseau supports a sharply increased tax on any property that is not necessary for a person to modestly support themselves and their family. For property that is necessary for support, there should be no tax at all. Rousseau agrees with Locke with regard to the illegitimacy of excessive wealth.

Adam Smith's Capitalist Manifesto

The Scot Adam Smith (1723–1790) is the grandfather of capitalism and of free enterprise economics. As a political economist and moral philosopher, he was among the first to emphasize free exchange and to present economics as an independent branch of knowledge. His best known and classic work, *The Wealth of Nations*, was published in 1776 and supported independence for economics and business in the same year that the American colonies declared their political independence from England. In an earlier book that is usually ignored, Smith

---

[26] Jean-Jacques Rousseau, *The Social Contract and Discourse on the Origin and Foundation of Inequality Among Mankind* (New York: Washington Square Press, 1967). See also the summary of Rousseau in Copleston, *History of Philosophy*, vol. 6, especially pp. 68–69 and 80–100.

had provided a humane foundation for the economic system with his emphasis on sympathy, virtue, and justice.[27]

In explaining economics Smith says, "Nobody ever saw a dog make a fair and deliberate exchange of one bone for another with another dog." Later he spells out the implications of this inability to exchange by showing that each animal is obliged "to support and defend itself, separately and independently, and derives no sort of advantage from that variety of talents with which nature has distinguished its fellows." Human beings, says Smith, are quite different in that they can take advantage of one another's unique genius. What one is good at he does in abundance, sells to others, and thus "may purchase whatever part of the produce of other men's talents he has occasion for." Smith's first and most familiar example is of the division of labor in pinmaking. One man, working alone and forming the entire pin, could perhaps "make one pin in a day, and certainly not make twenty." But when the operation is divided up into a number of separate operations so that "one man draws out the wire, another straights it, a third cuts it, a fourth points it, a fifth grinds it at the top for receiving the head," and so on, a group of pinmakers are able to make pins at a daily average of 4,800 pins per pinmaker, as Smith himself had observed.[28]

In addition to the value of exchange and the division of labor, Smith also examines the value of the free market, competition, and profit maximization. Smith was among the first to make a clear and plausible case that when morally conscientious individuals follow their own self-interest, it works to the benefit of society as a whole. As individual competitors pursue their own maximum profit, they are all thus forced to be more efficient. This results in cheaper goods in the long run. Free competition in all markets and with all goods and services is thus to be encouraged; government intervention serves only to make operations less efficient and is thus to be avoided. The same principles apply to international trade. There should be a minimum of government interference in the form of duties, quotas, and tariffs. Smith's is the classical argument in support of free trade.

Smith takes some of his basic inspiration from the English philosopher Thomas Hobbes (1588–1679). Hobbes had maintained that individuals act simply to gain that which gives them pleasure or to avoid that which causes displeasure. Since this may differ for each individual, there is no objective good or value in reality itself. Hobbes's view of human motivation is that of "egoistic hedonism." Since Hobbes's view is that human nature is largely self-seeking and that there is no objective morality, it is not surprising that he held that might makes right. It is important to have power to protect one's person and goods. Whatever a person has the power to take belongs to that person. Hobbes ac-

---

[27] Adam Smith, *The Wealth of Nations*, ed. J. C. Bullock (New York: Collier, 1909), pp. 19–23. On comparing the two works and on Smith's influence, see Patricia Werhane, *Adam Smith and His Legacy for Modern Capitalism* (New York: Oxford University Press, 1991).

[28] *Ibid.*, pp. 9–10.

knowledges that this leads to insecurity and even war but maintains that they are an inescapable part of the human condition. On the theme of trade and economic activity, Smith quotes Hobbes's claim that "wealth is power." Wealth enables its possessor to purchase what he or she wants, and this in itself gives that person considerable control over others. So it is in the interest of individuals to increase their wealth.

To explain profit maximization, Smith uses the example of rent. Even though the owner of the land contributes nothing to production beyond the fact of ownership, nevertheless the owner will strive for a contract stipulating the highest rent the tenant can possibly afford to pay. Contrary to the earlier principle of a "just price," the landlord will try to leave the tenant as little as possible of what he or she earns. Smith contends that this is as it should be. On some occasions the landlord may leave the tenant a bit more for him- or herself, but this is and should be exceptional; it is due to "the liberality, more frequently the ignorance, of the landlord."[29]

As the grandfather of modern economics, Smith spells out clearly and graphically most of the current major principles operating in economic and business theory. He illustrates the advantages of the division of labor, the free competitive market, and profit maximization and how they contribute to more efficient production. As individuals pursue self-interested goals, Smith's famous "invisible hand" guides economic and business activities so that they are more productive and cheaper and thus benefit society as a whole. Industry and commerce in the two centuries following Adam Smith have been extraordinarily successful. Moreover, business activities closely followed the model Smith described. The free market encouraged rapid economic growth. Economic motivation for most people up to Smith's time had been based more on obligations to a lord, proprietor, or to one's family and on threats, fears, and sanctions. The free market and potentially unlimited monetary rewards shifted the entire basis of economic activity.

The free market and the possibility of unlimited profits are at the heart of the system's greatest strength: It taps positive motivation and rewards. It draws a man or woman into greater activity and creativity and rewards those efforts. Furthermore, the rewards are tangible and measurable; by these standards there is little doubt as to who is a success. On the other hand, this new model for economic activity also includes the system's greatest weakness. It insulates a person from obligations to friends, family, fellow citizens, and the larger community, and replaces these obligations with an easily broken contract whose purpose is to obtain individual profit. Hence, individuals can much more readily come to feel that they are alone, that they are isolated, and that they are easily replaceable. Literature on the attitudes of managers and blue-collar workers

---

[29] *Ibid.*, pp. 153–71. See also Harold L. Johnson, "Adam Smith and Business Education," *AACSB Bulletin* (October 1976): 1–4.

alike shows that most have experienced this feeling of isolation and alienation.[30]

Put another way, Adam Smith and the Industrial Revolution that followed shifted people's view such that they tended to compare society to a machine instead of to an organism, as they had formerly. In earlier times, men and women knew they were part of something larger than themselves. Families worked together, and they cared for their neighbors. They were dependent upon one another—like parts of an organism. They had a stake in their community and they belonged. This was replaced by a situation in which one's own work was sold. One no longer belonged, and one's very self became just another commodity in the market system. Every individual can and will be replaced when he or she becomes obsolete, old, and inefficient, just as is the case with parts of a machine.[31]

Adam Smith provided an accurate and integrated picture of developing business activities. He detailed the advantages of free exchange. As such, he was to people of the nineteenth century the father of free market economics. Smith is still widely quoted and remains to this day a principal spokesperson for capitalism and free enterprise. The contribution of the European continent to values formed the foundation for the "New World." Let us now turn our attention to the growth of a new people across the Atlantic Ocean.

FOUNDATION FOR ENTERPRISE VALUES

The Europeans who crossed the ocean to this "New World" came as immigrants to a land they thought of as open and free. Yet Native Americans had been on the continent for scores of centuries before the Europeans arrived. Since they were few, they were ignored unless they got in the way of the newly arrived. In some cases the settlers made peace with the natives. In more instances there was a conflict between the farmers and the nomads, between the exploiters of minerals and those who reverenced the mountains. The way that the newcomers treated the native peoples reflected their practical, entrepreneurial, yet self-centered values.

The immigrants who came to the New World risked their lives and their fortunes in the hope of finding freedom and new opportunities. They came to a land that seemed to them to have limitless natural resources—timber, coal, and much good farming land. Clearing the land was backbreaking, but the result was good, fertile acreage that could be handed on to one's children. The chang-

---

[30] See evidence of this dissatisfaction, for example, in Theodore V. Purcell and Gerald F. Cavanagh, *Blacks in the Industrial World* (New York: Free Press, 1972), pp. 72–75, 236–38.

[31] For this and other insights, the author thanks Otto Bremmer. Concerning Smith anticipating and providing suggestions on the major moral failures of capitalism, see James Q. Wilson, "Adam Smith on Business Ethics," *California Management Review* (Fall 1989): 59–72.

ing climate encouraged work—it was brisk and invigorating—and the winters, when there would be no fruits or crops, demanded that settlers plan ahead and save something from the harvest. Two wide oceans provided natural defenses that allowed the New World to focus on its own needs and development without much fear of foreign intrusions.

All these natural characteristics affected the values and ideology of the people. But when the settlers came, they also brought with them their own values and ideals that heavily influenced their attitudes. Most of the early American immigrants were religious people. In fact, many of those who came to the colonies did so for religious reasons—many because of religious persecution in their native countries. They sought a land where they could live and pray as conscience dictated. The men and women who settled the new continent came from Europe and so brought with them the religion that predominated there—Christianity. The Spanish came first to Mexico and Peru, and founded cities, colleges, and businesses. But the English Puritans, who came a century later to the northern New World, had a more lasting influence on business values and ideology.

The Puritans fled Europe so that they might freely follow their antihierarchical religious faith and practices. To these men and women, who came well before the American Revolution, their work or their "calling" was an essential part of their total world view. To us today, the Puritan ideal is a delicate, even mysterious, paradox. Puritan preacher John Cotton (1584–1652) described it thus:

> There is another combination of virtues strangely mixed in every lively, holy Christian: and that is, diligence in worldly business, and yet deadness to the world. Such a mystery as none can read but they that know it.[32]

Puritans plunged into their work with a dedication that could come only because it was their calling. In John Cotton's words, "First, faith draws the heart of a Christian to live in some warrantable calling though it be of an hired servant."[33] Worship of God was not shown in hymn singing, colorful religious services, or sterile monasticism; worship was a simple, reverent prayer. Moreover, the Puritans' prayer was not separated from work, for work was their most effective means of giving glory to God. So work was disciplined and clear-eyed, because "when he serves man, he serves the Lord; he doth the work set before him and he doth it sincerely and faithfully so as he may give account for it." This early Puritan ideology strengthened the emerging social order by giving importance to every type of work. Again, in John Cotton's words, "[faith] encourageth a man in his calling to the most homeliest and difficultest and most dangerous things his calling can lead and expose himself to."[34] Self-discipline was also important, for Puritans were not to be caught up in their own success

---

[32] Perry Miller, *The American Puritans* (Garden City, N.Y.: Doubleday, 1956), p. 171.

[33] *Ibid.*, p. 173.

[34] John Cotton, quoted in Miller, *The American Puritans*, pp. 176–77.

or failure. They were ascetics in the world; although in it, they were detached from it.

Two generations later, Cotton Mather (1663–1728) was born into the same family of learning and clerical leadership. Like his grandfather, Mather held that

> A Christian has two callings: (1) a general calling to serve the Lord Jesus Christ, and (2) a particular calling which was his work or his business. Both of these callings are essential if the Christian is to achieve salvation. Contemplation of the good means nothing without accomplishment of the good. A man must not only be pious; he must be useful.[35]

The Puritan businessman fully integrated his work with his worship. Often he would mention God in his invoices, thanking God for a profit or accepting losses for God's greater glory. Moreover, each individual determined his or her calling, and work was generally done individually. In the same fashion, people achieved salvation individually.

American Puritans did not invent this position; they took the theology of John Calvin and spelled out in detail the implications for the businessperson. The businessperson in turn, eager for some justification of the efforts to which he devoted most of his waking hours, happily received the Puritan preacher's words. So there began the mutual understanding and support between preacher and businessperson that became a hallmark of New World society.

Benjamin Franklin's Way to Wealth

In the prerevolutionary period, Benjamin Franklin accepted the work values of the Puritans, shifted them from a religious to a secular foundation, and restated them for Americans. Franklin, especially in *Poor Richard's Almanack*, was incisive, mundane, prolific, and widely influential. Many of his homely bits of advice have become common sayings in our language. Franklin brought together 25 years of his *Almanack* writings on the world of work and business and published them in 1758 as the essay "The Way to Wealth."

> God helps them that help themselves. Diligence is the mother of good luck, as Poor Richard says, and God gives all things to industry. Then plough deep, while sluggards sleep, and you shall have corn to sell and to keep, says Poor Dick. Work while it is called today, for you know not how much you may be hindered tomorrow. Be ashamed to catch yourself idle. When there is so much to be done for yourself, your family, your country, and your gracious king, be up at peep of day; 'Tis true that much is to be done, and perhaps you are weak handed, but stick to it steadily, and you will see great effects, for constant dropping wears away stones and little strokes fell great Oaks.[36]

---

[35] A. Whitney Griswold, "Two Puritans on Prosperity," in *Benjamin Franklin and the American Character*, ed. Charles L. Sanford (Boston: D. C. Heath, 1955), p. 41.

[36] Benjamin Franklin, *The Autobiography and Other Writings* (New York: New American Library, 1961), p. 190.

In his own graphic way, Franklin focuses on the importance of saving and the need for capital when he notes that "a man may, if he knows not how to save as he gets, keep his nose all his life to the grindstone. If you would be wealthy, think of saving as well as of getting."[37] It was satisfying to Franklin's early American contemporaries to see him supporting the same values and justification for their work as did their ministers. He provided a rationale for work and a purpose for life; at the same time, he buttressed the existing social order.

Franklin's writings were best-sellers in his day and have exerted a tremendous influence up to the present. In his *Almanack*, his *Autobiography*, and his own life, Franklin embodied the Puritan virtues. He was eminently successful as an inventor, statesman, diplomat, and businessman and he espoused the same virtues as did the Puritan ministers. Although some aristocrats of his day, such as John Adams, resented Franklin's popular wisdom, he was held in esteem by the people. Harvard-educated John Adams, second president of the United States, was a New England patrician: brilliant and courageous but also haughty and stubborn. Adams conceded that Franklin was a genius, a wit, a politician, and a humorist, but he questioned his greatness as a philosopher, a moralist, or a statesman.[38] In spite of Adams's petty quarrels with Franklin, history shows Franklin to have had a greater influence on values. Thomas Jefferson agreed with the hard-working, individualistic ideals of Franklin, although Jefferson, who wrote the *Declaration of Independence*, was convinced that these virtues could best be fostered in, and the new nation grow best as, an agricultural society.[39] Jefferson felt that as long as one had one's own land to till and crops to care for, the economy would thrive and people would be happier.

At this time more than 80 percent of American workers were farmers, and if Jefferson had his way, that is how it would have remained. Jefferson was opposed to the industrialization he had seen in England. He would rather import finished manufactured goods than undergo the undesirable changes manufacturing inevitably brings: urbanization, landless workers, banking. In an agricultural society, where work and initiative immediately pay off for the individual and for the society as a whole, government intervention could be kept to an absolute minimum. Government would only retard the natural forces of growth with regulations and bureaucracy. In Jefferson's own oft-quoted words, "That government is best which governs least." The ambivalent feelings toward and even fear of business appear early, for business spawns cities. An agrarian society is simpler; duties and rewards are more easily seen and measured. Early Americans were therefore not always favorably disposed toward business or cities.

---

[37] *Ibid.*, p. 192.

[38] For this essay, see John Adams, "An Exaggerated Reputation," in Sanford, *Benjamin Franklin*, pp. 22–26.

[39] Arthur M. Schlesinger, "Ideas and Economic Development," in *Paths of American Thought*, ed. Arthur M. Schlesinger, Jr., and Morton White (Boston: Houghton Mifflin, 1963), pp. 108–9.

The American Frontier

The continuing westward expansion served to keep alive the simpler, measurable agrarian values. The effect of this westward movement and the frontier on the American character was spelled out by Frederick Jackson Turner just before the turn of the twentieth century. For successive waves of hunters, traders, ranchers, and finally farmers, there were always new lands to conquer. It seemed to be a world without limits. The Native Americans were nomadic, and there were fewer of them to offer resistance. For the brave and hearty immigrant, it was worth taking great risks, whether in moving or in building. Success brought wealth; failure provided the chance to try again somewhere else.

The new territories demanded the strenuous labor of clearing the land. The first farmers faced the difficult task of pulling out trees and building their homes and barns. Nevertheless, the rewards were great: They would have homes and incomes and could pass on their farms to their children. The rewards were clear, tangible, and permanent, and they gave settlers incentive and zest. The land is measurable and unambiguous. It is open to human effort; if one works harder, one will be able to produce more.

Turner himself sums up how the frontier has given the American intellect its striking characteristics:

> That coarseness and strength combined with acuteness and inquisitiveness; that practical, inventive turn of mind, quick to find expedients; that masterful grasp of material things, lacking in the artistic but powerful to effect great ends; that restless, nervous energy; that dominant individualism, working for good and for evil, and withal that buoyancy and exuberance which comes with freedom—these are traits of the frontier or traits called out elsewhere because of the existence of the frontier.[40]

Turner's thesis has been widely quoted and has had a great influence on thinkers and on women and men of affairs. Although there are few new physical lands to conquer, current challenges to all peoples demand the same kind of creativity, risk taking, energy, and sense of purpose.

Tocqueville's View of Americans

As anyone who has lived in another culture knows, the peculiar characteristics of that culture stand out in bold relief to the foreigner. In that same process, of course, one is also far better able to recognize the unique qualities of one's own culture. A people's characteristic values and ideology can best be understood in comparison with those of another culture. Thus a perceptive foreign visitor often is able to describe the values and characteristics of the host people with penetrating insight. As an example, Alexis de Tocqueville has remained one of the best commentators on the American character.

---

[40] Frederick Jackson Turner, *The Frontier in American History* (New York: Holt, 1920), p. 37.

A young French lawyer, Alexis de Tocqueville, came to the United States in 1831 to observe and learn from the people. His reflections, which are in his book *Democracy in America*, attained instant success not only in France but in England and the United States as well. Published in English translation in 1838, the book was immediately praised for its insight and lack of bias, and it is still regarded, 160 years later, as one of the finest commentaries on American life. Tocqueville tried to understand Americans on their own terms.

On arriving, Tocqueville noted the physical expanse of the new country: "The inhabitants of the United States constitute a great civilized people, which fortune has placed in the midst of an uncivilized country."[41] It was this same combination, of course, which was to help give rise to the independence, re-sourcefulness, and frontier spirit of which Frederick Jackson Turner was later to write. Tocqueville noticed that, preoccupied by the great task to be accom-plished, Americans tended to value facts more than consistent ideals, that which works more than the beauty of a comprehensive ideological system. He charac-terized the American "philosophical method," the American method of reflec-tion and learning, as "to evade the bondage of system and habit, of family max-ims, class opinions, and, in some degree, of national prejudices." Americans accepted tradition only as a starting point, the existing situation only "as a les-son to be used in doing otherwise and in doing better." Each person seeks to un-derstand for one's self. All these characteristics Tocqueville summed up as an individualism of thought: "Each American appeals only to the individual effort of his own understanding." This mentality shows that a generation gap is no new thing: "Every man there readily loses all traces of the ideas of his forefa-thers or takes no care about them."[42]

Tocqueville saw Americans as hardworking and individualistic. The only rationale they might have for their actions and attitudes is enlightened self-interest. They are not inclined to reverence tradition, to philosophize, or even to engage in much reflection. He focused on the same favorable attitude toward work that has been attributed to the Puritan, the immigrant, and the frontier set-tler. Americans see work "as the necessary, natural, and honest condition of hu-man existence." Labor is not only not dishonorable, it is held in honor among the people. Even the rich person feels the obligation to take up some sort of worthwhile work, whether this work be private or public.

When Americans were asked why they work, act, and think as they do, Tocqueville reported that they gave a rather consistent response:

> The Americans are fond of explaining almost all the actions of their lives by the principle of self-interest rightly understood; they show with complacency how an enlightened regard for themselves constantly prompts them to assist one another

---

[41] Alexis de Tocqueville, *Democracy in America*, trans. Henry Reeve, vol. 1 (New York: Knopf, 1946), vol. 1, p. 422.

[42] *Ibid.*, vol. 2, pp. 3, 4.

> and inclines them willingly to sacrifice a portion of their time and property to the welfare of the state.[43]

Although not unique to America, by the time of Tocqueville's visit enlightened self-interest had taken firm root here. In the generation following the publication of *Democracy in America*, social Darwinism was to make even more popular the doctrine that acting self-interestedly contributes to the common good, as we shall see later.

With remarkable insight, Tocqueville underscored both the strengths and the weaknesses of this philosophy. The principle of self-interest does not entail lofty goals, but it is clear and certain. It does not demand much of a person, yet acting in accordance with it does produce results. It is not difficult to understand for all sorts and classes of people. As a principle of human life, self-interest builds on peoples' infirmities:

> By its admirable conformity to human weaknesses it easily obtains great dominion; nor is that dominion precarious, since the principle checks one personal interest by another, and uses, to direct the passions, the very same instrument that excites them.[44]

The principle of enlightened self-interest produces no great acts of self-sacrifice, but it encourages a daily discipline of self-denial. By itself self-interest cannot make people good and virtuous and hence can hardly serve as a cornerstone of morality. Nevertheless, said Tocqueville, "it disciplines large numbers of people in habits of regularity, temperance, moderation, foresight, self-command."

Enlightened self-interest is closely related to individualism (for definitions, see Figure 2–2). Tocqueville's work was the first to discuss individualism and, in fact, the first to bring the word into the English language. It is characteristic of Americans that individualism was not a common word among them, even though it so well described some of their salient attitudes and values. People develop a vocabulary for those things of concern to them, those things they therefore want to discuss. Tocqueville suggested that there was probably no other civilized country in which less attention was paid to reflection and philosophy than the United States. Americans were not then, nor are they now, a very reflective people.

Tocqueville described individualism as a mature and calm feeling which disposes each member of the community "to sever himself from the mass of his fellows and to draw apart with his family and his friends." Each individual retreats to his or her own familiar turf and thus "leaves society at large to itself." The Frenchman contrasted individualism and selfishness, and he found both seriously deficient:

---

[43] *Ibid.*, vol. 2, pp. 122, 152.
[44] *Ibid.*, vol. 2, pp. 122–123.

> Selfishness originates in blind instinct; individualism proceeds from erroneous judgment more than from depraved feelings; it originates as much in deficiencies of the mind as in perversity of heart.
>
> Selfishness blights the germ of all virtue; individualism, at first, only saps the virtues of public life; but in the long run it attacks and destroys all others and is at length absorbed in downright selfishness.[45]

Tocqueville pinpointed possibly the most serious weakness of the American character. Enlightened self-interest and individualism narrow one's perspective. They encourage one to think less of public responsibilities, and they lead eventually to selfishness. He sounds like a contemporary critic reflecting on the weaknesses of the corporate executive or the bureaucrat. Tocqueville's sensitive assessment of the American character—its task-orientation and individualism; its impatience with tradition, reflection, and abstract ideals; its self-interest leading to selfishness—still stands as one of the great social commentaries. Later observers often use Tocqueville as a starting point, but few have done a better overall appraisal than he.

Social Darwinism and Herbert Spencer

Events of the latter half of the nineteenth century had a profound impact on attitudes and values. The Industrial Revolution, the growth of cities, and the beginning of the concept of evolution shook the foundations of life and thought. Spencer's theories of "social Darwinism" were based on the newly discovered theories of evolution.

Herbert Spencer (1820–1903) proposed a harsh "survival of the fittest" philosophy. Spencer's thesis was that the bright and able contribute most to society and so are to be encouraged and rewarded. The poor, the weak, and the handicapped demand more than they contribute and so should not be supported but rather be allowed to die a natural death. Contact with harsh and demanding reality is a maturing experience that should not be diluted by well-intentioned but in reality destructive charities and handouts. If "natural" principles were followed, evolution and the survival of the fittest in the competition of human life would be the result. Spencer did not set out to examine any particular society and its values; rather, his critique was proposed as "culture-free." According to Spencer, it applied to all people, for it was derived from basic, organic principles of growth and development. Spencer applied to society the same principles that Charles Darwin saw in biological life—hence the name *social Darwinism*.

Spencer and others who became prophets of the new evolutionary social ideology were impressed by the suffering of the poor, but they nevertheless felt that progress in an industrial society could come only through long hours of work, saving, self-discipline, and even the death of the less able. Rather than considering this a tragedy, they were convinced that through this process of nat-

---

[45] *Ibid.*, vol. 2, p. 98.

ural selection, those of greater talent, intelligence, and ability would survive and be successful. The physically and mentally handicapped, unable to compete successfully, are less apt to survive. It would be a mistake for a government to provide assistance to these handicapped and deficient persons. That would allow them to stay alive, and worse, to reproduce and so transmit their deficiencies to future generations.

Any attempt to minister to the needs of the poor or needy is misguided on several counts. It keeps alive those who are less able. It diverts the attention and abilities of able people who would be better off pursuing more fruitful careers. And, finally, it insulates the less able from a sobering contact with harsh reality and poverty, an opportunity that might jar them from their complacency and encourage them to work harder to better themselves. Although it might be painful to the weak in the short run, the overall good of society in the long run demands that these less fit individuals not be supported or encouraged. According to Spencer, society improves because of the survival of the fittest:

> The poverty of the incapable, the distresses that come upon the imprudent, the starvation of the idle, and those shoulderings aside of the weak by the strong, which leave so many "in shallows and in miseries," are the decrees of a large, farseeing benevolence. Under the natural order of things society is constantly excreting its unhealthy, imbecile, slow, vacillating, faithless members.[46]

It is especially clear in primitive societies that the strongest and cleverest survive best. But this is a natural process, and so it occurs in civilized societies, too. People would be wise to prepare themselves and their children for this struggle.

Society as a whole will benefit from this struggle for survival. Since the most intellectually and physically fit survive, the race will improve. Given a difficult and demanding environment, over several generations the ideal man and woman will develop. There should therefore be little state interference in this natural selection process. The state must not regulate industry, impose tariffs, give subsidies, establish a church, regulate entry into the professions, operate schools, or run the mail service. Most especially, the government must not provide for the poor, improve sanitation, or look to the health needs of the less able.[47]

An example of applying Spencer's views to social issues occurred in 1845–50. Ireland then experienced a blight of the potato—its staple food, which caused widespread famine, disease, and death. England had invaded and occupied Ireland for several hundred years, and the English took the most fertile land to grow grain for export back to England. At the time of the famine, grain was available from these fields in the Irish midlands. Members of British

---

[46] Herbert Spencer, *Social Statics* (London: Appleton, 1850), pp. 323–26, 353.

[47] See Donald Fleming, "Social Darwinism," in Schlesinger and White, *Paths of American Thought*, pp. 124–25.

Parliament were advocates of free markets and they used Spencer's arguments in debating whether to continue to send the grain to England or to release the grain to the Irish. Members of Parliament in London argued that the Irish race would be stronger and better if the weaker and less able did not survive. It is harmful in the long run for the government to intervene. So Parliament voted not to provide grain to those who were starving. More than one million people out of a prefamine population of eight million in Ireland died.[48]

Herbert Spencer's philosophy was even more popular in the United States than in his native England. His praise of the strong, clever, and aggressive individual was in keeping with the American spirit. Further, his theory of inevitable progress was received enthusiastically in a country already marked by general optimism. Spencer's thinking provided both a rational foundation for existing attitudes and a justification for many public and private practices. In the last third of the nineteenth century, Spencer was an influential leader of thought and a hero to many in the United States.

The personal attributes Spencer extolled are those that many hold to be necessary for a free enterprise system. The focus is on the hearty, adaptable individual in a hostile climate. Survival requires careful planning ahead, hard work, loyalty and responsibility to family, and individual self-sufficiency. And as radical as they may have seemed to his contemporaries, Spencer's theories are actually conservative. Spencer saw great good in the way things were; there was no need to change or to plan ahead on a national or local level. Since natural processes will inevitably produce the best people and the best society, any sort of government or even private intervention will only hurt society in the long run. Citizens must repress their feelings of pity for the poor and allow natural processes to work themselves out. Spencer's theories challenged the mainstream religious views of the time and were thus opposed by many. But to others his position seemed a natural extension of the traditional Puritan ethic, especially its secularized counterpart as expressed by Benjamin Franklin. It is no surprise that Spencer's theories were enthusiastically received by the business community of his day.

Struggle for Survival

The businessperson, and especially the entrepreneur, has always found the world to be nothing less than a struggle for survival. One may want to be humane and conscientious, but cannot afford to be. Herbert Spencer's theories of the survival of the fittest and what has come to be known as social Darwinism had an immense influence on the America of the late nineteenth century. In fact, it described the American experience.

---

[48] R. Dudley Edwards and Desmond Williams, *The Great Famine* (Dublin: Browne and Nolan, 1956), pp. 177–186, 243–246; also, E. R. R. Green, "The Great Famine (1845–50)" in *The Course of Irish History* ed. T. W. Moody and F. X. Martin. (New York: Weybright and Talley, 1967), pp. 268–74.

William Graham Sumner (1840–1910), a social science professor at Yale, was an advocate of Spencerism. Sumner's father was an immigrant English workingman who taught his children the Puritan virtues of thrift, self-reliance, hard work, and discipline.[49] His son was convinced that egalitarianism, made fashionable by the French Revolution and the freeing of the slaves, would undermine the initiative and independent spirit that encourage the best people to develop their talents fully. According to Sumner, the less able and adept are jealous of the successes of the more talented and through the political process they will require the latter to support them. This perversion undermines the creativity and motivation of the better and more talented people. Sumner applauded the era in which people would work and live, not because of inherited position and status, but because they themselves chose to do so through the new democratic device of contract. He clashed with Yale president Noah Porter when the latter objected to Sumner's assigning Herbert Spencer's book to students. Nevertheless, he won the long-term battle with probably the first clear statement of academic freedom within the university.

Sumner and Spencer urged a tight-fisted, unemotional aloofness. Both one's self and one's wealth must be saved and not spent without chance of a good return on investment. Free emotions and spontaneity were suspect; a person could lose all in a lighthearted or thoughtless moment. In the same vein, Sumner urged that government should not intervene in social and economic affairs. The environment should be kept clear of restrictions, taxes, restraints, and other needless and even harmful laws and regulations.

The opposition was led by Lester F. Ward (1841–1913). Ward's view, expressed in his *Dynamic Sociology*, is that people should control their environment, not allow it to control them. Evolution and natural selection as outlined by Darwin led to change without direction and without goals. According to Ward, the great value of evolution and natural selection was that they had brought people to the position in which they found themselves now. Moreover, it was precisely in the current era that individuals became able to control their own future and not leave it to blind chance. For him, it would have been the supreme paradox for men and women, now that they had discovered these natural laws and forces, to retreat and allow themselves to become victims of them. Ward labeled Spencerism a do-nothing philosophy.

Summary and Conclusions

From ancient times to the Middle Ages, Western attitudes toward work became progressively more positive. Biblical injunctions and monastic practices helped to integrate work, labor-saving devices, and a planned day into the average person's life. Then, in the sixteenth century, the Protestant Reformation made the

---

[49] Fleming, "Social Darwinism," *op. cit.*, p. 128.

successful performance of an individual's "calling" or occupation one of the primary duties of life. Although a joyless vision, it encouraged a focusing of energies that made possible rapid economic growth. The central importance given to private property and the freedom of the individual further supported this growth.

This chapter also examined the major values and ideals in American life and the inherited values, geography, and personal characteristics that contributed to the development of those values. The vast expanse of virgin land was a challenge to the righteous, task-oriented Puritans. Their moral theology supported their work ethic: early rising, self-denial, hard work, thrift. Furthermore, the favorable results of working hard showed that the individual was saved. Though not a Puritan, Benjamin Franklin found the work ethic attractive, and he presented a secularized version of it.

The values of American Puritans—hard work, saving, regular habits, diligence, self-control, and sobriety—still characterize the American work ethic to some extent. These values constitute what is known as the Protestant ethic, which will be discussed in greater detail in the next chapter.

Discussion Questions

1. How does a knowledge of history help the manager? How does it help in understanding the development of business values?
2. What were the attitudes of Plato and Aristotle toward work?
3. What influence did Jesus and the Gospels have on peoples' attitudes toward work?
4. What stand on work did the early Benedictine monasteries contribute? What meaning might these attitudes have for work today?
5. Describe how John Locke's position on private property influenced the Protestant ethic and early American attitudes. How does it influence current business values?
6. Did Martin Luther have a favorable view of business and commerce?
7. Did John Calvin look on work favorably? Why did Calvin think that the Protestant ethic would decay?
8. Why is Adam Smith called the grandfather of economics?
9. Compare Adam Smith's position on work and efficiency with that of Benjamin Franklin.
10. According to the Puritans, what constitutes a person's calling?
11. How did Benjamin Franklin alter the Puritan ethic?
12. Compare and contrast Benjamin Franklin's attitudes toward work and efficiency with those of Thomas Jefferson.
13. Describe the effect of the frontier on American values.
14. Outline Alexis de Tocqueville's appraisal of enlightened self-interest.
15. According to Tocqueville, what are the strengths and weaknesses of enlightened self-interest as a basic motive for people? To what extent are his assessments still valid today?

16. What is social Darwinism?

17. Why does Herbert Spencer maintain that evolution and the "survival of the fittest" are not to be thwarted?

18. Compare the effect of the frontier with the effect of social Darwinism on American values.

CASES
Tax-Free Camera

Eric has a work-study position in the marketing department at Northern University. At a local camera shop Eric is about to purchase a $250 camera for his personal use. He knows that if he tells the salesperson that he is purchasing it for university use, he will save $15 sales tax. Eric's friend, Joan, says, "Everyone does it. And the state has more money than they can use anyway." Eric agrees and tells the salesperson that it is for university use.

> What are the ethical issues in this case?
>
> Do you agree with Joan's statement?
>
> What should Eric do? Why?

Radar Detector

Louis Dwyer sells dashboard radar detectors to auto supply shops. He works for the largest firm that manufactures the devices in the United States. He is a bit troubled by the fact that the sole purpose of the "fuzz buster" is to evade the law on speed limits. He is a talented salesperson, and has other options for jobs. He comes to you for advice. What would you tell him?

CHAPTER

Factories, Immigrants, and Ideology

5

In the past the man has been first; in the future the system must be first.
—Frederick Winslow Taylor

The lives of people are strongly influenced by their history, as we have seen in the last chapter. Our ancestors' experiences in business and in life can help us understand current business values. This chapter continues to examine the people, events, and commentators that have influenced business values in the United States. It then focuses on the origin and content of business values and ideology.

Values and ideologies are not merely theoretical statements of purpose. They also motivate people to act. An ideology gives a rationale for action, and answers questions such as: What activities and values in my life are most important to me? How do I explain my life, my actions, and my values when they are questioned by others?

An ideology also embodies accepted ideals (for terms, see Figs. 1–1, 2–1, 2–2), the ultimate goals possessed by an individual or a society. Thus ideals can significantly influence values. Ideals are sometimes distant, whereas values affect actions. Unless ideals are integrated into an ideology, they do not have much influence on actions and choices. We can better understand our lives and values by examining how history has influenced those ideals and values. Let us now learn from our forebears.

135

THE PROTESTANT ETHIC AND BUSINESS PRACTICES

Let us continue our examination of the business values of a new nation. In Chapter 4 we surveyed the work values of Western civilization, and continued by viewing the Puritans and the writings of Benjamin Franklin. After independence, those values had an unprecedented opportunity to be realized. The new nation provided an ideal testing ground for enterprising farmers, traders, prospectors, entrepreneurs, and theorists. Business and commerce grew at an extraordinary pace. It is important to examine that growth briefly and, more to our purpose, the values that undergirded it.

The early days of the new republic were dominated by the farmer. The colonial merchant provided the link between early Americans, trading and transporting food and goods. From 1800 to 1850, wholesalers took the place of merchants. They "were responsible for directing the flow of cotton, wheat and lumber from the West to the East and to Europe."[1] The rapid growth of the American industrial system that was to make the United States the most productive nation in the world had begun by the middle of the nineteenth century. "In 1849 the United States had only 6,000 miles of railroad and even fewer miles of canals, but by 1884 its railroad corporations operated 202,000 miles of track, or 43 percent of the total mileage in the world." The number of those working in factories also grew very rapidly during this period. In terms of manufactured goods, "By 1894 the value of the output of American industry equalled that of the combined output of the United Kingdom, France, and Germany."[2] Growth continued to accelerate, until within 20 years the United States was producing more than a third of the industrial goods of the world.

Mining in the mountains of the far West provides a paradigm of the strengths and weaknesses of the American character: energetic, flexible, and enterprising, but also self-centered and with little concern for long-term consequences. Tales of silver, gold, and other minerals in the mountains thrilled the imagination of people across the continent. Mining called for strong, resourceful people. Hundreds of thousands took the challenge, risking their lives, their fortunes, and often their families to try to find the ore. Vast amounts of capital and superhuman energies were expended. The "get rich quick" spirit of these prospectors was a prelude to that of the entrepreneurs who came later. Virginia City, Nevada, was built over the famed Comstock Lode of silver ore. What had been bare desert and mountains in 1860 became within 5 years one of the most rapidly growing and thriving cities of the new West. The energies and genius of thousands sank dozens of shafts into the rock, supported them with timbers,

---

[1] Alfred D. Chandler, "The Role of Business in the United States: A Historical Survey," *Daedelus* 98, no. 1 (1969): 26.

[2] *Ibid.*, p. 27.

built flumes—and an entire city. Between 1859 and 1880 more than $306 million worth of silver was taken from the mountains.[3] The magnitude of the effort and the accomplishment can be gathered from this description:

> In the winter of 1866 the towns and mills along the Comstock Lode were using two hundred thousand cords of wood for fuel, while the time soon came when eighty million feet of lumber a year went down into the chambers and drifts. Since the mountains were naked rock, flumes had to be built from the forested slopes of the Sierras, and by 1880, there were ten of them with an aggregate length of eighty miles.[4]

Adolph Sutro owned a quartz mill on the opposite side of the mountains on the Carlson River, and he saw an easier way to get the ore out of the mountains. He envisioned a three-mile-long tunnel that would extend through the mountain from the river valley and intersect the Comstock mines 1,600 feet below the surface. The tunnel would drain the series of mines to that level and also enable the ore to be taken out through the tunnel for processing where fuel and water were plentiful. By 1866, Sutro had obtained contracts from 23 of the largest mining companies to use the tunnel when it was completed:

> After incessant effort, in which any man of less marvelous pluck and energy would have failed, he raised sufficient capital to begin the project. In 1869 he broke ground for the tunnel and set a corps of drillers upon the task that was to occupy them for eight weary years. It was the labor of a giant.[5]

Sutro finished his tunnel and put it in use in 1877. But within 3 years, the boom collapsed. The value of the silver mining stock sank from a high of $393 million in 1875 to less than $7 million in 1880. People slowly began to leave Virginia City, and today it is a ghost town, with only remnants of roads, homes, and a few of the more substantial large buildings left to remind us of what it once was.

Virginia City illustrates how the great talents and wealth of a society can be quickly channeled to accomplish tremendous feats; it also shows how such accomplishments are often short-lived and not designed to encourage stability. This sort of activity attracts energetic and fast-moving entrepreneurs; it does not appeal to people who desire family and neighborhood relationships. Virginia City illustrates both the strengths and the weaknesses of the American entrepreneurial spirit. The gold rush a decade earlier in California left a more permanent mark, since the new inhabitants did not leave when the gold ran out. The prospectors, miners, and fortune seekers converged from all parts of the country, disrupting communities and families. Before their coming, California had a

---

[3] Allan Nevins, *The Emergence of Modern America*, vol. 8 (New York: Macmillan, 1927), p. 137. For a discussion of these and other issues raised in this chapter, see Daniel T. Rodgers, *The Work Ethic in Industrial America, 1850–1920* (Chicago: University of Chicago Press, 1978).

[4] Nevins, *Emergence of Modern America*, p. 136.

[5] *Ibid.*, p. 137.

unique style. "To these California imperatives of simple, gracious, and abundant living, Americans had come in disrespect and violence." Exploitation of the land kept people moving, and left problems in their wake:

> Leaving the mountains of the Mother Lode gashed and scarred like a deserted battlefield, Californians sought easy strikes elsewhere. Most noticeably in the areas of hydraulic mining, logging, the destruction of wildlife, and the depletion of the soil Americans continued to rifle California all through the nineteenth century.
>
> The state remained, after all, a land of adventuring strangers, a land characterized by an essential selfishness and an underlying instability, a fixation upon the quick acquisition of wealth, an impatience with the more subtle premises of human happiness. These were American traits, to be sure, but the Gold Rush intensified and consolidated them as part of a regional experience.[6]

Throughout these years of rapid economic change, the role of entrepreneurs was central. Their brains, ingenuity, and willingness to risk gave us most of our economic success and growth. At the same time, their myopic desire for short-term gain caused many failures and much personal anguish. With this as background, let us return to the leaders of thought who have had a profound influence on American business values.

American Individualism Ralph Waldo Emerson Style

To this day, the American businessperson is characterized as an individualist. One articulate, persuasive, and most influential champion of freedom and the importance of the individual was Ralph Waldo Emerson (1803–1882). Coming soon after the French Enlightenment and Rousseau, Emerson is the best-known American proponent of individualism. He sees human nature as having natural resources within itself. Societal structures and supports tend only to limit the immense potential of the individual. Given freedom, individuals can act, grow, and benefit themselves and others. But they require an absence of restraints imposed by people, cultures, and governments. Emerson's friend Henry David Thoreau acted on this ideology and built a hut at Walden Pond, outside Boston, where he reflected and wrote alone in the unimpeded, open atmosphere of trees, grass, and water.

In Emerson's book of essays *The Conduct of Life, there is one entitled "Wealth."*[7] Here Emerson applies his philosophy of individualism to economics and the marketplace. A person should contribute and not just receive. If an individual follows his or her own nature, he or she will not only become a producer but will also become wealthy in the process. Individuals contribute little if they only pay their debts and do not add to the wealth available. Meeting only one's own needs is expensive; it is better to be rich and thus be able to meet one's

---

[6] Kevin Starr, *Americans and the California Dream* (New York: Oxford University Press, 1973), pp. 33, 63–66.

[7] Ralph W. Emerson, *The Conduct of Life and Other Essays* (London: Dent, 1908), pp. 190–213.

needs and add to wealth as well. And doing both coincides with one's own natural inclinations. Emerson insists that getting rich is something any person with a little ingenuity can achieve. It depends on factors the person has totally under his or her own control:

> Wealth is in applications of mind to nature, and the art of getting rich consists not in industry, much less in saving, but in a better order, in timeliness, in being at the right spot. One man has stronger arms, or longer legs; another sees by the course of streams, and growth of markets, where land will be wanted, makes a clearing to the river, goes to sleep, and wakes up rich.[8]

Emerson's heroes are the independent Anglo-Saxons. They are a strong race who, by means of their personal independence, have become the merchants of the world. They do not look to government "for bread and games." They do not look to clans, relatives, friends, or aristocracy to take care of them or to help them get ahead; they rely on their own initiative and abilities. Emerson's optimistic view of the potential of the free and strong individual released from the fetters of government and custom remains an important support of American values. While much of the Protestant ethic has changed, Emerson's view of the individual is still with us.

Children and Immigrants in Nineteenth-Century Factories

Before 1840, factory workers in the United States labored 12–14 hours a day, 6 or 7 days a week. An 84-hour workweek was common. By 1860, the average workday dropped to 10.6 hours a day, 6 days a week, but the 12–14 hour workday was still typical in many industries, including the textile mills of New England.[9]

In 1890, steel workers worked 12 hours a day, 7 days a week; most made $1.25 a day. Those wages went for rent, and there was little left to buy even food. Even if a steel worker worked 12 hours a day every day of the year, it was still not sufficient to support a family.[10] Therefore, many of these poor immigrants were single, and others left their families in Europe.

When the immigrants came, they knew that the work would be difficult and dangerous. They were at the bottom of the status ladder and therefore had to accept the hardest and most poorly paid work. A Hungarian churchman examined the conditions in Pittsburgh steel mills and said, "Wherever the heat is most insupportable, the flames most scorching, the smoke and soot most choking, there we are certain to find compatriots bent and wasted with toil."[11]

---

[8] *Ibid.*, p. 192.

[9] Gary M. Walton and Ross Robertson, *History of the American Economy* (New York: Harcourt Brace Jovanovich, 1983), pp. 280, 437.

[10] David Brody, *Steelworkers in America: The Nonunion Era* (Cambridge, Mass.: Harvard University Press, 1980), p. 98.

[11] *Ibid.*, p. 99.

Many young children also worked under some of these same conditions. In 1910 two million boys and girls, one-fifth of all American children 10 to 15 years old, worked 10 to 14 hours a day. In Syracuse, New York, factories would not hire children unless they were at least 8 years old.[12] Those who worked were the children of the immigrants and the poor, since their families needed the additional income. Child labor was a bargain for employers, since children's wages were less than those for adults. Further underscoring contemporary values and the acceptance of such factory conditions is the fact that before 1920 two laws passed by the U.S. Congress to restrict child labor were declared unconstitutional by the Supreme Court.

Working conditions were most often miserable and dangerous. Textile workers suffered brown lung disease, quarry workers breathed stone dust, coal miners suffered black lung disease and many deaths due to cave-ins, and many other workers inhaled toxic chemical fumes. The annual toll of those killed or injured in industry was roughly one million at the turn of the century.

At U.S. Steel's South Works in the Pittsburgh area in 1910, "almost one-quarter of the recent immigrants in the works each year—3,273 in five years— were injured or killed."[13] Working on the railroads was also very dangerous. In 1890, 2,451 railroad workers were killed, and this figure does not include many more civilians killed by trains.[14]

Companies often provided housing for their workers. Steel companies built good housing for better paid men and "shanties" (their own word) for the unskilled. Four men slept, ate, and washed in a 10-by-14-foot shanty. The annual rent charged was more than twice the cost of building the pine board shanty.[15] Steel owners and executives had ready responses to criticisms: The immigrants were eager for work, they made much more than they would have made in Europe, and their living conditions were poor because they used their salaries on beer and whiskey.

Given such low wages and poor treatment, it is not surprising that in the United States during this period the rich became richer and the poor became poorer. One percent of the population owned as much as the remaining 99 percent combined.[16]

From 1861 to 1865 Abraham Lincoln was president of the United States. Faced with a withdrawal of the confederate states from the union, a devastating civil war, and finding it very difficult to find a good general, Lincoln was nevertheless one of the outstanding leaders in United States history. His clear goals and strategies, decisiveness, concern for communicating with the ordinary citi-

---

[12] Walton and Robertson, *History of the American Economy*, p. 439.

[13] Brody, *Steelworkers in America*, p. 101.

[14] Otto L. Bettmann, *The Good Old Days: They Were Terrible!* (New York: Random House, 1974), p. 70.

[15] Brody, *Steelworkers in America*, p. 110.

[16] Bettmann, *The Good Old Days*, p. 67.

zen, ability to influence people through storytelling, and his honesty and integrity, all make him a model of leadership to our present day.[17]

Establishment Churches and Business

Churches have two roles to play in society: (1) to help people worship God and (2) to help them understand and deal with the moral issues of their everyday lives. These roles sometimes are in conflict. The second role involves sensitizing people to the moral problems that exist. Before 1920 this required calling attention to the abuses indicated above: child labor, dangerous working conditions, and working hours so long that decent family life was impossible. Yet as a church and its leaders become respected in society, they are easily lulled into blindness concerning the evils of the society that gives them increased status; they are thus deterred from acting as prophets and prodders of the public conscience.

A church has a responsibility to help all. Because of this mission most churches make special attempts to help the poor, since often the poor have desperate needs and lack a voice in society. Nonetheless, a church can be so influenced by its affluent members that it becomes part of the Establishment, and its leaders oppose change, "rabble rousers," and social justice. The church and its members risk losing too much if change occurred. We can learn a lesson for today by examining the actions of the more respected churches in the United States in the last century.

The dominant American Protestant churches in the nineteenth century, while preaching charity and concern for the poor, nevertheless vehemently defended the economic system that had grown up with the Protestant ethic. In this period, churches and schools had much more influence over American life and morals than is true today. The prestigious private colleges of the eastern Establishment taught the values of private property, free trade, and individualism. These religiously oriented schools (both Harvard and Yale were still Congregationalist at this time) generally taught conservative economic and business values along with their moral philosophy.

To many of the clergy, since God had clearly established economic laws, it would be dangerous to tamper with them. Francis Wayland, president of Brown University and author of the most popular economics text then used, intertwines economics and theology in stating his basic position: "God has made labor necessary to our well being." We must work both because idleness brings punishment and because work brings great riches; these are two essential, powerful, and immutable motives for work.[18] Wayland concluded from this simple principle that all property should be private and held by individuals. Charity should not be given except to those who absolutely cannot work, and the government should not impose tariffs or quotas or otherwise interfere.

---

[17] Donald T. Phillips, *Lincoln on Leadership: Executive Strategies for Tough Times* (New York: Warner Books, 1992).

[18] Henry F. May, *Protestant Churches and Industrial America* (New York: Harper & Row, 1949), p. 15.

In the last 25 years of the nineteenth century, the major Protestant churches went through an agonizing reexamination. Up to this time, the churches had wholeheartedly accepted Adam Smith's economics and canonized it as part of the "divine plan." They defended private property, business, the need to work, and even wealth. Then two severe, bloody labor disturbances occurred that forced the churches to reconsider their traditional survival-of-the-fittest theories.

The first of these conflicts followed a severe economic depression in 1877. Wages of train workers were cut by 10 percent, and they protested. They picketed and halted trains. Army troops were called to defend railroad property, and they fought with desperate mobs of workers. In the confusion, scores of workers were shot. The churches generally sided with the Establishment and self-righteously preached to the workers on the divine wisdom of the American economy. Hear the newspaper *Christian Union:*

> If the trainmen knew a little more of political economy they would not fall so easy a prey to men who never earn a dollar of wages by good solid work. What a sorry set of ignoramuses they must be who imagine that they are fighting for the rights of labor in combining together to prevent other men from working for low wages because, forsooth, they are discontented with them.[19]

The religious press, reflecting the attitudes of its patrons, took a hard line against what it saw as anarchy, riots, and support of weak and lazy men.

A decade later another serious confrontation occurred. On the occasion of a labor meeting at the Haymarket in Chicago, the police shot several of a group of strikers. A few days later, a bomb was thrown at the police. As is often the case in such situations, facts and circumstances were forgotten as near hysteria swept the religious press. The journal *Protestant Independent* was typical: "A mob should be crushed by knocking down or shooting down the men engaged in it; and the more promptly this is done the better."[20] Only when these strikingly un-Christian outbursts had ended did the clergy have the opportunity to reflect on what had happened and how they themselves had reacted. It then became clear how biased, inflexible, and violent had been their stance—hardly what one would expect of churches. During this period the clergy had been anxious to accommodate their churches' position to the new industrial movements. They changed no creeds or confessions but "progressively identified [themselves] with competitive individualism at the expense of community."[21] From the rubble of these mistakes and later recognized biases came the impetus toward a new social consciousness, specifically in the form of the Social Gospel.

---

[19] *Ibid.*, p. 93.

[20] *Ibid.*, p. 101.

[21] Martin Marty, *Righteous Empire: The Protestant Experience in America* (New York: Dial, 1970), p. 110.

Praise of Acquisitiveness and Wealth

Defense of free enterprise and praise of acquisitiveness and riches were not limited to the Establishment Congregational and Presbyterian churches. The Baptist preacher Russell Conwell traveled the country giving his famous speech "Acres of Diamonds." He delivered it more than five thousand times around the turn of the century to enraptured audiences eager to hear that to gather wealth was God's will.

Conwell's speech tells of a man who goes out to seek wealth; in the meantime his successor on the farm finds diamonds in the yard he had left behind. His message: Any man has it within his grasp to make himself wealthy if he is willing to work at it:

> I say that you ought to get rich, and it is your duty to get rich. How many of my pious brethren say to me, "Do you, a Christian minister, spend your time going up and down the country advising young people to get rich, to get money?" "Yes of course I do." They say, "Isn't that awful. Why don't you preach the gospel instead of preaching about man's making money?" "Because to make money honestly is to preach the gospel." That is the reason. The men who get rich may be the most honest men you will find in the community.[22]

Conwell here cites what to him was the happy confluence of deeply felt religious convictions and the life of the marketplace. Because of the more traditional religious values of poverty and humility, riches often brought qualms of conscience to believers. Conwell tries to wed faith and fortune: There can be no better demonstration of faith in God than to use one's abilities to their fullest, to be a success, and to accumulate the goods of the earth (to be used responsibly, of course). Conwell himself made a fortune from his lectures and, following his own advice on investment, used the money to found Temple University.

Praise of wealth not surprisingly also came from those who became wealthy. A handful of industrialists—called the robber barons—had an immense, enduring influence on America and American industry around the turn of the century. Among them, the immigrant Scot Andrew Carnegie enjoyed his role as industrial and "moral" leader. With the help of financier J. P. Morgan, Carnegie had put together United States Steel in 1901; he accumulated immense wealth in the process and loved to tell all who would listen why he deserved it. Furthermore, with his wealth Carnegie established libraries in every city and town in the United States, each proudly bearing the Carnegie name.

Carnegie had amassed a huge personal fortune, even though he was well aware that his own steelworkers were very poorly paid. He maintained that God gave him his wealth. Carnegie made no apology for the inequality and in fact defended it as the survival of the fittest. The millionaire's money would do no good if it were paid to the workers:

---

[22] Russell Conwell, *Acres of Diamonds* (New York: Harper, 1915), p. 18.

Much of this sum, if distributed in small quantities among the people, would have been wasted in the indulgence of appetite, some of it in excess, and it may be doubted whether even the part put to the best use, that of adding to the comforts of the home, would have yielded results for the race at all comparable.[23]

According to Carnegie, it is only the wealthy who can endow libraries and universities and who can best look after the long-run good of society as a whole. The money is much better spent when the wealthy accumulate it in large amounts so that with it they can accomplish great things.

For this reason, Carnegie felt that the wealthy person should "set an example of modest, unostentatious living, shunning display or extravagance." He should hold his money in trust for society and be "strictly bound as a matter of duty to administer in the manner which, in his judgement, is best calculated to produce the most beneficial results for the community." [24] Inequality and the accumulation of great fortunes are good for society, along with "the concentration of business, industrial and commercial, in the hands of a few." This concentration of wealth enables the most able to use the funds for the best interest of society.

Carnegie defended his fortune and his right to have it and dispose of it as he saw fit. Thus he was able to overlook the injustices he and his company supported. Of course, he was not entirely objective in his examination of the socioeconomic system; he profited much from it.

Manufacturing and Scientific Management

The growth of manufacturing did, in fact, provide a new and much faster means of attaining wealth and economic growth. With increases in productivity, higher wages could be paid and greater profits obtained for the owner at the same time. This was a considerable departure from past eras, when fortunes had been made by trade, transport, or lending (and, of course, wars and plunder). Thus in the past wealth had been considered more of a fixed quantity: What one person gained, another lost. The advent of manufacturing demonstrated clearly that the economy was not a zero-sum game—it was possible for each party in the exchange to benefit financially. Whether this occurred depended largely on increases in productivity.

Frederick W. Taylor, founder of scientific management, focused on better methods in manufacturing as a way to increase productivity. Productivity is, of course, the amount of a product that is produced per given input of resource—often per worker. Mechanization and careful planning would enable workers to

---

[23] Andrew Carnegie, "Wealth," in *Democracy and the Gospel of Wealth*, ed. Gail Kennedy (Boston: D. C. Heath, 1949), p. 6.

[24] *Ibid.*, p. 7. David M. Potter, in *People of Plenty: Economic Abundance and the American Character* (Chicago: University of Chicago Press, 1954), maintains that in an even more fundamental sense, a democratic system depends on economic surplus (p. 111ff).

produce more than they could without planning. This was Taylor's insight: Worker and management experience plus intuitive judgment are not enough. To achieve greater productivity, which would benefit all concerned, the work setting and even the motions of the job itself ought to be carefully studied to discover the most efficient tools, techniques, and methods.

As factory work became more complex, Taylor gained greater support for his view. No single person, worker or supervisor, could be aware of all the mechanical, psychological, and technological factors involved in planning even one job. Efficiency required careful planning by a team with various competencies. Intuition, experience, and seat-of-the-pants judgments would no longer do. Scientific management undermined Spencer's notions of survival of the fittest. Taylor pointed out that allowing the "best person" to surface naturally was inefficient. In the contemporary complex world, few people had the ability to achieve maximum productivity by themselves. Greater efficiency and productivity demanded the intervention of planners.[25]

Taylor was in favor of higher wages and shorter hours for workers, but he saw no need for unions. If scientific management is implemented and the best and most efficient means of production achieved, there will be no grounds for petty quarrels and grievances. Policies and procedures will be set by scientific inquiry into what objectively is most efficient. And that which is most efficient will benefit worker and management alike, since both will share in the results of this greater productivity: greater profits. In Taylor's scheme, the personal exercise of authority would be eliminated. Managers would be subject to the same policies, rules, and methodology as the workers themselves.

Although he agreed with the traditional managerial ideology that workers pursue their own self-interest and try to maximize their own return, Taylor challenged the notion that each person worked out this struggle in isolation, apart from and even in competition with other human beings. In an industrial organization greater productivity can be achieved only when each worker, along with management, cooperates to find the best means of production. Taylor pointed out how the returns to all were diminished if a single worker is not working at his or her most efficient job and pace. Taylor set out to help both worker and manager achieve maximum efficiency, which can be done only in cooperation. Up to this time a lazy man or woman had been penalized; now Taylor proposed to reward workers by enabling them to work to their greatest capacity and receive greater financial return.

Scientific management was not greeted happily by either workers or managers, because it tended to deprive each of a measure of freedom and judgment. Scientific management chronicled the shift from craft to industrial work. In the long run Taylor's methodology, and perhaps even more his ideology, have had

[25] Frederick Winslow Taylor, *Scientific Management* (New York: Harper & Brothers, 1947), pp. 36, 98, 99; see also Daniel Nelson, *Frederick W. Taylor and the Rise of Scientific Management* (Madison: University of Wisconsin Press, 1980).

an immense impact on industrial life.[26] In a sharp break from earlier American individualism, Taylor demonstrated that productivity and the system, in this case manufacturing, were more important than the lone individual. The emerging corporation itself bore additional testimony to the new importance of expertise, planning, and cooperation. In subsequent decades, often under pressure from labor unions, the corporation provided even more benefits to individuals: vacations, retirement, and medical care. Soon the majority of people worked with and cooperated with a larger group to achieve greater productivity, and this still characterizes American business.

Biased Management

The world and the ideals we have been discussing in this chapter are those of the business*man*. For centuries, business, commerce, and trade have all been largely "for men only." Women did not even obtain the right to vote until the twentieth century. Hence half of the potential technical and managerial talent was lost. Moreover, recent studies support the perception that effective leaders have masculine characteristics. Women who emerge as leaders tend to be androgynous; that is, while they may possess feminine characteristics, to be chosen as a leader they must also have masculine characteristics as well. Hence, "masculinity is still an important predictor of leader emergence."[27]

In addition, a glance at any firm's listing of its employees by rank and also by race and ethnic group, spotlights the results of centuries of racial prejudice. There are few blacks, Hispanics, or women in the "officials and managers" category and even fewer in top management. Moreover, it has been only within the past two generations that religious prejudice in the executive suites of the largest corporations has broken down; the WASP (White Anglo-Saxon Protestant) clique has cracked. Blacks, Jews, Catholics, and women are now climbing the managerial ladder into the executive suites.

Americans as Seen from Abroad

One who has visited another country finds sharp contrasts with one's own culture. An outsider viewing a culture is sensitive to elements to which members of that culture are often blind. While Alexis de Tocqueville is a foreigner who had superb insights about America, other visitors expressed important insights as well.

A century later another French observer, the Jesuit paleontologist Pierre

---

[26] See Martha Banta, *Taylored Lives: Narrative Productions in the Age of Taylor, Veblen, and Ford* (Chicago: University of Chicago Press, 1993).

[27] Russell L. Kent and Sherry E. Moss, "Effects of Sex and Gender Role on Leader Emergence," *Academy of Management Journal* (October 1994): 1335–46. See also *Competitive Frontiers: Women Managers in a Global Economy*, Nancy J. Adler and Dafna Izraeli, eds. (Cambridge, Mass.: Blackwell, 1994); and Phyllis Tharenou, Shane Latimer, and Denise Conroy, "How Do You Make it to the Top? An Examination of Women's and Men's Managerial Advancement," *Academy of Management Journal* (August 1994): 899–931.

Teilhard de Chardin, lived and worked in the United States for many years and noted many of the same qualities as did Tocqueville. Teilhard had a sympathetic view of the American character in spite of his own personal inclination for reflection and asceticism. Writing while on an expedition with some Americans in the Gobi desert Teilhard said,

> People here are inclined to treat the Americans as a joke, but the more I see of them the more I admire their ability to work and get things done, and the kinder and more approachable I find them. In my own branch of science it's the Americans who are showing us how we must set to work on the earth if we are to read its secret and make ourselves its masters.[28]

Granting the ability of Americans to get a job done, their orientation to action is also the source of criticism. Many foreign observers see Americans as individualistic, shallow, and materialistic—more wedded to things than to people, more inclined to do than to reflect. Let us examine some comments on the United States made by other foreign observers.

Albert Einstein, the brilliant mathematician and physicist, who came to live in the United States in the 1920s, admired the country. But in a caution that sounds contemporary, he said:

> The cult of individuals is always, in my view, unjustified. To be sure, nature distributes her gifts unevenly among her children. . . . It strikes me as unfair, and even in bad taste, to select a few for boundless admiration, attributing superhuman powers of mind and character to them. This has been my fate, and the contrast between the popular estimate of my powers and achievements and the reality is simply grotesque.[29]

Does the admiration today go to the top money makers, the "winners" in sports and entertainment, along with the likes of Bill Gates and Donald Trump in business?

Israeli writer Amos Oz adds that this individualistic view is spreading throughout the world:

> America has promoted and spread all over the world the simple ideal of individual happiness. Various religions, civilizations and ideologies throughout history regarded happiness as a collective rather than an individual experience. Almost all of them are losing ground to that triumphant American vision of private happiness. Hundreds of millions of people, from Tokyo to Leningrad, from Cairo to Buenos Aires, dream of being happy in the American way. But is the new global America, this international happiness-oriented village, a happy place? The popular American dream of living happily ever after, while dazzling the world, reminds me of the American landscape itself: plentiful, elusive, and forlorn.[30]

---

[28] Pierre Teilhard de Chardin, *Letters from a Traveller*, trans. Rene Hague et al. (New York: Harper & Row, 1962), p. 106.

[29] Albert Einstein, *Ideas and Opinions*, ed. by Carl Seelig (New York: Modern Library, 1994), p. 4.

[30] Quoted in "To See Ourselves as Others See Us," *Time*, June 16, 1986, p. 52–53. Quoted with permission.

Businesspeople are more positive about American values. Hear Akio Morita, the founder and former chairperson of Sony Corporation of Japan:

> What I like about the Americans is their frankness, their openness. In America, I feel I can openly express whatever opinion I have, and it is welcomed, even if it conflicts with other opinions. In Japan, even among friends we can't have a difference of opinion—disagreement destroys friendship. But in America, a difference of opinion can make friends, bring people closer together. That open-mindedness and frontier spirit is why I am so comfortable in the U.S.[31]

Foreign social commentators have felt the pulse of America and pointed to the strengths and weaknesses of the American character. They underscore the openness, flexibility, pragmatism, and respect for individuals. But they also see parochialism, lack of interest in other languages and cultures, materialism, and self-centeredness. It is essential that each person be aware of their own national character lest they uncritically be victims of their own biases. Such awareness is even more important if one is to influence one's own values and the values of one's nation. The necessity for informed changes that must occur if one is to live and compete in the global marketplace adds urgency to this task.

The events of history and social commentators provide insight into one's own origins and character. Examining these foundation values helps one to get a better grasp of current business values. In the past, the geography of the United States, combined with the attitudes and values of the people who settled it, gave the country a unique world position. It had rich and abundant farmland, protected east and west borders, a slowly retreating frontier, and a people imbued with the Puritan ethic. The geography and history of a land and the personality of its people provide a foundation for values that are shared by a people.

IDEOLOGY AND VALUES

A system of values that provides a group with life goals and personal values is called an ideology (for terms, see Figures 1–1 and 1–2). For an individual or a group, an ideology answers such questions as: What is most important to us? Why are we doing this? How can I explain my life and my society to myself and to others? An ideology is a coherent, systematic, and moving statement of basic values and purpose. It is a constellation of values generally held by a group, and members of the group tend to support one another in that ideology.

An ideology is an explication of values. It is a spelling out of attitudes, feelings, and goals. Without an explicit ideology, a nation or group is left without clearly stated purposes and hence without a consensus or the drive that comes from purpose. When an ideology is spelled out, it can be examined, challenged, and altered as conditions change and new needs arise. It is then in the open for all to accept or reject as they see fit. When an ideology is not explicit,

---

[31] Quoted in "To See Ourselves."

it is sometimes claimed that there is no ideology; but this is hardly true. The ideology is merely implicit, unspoken, and hence unexamined. This is a precarious position for any society, since difficult questions which arise can thus cause confusion and chaos.

Ideologies possess certain common features. They are selective in the issues they treat and in the supporting evidence and arguments they use. They are straightforward and uncomplicated, even when the actual material is quite complicated. Their content is limited to what is publicly acceptable. Finally, although ideologies are answers to questions and hence address the intellect, they nevertheless do so in a manner that also engages the emotions. They can inspire and motivate men and women to cooperate and even undergo great hardship for the sake of a compelling goal.

The positive effect of an ideology is that it gives a people direction, coherence, norms, and motivation. It can bring clarity and assurance to the mind and hence vigor and enthusiasm to life and work. These are great advantages, especially to a people troubled by doubts, lessened confidence in institutions, and inadequate leadership, as is often the case in contemporary societies. A group possessing an ideology is thus given meaning, direction, and drive. Nations and peoples have left their mark on history, whether for good or ill, to the extent to which they have fashioned for themselves a comprehensive and compelling ideology—for example, ancient Rome (Pax Romana), Victorian England (Mother England), and Nazi Germany (master race).

Most of the important things we do stem from an often implicit ideology, everything from raising children to going to work, from conducting foreign policy to meeting neighbors. Even a position that ideologies are unnecessary or demeaning or oppressive is itself an ideology. Subgroups within a society, such as the Rotary Club, possess some constellation of values, however limited or narrow. Generally, the more embracing a group, a movement, or a state, the more comprehensive will be its ideology.

On the other hand, ideologies have some disadvantages. They can rigidify. They tend to lock persons and systems into classes, roles, and expectations. A doctrinaire ideology can cause fanaticism, intransigence, and uncompromising attitudes. It can impede progress and cause problems for those in the group who find difficulties with the ideology, often those who are the most creative and talented. The group as a whole then tends to expend a great deal of effort defending its position instead of looking to the future.

It benefits people of every nation to examine their place in history and spell out national values and the ideology in which they are embedded. Demands for an exposition of one's ideology come from a variety of sources:

1. Many are asking themselves, their peers, and their national leaders, What are we about? What are our goals? What is worth living for? Why?
2. Any effort to lessen government regulation demands that individuals and organizations have their own sense of goals, ethics, and self-discipline—which take into account the public interest and the common good.

3. As the population increases and we live closer together, we find that what one person does often infringes on others. Many actions place burdens on *other* people, for example, building a shopping mall on previous farmland, driving a smog-producing automobile, or moving a plant to the water-scarce sunbelt. As managers, citizens, or government officials, we need criteria for making such decisions that impinge upon others.

4. Disagreements over public policy—for example, taxes, support for the poor, and pollution control—force us back to the earlier questions as to what kind of society we want, what our collective priorities are, and what tradeoffs we are willing to bear. Special interest groups plead their own specific cause but do not address the common good. Under such conditions, people often find it easier to know what they dislike than the far more important issue of what they like: their positive values, goals, and policies.

We all need to answer these questions in order to clarify personal and corporate values and goals. Each person is challenged to work out her or his own answers to basic value questions, to formulate her or his own constellation of values. Some consensus is necessary on these values in order to have effective and consistent national policies. Without an agreed upon ideology, decisions are made on the basis of special-interest groups, unexamined and short-run criteria, popular myth and shallow values. The agreed-upon values, especially those that touch upon the issues of public life, are called an ideology. As such, they provide direction and verve. And an awareness of the dangers of any ideology—for example, that it may mask privilege or that it may rigidify—should better enable us to avoid those dangers. There is a similar need for a mission statement or a creed for business firms, and this will be discussed in Chapter 8.

Origin and Impact of Ideology

An ideology that is a rationalization of the existing order defends the status quo. An ideology based on ideals that aim to change that status quo into something that is viewed as better is called utopian. To Americans, utopian has an idealistic, pie-in-the-sky, pejorative connotation. Here we will use it as a descriptive term only.

Karl Mannheim, in his classic *Ideology and Utopia,* says that a state of mind is utopian if it has ideals that transcend reality. He says that ideologies become utopian when groups act on them and challenge the existing order. When these ideals pass over into conduct, they "tend to shatter, either partially or wholly, the order of things prevailing at the time."[32]

Many utopias of today become the realities of tomorrow. The principles of democracy and freedom were utopian in the minds of those who founded the United States. Their notions of representation and individual rights were ideals

---

[32] Karl Mannheim, *Ideology and Utopia*, trans. Louis Wirth and Edward Shils (New York: Harcourt, Brace & World, 1936), p. 192. Quoted with permission.

which, when they were written into the *Declaration of Independence* and *The U.S. Constitution* and acted upon, challenged the status quo, shattered the existing order, and caused a revolution. A utopian ideology of freedom and equality became translated into the civil rights movement of the 1960s. Looking back over the period of rising aspirations, especially in the Western world, Mannheim calls the prevailing ideology of freedom a utopia:

> The utopia of the ascendant bourgeoisie was the idea of "freedom.". . . Freedom in the sense of bursting asunder the bonds of the static, guild, and caste order, in the sense of freedom of thought and opinion, in the sense of political freedom and freedom of the unhampered development of the personality became . . . a realizable possibility.[33]

Generalizing, Mannheim points out that any nation or group which wants to translate its ideals into reality must formulate an ideology that builds on the existing values, needs, and aspirations of the people. This utopian ideology may then catch the imagination of people and be the inspiration for change. The "New Deal" (unemployment insurance, minimum wage, etc.), the Civil Rights movement in the United States, and other social movements all possessed an ideology; and each left a positive imprint on society. For every utopian ideology that eventually becomes reality, there are many others that never get beyond the state of ideas. However, they may have caused some discord in society, and their adherents considered fanatical.

There are dangers inherent in any ideology in addition to those pointed out earlier. The dangers of being closed to facts and of fanaticism are highlighted by Mannheim: "Nothing is more removed from actual events than the closed rational system. Under certain circumstances, nothing contains more irrational drive than a fully self-contained intellectualistic world view." Some environmental groups, skinheads, survivalists, and the rural militia are examples of fringe groups that get their direction and enthusiasm from an ideology. The lack of meaningful general goals and an ideology among people as a whole encourages such groups. Moreover, the absence of a general ideology often results because many feel they are well adjusted to the current state of affairs, and thus have little incentive to theorize, according to Mannheim. These "conservatives" are happy with their situation, and so they defend the status quo.

Mannheim points out that as long as people are content, they do little reflecting about situations in which they find themselves. They then tend to regard their current situation as part of the natural order of things; the way things are is the way they ought to be. They then tend to emphasize practical "how to do it" concerns—the means of coping within existing structures. It is only in the face

---

[33] *Ibid.*, p. 203. A comprehensive presentation of empirical work on ideologies, along with some synthesis is Chapter 2 of Harrison M. Trice and Janice M. Beyer, *The Cultures of Work Organizations* (Englewood Cliffs, N.J.: Prentice-Hall, 1993), pp. 35–76. Unfortunately Trice and Beyer neglected the empirical work on these subjects from the social issues in management literature.

of challenges to the status quo that conservatives do much reflecting. So the reflection and therefore the ideology of conservatives are generally not as profound or comprehensive as that of the challengers. Thus the "most recent antagonist dictates the tempo and the form of the battle."[34]

Challenge Brings Understanding

A valuable by-product of this type of challenge of goals and ideologies is that people are compelled to examine themselves. Making ideology explicit can clarify goals for individuals and society as a whole. A society with a weak ideology, or one in which ideology seems unimportant, is generally stable, complacent, and at ease with its inherited laws, customs, and ideals. Making a key point, Mannheim paints a sad, even desperate, picture of a society or a people without a utopian ideology:

> The disappearance of utopia brings about a static state of affairs in which man himself becomes no more than a thing. We would be faced then with the greatest paradox imaginable, namely, that man, who has achieved the highest degree of rational mastery of existence, left without any ideals, becomes a mere creature of impulses. Thus, after a long, tortuous, but heroic development, just at the highest stage of awareness, when history is ceasing to be blind fate, and is becoming more and more man's own creation, with the relinquishment of utopias, man would lose his will to shape history and therewith his ability to understand it.[35]

Mannheim presents an impersonal, alienating, and frightening prospect of a world without utopias—without ideals or engaging goals.

On the other hand, injustices can also be perpetrated in the name of an irrational but compelling ideology. Any strong, moving ideology risks being gross, oversimplified, and even unjust. Mannheim's own Germany a few years later was to undergo a tragic revolution in the name of "Aryan superiority" and the "master race." "Ethnic cleansers" in Bosnia, armed citizen militias in the United States, and neo-fascists in many countries are confident, closed, paranoid, and often not well educated people. Each of these ideologies fills a vacuum. In Iran and Iraq two opposing ideologies face each other across a common border.

In sum, an ideology is required for a stable society. Without an ideology people lose direction and enthusiasm for life. In addition, a *utopian* ideology is needed for a society to better itself. Such an ideology, with ideals that are as yet unattained, is needed in order to question the status quo. Without a utopian ideology, people cease questioning themselves and their goals. So little new is accomplished on any significant scale and society does not improve.

---

[34] *Ibid.*, pp. 219, 229, 231.

[35] *Ibid.*, pp. 262–63.

Suspicion of Ideology

Many people in industrialized nations share an abiding distrust of ideology. In an attempt to outline what has caused the rapid economic development of the United States, Arthur Schlesinger, Jr. acknowledges the physical advantages of the continent. But he points out that the fertile lands and natural resources were there for the native Americans, too, but were never exploited.[36] Schlesinger maintains that the most important element in the success story of the United States was the spirit of the settlers. He contends that this spirit manifested itself in three important ways. The first was a faith in education. Investment in people through education results in increases in productivity. A second factor encouraging development was the commitment to self-government and representative institutions. Democracy was important for releasing people's talents and energies.

The third uniquely favorable element in the American spirit, and probably the most important one according to Schlesinger, was a rejection of ideology: "America has had the good fortune not to be an ideological society." Schlesinger defines ideology as "a body of systematic and rigid dogma by which people seek to understand the world—and to preserve or transform it." Many agree with Schlesinger that ideology narrows and distracts one from reality. They would not allow ideology to "falsify reality, imprison experience, or narrow the spectrum of choice."[37] This attitude discourages innovation and experiment, part of the dominant empirical and pragmatic American approach.

The principal difficulty with an ideology is that it is a partial depiction of reality. Certain elements are emphasized and others neglected. When decisions are made, they can thus be biased or even wrong. The dominant American philosophy, pragmatism, is not heavily theoretical. It stays close to the facts; to simplify, it holds "that which works is true." Schlesinger rightly rejects rigid dogma that would subjugate people and facts to an ideology. Americans have achieved much success in being flexible, open, and risk taking in a pluralistic society.

Schlesinger may not like ideology, but his own position is itself an ideology. It is an ideology that values freedom, laissez-faire, and selective nonintervention. Moreover, that freedom is especially for me and mine. It does not apply to the Native Americans, who, in spite of the fact that they did not "exploit" their lands as Schlesinger would have liked, were pushed off those lands. Native Americans did not have the freedom to decide how they would use their lands. This double standard calls for government intervention at home and abroad to preserve *my* freedom and prerogatives; it calls for nonintervention when government intervention does not benefit *me*, restricts *my* freedom or the freedom of *my* organization.

---

[36] See "Epilogue: The One Against the Many," in Schlesinger and White, *Paths of American Thought*, pp. 531–38.

[37] *Ibid.*, pp. 532, 533.

Many people hold that if each person or group uses its talents, intelligence, and resources to pursue its own long-term self-interest, it will work out most favorably for all. By any definition, this is an ideology. However, its long-run value and effectiveness is questioned by many around the world, especially those whose own freedom and best interests have not been served.

Values in Modern Life

We will now attempt to outline some basic human values, then give special attention to those values that characterize industrial societies. As a basis for his synthesis, John Piderit in *The Ethical Foundation of Economics* presents seven "basic goods, elemental values, or essential goals" that come from the natural law ethics tradition. These are common to all people and are: knowledge, beauty, life, friendship, playfulness, practical reasonableness, and religion. These goals are so basic that an "examination of experience reveals that a person understands that he is under a moral obligation to pursue these values in appropriate circumstances and that he should never perform an act that is directly opposed to them."[38]

Focusing specifically on business and the society it serves, William C. Frederick, in his very helpful synthesis, *Values, Nature and Culture in the American Corporation*, has identified two basic values of business, "economizing values" and "power aggrandizing values." He finds that these values are in tension with the third and more important value of society, which he calls "ecologizing values." Economizing is essential to any organization, especially business, and the efficient use of resources and the profit orientation are rooted in this value. "Power-aggrandizing" is also common in organizations; it operates when executive, manager, or others are concerned with accumulating power and status. Not surprisingly, power aggrandizing often thwarts efforts to economize. While economizing and power aggrandizing are found to varying extent in all business organizations, these values are not sufficient. The basic value of society is that of ecologizing. Ecologizing is preserving life and what is necessary for life, and it is thus even more basic than the other two. Often ecologizing goals are opposed and hindered by economizing and power-aggrandizing values. Nevertheless, ecologizing values must be recognized by executives if business is to aid, and not injure, people in the long-term.[39]

We will now attempt to enumerate values that build upon the above values. The following values are more a part of our direct experience and hence our vocabulary, and as such are probably more easily recognizable. Individualism and enlightened self-interest remain basic values. Moreover, these values affect entire life-styles, not merely work attitudes. Whenever pre-

---

[38] John J. Piderit, S.J., *The Ethical Foundations of Economics* (Washington, D.C.: Georgetown University Press, 1993, pp. 54–69.

[39] William C. Frederick, *Values, Nature and Culture in the American Corporation* (New York: Oxford University Press, 1995).

dominant American values are listed, it is no accident that so many of them support work attitudes and are directly related to individualism and enlightened self-interest. The current serious challenge to some of these values will be discussed in later chapters. Here, let us attempt to indicate what these values are.[40]

Achievement and success. American culture has been and still is characterized by a stress on individual achievement. Horatio Alger, who rose from rags to riches, is a legend. The American myth says that anyone who works hard enough can succeed in what he or she sets out to do. Moreover, when we meet a successful person, we are more impressed if he or she did not inherit wealth. Someone who was born poor and then worked hard to obtain what he or she has is a model. It is embarrassing to be reminded that several of our recent presidents were born into wealthy families.

Money and wealth are valued for the comforts they bring, but even more because they are symbols of success. Income is a measure to the owner and to the world of one's own personal worth. People desire growing businesses, large homes, and luxury automobiles; they signal success. This achievement and success ideal is manifested most extensively in business. The drive to achieve is especially strong among business managers, and this will be discussed in greater detail in Chapter 7.

Activity and work. A devotion to work on the part of both the unskilled worker and the executive has provided most of the wealth we now enjoy in the United States. Work is respected not only because it results in wealth but also for its own sake—"The devil finds idle hands." In the United States a person's self-respect is damaged when he or she is without work. Americans have traditionally not valued leisure for its own sake; it is valued if afterward a person can work better. It is recreation, and it, too, has a purpose. Task orientation has become a compulsion for which Americans are frequently criticized.

Unskilled workers know that even though they are ahead of schedule with their job, they had best appear busy. To call a person lazy is a serious criticism, especially because the amount of activity is something over which a person seems to have control. Americans set out to shape and control their own lives and their world. They heed the biblical injunction "to subdue the world."

Efficiency and practicality. Closely related to the foregoing cultural values are efficiency and practicality, which are concerned more with methods of working and acting. We have seen how Tocqueville was much impressed with American ingenuity and ability to "get the job done." Americans are often criticized for an overemphasis on technique, with little reference to goals.[41] Critics say that en-

---

[40] For a basic work to which the author is indebted, see the chapter "Values in American Life" in Robin M. Williams, Jr., *American Society: A Sociological Interpretation*, 3rd. ed. (New York: Knopf, 1970), pp. 438–504.

[41] For a classic statement of this position, see Jacques Ellul, *The Technological Society* (New York: Knopf, 1964).

gineers and accountants run our society and that their values are at best instrumental and thus only means. They may know how to accomplish a specific task but rarely consider whether it is a good thing to do. A practical person, focusing on efficiency, assumes the basic worth of the task and of the economic and social order itself. A practical orientation demands only short-range adjustments to immediate situations.

Americans are known as people who can quickly and effectively search out the best way to accomplish the task. They are active in the search for solutions and are rarely reflective or contemplative. To call an American a "dreamer" or "impractical" is a severe criticism. Characteristically, the best-known American philosophers, such as Dewey, Peirce, and William James, are not idealists but rather pragmatists.

Equality. The American emphasis on equality originates with early constitutional ideals: All people are created equal. Citizens of the new world witnessed the elimination of indentured servitude, imprisonment for debt, primogeniture, slavery, and property requirements for voting and public office. New immigrants were able to acquire land and a free public education, and minorities and women have gained many important civil rights.

Observers remark on the unusual informality, frankness, and lack of status consciousness in American interpersonal relations. Such open and direct relations can endure only if they are supported by the values of the equality and importance of each person. But the value of equality can run counter to that of freedom. When people pursue freedom in the rugged individualist climate in which the fittest survive, it results in some becoming rich and others remaining desperately poor. Varying opportunities, talents, and effort will influence what a person can achieve.

Of all the government and corporate policies that have been developed to bring about better equality of opportunity in the workplace, none meets more opposition than "affirmative action." In order to compensate for past discrimination in the workplace, many contend that when an equally qualified minority or woman is presented for promotion, the minority person or woman should be chosen. Ironically, both the reason for the practice (to compensate for past discrimination) and the major objections to it (reverse discrimination) stem from the American ideal of equality, especially equality of opportunity.[42]

External conformity. Visitors find a uniformity in speech, housing, dress, recreation, and attitudes in the United States. Observers point to a certain flatness, to homogeneity, to a lack of serious dissent and challenge. Witness the "uniform" of blue jeans on young people and books written on dressing for success.

---

[42] See the detailed discussion of this complex question in Theodore V. Purcell and Gerald F. Cavanagh, *Blacks in the Industrial World: Issues for the Manager* (New York: Free Press, 1972), especially Chapter 10, "Equal Versus Preferential Treatment," pp. 275–93.

To rugged individualists, these comments may seem unfair. Yet, on closer examination, American individualism consists largely in the rejection of government restrictions on personal and business activity.

Freedom.   Freedom is a prime value in American life. It is also the most discussed American value. The individual has freedom to operate in the social Darwinian world in which the fittest survive best, as we have seen earlier. He or she may freely choose a marriage partner, friends, a home; change jobs; or move. Freedom is the bedrock value not only of our laissez-faire, free enterprise economic system, but for most of the rest of American life. Freedom has been touted alike by the Founding Fathers and the members of the local block club. American individualism, of course, is possible only when freedom is the foundation value.

The value of freedom has inspired the women's and civil rights movements. Cultural norms that bind persons to expected roles can be oppressive. Freedom urges the elimination of these one-sided and unjust bonds. Defense of freedom is a foundation of American foreign policy, and freedom is the cornerstone of the business system—*free* enterprise. As pointed out earlier, this freedom is primarily for me and mine. Freedom so permeates business ideology that it is discussed in almost every chapter of this book.

Material comfort.   As indicated above, Americans place a high value on the luxurious automobile, a spacious home in the suburbs, and a good meal. The fact that these things are material comforts and that they are highly valued does not tell us why they are valued. For each item, the underlying reasons may range from its being a symbol of achievement to its providing hedonistic gratification in its own right. Younger generations are more likely to spend their income on items that bring them comfort than to save for some future need.

The rise in popularity of television, rock concerts, spectator sports, packaged tours, film, and alcohol indicates a greater passivity on the part of people. There seems to be less active participation and more passive desiring to be entertained. The drug culture and chemically induced pleasure take this tendency to its limit. Seeking pleasure coincides with a decline in the Puritan values of self-denial and asceticism.

Moral orientation and humanitarianism.   Although Americans are eminently practical, they still see the world in moral terms. Conduct of self and of others is constantly judged: honest, trustworthy, "a comer," lazy. Basic honesty and frankness are also part of our moral and humanitarian value orientation. Foreign commentators are often surprised at how open and straightforward they find Americans to be. American charities, along with our social legislation since the 1930s, are evidence of humanitarian attitudes. Social security, the minimum wage, and medical care for the poor are examples of our attempt to take care of the less fortunate. However, a moral person can become cynical when his or her moral code is found to be superficial, inapplicable, or too idealistic.

Patriotism.   Every society has a sense of the greater value of its own people. Anthropologists tell us how in tribal societies the rules of respect for another's person and property do not apply to "outsiders." They apply only to the members of one's own tribe. Racism and sexism stem from these same parochial values. In the United States our loyalties in the early days of the republic were with local cities (Boston, Philadelphia) and then with the states; finally, for business and defense reasons, our loyalties lie with the nation-state. Individual patriotism is often made a moral issue.

Rationality and measurement. This value is probably best exemplified when approaching a problem. A person is expected to be objective, to gather the facts first, and not to be unduly influenced by bias or emotions. The "scientific method," which embodies this approach, is the model for problem solving. If data for a solution can be measured, that will make the solution more objective and therefore acceptable.

The value of science is demonstrated in its intelligent use in mastering our external environment. This orientation is compatible with a culture that does not value emotion, and looks on the world as open to eventual control.

Optimism and the inevitability of progress. The combination of an immigrant people willing to work hard with what seemed like unlimited natural resources and the existence of the frontier created an optimistic atmosphere. Anything could be accomplished if only one put one's mind to it. The result was a growth of jobs, products, and cities.

The optimistic euphoria that enveloped the American people in the post World War II era has dimmed. We defined progress largely in economic terms.

FIGURE 5–1 Changing Importance of Basic American Values

	Increase or Decrease[*] *1945–1996*
Achievement and success	+ −
Activity and work	−
Efficiency and practicality	+ −
Equality	+
External conformity	+
Freedom	+ −
Material comfort	+
Moral orientation and humanitarianism	−
Patriotism	−
Rationality and measurement	+ −
Optimism and the inevitability of progress	−

+ = increase;   − = decrease;
+ − = indicates evidence of both.

[*] Adapted from Robin M. Williams, *American Society, op. cit.;* and Harrison Trice and Janice Beyer, *The Cultures of Work Organizations, op. cit.*

As long as sales and the gross national product were increasing, progress was occurring. For an attempt to chart the change in the strength of each of these values, see Figure 5–1. The problems of global competition, the required downsizing, the danger of wastefully using finite resources, the necessity of rethinking what "progress" is, and the impact these issues are having on business and business values will be discussed in greater detail in Chapters 8 and 9.

THE NECESSITY OF AN IDEOLOGY FOR BUSINESS

Let us now examine the importance of an ideology for business.[43] An ideology is essential for any social system. Within a business firm an ideology, more commonly called a mission statement with shared values, facilitates decisions, operations, and cooperation.[44]

An ideology is especially important for business in our complex international world, because it can provide a useful response to several problems:

1. Global markets demand that a firm be flexible and able to quickly meet new needs. An ideology provides goals but not a straitjacket.

2. Executives are criticized for managing for short-term results and neglecting long-term planning and investment for the firm. An ideology and mission statement help managers to focus on the long-range goals of the firm.

3. Scholars and citizens have long questioned the legitimacy of the corporation. Where resides the ultimate authority in the corporation, and where resides the responsibility that goes with it? An ideology helps answer this question.

4. Some critics question the free enterprise system, because of its inequities. An ideology clarifies the goals and beneficiaries of free enterprise.

Without a mission statement and goals, it is very difficult for businesspeople to make decisions, establish new policies, to rectify abuses, and defend themselves against unfair attacks. An ideology will guide the successes of business and support whatever stature and power it possesses.

---

[43] Richard M. Weiss, in *Managerial Ideology and the Social Control of Deviance in Organizations* (New York: Praeger, 1986), presents ideology as a social control mechanism in the rehabilitation of alcoholics and other "troubled" employees.

[44] Janice M. Beyer, "Ideologies, Values, and Decision Making in Organizations," in *Handbook of Organizational Design*, ed. Paul C. Nystrom and William H. Starbuck, vol. 2 (New York: Oxford University Press, 1981), pp. 166–202. This comprehensive article provides an overview of social science research on values and ideologies in organizations, along with several varying definitions. See also Richard M. Weiss and Lynn E. Miller, "The Concept of Ideology in Organizational Analysis: The Sociology of Knowledge or the Social Psychology of Beliefs," *The Academy of Management Review* 12 (January 1987): 104–16.

Managers and scholars alike know the vital importance of organizational legitimacy.[45] Without an ideology, the corporation risks losing its privileged position in the United States, perhaps even its legitimacy. Adolph A. Berle expressed his classic position on the corporation,

> Whenever there is a question of power there is also a question of legitimacy. As things stand now, these instrumentalities of tremendous power have the slenderest claim of legitimacy. . . . Legitimacy, responsibility and accountability are essential to any power system if it is to endure.[46]

Notice how Berle links the issues of legitimacy, responsibility, and accountability. In clarifying these basic issues, the corporation is on weak ground. Without reviewing the classic position of Berle and Means,[47] suffice it to say that the corporation is responsible to no one. Management, often with little ownership or legitimacy, makes decisions. With the exception of periodic actions of fund portfolio managers, shareholders generally have no input into major corporate decisions. The board of directors is elected from a slate chosen by the board itself.[48] If there are three directors to be elected, only three candidates are on the ballot; elections are like those in autocratic states. The annual meeting of stockholders is a public relations event, and the actual owners exercise little real power. If a shareholder does not vote, the abstention is often counted as support for management.

Questioning the corporation's power and legitimacy goes to the heart of its purpose, role and responsibilities. The role and responsibilities of the chief executive officer and the board of directors will be discussed in more detail in Chapter 8. As we will see, assessment of these issues requires understanding the purpose, rationale, and responsibilities of the corporation, its very reason for existence—its ideology.

An ideology for the individual firm and for business in general will enable executives and others to answer these questions. Even the pro-business Republican Congress manifests a lingering distrust of big business. Without accountability and a clear statement of purpose, business risks losing its respected position in American society. A firm's statement of purpose must be understandable to its many stakeholders and the firm must be held accountable to act in accordance with it. If this does not occur, the rebuilding of trust in business will not happen. The following chapters are intended to aid that rebuilding.

---

[45] See Mark C. Suchman, "Managing Legitimacy: Strategic and Institutional Approaches," *Academy of Management Review* 20 (July 1995), pp. 571–610.

[46] Adolph A. Berle, *Economic Power and the Free Society* (New York: Fund for the Republic, 1958), p. 16.

[47] Adolf A. Berle and Gardiner C. Means, *The Modern Corporation and Private Property* (New York: Macmillan, 1932). David Cowan Bayne, a disciple of Berle, maintains that trust is the essential controlling element of corporate power. See his *Philosophy of Corporate Control* (Chicago: Loyola University Press, 1986).

[48] Harold S. Geneen, "Why Directors Can't Protect the Shareholders," *Fortune*, September 17, 1984, pp. 28–32.

Summary and Conclusions

The business values described in this chapter were ideal for a period of expansion, rapid growth, and exploitation of land and resources. It gave the poor an opportunity and exploited the immigrant's eagerness for work. It also gave a new nation its railroads, mines, banks, manufacturing firms, and cities.

Perceptive visitors during the last century and a half noted an honesty, frankness, and directness in Americans. They found a pragmatic people with little time for unproductive theorizing. Freedom is a bedrock value that has been institutionalized in our Constitution, laws, and attitudes.

Several elements converged to fashion this new vision called the American business ideology:

1. The *frontier* provided opportunities to the immigrants who had come to the New World looking for a challenging new life in farming, mining, or manufacturing, where potential rewards were immense.
2. The *Protestant ethic*, which underscored the value of hard work in a person's occupation, was carried to the New World by the Puritans and translated into a secular vision by people like Benjamin Franklin.
3. Faith in *free enterprise* gave the individual confidence and vigor. The system worked well in encouraging economic growth and, moreover, was shown to be intellectually sound by the classical economists.
4. *Competition* became more explicit and central with the advent of the theory of evolution and the recognition of the principles of natural selection and the survival of the fittest. Natural forces, if allowed to operate without constraint, would provide the efficient firm.
5. The *role of government* was to apply as few constraints as possible to business activity; its central purpose was to protect the private property of its citizens. On this Thomas Jefferson is often quoted: "That government is best which governs least."

It is an irony of history that emphasis on the rugged individualist peaked during the latter half of the nineteenth century, just at the time the business scene was dominated by oligopolies and trusts. One or a few firms in each industry virtually controlled production, prices, and even wages. It was difficult for an individual, no matter how rugged, to raise the capital necessary to compete. At that time and since then, it has become apparent that this American business ideology, although it may provide a motivation and a vision for the enterprising individual, is not entirely accurate in its description of the marketplace. For the market is not totally free.

The values of American Puritans—hard work, saving, regular habits, diligence, self-control, and sobriety—are still somewhat present in the American work ethic. These values constitute what is called the Protestant ethic. It was an ideology that advocated hard work, competition, self-reliance, self-discipline, individualism, saving, and planning ahead. These were called forth by a vision preached in church, school, and town meeting, a vision of growth, superiority, and improvement of the world for the next generation.

With this history as background, we assessed the major values of Americans. This examination of American values provides a framework for considering business values and ideology. We examined ideologies, including their function and their effects. Business values exist in society, and we see how well U.S. society's ideals support the values of its business community. Nevertheless, there is considerable suspicion of business, especially big business. An adequate response to these issues is possible only by spelling out a purpose and an ideology for business firms that is in better harmony with what society expects.

The goal of the traditional American business ideology is expansion and growth; its focus is on material reward for the individual. But the assumption that an individual always wants more material goods leads to further questions. Is the goal of more material goods sufficient to motivate emotionally and morally mature people to give most of their physical and psychic energy to the business enterprise? Are there other values of the individual in an affluent society that must be tapped if we are to continue to be economically healthy? From another perspective, to what extent will one's "calling" continue to be central in one's life? Or consider a question that will have profound impact on national policy: Is a goal of material growth necessary for a business creed for the future? If so, what sort of growth? These and other, similar questions will be addressed in the following chapters.

Discussion Questions

1. Citing historic events and attitudes, indicate what characteristic American values were illustrated during the silver-mining days at Virginia City, Nevada.
2. According to Ralph Waldo Emerson, how does one achieve success and wealth?
3. Describe the attitude of people in the establishment churches to the new immigrant laborers in the United States in the 1800s.
4. Compare the values shown by the mine owners with those of the Establishment churches during the same period (i.e., roughly 1860–1890).
5. What are the similarities and dissimilarities between the Protestant ethic and American individualism?
6. Outline how the Protestant ethic aided in the economic development of the New World.
7. Describe the hours, wages, and working conditions of poor people, immigrants, and children before 1920.
8. What are the two conflicting responsibilities of churches? How does your church meet each of these responsibilities?
9. Outline the arguments of Conwell and Carnegie on the goodness of acquisitiveness and wealth.
10. What was Andrew Carnegie's position on wages? What was his justification for the wealth of the rich? Is this position held today?

11. Compare Carnegie's attitudes on work with those of Frederick W. Taylor (scientific management). What do they have in common? How do they differ?
12. What are the insights of Teilhard de Chardin, Albert Einstein, Amos Oz, and Akio Morita on the American character? Do their observations have a common theme?
13. Distinguish among values, goals, ideals, and ideologies.
14. How do values relate to an ideology?
15. What is an ideology? What does a utopian ideology do for a society?
16. What are the advantages and disadvantages to a society of having a well-articulated ideology? What happens to a society without such an ideology?
17. Are the American values outlined in this chapter predominant for the average American? For people in your environment? For you?
18. Do businesses today possess a consistent ideology? What are the disadvantages of not having a business ideology?
19. What is the ultimate purpose of a business? Is it to make a profit? Or is it to provide jobs and family income, along with quality goods and/or service at a low price? What is the difference?
20. Does your firm have a mission and goal statement? Is it comprehensive and motivating?

CASES

Educational Reimbursement

Rob Stewart, an assistant professor of marketing, is teaching the introductory marketing course for the fall term at Southwestern State University; there will be about 600 students in the course. Stewart can select from among six basic marketing texts, and he negotiates with various publishers to determine which will provide the best "educational reimbursement" (i.e., gifts to a person or department of computers, teaching equipment, or dollars). The publishing house of Smith and Luster agrees to $600 worth of reimbursement, and Stewart decides on its text even though it is not as good as another text. How do you judge the ethics of Stewart's decision? Is there a conflict of interest here? Explain. Who benefits? Make any necessary distinctions.

Safe Drug

Your firm has developed a prescription drug that cures the flu. The Food and Drug Administration has delayed giving it clearance. Your own scientists think that the drug is safe, and that the FDA is overly cautious. Other governments, with high standards for safety, have approved the drug for sale in their countries. Should your firm market the drug overseas? Or should you wait for U.S. approval?

CHAPTER

Critics of Free Enterprise

6

Materialism failed as an ideology in the East, but has triumphed as a matter of practice in the West. In exchange for the prospect of prosperity and security, many Europeans forgot about the bigger Europe of spiritual values, humanistic ideals and intellectual integrity.
—Vaclav Havel, President, Czech Republic

We have seen in earlier chapters that the free market system has remarkable strengths and also severe weaknesses. Hence free enterprise has numerous critics; and no critique has proven as perceptive, trenchant, or appealing as that of Karl Marx. Marx raises serious questions about the moral and social consequences of the economic system we have adopted. He had an extraordinary ability to pinpoint and articulate the deficiencies of the free market system. Marx also offers an alternative set of values for a socioeconomic system, but followers of Marx have not been successful in providing a realistic, workable alternative to capitalism.

For much of the twentieth century, Eastern Europe, the Soviet Union, and other nations had collectivist, communist economies, and Marxist governments. These economies achieved much in developing industry and providing jobs. Marxism became the banner around the world for many who sought to support the plight of the poor. However, because of arbitrary imprisonment of critics, trampling on individual rights, favoritism, and other abuses of the system in these countries, along with inefficiencies, the governments fell in the early 1990s.

These countries, along with China, now have free market economies. Unfortunately, the market system in Russia, Ukraine, and other nations is now dominated by the worse elements of the market system: a few huge fortunes and many unemployed; products, contracts, and advertisements that cannot be trusted; pollution, bribery, favoritism, and organized crime.

Nevertheless, Marxism, along with the variety of other attempts to organize people and production along communal lines, are important movements in world history and deserve special attention. Their ideology stands in marked contrast to the ideology of self-interest and free markets. There is much that is admirable in the way of shared living that they advocate. Moreover, we can learn from their valid criticisms of free enterprise, and the alternative values which they espouse.

Free enterprise, or capitalism as it is called by its critics, is the socioeconomic system of the developed, industrialized countries. The countries of North America, Western Europe, and Japan are now joined by the rapidly developing countries of Asia, Eastern Europe, and the nations of the former Soviet Union.

Many communities worldwide have been and are built on cooperative, rather than competitive, ideals. Medieval European communities were more cooperative than their contemporary counterparts. Guilds, stable populations, and extended families, who all lived within walking distance, gave these early communities cohesion. On the other hand, they also had a rigid hierarchical social system. If the father was a butcher, so too was the son. We will discuss examples of cooperative economic systems later in this chapter.

Before examining the criticisms of capitalism, let us step back for a moment to probe some of our *own beliefs* and presuppositions. Each of the following questions can be asked of any of the major leaders of thought discussed in this book. To obtain additional clarity on your own goals, beliefs, and value system, ponder these questions. What do *you* believe regarding the following fundamental issues:

1. Are human beings headed for progress and a better life or for poorer living conditions and a decline of civilization?

2. If neither progress nor decline is inevitable, do we have it in our power to affect future societies (e.g., societies existing 10 years hence)? If so, in what way?

3. Is anything always morally right or always morally wrong (e.g., murder)? Is lying or stealing always, or generally, wrong, or is it all relative, a matter of social expectations and the law?

4. Are human beings essentially good, needing only support and encouragement for their development, or are they essentially self-seeking, such that an economic system is wise to build on this selfishness and make best use of it?

5. Is competition the most effective motivator for you? Is cooperation more effective, or do you respond to some combination?

6. Does life end at death? Is there an afterlife? How does this influence your life, work, and attitudes?

7. Have you ever thought about the above questions or do you put them aside—either because you do not understand their relevance or because they are too difficult?

Your answers to these questions may expose the framework you use in making daily and long-term decisions. Your answers also affect your goals, values, and ethics. On the other hand, you may not have thought much about these questions. Perhaps your values and ethics have been taken from other people, superiors at work or the media. In that case you are making daily decisions, some with far-reaching implications, without having examined the presuppositions beneath those decisions. Problems which stem from this posture, and how people cope or fail to cope, will be discussed in the next chapter.

If we raised these questions to Bernard of Clairvaux, John Calvin, Benjamin Franklin, Adam Smith, Karl Marx, and others, what would they say? But let us now continue with our examination of the criticisms of capitalism.

THE MARXIST CRITIQUE

Karl Marx (1818–1883) first forged a theory of communism. Marx's criticisms of the capitalist system were incisive and based on careful empirical studies. His language was intentionally polemic, and he and his followers used terms like *exploitation, imperialism,* and *alienation.*[1]

The criticisms come from a viewpoint that is designedly quite foreign to that of the American business community. But despite the differences in language, values, and attitudes, the Marxist critique leads us to examine our own national priorities and the values that govern our economic, political, and social policies. If we strive for an objective examination of the goals and values of free enterprise, we must not neglect its critics.

A man of real genius, Marx combined analytic power with an ability to weld his ideas into an overall theory of history. According to his theory, economic forces are the primary determinant of history. Economic structures give rise to class differences; class conflicts provoke social and political struggles. Marx thought class conflict between workers and owners would inevitably erupt in revolution and usher in a new socialist system of production.

Marx points out that economists view economic factors (capital, labor, prices) as things. Marx insisted that economics does not deal simply with things; it deals with social relations. Every commodity produced and sold, every wage paid, involves very definite relationships between human beings. In failing to recognize these social relations, capitalism and capitalist theory ignore the real effects of the system on human society.

This basic critique can be divided into several accusations made by critics of the capitalist system. Some may find these accusations exaggerated and one-sided. But we present them in the conviction that intelligent criticism often leads to a reexamination of views.

---

[1] John E. Elliott, "On the Possibility of Marx's Moral Critique of Capitalism," *Review of Social Economy* 44 (October 1986): 130–44.

Exploitation of the Worker

The free enterprise system operates on the theory that when people work for their own self-interest, they will simultaneously contribute to the welfare of all. Everyone profits from economic growth, and each person receives monetary rewards in proportion to his or her efforts and skill. Marxists challenge these assumptions. That economic growth has occurred since the beginning of the modern industrial age is evident. That all have profited from this growth proportionate to their work is dubious. For Marx, who knew the Industrial Revolution during its grimmest stage, it was difficult to see how workers benefited much from their labors. As we saw in the last chapter, factory workers lived in hovels, worked exhausting 12-hour workdays 6 days a week, and died prematurely. Marx's classic work, *Capital*, chronicles the price paid in human suffering for industrial growth: workers suffering from pulmonary diseases caused by the dust and heat of factories, small children working 15-hour days, a young girl dying of exhaustion after 26 consecutive hours of work.[2] Workers were forced to live on subsistence wages while owners acquired fortunes and lived in luxury.

In developed countries the extremes that exist now between the impoverished and the wealthy may not be as obvious as they were a century ago. Labor unions and government legislation have brought higher wages and better working conditions, which have raised the standard of living of many workers. But if one looks to the *distribution* of wealth and income, very large inequalities remain, and those gaps are now increasing. In a study of incomes of 16 industrialized countries during the last 2 decades, the United States had the *greatest inequality* of all. The income gap between the rich and the poor was wider in the United States than in any other industrialized country, according to this comprehensive study of incomes.

Following the United States in income disparity were Ireland, Italy, Canada, Australia, and Britain, in that order. Finland had the least disparity, followed by Sweden, Belgium, Netherlands, Norway, and West Germany. More specifically, in the United States, a person at the tenth percentile of income (10% down from top income) earned two times (206%) the U.S. median income, while in Finland a person in the tenth percentile earned about one and one-half (150%) the Finnish median income. In addition, an American at the nintieth percentile earned only 35 percent of median income, while in Finland someone at the nintieth percentile earned about 60 percent of the Finnish median. During the decade of the 1980s, inequality in income rose markedly in the United States, Japan, Australia, and Britain, and showed lesser increases in five other European countries. Income disparity actually fell in Italy and Portugal.[3]

---

[2] Karl Marx, "The Working Day," *Capital*, vol. 1 (New York: International Publishers, 1967), pp. 244–54.

[3] *Report of the Organization for Economic Cooperation and Development*. See *New York Times,* October 27, 1995, p. C2. This study used data provided by the governments involved, and was also funded by the governments. Each government also had the opportunity to critique a draft of the report.

For a Marxist, the reason for this gap is clear. Workers can only bargain for higher wages. Managers determine compensation: wages, executive salaries, and dividends to stockholders. The manager controls the system, and the great inequalities are a result of that control. Workers are not paid the real value of their work contribution, according to Marx. The difference, the surplus value, between what workers add to the product and their actual wage is the real source of profit.

Marx argues that profit is the surplus after all costs have been met. Marxists recognize the need for investment in new equipment and research; their quarrel is with its private possession and control. If workers are the prime source of production, then they, not owners, should be the prime beneficiaries, and they should also have a significant voice in the production process. The fact that labor unions have reduced the inequities between wages and profits does not alter the basic fact of exploitation for a Marxist. The manager still seeks to pay as little as possible for workers' services. The resulting profits or "surplus" are not the rewards of the capitalist's hard work or enterprising spirit, but result simply from ownership of property and control over the work of others.

Sweatshops continue to exist in Asia and Latin America as well as in New York City and California. Manufacturing workers labor 12 hours a day 6 days a week for less than minimum wage, and are often kept in virtual slavery. Young girl workers sew name brand garments and shoes, and in the United States, they are generally illegal immigrants. U.S. citizens often resent the fact that "these illegals are taking our jobs." The garments and shoes are sold at premium prices, with the profit going to owners.

Marx challenges the contention that wealth has really been the product of "free" enterprise. Can the wealthy really be said to have "earned" their total income in the past without acknowledging the takeover of native lands, slavery, or the minimal wages paid immigrant workers? Or in the present, do low-paid service workers receive a wage proportionate to their work when top executives of the same company earn 100 times or more their salary?

The income gap between top managers and others in the firm continues to increase. According to a survey commissioned by *The Wall Street Journal*, in 1994 the average chief executive's cash pay increased 11.4 percent in just 1 year, compared with only a 4.2 percent increase for other white collar employees. That year the median total compensation for the 350 CEOs surveyed was $1,779,663.[4]

These large salary increases were bestowed at a time when many of these same executives were asking others to accept pay reductions and they were cutting jobs. Two examples illustrate different approaches. Ronald W. Allen, CEO of Delta Airlines, in 1993 announced the reduction of 15,000 jobs, about 20

---

[4] "Pay Trends," *Wall Street Journal,* April 12, 1995, p. R8.

percent of the workforce; Allen did not take a bonus and actually took a pay reduction himself. He said that if flight attendants, reservation clerks, and others were taking pay cuts, he should do the same. Allen has worked for Delta all his life, and he wants to maintain solidarity with the rest of the workforce and support their loyalty.

On the other hand, Albert J. Dunlap, CEO of Scott Paper, announced cuts in the Scott workforce of about one-third or 11,200 jobs. He then received $3,500,000 in salary and bonus, while his predecessor the previous year had received but $618,000. He argues that he added much to shareholder value. Concern for solidarity and loyalty of the workforce were not considerations for Dunlap; he left Scott shortly thereafter. Edward Brennan of Sears Roebuck announced job cuts of 50,000 and then received a 198 percent increase in compensation the following year to $3,000,000. George David, CEO of United Technologies, cut 10,600 jobs, and then received a 115 percent increase in pay. Most CEOs take pay increases in spite of cutting jobs and asking for sacrifice in order to cut costs.[5]

Critics of free enterprise argue that investments produce more income than work itself. A study of people who reported incomes of $1 million or more showed that only 4 percent of their income came from salaries; the rest came from dividends and capital gains.[6] As important as these issues are, Marx was concerned about more than the distribution of wealth and a fair wage for work done.

Alienation of the Worker

Dissatisfaction with one's job and a lack of commitment and loyalty are common among working people today. Marx saw the roots of this when he charged that work was forced and dehumanizing. The work is forced because jobs are scarce and the average worker, though theoretically free to accept a job or not, has little choice but to take the job. Nor do workers have much freedom in the way they carry out the work. They do the work assigned often even at the pace designated. The work is thus dehumanizing because it does nothing to develop the human potential of the workers (e.g., their ability to be inventive, to make decisions, to develop different skills). The worker is simply an appendage to a machine. He "does not affirm himself in his work but denies himself, feels miserable and unhappy, develops no free physical and mental energy but mortifies

[5] Hugh M. O'Neill and D. Jeffery Lenn, "Voices of Survivors: Words that Downsizing CEOs Should Hear," *Academy of Management Executive* 9 (November 1995): 23–34. Also Molly Baker, "I Feel Your Pain: When the CEO Orders Massive Layoffs, Should He Get a Pay Raise?" *Wall Street Journal*, April 12, 1995, p. R6.

[6] Richard C. Edwards, Michael Reich, and Thomas E. Weisskopf, eds., *The Capitalist System* (Englewood Cliffs, N.J.: Prentice-Hall, 1986), pp. 223–24, and Ferdinand Lundberg, *The Rich and the Super-Rich* (New York: Bantam Books, 1968), pp. 43, 935–36.

his flesh and ruins his mind."[7] The capitalist works him as he would "a horse that he has hired for a day."[8]

Critics charge that free enterprise values efficiency and profit maximization more than humanizing work. In most traditional societies one's work was one's life. Work, play, and social life flowed into each other. Work meant simply tasks to be done, and there was no division of life into work and nonwork. For most moderns, in contrast, work has unpleasant connotations. Note the number of people who take early retirement. With increasing specialization, a worker is assigned to a narrower portion of a task. The work is completed by another: out of sight and out of mind. There is little sense of satisfaction from work. Moreover, few jobs challenge one's real skills, imagination, or spirit. Many jobs simply call for a capacity to follow exact routines in an orderly way, as with fast food work. As a result, work does not mean much to those people and they do not enjoy it.[9]

Workers are not asked to use their mind or to be creative. Scientific management which Frederick Taylor proposed in the late nineteenth century (see Chapter 5), and which influenced the U.S. system of production, deliberately divorced mental and material labor. Taylor wrote,

> The managers assume the burden of gathering together all of the traditional knowledge which in the past has been possessed by the workmen and then of classifying, tabulating, and reducing this knowledge to rules, laws, and formula. All possible brain work should be removed from the shop and centered in the planning or laying-out department.[10]

Assembly lines carried this concept of mechanized labor to its fullest expression. Henry Ford's decision in 1914 to raise workers' pay to 5 dollars a day was hailed as an enlightened, progressive move done to enable workers to become more affluent customers. Critics maintain that this view overlooks the fact that Ford faced an angry revolt by workers against his new assembly lines. The turnover rate in 1913 had forced the Ford Motor Company to hire 963 workers in order to keep 100 jobs filled.[11] The lack of creativity allowed is true not only in manual work but in clerical work as well. The drive for speed and efficiency has reduced work to simplified, routinized, and measured tasks.

Although work is sometimes inhumane, unemployment proves far more degrading still. To speak of *only* 5 percent unemployed does little to describe the

---

[7] Loyd D. Easton and Kurt H. Guddat, trans. and eds., *Writings of the Young Marx* (Garden City, N.Y.: Anchor, 1967), p. 292.

[8] Marx, *Capital*, vol. 1, p. 185.

[9] Kenneth Keniston, "The Alienating Consequences of Capitalist Technology," in Edwards, Reich, and Weisskopf, *The Capitalist System*, pp. 269–73; see also Herbert Gintis's essay on alienation, which follows Keniston's.

[10] Harry Braverman, *Labor and Monopoly Capital: The Degradation of Work in the Twentieth Century* (New York: Monthly Review, 1974), pp. 31–39, 112–18.

[11] *Ibid.*, p. 149.

frustration, powerlessness, and anxiety of millions of unemployed people. Unemployment benefits may permit an income on which to live for a short time, but it is dehumanizing. From a Marxist perspective, worker exploitation and alienation are among the most serious failures of the free enterprise system. The work environment's effects on workers will be discussed in the next chapter.

Big Business Dominates National Goals

Americans take pride in their democratic system: "Whatever its faults, it's the best in the world." Every citizen has a voice in the government. All can vote; all can aspire to political office. The two-party system offers choices in policies and candidates. The division of executive, legislature, and judiciary is a model of balance of power.

Critics challenge this faith in U.S. democracy. Their quarrel is not with the ideals and values of democracy but with claims that they have been realized in the United States or other free market nations. Marx argued that political freedoms created only an "illusion" of true human freedom. People's lives are determined far more by the conditions in which they live in society than by abstract political rights. Political power, moreover, reflects economic power. When John Locke, the seventeenth-century English philosopher, stated that the chief end of persons uniting to form a government was "the preservation of property," he reflected the goals of his social class of wealthy people. The democratic state in market societies claims to represent the common good of all its citizens, and indeed periodically it passes legislation to legitimize that claim. But it serves primarily to further the interests of the powerful and wealthy.[12]

The most obvious evidence for this position is the disproportionate representation of the wealthy in high office. In theory anyone can be president of, for example, the United States. But in fact multimillionaires, though they constitute a small fraction of the population, have regularly been elected over the last 50 years—Franklin D. Roosevelt, John F. Kennedy, Lyndon Johnson, Richard Nixon, Jimmy Carter, Ronald Reagan, George Bush. In addition, cabinet members, ambassadors, and even members of Congress come disproportionately from the ranks of millionaires.

The presence of wealthy men in high office is not the only objection of critics. Many stress far more the support of the state for large corporations. Corporations may complain of government regulations and taxes, but there are many ways in which government subsidizes big business.

The state assists big business both by creating a climate for its accumulation of capital and by bearing much of the burden of social expenses (e.g., education and health care). Government subsidy of private industry is illustrated by the automobile industry. Cars need roads, but private industry does not bear the cost

---

[12] "The Communist Manifesto," in *The Marx-Engels Reader*, ed. Robert C. Tucker (New York: W. W. Norton, 1972), p. 337.

of building them. The federal government paid 90 percent of the cost of interstate freeways and 50 percent of the cost of all other primary roads. Eighty percent of the funds earmarked for the redevelopment of Appalachia went into roads.[13]

The state subsidizes business, and hence profits, in a variety of ways: subsidizing exports, helping to finance land development and building; and funding research and providing tax exemptions for building depreciation and oil exploration. By providing unemployment, welfare, and medical benefits, it tempers the discontent created by unemployment. It pays for much of the cost of cleaning up industrial pollution. Government picks up much of the responsibility that business escapes through bankruptcy and negligence. Government support of business is summarized:

> Over the past three decades, the government has helped to build ten million units for the better-off and 650,000 units of low-cost housing for the poor. . . . there were $2.5 billion in subsidies for the urban freeways, which facilitated the commuting of the privileged, and only $175 million for mass transit. All of this made good commercial sense even though it helped to perpetuate the social disaster of the disintegration of the central cities, the consequent isolation of the racial and ethnic minorities, the subversion of the passenger-rail system, and so forth.[14]

Government policies regarding farming reveal the same priorities. From 1940 to 1985, the number of farms in the United States decreased by 60 percent and the size of the average farm increased by 160 percent. The "family farmers" included ITT, Gulf+Western, Boeing, and other large corporations. Moreover, it was these giant agribusinesses which were the prime recipients of federal subsidy.[15]

Charles Lindbloom, in his classic *Politics and Markets*, focuses on the influence of big business on the state. Though he defends the market economy, Lindbloom believes that giant corporations are inconsistent with democracy. Business executives and not government officials, he argues, make most of the public policy decisions that affect the economic life of the nation. Their decisions, in turn, affect almost every aspect of life—jobs, homes, consumer goods, leisure. These executives determine income distribution, allocation of resources, plant locations, the pattern of work, the technologies used, goods produced, the quality of goods and services, and of course executive compensation and status.[16] These major decisions are turned over to business leaders and taken off the agenda of government. Thus citizens have no vote at all on policies that affect every sphere of their lives.

---

[13] James O'Connor, *The Fiscal Crisis of the State* (New York: St. Martin's Press, 1973), pp. 105–6.

[14] Michael Harrington, *The Twilight of Capitalism* (New York: Simon & Schuster, 1976), p. 224.

[15] *Statistical Abstract of the United States–1986,* p. 632; see also Douglas F. Dowd, *The Twisted Dream: Capitalist Development in the United States Since 1776* (Cambridge, Mass.: Winthrop, 1977), pp. 177–78.

[16] Charles Lindbloom, *Politics and Markets: The World's Political-Economic Systems* (New York: Basic Books, 1977), p. 171.

But these major decisions only begin to indicate the public role of business leaders. Their influence on government is quite different than that of any other group in society. Public functions in the market system rest in their hands. For example, jobs, prices, production, growth, the standard of living, and the economic security of everyone is under their influence. Business leaders are not just representatives of one or more special interest groups; the welfare of all people in a society depends on what they do. When business leaders ask for tax reductions to stimulate investment, subsidies for overseas exports, transportation and research, for troops to protect investments in foreign countries, or for similar advantages, the state often responds favorably.

All citizen groups can compete in politics, but they must use their members' own incomes and energies. Business corporations can spend corporate funds and work on company time, and can use professional lobbyists to influence legislation. Business has myriad avenues by which to present its own point of view. Through lobbying, gifts, entertainment, and real or threatened litigation, business uses its resources to confirm its position and gain approval. Roughly $130 billion a year is spent on advertising and other sales promotion.[17] All of this promotes a firm and a brand, and some of it is corporate advertising with an overtly political content. This matches all the funds spent on education or health in the country. Few dissenting voices even exist to compete with dominant business views. The large private corporation, Lindbloom concludes, is not consistent with democratic theory and vision.[18] Critics point out that this same business control now extends to the entire world.

Corporations Exploit Other Countries

Much criticism of free enterprise has been directed against the influence of capitalism in poor countries. When people praise the achievements of free enterprise, they point to the overall affluence of Japan, Western Europe, and the United States, and the political democracy which accompanies it. But in Latin America, Asia, and other parts of the world, free enterprise often accompanies desperate poverty for the majority, right-wing rule, corruption, and exploitation by foreign companies. For example, in El Salvador, free enterprise means 2 percent of the population own 60 percent of the land and 8 percent receive half of all personal income. The remaining 92 percent of the population live in poverty and three-fourths of the children suffer from malnutrition. Yet efforts at reform have been crushed by right-wing death squads, often trained in and by the United States.

Critics argue that capitalist countries want to maintain the status quo in developing countries in order to exploit them. Exploitation has profit as its motive. Less developed countries of the world provide natural resources and cheap

---

[17] *Statistical Abstract of the United States—1994* (Washington D.C.: U.S. Department of Commerce, 1994), p. 543.
[18] *Ibid.*, pp. 172ff, 195, 214.

labor which make investment very profitable if the political regimes are favorable. Economic development has brought some jobs and income for the poor, and also huge financial rewards to the wealthy elite in Brazil, Colombia, Indonesia, India, and other developing countries.

The very beginnings of capitalism in Europe, many contend, was made possible by the plunder of gold, silver, and other minerals from countries of the southern hemisphere. Then specialized economies which are less flexible were developed by foreign investors. Today we associate certain products with specific countries—coffee in Brazil, tin in Bolivia, copper in Chile, sugar in Cuba. But the specialization in such commodities did not result from initiatives within those countries. The economies of these countries were focused by European and U.S. companies to meet needs in the "developed world." The concentration on one or two products generally upset a natural balance of production and created "one-crop" economies dependent on the fluctuating prices in the world market for that one crop. For example, Brazil's northeast was once that country's richest area; now it is its poorest. Portugal granted lands to Brazil's first wealthy landlords, and sugar production flourished for a few generations. When washed-out soil and eroded lands resulted, the landlords then left with their cash.[19] Barbados, in the West Indies, suffered the same fate. It once produced a variety of crops and livestock on small holdings: cotton, tobacco, oranges, cows, and pigs. Cane fields devoured all this; the soil was then exhausted and unable to feed the population. The story is similar in Africa. Gambia once grew its own rice on land now used to grow peanuts. Northern Ghana grew yams and other foodstuffs on land now devoted to cocoa. Much of Liberia and Vietnam were turned over to rubber plantations. Seizures of land, taxation, undercutting of domestic prices, and forced migrations were all employed by colonizers to gain control of the land.[20]

This has left a world divided between a few who live in opulent affluence and the many who live in "dehumanizing poverty, servitude, and economic insecurity." While chief executive officers, investment bankers, financial speculators, entertainers, and athletes bring in incomes of well over $1 million each year, about 1 billion of the world's people "struggle in desperation to live on less than $1 dollar a day."[21]

The countries and the people who are already wealthy control the priorities and determine what is to be made, financed, and traded. They have the power to make the rules and make the rules to suit their own interests. Consider the following data:

---

[19] Eduardo Galeano, *Open Veins of Latin America: Five Centuries of the Pillage of a Continent*, trans. Cedric Belfrage (New York: Monthly Review, 1973), pp. 72–75.

[20] Frances Moore Lappe and Joseph Collins, *Food First: Beyond the Myth of Scarcity* (Boston: Houghton Mifflin, 1977), pp. 78ff.

[21] David C. Korten, *When Corporations Rule the World* (San Francisco: Kumarian Press and Berrett-Koehler, 1995), p. 20. Korten provides a well documented and carefully reasoned critique of current global economic policies.

El Salvador and Costa Rica . . . grow export crops such as bananas, coffee and sugar on more than one fifth of their cropland. Export cattle ranches in Latin America and southern Africa have replaced rain forest and wildlife range. At the consumer end of the production line, Japan imports 70 percent of its corn, wheat, and barley, 95 percent of its soybeans, and more than 50 percent of its wood, much of it from the rapidly vanishing rain forests of Borneo . . . (meanwhile) millions of pigs and cows are fattened on palm-kernel cake from deforested lands in Malaysia, cassava from deforested regions of Thailand, and soybeans from pesticide-doused expanses in the south of Brazil in order to provide European consumers with their high-fat diet of meat and milk.[22]

Does not the presence of foreign mining firms, manufacturers, fruit growers, and banks bring needed capital, technology, and know-how to poor countries? To some extent, yes. However, the income that comes back to the richer country from private investment in poor countries exceeds that going into initial investment by more than 80 percent.[23] In a typical year, only 30 percent of the earnings generated in developing countries is reinvested in those countries. The remainder is sent back to the wealthy country. This compares with 63 percent of similar earnings reinvested in developed countries.[24] Putting the situation graphically, if a box of bananas retails at $13.45 in the United States, producers in Honduras receive roughly $1.49; this covers tending the bananas, cutting, and packing them. Chain supermarkets in the United States gross $4.23 on that same box.[25]

The global economy has created a market in which competition among communities is as real as competition among firms. Moore County, South Carolina won a bid in the 1970s to bring a Proctor Silex plant to their community. They later floated a $5.5 million bond to finance sewer and water for an expansion. Then in 1990, the firm moved to Mexico, leaving behind 800 unemployed Moore County residents.[26] This same sort of competition exists among cities, when they vie with one another to subsidize stadiums for professional athletic teams, in effect subsidizing the players who are paid an average of $1.5 million dollars each.

"The market will decide" and "consumer sovereignty" are bywords justifying such free enterprise and global markets. But the consumer who decides is the consumer who has money. The poor and hungry cannot pay enough for food to match the profits that can be made on exports. Therefore, Central America sends its vegetables to the United States, where large quantities are dumped or used as animal feed because their quality is not good enough or markets are

---

[22] Alan Durning, *How Much Is Enough? The Consumer Society and the Future of the Earth* (New York: W. W. Norton, 1992), p. 56. Quoted in Korten, p. 30.

[23] "U.S. Direct Investment Abroad," *Survey of Current Business*, August 1986, p. 70.

[24] *Ibid.*, table 4, p. 42.

[25] Lappe and Collins, *Food First*, pp. 194–98. The dollar figures have been adjusted for the rise in prices.

[26] Korten, *When Corporations Rule the World*, pp. 128–29.

oversupplied. Mexico grows strawberries, cantaloupes, and asparagus for Del Monte and other global corporations to sell in the United States. Colombian private owners grow flowers for export because one hectare of flowers brings nine times the profit that wheat or corn could. Because the market in the United States and Europe demand it, cocaine now brings far greater profits to Colombian farmers.[27]

When poorer nations attempted to achieve a democratic, fairer society, the United States often intervened. The United States sent Marines into Guatemala in 1954, supported the military overthrow of Goulart in Brazil in 1964, used the CIA to subvert and overthrow the elected Allende government in Chile in 1973, and supported the extreme right-wing dictatorship in El Salvador until 1988. In Cuba, before Castro's revolution, U.S. companies controlled 80 percent of Cuba's utilities, 90 percent of its mines, and almost 100 percent of its oil refineries. U.S. firms received 40 percent of the profits on sugar, a crop that represented 89 percent of all Cuban exports. It was this argument that Castro made that garnered him the support of the people. More recently, the invasion of Panama was to protect the Panama Canal and the war in Iraq was to protect our supply of petroleum. The reason for many military interventions is the protection of U.S. business investments.

Finally, if foreign policy and military intervention protect overseas business, the defense industry is thus essential to free enterprise. In addition, it sells planes, missles, tanks, guns, and other equipment to friendly poor countries. Defense contracts, in turn, provide jobs, business, and reelection for government representatives. Hence we see that exploitation of other countries, military support of business interests, and a large "defense" industry are essential elements of contemporary "free markets."

Social Consequences of Capitalism

Social problems abound around the world that are the direct consequence of subordinating social concerns to profit making. These problems are familiar. The United States has killed 85 percent of its wildlife and destroyed 80 percent of its forests; millions of acres of farmland have been misused, paved over, and lost. Pollution is rampant. New York City dumps 200 million gallons of sewage into the Hudson River each day. High national infant mortality rates reflect the poor medical care poor people receive. Crime and violence undermine urban life. Armed robbery in Washington, D.C., is 20 times that of London. Drugs, poor public schools, inadequate housing, broken families, racial prejudice, unemployment, and great disparities in income are common problems in most market economies.

The United States, Western and Eastern Europe, and now increasingly Japan are plagued by serious social problems. Japan, Western Europe, and the

---

[27] *Ibid.*, pp. 255–56.

United States pride themselves on enjoying a very high standard of living. Their citizens enjoy far more material benefits than any other people in history. But many question even this achievement. How much of what we consume corresponds to real needs? Our consumer-propelled economy demands the creation of mostly false "needs."[28] Advertisements keep us in a state of perpetual dissatisfaction with what we do have. So new "styles" become the selling point. Advertising seeks to convince us of our "need" for ever-drier deodorants, electric toothbrushes, and automatic garbage compactors. Vacation advertisements try to convince us to go to ever more exotic and expensive places. Meanwhile, in Mexico, India, Indonesia, and other poor countries, the poor flock to the cities seeking work. Unable to find it, they subsist in shantytowns with no water, electricity, or roads. It is hardly the place to raise children.

The charges made by critics about our economic and political system are many. The profit produced by industry goes to owners and executives in far greater share than to workers. Return on investment multiplies the disproportionate distribution of wealth. Factory work often stunts the capacities of workers engaged in it. Initiative, self-determination, and a voice in decision making are not often given to workers. Competitive self-interest characterizes work at every level. Poverty and unemployment become stigmatized and are considered to be one's own fault. A wealthy, powerful elite controls the highest public offices. Laws favor the wealthy and protect their incomes by tax loopholes. Women are often still subservient. Pollution, crime, drugs, racial discrimination, and false needs are by-products of an economy directed only toward more and more goods and profits.

Critics ask why we have allowed ourselves to be duped into thinking that promiscuous growth is the only way. Why not instead "concentrate on ending poverty, improving our quality of life, and achieving a balance with the earth. We can achieve these goals—if we can free ourselves from the illusion that growth is *the* path to better living."[29]

Critics are often perceptive and eloquent in pointing out the flaws in the free market system. As critics, they tell us much. If we ignore the critics, our weaknesses will undoubtedly not go away, but become worse; this could bring instability and potential undermining of the system itself. We are wise to hear the critics, and try to repair the flaws in the system. Giving priority to developing a sustainable economy that meets all peoples' needs, both in developing countries and around the world, is an important goal. Although there are trade-off costs, when understood, such goals appeal to most people.

---

[28] Herbert Marcuse, *One Dimensional Man: Studies in the Ideology of Advanced Industrial Society* (Boston: Beacon Press, 1964), pp. 225–46.

[29] Korten, *When Corporations Rule the World*, p. 38. See also Roger Terry, *Economic Insanity: How Growth-Driven Capitalism Is Devouring the American Dream* (San Francisco: Berrett-Koehler, 1995) for a current, cogent statement of the case.

Cooperative Versus Competitive Market System

Designing an economic system or even specific programs to deal with an unjust distribution of wealth and income generally results in a loss of efficiency and productivity. Government programs require planning and administrators. They are expensive, are influenced by political interests, and do not always achieve their intended goals. Moreover, such programs can have a negative effect on the incentive to work for both low- and high-income people. On the other hand, critics accuse capitalism not only of exploitation and alienation of the worker but also of encouraging selfishness. Excessive competition and selfishness among individuals can hinder the efficiency of a firm and the liveableness of a society.

Two ideals of a democratic society, justice (or equality) and efficiency, are thus often placed in opposition to one another. That is, in the minds of most people, increasing one requires sacrificing some of the other.[30] The ideals of *justice* are basic to any society, especially to a free, democratic one: All men and women have a right to the basics of food, shelter, and some education; all men and women should have an equal opportunity to work and should be treated fairly at work; all people should be treated equally before the law; and there should not be a great disparity among families in income and wealth.

The ideal of *efficiency* is an intermediate, pragmatic goal of industrialized societies. It includes the following convictions: A more efficient and productive society yields more jobs and income for all; all individuals should work hard according to their abilities; rewards should be proportionate to an individual's work and merits; and people, material, and capital should be able to move freely.

These two goals of justice and efficiency are basic. Although we fail in one or the other from time to time, it is also true that both remain explicit and real goals for Americans and others in industrialized societies. Total achievement of one may occur only at the expense of the other, yet we also know that it is unwise to undermine seriously either justice or efficiency. Both are essential to any society. This follows from Kohlberg's Level III values, as we saw in Chapter 2.

Increasing productivity is a standard measure of efficiency. We often define productivity as output per person-hour. That is, productivity increases as the amount of labor expended to produce a good or service decreases. Less often do we define productivity as a function of raw materials or energy used. Yet materials and energy are scarce, becoming more valuable, and are essential to a sustainable economy. Perhaps we need new terminology (maybe *energy productivity* and/or *materials productivity*) to describe moving toward fuller employment and using less energy and materials to produce the goods.

The suggestion that a modern economy can be "unregulated" is mistaken. Government regulation provides protection which is necessary for business to

---

[30] See Arthur Okun, *Equality and Efficiency: The Big Tradeoff* (Washington, D.C.: Brookings Institution, 1975).

operate. Regulation prohibits monopolies, limits toxic pollution, and insures, for example, truthful advertising, accurate information on pharmaceuticals, and financial disclosure of publicly held firms. Bankruptcy legislation even protects owners from going to debtors prison. Government legislation "levels the playing field" to assure fair business dealings for consumers, producers, and investors. Without such government regulation the business environment would be a jungle. Business planning and growth would be impossible.

Every economy operates according to certain priorities and a resulting set of rules. Thus, the important question is, on what priorities are the rules devised? For example, ideally every society assesses taxes and provides subsidies in order to be of the greatest benefit to the people as a whole. That is, legislation, taxes, and other government activities are to be directed to the common good.

Rules or legislation directed to the common good often require that some individuals or groups must sacrifice some immediate benefits. For example, taxing people to pay for fire protection and parks is a cost to those who may never use the fire department or the park.[31] Thus, this demands a political decision that fire protection and parks are important goods for which all people should pay whether or not they directly benefit from these services.

Such political decisions in a democracy require an objective and far-sighted approach to assessing the common good. Legislative decisions sometimes are made that will infringe upon, and hence will not be popular with, certain groups of citizens. These groups may be quite powerful, either because of their money, their influence, or both. Such legislative decisions are becoming harder to make because of lobbyists, special interest groups, and political action committees that contribute to a candidate's campaign. It is difficult for a representative or senator to support legislation that would result in a long-term benefit for most people, if it results in a short-term cost for a powerful segment.

For example, it would benefit most citizens of the United States if we could simultaneously lower both pollution and our excessive purchases of goods overseas. An energy plan that would encourage consumers to be more efficient in their use of the nonrenewable resource of petroleum would accomplish this. Such an energy plan would aid city planning, slow urban sprawl, preserve farmlands, reduce pollution, and reduce the amount of petroleum we must import. The $50 billion or more that we spend annually for imported petroleum is a principal cause of our balance of payments deficit. Japan and the European nations have enacted a 2 to 3 dollars per gallon tax on gasoline for the above reasons. Such a tax would enable the United States to balance the budget and lower income taxes at the same time. In spite of the above evidence, the U.S. Congress does not have the will to tax petroleum to encourage more efficient

---

[31] For a detailed discussion of the common good as an economic objective, see John J. Piderit, S.J., *The Ethical Foundations of Economics* (Washington, D.C.: Georgetown University Press, 1993).

consumption.[32] The United States stands apart from other developed nations and has earned their disapproval because of its voracious use of petroleum and its refusal to deal with this long-term common good.

Enlightened self-interest can lead the entrepreneur to provide the products and services that people want—and to do so efficiently. But enlightened self-interest also encourages individuals to become more selfish. An infant is born self-oriented, but as it grows it comes to recognize the importance of other people. This realization comes gradually with maturity, as we have seen in Chapter Two. Excessive stress on self-interest can stunt a person so that he or she remains at the stage of early adolescence, with a focus on "me and mine." Hence enlightened self-interest must often be guided in order to achieve the common good, especially in contemporary society, where so many of our actions affect others (e.g., noise, pollution, and the use of scarce resources). These issues were also discussed in Chapters 1, 5, and 7.

The case for private ownership of large firms is justified primarily in the name of efficiency. The large disparities in income and wealth that we witness in the United States and Europe are also defended on the basis of efficiency: Money motivates people to work and to work harder. The private sector is generally more efficient than the public sector. That large disparities in income and wealth also bring about greater efficiency is difficult to establish. In fact, there is much evidence that such disparities within a firm bring discontent, jealousy, and a lack of loyalty. Here we find one of the most clear-cut conflicts among our basic values: justice versus efficiency. We will go into more detail on executive compensation in Chapter 8.

FREE ENTERPRISE QUESTIONED FROM WITHIN

People typically consider rising gross domestic product and rising median family income as earmarks of a successful society. It is true that we have been successful in the production and consumption of material goods, so it is probably not surprising that we would like to make that the measure of success for all cultures. Frederick Winslow Taylor, the founder of scientific management, put it succinctly when he said, "In my judgment the best possible measure of the height in the scale of civilization to which any people has arisen is its productivity."[33]

An opposing point of view was presented a generation before Taylor, when England was at its height as an industrial and world power. Matthew

---

[32] For the same reasons, several well-respected national journals consistently have advocated a gradual but substantial tax increase on gasoline. See *Business Week*, August 23, 1993, p. 14; September 16, 1991, pp. 86–92, 128; September 3, 1990, p. 118; November 23, 1981, p. 152; *U.S. News and World Report*, August 27–September 3, 1990, p. 88; November 5, 1979, p. 92; *New York Times*, June 28, 1988, p. 29.

[33] Frederick W. Taylor, *Hearings Before the Special Committee of the House of Representatives to Investigate the Taylor and Other Systems of Shop Management*, vol. 3 (Washington, D.C.: Government Printing Office, 1912), p. 1471.

Arnold pointed to those who said that England's greatness was based on its railroads and its coal. He went on:

> If England were swallowed up by the sea tomorrow, which, a hundred years hence, would most excite the love, interest, and admiration of mankind—and which would most, therefore, show the evidences of having possessed greatness?

Arnold asked whether it would be the England of the preceding two decades, a period of industrial triumph, or would it be an earlier period when culture was more valued? Arnold answered for his contemporaries:

> Never did people believe anything more firmly than nine Englishmen out of ten at the present day believe that our greatness and welfare are proved by our being so very rich.

And then he goes on to give his own response:

> The use of culture is that it helps us, by means of its spiritual standard of perfection, to regard wealth as but machinery, and not only to say as a matter of words that we regard wealth as but machinery, but really to perceive and feel that it is so.[34]

This same issue faces all people as we come to the year 2000. How are we to judge the success of our civilization? What is our goal and what are our criteria for judging whether or not we are successful? Frederick Taylor says it is productivity; Matthew Arnold says productivity and wealth are merely tools to achieve something more. In this perennial debate, on which side do we stand? Or must we fashion some middle ground? A purpose of this book is to help each of us to provide some answers to these questions.

Schumpeter's Prediction of the Decay of Capitalism

Fears of the decay of free enterprise and the capitalist system were voiced as long ago as the sixteenth century by religious reformers John Calvin and John Wesley. Those who fashioned the ideals underlying the Protestant ethic foresaw the ultimate collapse of that system (see Chapter 4). They predicted the collapse of the system once the goals of more material goods, greater financial rewards, and better efficiency in production would be attained. One of the first economists to predict such a collapse was Joseph Schumpeter, who wrote more than 50 years ago.

Schumpeter provides a detailed description of the decay of capitalism. He points out that the very success of the capitalist economic system in providing goods and income paradoxically lessens dependence on the system. As free enterprise is successful, human needs are satisfied and opportunities for investment are fewer. That same success undermines the need for, and so the position

---

[34] Matthew Arnold, *Victorian Prose*, ed. Frederick William Roe (New York: Ronald Press, 1947), p. 399.

and prestige of, the entrepreneur, who is no longer dominant or even highly respected in society.[35]

Contributing to the growing hostility to capitalism are the intellectuals. Academics and intellectuals are quick to see inequities and evils in any system. The problems are there to see, and it is the vocation of the intellectual to point them out. Intellectuals and youth are the principal critics of totalitarian regimes worldwide. However, Schumpeter says that most intellectuals have had no experience in trying to manage an organization, so they do not possess the practical wisdom of those who have gotten their hands dirty. In addition, they have a captive audience in the universities and thus have a ready-made forum for their critical views. Schumpeter was convinced that the intellectuals were undermining capitalism.

Moreover, the professional manager does not have the same long-term vision as the owner he or she replaces.[36] A manager need not stay and fight for the integrity of a firm; he or she will move on to another job that offers greater financial rewards. Schumpeter's indictment is a broad-gauged one; he even goes into some detail as to how capitalism and its attendant attitudes tend to undermine family life and child rearing. In his view, capitalism faces imminent death.

Schumpeter picks out another weakness of capitalism: It has no compelling, motivating, all-embracing ideology and set of values. It is a pragmatic system, designed and pursued for a narrowly conceived end—economic growth. He then contrasts capitalism with Marxism. Marxism has a vision of the world and a systematic ideology; it calls on its followers to sacrifice for the sake of the poor and the oppressed and for a more equal distribution of goods. This vision inspires people. In contrast, capitalism promises only a higher standard of living and is not directly concerned for the poor and disadvantaged. It is effective in production but crass and parochial in its view of people and their world. Schumpeter's critique was widely quoted in his own day. Is it still relevant today?

Argument for Free Markets: A Rebuttal

A counterargument to critics is a defense of capitalism and free markets. The most respected and articulate contemporary spokesperson for this free market ideology is Nobel Prize-winning economist, Milton Friedman. He considers freedom the most important value in any economic or political system, and he sees economic freedom as absolutely essential to political freedom.

Friedman's position in defense of the free market and in opposition to government intervention goes all the way back to Adam Smith. His is the now familiar position that allowing every person the opportunity to buy and sell openly and without restriction will ensure that people will obtain the goods and

---

[35] Joseph A. Schumpeter, *Capitalism, Socialism and Democracy* (London: Allen & Unwin, 1943), pp. 131–39.

[36] *Ibid.*, pp. 143ff, 156.

services they need at the lowest possible price. Free competition in the market-place will bring about the greatest efficiency in producing the goods society is willing to pay for. The corporation, as the predominant economic institution, is a focus of Friedman's concern. He sees a corporation as solely economic, responsible primarily to its stockholders. The agents of the corporation, corporate management, have no right to dispose of stockholders' profits in any manner that does not directly benefit the corporation. Management has no right to spend to make the workplace safer, to install pollution-control equipment or to give money to universities, unless in some way these actions benefit the corporation itself, at least in the long-term.

Friedman is convinced that government has no role in central economic planning. He speaks disparagingly of the government exercising control over the market in the "public interest." Moreover, on the whole he finds that citizen public interest groups have a negative influence:

> Whatever the announced objectives, all of the movements in the past two decades—the consumer movement, the ecology movement, the protect-the-wilderness movement, the zero-population-growth movement, the "small is beautiful" movement, the antinuclear movement—have had one thing in common. All have been antigrowth. They have been opposed to new developments, to industrial innovation, to the increased use of natural resources.[37]

Although the details of Friedman's indictment are not entirely accurate, it is clear that he believes these public interest movements have hurt rather than helped the operation of the market.

Problems such as product reliability, worker safety, and industrial pollution must be addressed. If government legislation and regulation are to be kept to a minimum, and if public interest groups do more harm than good, then the only alternative for solving such problems is management initiative. Yet Friedman is also convinced that management has no right to take the initiative on these issues out of a recognition of the common good. Friedman vehemently denies that corporations do have, or even *can* have, social responsibilities: "The only entities who can have responsibilities are individuals; a business cannot have responsibilities."[38] To presume that a corporation can have social responsibilities

> shows a fundamental misconception of the character and nature of a free economy. In such an economy, there is one and only one social responsibility of business—to use its resources and engage in activities designed to increase its profits so long as it stays within the rules of the game, which is to say, engages in open and free competition, without deception or fraud.[39]

He is convinced that the growing sense of corporate social responsibility undermines basic freedoms:

---

[37] Milton Friedman and Rose Friedman, *Free to Choose: A Personal Statement* (New York: Harcourt, Brace, Jovanovich, 1980), pp. 54–56, 95, 191.

[38] Milton Friedman, "Milton Friedman Responds," *Business and Society Review* 1 (Spring 1972): 6.

[39] Milton Friedman, *Capitalism and Freedom* (Chicago: University of Chicago Press, 1962), p. 133.

Few trends could so thoroughly undermine the very foundations of our free society as the acceptance by corporate officials of a social responsibility other than to make as much money for their stockholders as possible. This is a fundamentally subversive doctrine. If businessmen do have a social responsibility other than making maximum profits for stockholders, how are they to know what it is?[40]

He then points out the difficulty in making such a determination, citing the fact that some German business executives contributed to the Nazi party in the early 1930s. Managers thus wrongly presumed an authority and a wisdom they did not possess.

Friedman argues for the abolition of all corporate taxes and for ensuring that corporate profits are returned to the stockholders, who can then as individuals decide how they will spend their money. It is their money, so it should be their decision whether or not to use it for community purposes. His position is simple, straightforward, and consistent: The interests of stockholders, consumers, and citizens as a whole are best served if the corporation sticks to its traditional role of producing goods and services and does that as efficiently and inexpensively as possible. This is the best long-run service that the business firm can provide for society. He does, however, recognize the problem of unemployment and disability, and he was one of the first to propose a guaranteed minimum income (or "negative income tax," as he calls it) for all those of wage-earning age in the economy. He would substitute a minimum income for the variety of welfare, disability, and unemployment programs that have proliferated, all of which now require separate, expensive, and inefficient administrative apparatuses.

The same principles apply to such diverse areas as schooling and medical care. Friedman does not think the government should be in the business of education, for public education then becomes a monopoly insulated from the challenges to excellence and efficiency that come from free competition. Rather, the government should provide redeemable tuition certificates for parents and children to use at the school of their choice. As with the production of goods and services, he is convinced that better and more effective education will result when there is free competition.[41] His position on medical doctors and the monopoly that certification gives to the American Medical Association is the same. Better, more efficient, and cheaper medical service would result if there were no monopoly. If anyone with some medical knowledge could hang out a shingle, the public would eventually find out who was giving better service and who should not be patronized. Friedman criticizes the guru status we have bestowed on medical doctors, and he claims this hinders finding the most effective and efficient treatment.

---

[40] *Ibid.*

[41] Friedman and Friedman, *Free to Choose*, pp. 150–88.

Milton Friedman acknowledges that his views on the corporation and the socioeconomic system do not possess the depth, insight, or balance of his Nobel Prize-winning work in economics. He fails to grapple with the basic criticisms of free enterprise: It results in costs to third parties, serious inequities, and encourages selfishness. Furthermore, Friedman has little patience for any of the major alternative solutions: public interest group pressures, voluntary actions by management, or government regulation. He is even less interested in cooperative methods of organizing an economy, which were very popular in the last century and continue to be at present.

ALTERNATIVES TO INDIVIDUALISM AND CAPITALISM: COOPERATIVES

Some people who immigrated to the United States organized their economic life cooperatively rather than competitively. In fact, many immigrants, after having experienced life threatening work, exploitative bosses, and child labor, came to the New World precisely to pioneer cooperative living. Hundreds of cooperative communities were formed in the United States during the last 150 years.[42] Each of these communities eventually counted their members in the hundreds and sometimes thousands. The members shared work and income equally. They were opposed to the competition encouraged by capitalism and felt that only through cooperation could a truly human and Christian community develop.

The Shakers were a religious group that began in the United States in 1774 and by the early 1800s had grown to nineteen separate communities scattered throughout New England and the Midwest; their land holdings totaled nearly 100,000 acres.[43] The suburb of Cleveland called Shaker Heights takes its name from the Shaker community that was there. Its beautiful Shaker Lakes were built as millponds by the Shakers. The men and women lived in separate communities; there was little contact between them at work or socially. There was no marriage; new members had to be converted. In the early days there were many converts, and the number of Shakers reached 6,000. They called themselves the *Millennial Church*. It was outsiders who, observing the long, loud, and active shaking movements in their prayer services, dubbed them *Shakers*. Another example of the many communal ventures was Brook Farm, which was located in West Roxbury, within the city of present-day Boston.

---

[42] Rosabeth Moss Kanter, *Commitment and Community* (Cambridge, Mass.: Harvard University Press, 1972); see also David French and Elena French, *Working Communally* (New York: Russell Sage Foundation, 1975), and an earlier account by William A. Hinds, *American Communities* (Chicago: Charles Kerr, 1902).

[43] William A. Hinds, *American Communities*, p. 27; see also Marguerite F. Melcher, *The Shaker Adventure* (Princeton, N.J.: Princeton University Press, 1941), p. 302.

Most of the members of these communities farmed, but many other skills were present. Notable among communities where manufacturing began is the Oneida Community in New York State, which was founded by the minister John Humphrey Noyes in 1848. Although it is no longer a commune, it has paradoxically developed into a multimillion-dollar international company and is now the largest maker of stainless steel tableware in the United States.[44]

Probably the best known communal experiment was New Harmony, Indiana, a community started by Robert Owen. Owen, a wealthy British factory owner, was the first in England to limit the workday to 10 hours. He both advocated and initiated among his employees other work and social reforms. Owen's dream was a community in which all work, life, and leisure would be shared. Unlike most other early commune organizers, Owen's vision was not religious in origin. In 1825, Owen purchased a set of buildings built by a religious community called the Rappites and renamed it New Harmony. He advertised for members and accepted almost all comers; more than 900 arrived, among them some talented and well-known professional people. But because of his other obligations, Owen himself found little time to be at New Harmony. Farming and other basic skills were scarce among the community members, and lack of a common vision and subsequent discord brought the community to an end in 1827, after only 2 years. It was a noble, highly publicized, and expensive experiment, but it was shorter lived than most cooperative communities.

Communities to Aid Others

A much older example of cooperative life are the Benedictine monks, whom we discussed in Chapter 4. Very early, Christians called for sharing one's goods with one's sisters and brothers (Acts 2:44–47). Monastic living is an enduring model of living and working together and sharing goods. However, Catholic orders of women and men, which depend on shared religious values and a lifelong commitment, were never intended for everyone; they are voluntary associations for those who choose them.

In this spirit, there are today within the Roman Catholic Church tens of thousands of women and men in almost every country of the world who choose to live a life together in religious communities. They choose to sacrifice in order to be of greater service to men, women, and God. Examples of these groups are the Religious Sisters of Mercy, Sisters of St. Joseph, Franciscans, Dominicans, Benedictines, Society of Jesus (Jesuits), and hundreds of other groups.

They are led by Jesus Christ in the Gospels to help other women and men, especially those who are poor and most in need, and to try to make the world a better place. They work in hospitals, schools, colleges, and social service agen-

---

[44] Hinds, *American Communities*, pp. 173–214. Concerning its more recent economic success, see "It Started Out as a Commune in 1848, and Today Oneida Is a Thriving Business," *Wall Street Journal*, April 4, 1973, p. 8.

cies. They choose to hold property in common (e.g., salaries, savings, housing, autos, televisions, VCRs, etc.), live in a community in place of having a family, and plan their lives with others in that community. Thus, they seek to be a witness that one can live without being caught up in our most common vices: self-centeredness, materialism, and an overemphasis on sexuality. The author of this book is a member of the Society of Jesus (Jesuits). There remains a steady stream of dedicated young women and men who are entering the vowed Catholic religious communities, and the numbers are increasing in countries like India and Indonesia, where Catholics are a small minority in the total population.[45]

In summary, all of these successful religious and secular cooperative communities began with strong leadership; most were religious in origin. For a community to survive, it must continue to attract vigorous and talented people, not merely the weak and those who are looking for a refuge from the problems of the outside world. Self-discipline and order are necessary to solve the multitude of differences that arise in a community, yet these are impossible to sustain without a shared vision. Many of the early American communes failed after the original leader was gone and the early goals and inspiration for the community began to fade. The Catholic religious communities are much more long-lasting. Communes are not a new social phenomenon. They are a reflection of a deep-rooted desire that people have for humane relationships, cooperation, and communication based on shared values.[46]

Shared Values in a Community

The need to encourage cooperation exists especially in free market societies, where enlightened self-interest pushes people toward individualism and selfishness. Religion is an aid in all societies in bringing people together, giving purpose to life, helping people formulate long-range personal and group goals, and forming character. However, because of its secular bias, Western countries have kept religion at the periphery of public policy and public debate. This placed Western societies in a secular limbo, without strong religious values to support

---

[45] For additional information, see Patricia Wittberg, S.C., *Creating a Future for Religious Life: A Sociological Perspective* (New York: Paulist Press, 1989); Wade Clark Roof, *A Generation of Seekers: The Spiritual Journeys of the Baby Boom Generation* (San Francisco: Harper, 1993); Francis Kelly Nemeck and Marie Theresa Coombs, *Called by God: A Theology of Vocation and Lifelong Commitment* (Collegeville, Minn.: Liturgical Press, 1992). For additional information on specific religious communities, those mentioned in the text and others, check those subject headings in library.

[46] See the special issue of *Business Horizons*, July–August 1991. "Creating the Good Society: To Whom is the Corporation Responsible?" The entire issue, with articles by many leaders in the field, is devoted to the corporation as responsible to society. For a sociological analysis of American communes, see Benjamin Zablocki, *Alienation and Charism: A Study of American Communes* (New York: The Free Press, 1979). A well-written, carefully researched first-hand account of scores of communes of the 1960s in the United States is Robert Houriet's *Getting Back Together* (New York: Coward, McCann & Geoghegan, 1971).

them. Nevertheless, the tide has turned, and in recent years religion is newly respected as a shaper of public and political values.[47]

Excessive individualism in Western countries has spawned problems of crime, the breakdown of the family, and a deserted central city, according to a respected new group. They call themselves *communitarians*. This new group calls for building upon shared values and mutual understandings in order to address our problems. The founder of the group, Dr. Amitai Etzioni, has written *The Spirit of Community*,[48] and has founded a journal, *The Responsive Community* in order to provide a forum for this point of view. Communitarians contend that any society must limit some of what some people claim as "rights," in order to achieve the common good. For example, Etzioni argues that allowing everyone to "do their own thing" undermines both character formation for children, and also long-term public policy. This group of respected people in government and universities is trying to build bridges between the feuding factions of Western society. The attention that communitarians have received indicates that they are espousing the values and goals that many people share.

There are other cooperative models for organizing free markets. Two of these are: (1) European social democracy, and (2) the Mondragon model of cooperative work. The social democracy model is best known in Sweden, Norway, Holland, Germany, and Austria. These societies see government as the conscience of the free market. Jobs are considered the bedrock essential of a society, so Sweden keeps unemployment at less than 2 percent. The Swedes elect to pay 50 percent of their taxes for education, health, housing, and so on. One downside to this system is a decline in caring and volunteerism among ordinary citizens; many come to expect the government to do it all. Another problem is the growth of government bureaucracy.

Mondragon is a group of worker-owned and managed firms in northern Spain. Founded by a Catholic priest, the cooperative businesses have been remarkably successful for more than 60 years. Mondragon now includes more than 100 manufacturing firms, banks, schools, universities, stores, and hospitals and employs thousands of workers. These institutions have also been financially successful. When layoffs are necessary, the cooperative provides 80 percent of salary until they return to work. For those with suitable job skills, Mondragon provides a fine example of prosperity for both individuals and the community.[49]

---

[47] Note the widely acclaimed commentary by Stephen Carter, *The Culture of Disbelief: How American Law and Politics Trivializes Religion* (New York: Basic Books, 1993).

[48] Amitai Etzioni, *The Spirit of Community* (New York: Touchstone Books, 1994). Etzioni's proposal for a less egoistic economic model is favorably reviewed by Bill Shaw and Frances E. Zollers, "Managers in the Moral Dimension: What Etzioni Might Mean to Corporate Managers," *Business Ethics Quarterly* (July 1993): 153–68.

[49] For an overview of these two models, see Charles Derber, "Communitarian Economics: Criticisms and Suggestions from the Left," *The Responsive Community* (Fall 1994): 29–41.

Cooperation in the Workplace

There are many other current attempts to encourage greater cooperation and commitment among members of business firms in order to attain better product quality, create a more humane workplace, and achieve greater profitability. A producer cooperative is an entire work setting built on cooperative ideals. Participative management, employee stock ownership plans, flexible work schedules, and profit sharing are all designed to build greater commitment and cooperation among workers in organizations that are based on the free market model.[50] United Airlines is an example of a firm that is owned by its employees. Employees purchased the firm for $5 billion in 1994, and there is now undreamed-of cooperation to make the airline more efficient and more effective.[51]

A rationale for cooperation with workers, as well as partnership with other "factors of production" comes from the "stakeholder" theory of management. Employees, creditors, suppliers, customers, local communities, government, and other groups all have a "stake" in the business operation, and so deserve consideration. Some stakeholders may share in the appropriate decisions of the firm. Doing this successfully gives a firm legitimacy in society. It demands that executives possess political, as well as management, skills.[52]

Some people perform best when they work cooperatively, while others do better with individual incentives. Individualists are happier and work better when they are given individual tasks to perform and are rewarded with individual incentives. On the other hand, others are more satisfied and operate better when they work cooperatively in a group and are rewarded with group incentives. Collectivists perform more poorly when working alone or in an outgroup than they do working in an ingroup. Thus it is important to know what motivates a particular group of workers. These differences also have implications for managing and setting up incentive systems in different cultures.[53] Why people work, how work can be more satisfying, and the effect of the organization on motivation will all be discussed in the next chapter.

---

[50] See Jon Pierce, Stephen Rubenfeld and Susan Morgan, "Employee Ownership: A Conceptual Model of Process and Effects," *Academy of Management Review* (January 1991): 121–44; Douglas E. Booth, "The Problems of Corporate Bureaucracy and the Producer Cooperative as an Alternative," *Review of Social Economy* 43 (December 1985): 298–315. For a summary of these participation programs, see Chapter 3, "Work and Job Satisfaction," in Gerald F. Cavanagh and Arthur F. McGovern, *Ethical Dilemmas in the Modern Corporation* (Englewood Cliffs, N.J.: Prentice-Hall, 1988).

[51] "United We Own: Employee Ownership is Working at the Airline," *Business Week*, March 18, 1996, pp. 96–103, 124.

[52] The classic exposition of stakeholder theory is R. Edward Freeman, *Strategic Management: A Stakeholder Approach* (Marshfield, Mass.: Pitman, 1984). See also Freeman, "A Stakeholder Theory of Modern Corporation," in Thomas Donaldson and Patricia Werhane, *Ethical Issues in Business* (Englewood Cliffs, N.J.: Prentice-Hall, 1993), pp. 166–171.

[53] R. Christospher Early, "East Meets West Meets Midwest: Further Explorations of Collectivistic and Individualistic Work Groups," *Academy of Management Journal* (April 1993): 319–48. This research was done using Chinese, Israeli, and American subjects.

Summary and Conclusions

Karl Marx pinpointed the weaknesses of the capitalist economic system. He and his followers have shown that a free enterprise economic system has some undesirable consequences. According to Marx, capitalism results in

1. Exploitation of the worker,
2. Alienation of the worker,
3. Big business dominating national policy,
4. Corporations exploiting other countries.

Marxists are at their best in criticizing capitalism. Negative economic and social consequences, such as poverty, unemployment, and crime are certainly not advocated by the defenders of free enterprise. Nevertheless, a critique of capitalism and the market system does raise the question of how priorities are formulated. Who decides what goals of a society are primary? Priorities are discussed only in the political sphere, if at all. And government can regulate and subsidize, but it does not set specific economic goals. Free enterprise advocates defend this nonintervention as more efficient. In theory, free enterprise recognizes only one priority: "Will a given product, service or action return a profit?" The system does not ask how important the need is that is being fulfilled; it has no method of rating products or services on any scale of values other than dollars. Moreover, there are many goods, such as streetlights, police, parks, and public transportation, whose market value does not reflect their long-term value to society as a whole.

Perhaps profits should be the sole concern of business. If that is true, in free market countries, who sets national priorities and implements them? Do individual consumers collectively have the vision to look after the long-term good of themselves and future generations? How did we decide that we should spend more on advertising than on education, or on dog food and cosmetics than on helping hungry peoples feed themselves? How did we decide that automobile travel was better than using urban rapid transit? As we will see in Chapter 8, in a market economy it is not clear where the responsibility for such decisions lies. Those advocating greater business responsibility have pointed to the negative moral and social consequences of some business policies, such as those regarding toxic waste, product safety, plant closings, and energy and resource use. But the issue of national priorities goes beyond these policies.

Efficiency and justice are both important goals for any society. Competition encourages flexibility and efficiency. However, paradoxically self-centeredness and competition by individuals and firms often brings a decline in efficiency. A concern for others and cooperation undergird justice.

In short, it appears that some of the values that we cultivate in the name of efficiency and success now make us less efficient and less successful. Moreover, in the process we can become blind to the importance of cooperation and justice. This much can be gained from considering critiques of free enterprise: an incentive to examine our own personal and national priorities. It helps us to see the inadequacies of our own ideology, so that we may amend it and thus improve our personal and collective ability to live a decent and happy life.

Discussion Questions

1. How do you respond to each of the seven questions posed at the beginning of the chapter?
2. What evidence does Karl Marx provide that capitalism exploits the worker? Is the argument valid? Does income tax rectify the inequality?
3. What evidence does Marx use to sustain his claim that capitalism alienates the worker? Evaluate this claim with respect to the contemporary workplace.
4. How does big business dominate the formulation of national goals? Provide evidence for your answer.
5. How do large corporations exploit poor countries? Cite evidence and explain.
6. Do the four major problems of capitalism cited by Marx stem primarily from capitalism or industrialization? Why?
7. Marxism claims to be materialistic. Is it more materialistic than capitalism or free enterprise? In what way do the goals that Marxism holds out for the average worker transcend materialism?
8. How does one measure the success of a society? By its gross national product? By the average per capita income of its members? By its literature or art? By its care for the poor and disadvantaged? What criteria should be used?
9. Why did Joseph Schumpeter say that capitalism would decay? Compare his views on this subject with those of John Calvin.
10. Describe the origins and characteristics of early American communal societies.
11. How do Catholic and Christian religious orders differ from the early American communal societies in their motivation? In their work ethic? In their ability to last?
12. What elements in a communal society tend to support its continued existence?
13. Outline the comparative advantages and disadvantages of a) cooperative and b) competitive economic systems.
14. Does the current concern for teamwork and worker participation undermine competitive free enterprise?

Exercise:
International Management Consultant

Business today is global. To be successful, businesspeople must understand other cultures and other peoples. A fellow student from another country is a resource for learning about that person's country and its issues. The purpose of this project is to learn about the climate for living and doing business in a country with different customs, expectations, laws, and language. Consult a fellow student from another country for information and help.

Procedure

I. Find a student from another country who will help you. Try not to overburden the consultant.

II. Examine a social issue that faces business, for example:
   A. Equal employment opportunity (minorities or women)
   B. Air or water pollution
   C. Marketing or advertising practices
   D. Safety of products or workplace
   E. Bribery, kickbacks, tax evasion, or other practices
   F. Operation of foreign firms within the country
   G. Host government regulations
   H. Other (check with instructor)

III. Prepare a summary report on a single sheet of paper outlining the following:
   A. Country chosen
   B. Name of international student consultant
   C. The issue or problem examined, with some background
   D. Any special industry or firm involved
   E. Proposal to address the difficulty

CASES
California Sweatshop

On August 2, 1995 authorities raided an El Monte, California, sweatshop that employed 72 illegal immigrants from Thailand. They were often forced to work 17 hours a day, were closely guarded, and held against their will; if they refused to work, they were sent back to Thailand. The Thai workers were making clothing that was sold at retailers like B.U.M. and Mervyn's. Federal authorities had heard about the situation 3 years earlier, but failed to investigate.

After their release, lawyers defending the Thai immigrants obtained more than $1 million in back wages. Government officials said that they thought that the raid and providing back pay would encourage other illegal immigrants to come to the United States.

What ethical norms are involved in this case? Discuss the ethics of the: (a) owners of sweatshop; (b) Thai illegal immigrants; (c) government authorities; (d) clothing retailers.

Superior's Expense Report

Sara McIntyre, a young management accountant at Tuloc, Inc., receives an expense report for reimbursement from Elmer Cole, vice president of the division. The report requests $3,100 for a 2-day trip to Boston, and most of the items have no receipts and seem inflated to McIntyre. What should McIntyre do? What are her obligations and to whom?

CHAPTER

Personal Values Within the Firm

Man is by instinct a lover, a hunter, a fighter, and none of those instincts are given much play at the warehouse!
—Tennessee Williams, *The Glass Menagerie*[*]

Freedom is not the power of doing what we like, but the right of being able to do what we ought.
—John Paul II

T he groups and organizations we are members of—from family to corporation—have a profound influence on our personal values, goals, and ethics, although we are seldom explicitly aware of this influence. Personal values, which are among the basic components of personality, develop from exposure to others. Values are often received uncritically from parents, peers, teachers, and the media. A loving and listening parent encourages values that are quite different from those engendered by a parent who is annoyed, distracted, or absent.

Later, during working years, we often so identify with an organization that success within it becomes a primary measure of personal worth. Performing well at Hewlett-Packard or Dow Chemical tells me what sort of a person I am. When I am with a firm that encourages pride in good work, autonomy, new ideas, and risk taking, that can give me self-confidence and joy in doing my work. On the other hand, personal values are sometimes compromised by a

---

[*] Tennessee Williams, *The Glass Menagerie*, ed. Gilbert L. Rathbun (New York: Random House, 1965). Quoted with permission.

195

business climate that condones unethical acts.[1] Moreover, an individual may identify too closely with work and make "success" on the job the total measure of self-worth. Realization of the inadequacy of that measure often does not come until midlife, and then it brings with it profound anxieties, frustrations, and even serious physical ailments. We discussed stress on the job and the midlife crisis in Chapter 2.[2]

A business firm can and should meet vital individual and social needs. It can enable an individual to achieve a sense of identity and "develop the skills and loyalties that are necessary to sustain the social structure of responsible and ethical organizational life."[3] Ford Motor Parts and Service Division calls itself "the loving and caring division." Levi Strauss encourages all of its employees to use ethics in their actions; it also seeks employee input on all work-related issues. Canon's CEO, Ryuzaburo Kaku, encourages a sense of working and living together for the common good in all business decisions. Avis began employee participation groups when it became 100 percent employee owned, and earnings and stock prices jumped immediately. Domino's Pizza encourages its employees to use the Golden Rule in the workplace. This reinforces human values learned in the family and neighborhood and encourages concern for people— whether they be neighbors, coworkers, suppliers, customers, or subordinates. Each of these firms thus helps their people to maintain an integrated personality, not separating the values of family life from those of the workplace.

Some business firms, and even some universities and hospitals, show little social concern. As we will see later in this chapter, managers of such institutions tend to be more self-centered and show less concern about social conditions and are not willing to make personal gain secondary to helping other people. The values of these managers contrast with the self-image most Americans have of themselves as generous. When personal values are held uncritically, they contain the seeds of potential conflict and anxiety. Leaders of organizations who make decisions based on self-centered values often cause severe social disruption. Note the greedy trading activities of some financial bankers or the "kiss and tell" books by friends and ex-members of the Reagan and Clinton administrations. This is a paradox, since managers conceive of themselves as objective, rational, and not led by personal whim. A good manager insists on a careful analysis of all the facts before coming to a judgment. The use of market surveys, outside consultants, product planning groups, and computer analyses indicates the high priority that rational decision making has within firms. Yet these same managers are

---

[1] William C. Frederick and James Weber, "The Values of Corporate Managers and Their Critics: An Empirical Description and Normative Implications," in *Research in Corporate Social Performance and Policy*, ed. William C. Frederick, vol. 9 (Greenwich, Conn.: JAI Press, 1987), pp. 131–51.

[2] For a more complete description of work and job satisfaction issues, see Gerald F. Cavanagh and Arthur F. McGovern, *Ethical Dilemmas in the Modern Corporation* (Englewood Cliffs, N.J.: Prentice-Hall, 1988), pp. 34–63.

[3] Timothy L. Fort, "Business as Mediating Institution," *Business Ethics Quarterly* 6 (April 1996): 149–63.

often unaware of how much their unexamined personal values bias their decisions; they thus hurt both themselves and their organizations.

Managers are often unaware that the decision-making process itself rests on unexamined assumptions. For beneath this rational structure lie certain presuppositions about the purpose of the firm—to maximize profits, to expand market share, and so on. These very ideological assumptions upon which rational decision making is based are often accepted unquestioningly, much as we accept traditional cultural norms.

Each organization develops a life and norms of its own. Schools give values to children before they are in the workplace. Consider the environment and the values communicated when teachers in two different eras were asked what were the major problems in school (see Fig. 7–1). In 1940 teachers said that major problems were such things as talking out of turn, cutting in line, chewing gum, and running in the halls. In 1992 teachers said that the major problems were such as: alcohol abuse, pregnancy, suicide, and assault.[4]

Just as ethical norms and expectations within schools are affected by the serious problems listed, so too a business is affected by the problems that it faces. An organization's struggle for survival and growth can give apparent legitimacy to many activities that would not be undertaken if subjected to more careful and conscientious scrutiny. These activities often conflict with the personal values of honesty, integrity, and concern for others that are possessed by members of the organization. This conflict may then cause members to reflect on the inconsistency of these personal and organizational values. The inadequacy of an exclusive reliance on market values often does not appear until the values of the firm come into conflict with the values of the larger society. Many of these issues will be discussed in greater detail in Chapter 8.

FIGURE 7–1 Student Discipline Problems

Teachers' Listing of Discipline Problems in School

1940	*1992*
Talking out of turn	Drug abuse
Making noise	Alcohol abuse
Cutting in line	Pregnancy
Littering	Suicide
Chewing gum	Rape
Running in halls	Robbery
Dress code infractions	Assault

Source: Congressional Quarterly Researcher, September 11, 1992.
Quoted with permission.

---

[4] *Congressional Quarterly Researcher*, September 11, 1992. Quoted in *The Responsive Community* (Summer 1993): 56.

This chapter will examine *personal values in the workplace*, including the following topics:

1. the influence of *organizational values, climate, and expectations* on the values of individuals;

2. *goals and motives of individuals* and how motives are affected by personal values and ethics;

3. *accomplishment and pressures* within the organization, and how these contribute to personal health or illness.

THE ORGANIZATION'S FORMATIVE INFLUENCE: SOCIALIZATION

Any group of people working together must share goals and values, otherwise they experience confusion and conflict. Hence socialization is essential in any human endeavor. Formal socialization (see Fig. 7–2) is the planned and deliberate attempt by the organization to affect the attitudes of members. Informal socialization takes place among members through ordinary interaction. Many values are introduced in orientation and training programs, but they are specified by exposure to the expectations of superiors and peers 40 hours a week. Socialization takes place through language, stories, songs, and myth that are passed down through the organization.[5] When coupled with the perceived importance of success in the firm, such socialization brings changes in and rein-

FIGURE 7–2 Socialization Within the Organization

Types of Socialization	*Methods of Socialization*
FORMAL	1. Orientation program
	2. Job descriptions and work procedures
	3. Management development and training programs
	4. Codes of behavior
	5. Performance appraisal and feedback
INFORMAL	1. Expectations of superiors
	2. Actions of and conversations with peers
	3. Unwritten norms
	4. Organizational culture

[5] For current research on socialization and related issues, see Harrison M. Trice and Janice M. Beyer, *The Cultures of Work Organizations* (Englewood Cliffs, N.J.: Prentice-Hall, 1993), esp. pp. 129–73. Also Gareth R. Jones, "Socialization Tactics, Selfefficacy, and Newcomers' Adjustments to Organizations," *Academy of Management Journal* 29 (June 1988): 262–79; Douglas T. Hall, "Careers and Socialization," *Journal of Management* 13 (April 1987): 301–21.

forcement of values. For example, Disney Productions, both through formal and informal socialization, insures that new members know how to make "guests" feel welcome and comfortable.

The organization has its own demands, which arise from the activities directed toward maintaining the health of the organization. These activities are often determined by the market values of profitability, market share, and return on investment. Organizational maturity and stability, without profitability and growth, are not acceptable goals for the long term; chief executive officers have been fired for having such unaggressive goals. Moreover, organizations affect almost every segment of our lives, and hence our moral lives also. As some put it, "Because modern organizations have created and have largely defined the American value system, they must be considered the most important socializing agencies in America."[6]

Work climates have a strong influence on the ethical values and thus the actions of members of an organization. Expecially in earlier decades this fact was not well recognized, but has recently generated much interest among scholars.[7] From 1950 to 1980, which were years of American business success, many American firms became large and bureaucratic. They are now trying to be more innovative and flexible in order to meet international competition. But organizations generally change their goals and values only in the face of new demands from the outside. Without such challenges, they tend to continue to operate in ways that were successful in the past, and they thus become more rigid as the years go by.

Organizations are generally effective in selecting individuals and then socializing them into persons who "fit well" into the system. Each organization has a subtle but potent influence on its members' attitudes, values, and ethics. As sociologist Robert Merton puts it,

> The bureaucrat's official life is planned for him in terms of a graded career through the organizational devices of promotions by seniority, pensions, incremental salaries, etc., all of which are designed to provide incentives for disciplined action and conformity to artificial regulations. The official is tacitly expected to and largely does adapt his thoughts, feelings, and actions to the prospect of his career. But these very devices which increase the probability of conformance also lead to an overconcern with strict adherence to regulations which induce timidity, conservatism, and technicism. Displacement of sentiments from

---

[6] Deborah Vidaver Cohen, "Moral Climate in Business Firms: A Framework for Empirical Research," in *Academy of Management Proceedings—'95*, ed. Dorothy P. Moore (Vancouver, B.C., 1995). The original quote is from William G. Scott and David K. Hart, *Organizational America* (Boston: Houghton Mifflin, 1979), p. 36.

[7] For an overview of this work, see James Weber, "Emphasizing the *Ethical* in Ethical Work Climates," paper presented at National Academy of Management—1993, Atlanta; also Linda K. Trevino and G. Weaver, "Business ETHICS/BUSINESS Ethics," *Business Ethics Quarterly* 4 (1994): 113–28; Bart Victor and John Cullen, "The Organizational Basis of Ethical Work Climates," *Administrative Science Quarterly* (March 1988): 101–125.

goals onto means is fostered by the tremendous symbolic significance of the means [rules].[8]

Another sociologist, Robert Jackall, paints an unflattering picture of American corporate bureaucracy. On the basis of extensive interviews with managers, he points out that managerial decisions are made on a short-term basis. Moreover, most firms reward this short-term perspective, and generally reward on the basis of political considerations rather than performance and merit. The most important thing that is learned in the corporation is mastering expectations and fitting in.[9]

Most large organizations offer many examples of such shortsighted and inflexible behavior. For example, banks tend to be conservative and bureaucratic. Risk taking and flexibility traditionally were not as important for banks. A large, rigid organization develops a life of its own, protecting its own special interests and being jealous of its own position, power, and prerogatives. The corporation's procedures, especially when they have been successful in the past, can become rigid and ossified. Each individual is expected to "learn Mitsubishi's way of doing things." Managers select for promotion subordinates who have values like their own. Although these managers pride themselves on making objective and rational decisions, there is evidence that personal likes and values play an important role.

In large organizations, coordination between people and business units is essential. As various responsibilities are spelled out in writing, there is less room for individual judgment. Even in decentralized companies that are trying to be more flexible, standard practices and procedures limit new ideas and initiatives. Deviant values are eliminated, either in the selection process or through socialization. It thus becomes clear which values are accepted and which are not, for example, whether it is preferred behavior to wear a tie or not, to come to work early and stay late, or to file for overtime.

In any organization, the competitive, achievement-oriented manager wants to be noticed quickly as a success. Such a manager then tends to focus on short-run performance, as it is more easily measured and will provide early favorable notice to top management. Market values tend to crowd out personal and social values.

Accomplishment and Loyalty at Work

In an attempt to address the above problems of bureaucracy and the inefficiencies that go with it, many firms have engaged in "reengineering." During the

---

[8] Robert K. Merton, "Bureaucratic Structure and Personality," in *Organizations: Structure and Behavior*, ed. Joseph A. Litterer, 3rd ed. (New York: Wiley, 1980), pp. 232–33. For one attempt to overcome these attitudes through training, see "How Am I Doing: The Creative Management Approach Uses Tough Love," *Business Week*, Oct. 23, 1995, pp. 72–74.

[9] Robert Jackall, *Moral Mazes: The World of Corporate Managers* (New York: Oxford University Press, 1988).

first seven months of 1993, more than 350,000 workers lost their jobs.[10] In order to cut costs to meet world competition, AT&T, GM, Briggs & Stratton, and hundreds of other firms have engaged in extensive layoffs. Job reductions continue at a rapid pace. Partially as a result of these new efforts, productivity and profits have increased, yet wages are not increasing.[11] The downsizing has had an immense human cost. As *Business Week* put it:

> Today's corporation is no longer a secure or stable place. It's an uncertain, turbulent environment where managers often find their compassion and humanity in conflict with pressures of competition and ambition. Fear is almost palpable in the corridors of the reengineered work place, where loyalty takes a backseat to survival and personal advancement.[12]

Acknowledging that much job security and loyalty have now evaporated, some maintain that if an employer is honest and provides satisfying work they can expect a new form of commitment from workers. In spite of their insecurity, people still hope that their work will provide satisfaction and fulfillment. Satisfaction generally comes from doing a job well and contributing to the happiness of others.[13] This conviction that one's life is worthwhile gives not only satisfaction but also energy and focus to one's work. Large organizations and efficiency demand specialization of tasks and interchangeability of personnel. As work is divided up and depersonalized, much of the joy of successfully accomplishing tasks is taken away. Whether manufacturing products or providing services, workers rarely produce finished goods by themselves. They perform a small portion of the entire job, since specialization of labor lowers costs. The large firm often furthers this segmenting of labor, creating a greater physical distance between the individual worker and the finished product.

As a result, in industrial society something that is vital and essential for human life is neglected and repressed. Satisfaction, pride in work, and a sense of ownership are lacking. The goals of a firm—production and growth—take precedence over the goals of individuals. When nonhuman objectives are valued over persons, the result is isolation, loneliness, and alienation. Even though there are more conveniences and more wealth, life is often less fulfilling.

Our expectations have been raised by advertising only to be dashed by reality. In the act of accumulating wealth and developing sophisticated technology,

---

[10] Michael Hammer and James Champy, *Reengineering the Corporation* (New York: Harper, 1994). The figures are from W. McKinley, C. Sanchez, and A. Schick, "Organizational Downsizing: Constraining, Cloning, Learning," *Academy of Management Executive* (August 1995): 32–39; see also "Reengineering: the Hot New Managing Tool," *Fortune*, August 23, 1993, pp. 41–48.

[11] "The Wage Squeeze: Productivity and Profits Are Up a Lot. Paychecks Aren't," *Business Week*, July 17, 1995, pp. 54–62.

[12] "The Pain of Downsizing," *Business Week*, May 9, 1994, pp. 60–69. The harsh effect on supervisors of implementing layoffs is told in Lee Smith, "Burned-out Bosses," *Fortune*, July 25, 1994, pp. 44–52.

[13] Brian Dumaine, "Why Do We Work?" *Fortune*, December 26, 1994, pp. 196–204; also Brian O'Reilly, "New Deal: What Companies and Employees Owe One Another," *Fortune*, June 13, 1994, pp. 44–52.

we often lose a sense of achieving and contributing to something worthwhile. We repeatedly emphasize material wealth more than the person. This tension is one of the causes of "career crises." It is important for all who are employed, whether with their hands or their minds, to have work that is meaningful.

One reason for our lack of satisfaction is that our work ethic no longer has a foundation. When the Protestant ethic was the basic value system for Americans, personal values supported work values. As Daniel Bell sees it, this is not now the case:

> What this abandonment of Puritanism and the Protestant Ethic does is to leave capitalism with no moral or transcendental ethic. It also emphasizes an extraordinary contradiction within the social structure itself. On the one hand, the business corporation wants an individual to work hard, pursue a career, accept delayed gratification—to be, in the crude sense, an organization man. And yet, in its products and its advertisements, the corporation promotes pleasure, instant joy, relaxing and letting go. One is to be "straight" by day and a "swinger" by night.[14]

This paradox is demonstrated in self-seeking individualism, which tears apart families, neighborhoods, and business firms.

Money As the Goal

Corporate and material values influence many Americans. To foreign observers, it sometimes appears as if everything Americans do is directed toward providing and acquiring material goods. A few manifestations of this orientation are advertising, the centrality of work life, and designer clothes. Americans act as if they believed that "happiness is a new minivan or a vacation home." We conceive of ourselves in terms of the goods we purchase and use. For example, consider the attitudes of today's college students, who mirror our cultural values. More than 73 percent of college freshmen surveyed around the United States believe that being financially well-off is a very important goal. This number has remained stable for about 2 decades, since it rose from a low of 40 percent in 1970. Compare this with another goal. In 1970, 83 percent of college freshmen thought that developing a meaningful philosophy of life was very important; in 1994, the percentage was only 43 percent.[15]

The goals of college frosh reflect the goals of their elders. Consider the salaries of entertainers, sports figures, and CEOs; their compensation is immense and disproportionate to their contribution. Encouraging shortsightedness and greed, a national U.S. business magazine ran a cover story with the title: "Are You Paid Enough?—Unless You Earn Four Times Your Age, The Answer is Probably NO." Derek Bok, former president of Harvard University, is trou-

---

[14] Daniel Bell, *The Cultural Contradictions of Capitalism* (New York: Basic Books, 1976), pp. 71–72.

[15] "Disengaged Freshman: Interest in Politics Among First-year Students Is at a 29-year Low," *Chronicle of Higher Education*, January 15, 1995, pp. A29–31.

bled by the immense salaries of corporate CEOs.[16] We will discuss executive compensation in the next chapter.

Economic goals and business values can have a profound influence on our political values as well. Business lobbying often has a decisive influence on domestic legislation and foreign policy. Economics is dominant when we go to war in Kuwait to prevent our oil supply from being cut off.

In the last chapter we examined Karl Marx's position that an industrial society separates people from their work and alienates them. Is working in fact an attractive and rewarding activity for most people? We know that assembly line work, along with repetitive work in fast food and other organizations, provide little job satisfaction. Lack of satisfaction occurs when work is cut into small segments, supervisors are distant and impersonal, and there is little pride in the final product. In many of these jobs, workers are used like single-purpose tools. Such jobs thus demand little intelligence or imagination, and the workers have little control over the work or the work setting. Productivity and efficiency are valued over pride, responsibility, and the joy that can be gotten from work.

Job satisfaction is reduced by job specialization. A firm spends thousands of dollars training an employee for a specific position. As years go by, the employee desires a job that is more challenging. However, the firm has an investment in this employee. It is to the firm's short-term advantage not to make a change, since it is expensive to train another employee and would take time for a new person to gain competence. Therefore, the firm does not make a change. The employee thus remains in the position and becomes bored and dissatisfied with the job, and frustrated with self and the company.

Another factor that has undermined respect for work is its presentation on TV. When did you last see a film or a TV program that showed a businessperson who worked hard, produced a valuable product, built teamwork among her colleagues, and was satisfied with her work? A PBS documentary entitled, "Hollywood's Favorite Heavy: Businessmen on Prime Time TV," was partially underwritten by Mobil Oil. In their own editorial Mobil cites the findings of the documentary, "By the age of 18, the average kid has seen businessmen on TV attempt over 10,000 murders." The narrator says that businesspeople on TV "seem to make an awful lot of money, without ever having to work hard or produce useful products. To succeed, all they seem to do is lie, steal, cheat, blackmail, even murder." The documentary then shows film clips of popular TV shows in which all of the above take place.

On the other hand, in most TV shows school and work are both treated as frustrating, boring, trivial, and/or a joke. One who works in TV and who is also a critic names many specific shows that place work in a poor light. He then asks why we cannot have some TV that shows work as a worthwhile human activity:

---

[16] Derek Bok, *The Cost of Talent* (New York: Free Press, 1993); and *Fortune*, June 26, 1995, pp. 66–76.

People smart enough to make brilliant shows like "Cheers" or "The Wonder Years" or "Cosby" or "L.A. Law" easily have it in their power to do what Arthur Miller did in *Death of a Salesman*, what Norman Lear did in "All in the Family," and what many other writers have done before them: to show that discipline, work, and all the habits that make people and nations self-sufficient and proud of themselves are not for losers but for winners.[17]

When faced with poor quality and low productivity, American firms encouraged more input from workers through job redesign, job enrichment, and total quality management. Workers in production often have creative ideas on how to produce the product efficiently.

Executives often demonstrate a lack of concern for people. Managers sometimes think that their attention must be restricted to the short-term, bottom-line goals of better productivity, higher return on investment, and a larger share of the market. The individuals who are attracted and make it to the corporate executive suite have a great need for success. To attain their goals, they must be able to make decisions unencumbered by emotional ties to persons or groups. They must always be ready to move to a new location and leave old friends and associations behind. They must have sufficient detachment from their friends and neighborhoods. In fact, for many there is little point in making deep friendships or getting involved in local activities; it would only make parting more difficult. In his study of the executive personality, William Henry concludes,

> The corporate executive is a special type, spawned on impersonality and hurried into the task of defending his individuality in the diffuse and open competition of nonfamily life. His energy to prove his competence again and again is extreme, and his need to re-create a safe and personalized nest is minimal. Undeterred by other than the purely conventional in personal life, he is able without sense of loss to devote his entire life to the executive task.[18]

Those attracted to corporate executive work are often people who do not depend on close personal relationships. They obtain their major satisfaction from completing a task. Their personal values set the tone for the organization; these values are communicated to others in the firm. It is clear to all that the successful people are more task- than person-oriented.

Winners and Self-Developers Among Managers

After interviewing managers in large, high-technology companies, Michael Maccoby concluded that such people were not primarily interested in skills, power, or loyalty but rather in "organizing winning teams."[19] Hence he charac-

---

[17] Benjamin Stein, "Work Gets No Respect on TV," *The Responsive Community* (Fall 1993): 32–37.

[18] William E. Henry, "Executive Personality and Large-scale Organizations," in *The Emergent American Society*, ed. W. Lloyd Warner et al., vol. 1 (New Haven: Yale University Press, 1967), p. 275.

[19] Michael Maccoby, *The Gamesman: The New Corporate Leaders* (New York: Simon & Schuster, 1976), p. 34.

terized successful managers as "gamesmen." Gamesmen develop many positive intellectual characteristics to aid in "winning the game" (e.g., analysis, problem solving, and policy development), but at the same time they allow their emotional life to atrophy. They are more detached and emotionally inaccessible than others in the corporate hierarchy.

Gamesmen do not have a "developed heart." They lack compassion and appreciation for suffering—they cannot even bear to look at suffering. Maccoby calls them "weak hearted." Most younger managers are weak-hearted gamesmen. For Maccoby, a strong-hearted manager is able to understand and to empathize with the suffering that may come from a particular business decision. The strong hearted make the best executives in Maccoby's judgment.

Gamesmen also have little sense of social responsibility. Unaware of and hence unconcerned about the social and human effects of their actions on others, they operate on the primitive notion that the growth of their organization will automatically benefit poor people. They refuse to consider undesirable secondary effects.

Although most of the gamesmen that Maccoby interviewed indicated that they wanted friendship and help from their friends, fewer than 10 percent said that helping others was a personal goal. This contrasts with more than half of a group of factory workers who mentioned helping others as a personal goal. Maccoby found managers in Mexico to be "more aware than Americans that their careers protect them from the poor, but even the Mexican executives are not aware that within their enclaves they are becoming more alienated from themselves." Around their houses they have built walls, and on top of those walls they put broken glass or spikes to prevent the intrusion of "outsiders." In a similar way, many affluent neighborhoods in the United States and in other countries now have walls and guardhouses to separate the wealthy from poor people.

Gamesmen set out to be "winners." Their alert, aggressive behavior does make them successful in focused tasks at work. However, they trade off much of their affective life. The fatal danger of gamesmen is to be trapped in perpetual adolescence, striving to be a winner at the game throughout adulthood.[20]

In a later study, Maccoby identified a growing group among young managers: self-developers.[21] Self-developers value opportunities to learn, grow, and gain a sense of competence and independence in an egalitarian workplace. Wary of being swallowed up by work, they are less likely to become corporate chiefs than are gamesmen. More concerned with learning and cooperation, they are motivated to succeed in family life as well as in their careers and to balance work with play. In the future, with fewer layers of middle management and more moving from one firm to another, it will be important that people be able

---

[20] *Ibid.*, pp. 109, 203.
[21] Michael Maccoby, *Why Work?* (New York: Simon & Schuster, 1988).

to manage themselves. The self-developers have those qualities, and seem better adapted to business in the year 2000 than do gamesmen.

Dissent in the Organization

The importance of independent judgment has always been recognized by Americans. But although we mouth our support of independent judgment, experience and research indicate that it does not hold the high priority we claim for it. In fact, the attitudes of the group have a profound influence on the individual through informal socialization. Individuals are often willing to deny their own perceptions and judgments because of the attitudes of their group.

One of the classic experiments in studying the influence of groups on the judgment of members was done by Solomon E. Asch.[22] Asch gathered groups of seven to nine engineering students at MIT for "psychological experiments in visual judgment." Members of each group were shown two cards simultaneously; one card bore a standard line, the other bore three lines, one of which was the same length as the one shown on the first card (See Fig. 7–3). They were asked, which line is the same length as line X? Is it A, B, or C? In each group, all but one member were "confederates" (i.e., instructed ahead of time to pick the same incorrect line). The remaining member was "naive" and was the only real subject of the experiment. The question at issue was: How often would a group member pick the right line even in the face of unanimous agreement by the rest of the group that another was the right one? It was visually quite clear which line was the same length as X, and ordinarily only 1 percent of the subjects would pick the wrong line. The subject was seated near the end of the group so that most of the others had responded by the time it was the subject's turn to do so.

FIGURE 7–3 Line Perception Experiment

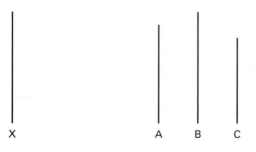

Is line X the same length as A, B, or C?

---

[22] Solomon E. Asch, "Opinions and Social Pressure," in *Science, Conflict and Society* (San Francisco: Freeman, 1969), pp. 52–57.

For our reputedly individualistic society, the findings are significant: Faced with incorrect answers by the majority, 75 percent of real subjects erred as well. Only 25 percent braved conflict with the group and held to their own perceptions. As Asch points out, when a majority of reasonably intelligent and educated young students will call black "white" when faced with the opinions of the group, it is obvious that we lose much of the benefit of individuals' independent assessments of reality. The opinions and values of the majority can become a tyranny. We can easily see this in Cuba or Iran but are less able to see it in our own society.

In spite of their positive contributions, persons who exercise independent judgment are not always popular in an organization. This was shown in experiments with problem-solving groups. A "deviant," a person whose values and attitudes did not coincide with those of the group, was placed in half the groups. In every case, the groups with a deviant had a better solution to the problem they were given than did the homogeneous groups. Each group was then asked to eliminate one member of the group before receiving the next problem. In every case, the deviant was thrown out, and this in spite of the fact that it was fairly clear the deviant had contributed significantly to the work they had done.[23]

Groups generally value harmony and unity more than new information and challenge. This behavior is sometimes called *groupthink*. It describes a deterioration of an individual's mental efficiency, reality testing, and moral judgment as a result of group pressures.[24] The suppression of dissent among those in working groups results in failure, often disastrous failure, as important information and options are not brought forward. Hence it is important to provide a vehicle for the expression of dissent. For example, the lack of a means by which the Morton Thiokol engineers could have warned the managers of the Challenger space launch about the dangers of a launch at below freezing temperatures resulted in disaster and loss of life. In order to lessen the danger of such blockage of vital information and other problems, General Dynamics has established an ombudsman and an ethics hotline at each company facility. Both can be called anonymously to ask questions or to report information.

Other experiments have shown that in a group, individual competitive behavior (individuals looking exclusively to their own success and satisfaction) often leads to disruption and inefficiency in the group's effort. Competitive behavior may lead to greater efficiency when the job can be done entirely by an individual working alone. So, in spite of the American myth, in most settings, including business, cooperative behavior leads to greater efficiency than does overly competitive behavior.[25]

[23] Elise Boulding, *Conflict: Management in Organizations* (Ann Arbor, Mich.: Foundation for Research on Human Behavior, 1964), p. 54.

[24] I. L. Janis, *Groupthink* (Boston: Houghton Mifflin, 1982); see the discussion of groupthink in Stephen P. Robbins, *Organizational Psychology* (Englewood Cliffs: Prentice Hall, 1993), pp. 348–50.

[25] Alfie Kohn, "How to Succeed Without Even Vying," *Psychology Today* (September 1986): 22–28.

In sum, corporations tend to inculcate and thus perpetuate their own values. Like other organizations, corporations have the goals of survival and growth. These goals, plus the private enterprise goals of profit and return on investment, have a profound influence on the attitudes and values of a corporation's members. Members learn to accept the rules of the game that exist implicitly in their organization. Although creativity is of long-term benefit to the firm, it is not easily tolerated. The material goals of the firm often force individuals into judging the success of their work in numerical terms: numbers of product and dollars of profit. The bias toward the concrete and measurable is widespread because of their objectivity. But this bias can easily undermine long-range and human values, such as creativity, trust, and openness.

WHY PEOPLE WORK: MOTIVATION AND IDEOLOGY

Why people work is no mere academic question. Hundreds of studies of motivation are done each year, and there are few academic quests that have such practical implications. Executives regularly ask how to better motivate their associates and workers.

One of the challenges for the concerned executive and the researcher is to determine how a firm can pursue its objectives effectively and at the same time encourage the development of its members as persons. From the viewpoint of the person, social scientists have demonstrated that an individual can grow toward full maturity and achieve self-actualization only in an interpersonal atmosphere of complete trust and open communication.[26] Open, trusting interpersonal relationships are essential to maturation. Working relationships can seldom attain the necessary openness and trust. Moreover, if the working climate inhibits personal growth, it will result in frustration and, eventually, a poor working environment. Managers are therefore especially concerned about the quality of working relationships within the organization. From the viewpoint of the firm, Charles Handy summarizes the issue, "The organization which treats people as assets, requiring maintenance, love, and investment, can behave quite differently from the organization which looks upon them as costs, to be reduced wherever and whenever possible."[27]

Many business executives have become interested in supporting the personal growth of their employees. At 3M, Levi Strauss, and Digital, for example, executives know that the abilities of their employees can best be tapped by

---

[26] Herbert A. Shepard, "Changing Interpersonal and Intergroup Relationships in Organizations," in *Handbook of Organizations*, ed. James G. March (New York: Garland, 1987), pp. 1122–37. For recent research, see Roger Mayer, James Davis and David Schoorman, "An Integrative Model of Organizational Trust," *Academy of Management Review* (July 1995): 709–734.

[27] Charles Handy, *The Age of Unreason* (Boston: Harvard Business School Press, 1990), p. 24.

means of such support. It has even been shown that such support can indirectly improve flexibility, innovation, and product quality. The case for shared decisions and for encouraging individual initiative and creativity has been building for decades. One indication of the concern firms have for these issues is the size of their training budgets and the amount of time and effort they spend encouraging shared decision making and cooperation on the job. A variety of theories of motivation have been proposed over the years. Here we will examine a few that take account of the role of values and ideologies.

Personal Growth Within the Organization

People in firms ask for more communication, more participation, and more opportunity for individual initiative. Yet executives are not always able to perceive the importance of providing challenging and satisfying work, encouraging a sense of ownership, allowing flexibility, and motivating employees to make their best effort.[28] It is important to note that everyone benefits from the working environment that results. These policies not only serve the individual need for self-development but also provide the foundation for improved product or service quality, new ideas, and greater efficiencies.

When psychologists ask why people work, they now generally look at values. What sort of values move the employee to work?[29] Most older theories of motivation popular with businesspeople rarely discussed values, goals, or ideologies. These theories generally presupposed traditional goals. By ignoring values and goals, motivational theorists implied that they were unimportant; they thus did both people and business a disservice. Among the questions we might ask about popular theories and practices of motivation are these: To what extent do they imply values and goals? Do they presuppose goals or predispose one toward certain goals? Do these theories aid in a search for values and goals or do the theories mask their absence?

But businesspeople now know that there is an intimate relationship between personal values and motivation. Product quality and production efficiencies depend on the values and goals of the firm as articulated by the chief executive. The recent and highly popular books and lectures of Stephen Covey, Tom Peters, Peter Senge, and others demonstrate that effective leadership is based on

---

[28] Robert C. Ford and Myron D. Fottler, "Empowerment: A Matter of Degree," *Academy of Management Executive* (August 1995): 21–31. Robert H. Rosen, *Healthy Companies: A Human Resource Approach* (New York: American Management Association, 1986); also "Managers Underrate Employee Values," *Administrative Management* (July 1987): 8.

[29] For an overview of the literature on motivation, see Stephen Robbins, *Organizational Behavior*, 6th ed. (Englewood Cliffs: Prentice-Hall, 1993), especially pp. 203–281; and Richard M. Steers, *Introduction to Organizational Behavior* (Glenview, Ill.: Scott, Foresman, 1988), esp. pp. 153–76, 181–209.

clear values and goals that are utilized by all managers in the firm.[30] The current increased interest in motivation has coincided with, and perhaps partially caused, an increased interest in values, ethics, and ideologies.

Ideologies are, as we have seen, products of deliberate reflection and articulation. However, social scientists warn us to be suspicious of stated reasons for actions. We are often victims, they remind us, of unconscious motives that have a powerful influence on our actions. We may think we know why we do something and respond with an answer when asked. But according to psychologists, we may not even know the real reason at all. In short, the inquiry into values is not aided by psychologists who imply that straightforward verbal statements are generally self-deceiving and untrue. We now turn to several psychologists who have classical theories of motivation that are highly influential. We are especially interested in how they treat the relationship between motivation and values.

Self-Actualization

Abraham H. Maslow proposed that motivation arises from a hierarchy of needs. Maslow based his theory of motivation on observations of healthy, mature persons. For individuals to develop their own internalized philosophical and religious values, "lower needs" (food, water, safety, and security) must be somewhat satisfied. Maslow found that as lower needs were satisfied, they ceased to be motivators. The person then moved on to "higher needs" (belongingness, love, self-esteem, and self-actualization), so that healthy persons are primarily motivated by their needs to develop their capacities and actualize their potentialities to the fullest.[31]

The higher needs are not dominant, according to Maslow. For all peoples these needs are important for the person, but they often do not emerge in people who do not have enough to eat or a roof over their heads. In Maslow's words, "The human needs for love, for knowledge or for philosophy, are weak and feeble rather than unequivocal and unmistakable; they whisper rather than shout. And the whisper is easily drowned out."

Maslow maintains that as individuals become more mature and accepting, they will establish their own values. He concludes that a firm foundation for a value system is furnished by open acceptance of one's own self, "of human nature, of much of social life, and of nature and physical reality." A society made up largely of self-actualizers is characterized by more free choice and nonintru-

---

[30] Stephen R. Covey, *Principle Centered Leadership* (New York: Fireside, 1992), and his *Seven Habits of Highly Effective People* (New York: Fireside, 1990); Peter Senge, *The Fifth Discipline* (New York: Currency, 1995); also Thomas J. Peters and Robert H. Waterman, Jr., *In Search of Excellence* (New York: Harper & Row, 1982).

[31] Abraham H. Maslow, *Motivation and Personality* (New York: Harper & Row, 1954), pp. 35–58.

siveness. Under these conditions, "the deepest layers of human nature would show themselves with greater ease."[32]

Maslow goes on to describe the personal characteristics of the people he has examined—those whom he calls self-actualizers. They tend to be "strongly focused on problems outside themselves"; they are problem-centered rather than ego-centered. Most often these mature, self-actualized individuals have "some mission in life, some task to fulfill," a task outside themselves that enlists most of their energies. Such tasks are generally unselfish; they are directed primarily toward the good of others. Furthermore, self-actualizers have wide horizons; their major concerns are not ego-centered, tribal, or petty. They seem to have a stability that enables and encourages them to address large ethical and social issues.

Maslow describes in detail their ethical values. Self-actualizers "are strongly ethical, they have definite moral standards, they do right and do not do wrong." They are less confused about their basic values. It is easier for them to distinguish right from wrong, although their judgments do not always coincide with those of the accepted, conventional, surrounding culture.

Maslow holds that as persons grow and mature, they will become less selfish and more concerned with other people and larger problems. Their values will become clearer, more explicit, and highly ethical. Indeed, although Maslow finds that these people are not always theists and that some have little loyalty to an institutional church, they are nevertheless the sort who could be described as godly or devout people.[33]

Maslow is convinced that ethical values emerge as a person matures. In fact, he implies that the development of unselfish goals and internalized ethical principles can only occur as a person matures. He therefore has little sympathy for a study of values, ethics, asceticism, or a spirituality that seeks to develop unselfish ethical principles and goals. In Maslow's view, people must become self-actualized before unselfish goals and policies can be developed. However, two questions: Will such moral development and maturity ever characterize most leaders and policy makers? Can the problems that face people and nations wait for this maturity to come about? We now turn to theories of motivation that explicitly inquire into the effect of the values of businesspeople.

Need for Achievement and Power

A need for achievement and a need for power are often strong motivations for businesspeople. Entrepreneurs generally have a high need for achievement; corporate executives often have both a high need for achievement and a high need

---

[32] *Ibid.*, pp. 276–78.

[33] *Ibid.*, pp. 168–69. Some empirical verification of Maslow's model is provided by Jean Davis-Sharts, "An Empirical Test of Maslow's Theory of Need Hierarchy Using Hologeistic Comparison by Statistical Sampling," *Advances in Nursing Science* (October 1986): 58–72.

for power. David C. McClelland has examined the need for achievement and the need for power. He finds that the success of an individual or a society is generally positively correlated with a high need for achievement. A person's need for achievement can be measured; it can even be increased, according to McClelland.

McClelland examines the long-range impact of a person's ideology on motivation. Just as we did in Chapter 4, McClelland cites Max Weber on the contribution of the Protestant ethic to attitudes that support modern capitalism.[34] Protestantism encouraged independence and self-reliance. Since the church was no longer the central agency for communicating values, individuals became independent.

Attitudes of independence, self-reliance, and the need for achievement are influenced by the manner in which parents bring up their children. From the content of children's stories, dreams, daydreams, and fantasies, McClelland is able to determine whether there is a high or a low need for achievement. Since parents' own values and ideology influence which stories they tell their children and which books they give them, parents thus have a profound effect on their children's motivation. In experimental work, researchers found that boys who showed a high need for achievement had mothers who expected their sons to master a number of activities early in life—to know their way around the city, be active and energetic, try hard to get things for themselves, do well in competition, and make their own friends.[35] On the other hand, the mothers of boys with a low need for achievement reported that they had restricted their sons more. These mothers did not want their sons to make important decisions by themselves or to make friends with children not approved by their parents.

McClelland theorizes that the Protestant Reformation encouraged a new character type possessing a more vigorous and independent spirit. This spirit of self-reliance was then passed on through child-rearing patterns, and McClelland holds that self-reliance forms the foundation for modern capitalism. He cites evidence that the need for achievement is increased as an effect of an ideological or religious conversion, for example, to Fundamentalism, Marxism, or Catholicism.[36] In the wake of the reflection and forced reassessment a conversion entails, a felt challenge and a resulting need for achievement emerge. According to McClelland, religion, ideology, and values are inextricably intertwined with motivation, especially the need for achievement. Their relationship is especially close when a person reassesses and changes his or her values.

McClelland cites Florence in the late Middle Ages as an example of a society where the need for achievement was expressed in art. When one sees the cathedrals of Europe built in the Middle Ages, or the magnificent extant reli-

---

[34] Max Weber, *The Protestant Ethic and the Spirit of Capitalism*, trans. Talcott Parsons (New York: Scribner, 1958).

[35] David C. McClelland, *The Achieving Society* (Princeton, N.J.: Van Nostrand, 1961), pp. 46–50.

[36] *Ibid.*, pp. 406–17.

gious temples built by the ancient civilizations in Mexico, it becomes clear that for many cultures religion was the major means of expressing achievement. However, in modern societies business may be *the* major outlet for the need for achievement. So McClelland's practical criterion for the success (and hence implicit goal) of the achiever today is economic growth. In using this criterion, McClelland accepts traditional business ideology and the prevailing social norms of industrial society—that economic growth is the final goal of a people.

McClelland acknowledges that achievement is measured in money, but he denies that the businessperson with a high need for achievement is motivated by money.[37] Money is a *symbol* of success. An increase in salary is a sign of success and is the reward to one who achieves; it is often demonstrated to friends and neighbors by a new sport-utility vehicle, an Armani suit, or a home in Aspen. Some observations by Erich Fromm on money as a measure of personal success will be examined later in this chapter.

People with a high need for achievement are more likely to achieve when they can be their own boss. Someone who begins a business—an entrepreneur—is motivated by a high need for achievement. Executives with a high need for achievement tend to centralize power and want credit for their achievements.[38] Given that most new jobs are created in firms with less than 100 employees, business (and hence society as a whole) depends heavily on individuals with a high need for achievement.[39]

Most of McClelland's work was done with males. More recent experimental work shows that males have a high need for achievement and a high need for power, whereas females have a high need for affiliation (relations with others). Females tend to show achievement through nurturing and support. Women face a greater dilemma than do men in their business careers. Although a woman's career is quite important to her, marriage and having children increase in importance as a woman progresses in her career.[40] This calls for major decisions and sometimes creates stress.

McClelland later turned his attention to the need for power and influence. The need for power is the desire to have an impact, to be strong or influential. McClelland found that top managers in large companies possess a need for power even higher than their need for achievement. This need for power must be "disciplined and controlled so that it is directed toward the benefit of the in-

---

[37] *Ibid.*, pp. 232–37.

[38] Danny Miller and Cornelia Droge, "Psychological and Traditional Determinants of Structure," *Administrative Science Quarterly* 31 (December 1986): 554.

[39] David L. Birch, Job Creation in America: *How Our Smallest Companies Put the Most People to Work* (New York: The Free Press, 1987).

[40] Brooke Banbury-Masland and Daniel J. Brass, "Careers, Marriage, and Children: Are Women Changing Their Minds? " *Business Horizons* (May–June 1985): 82–86; Janet T. Spence, "Achievement American Style," *American Psychologist* (December 1985): 1285–95. For limitations of McClelland's thesis, see R. Scott Frey, "Need for Achievement, Entrepreneurship, and Economic Growth: A Critique of the McClelland Thesis," *Social Science Journal* 21 (April 1984): 125–34.

stitution as a whole and not toward the manager's personal aggrandizement."[41] Some suggest that the huge salaries of top executives reflect less their merit than their need for power. We will discuss executive compensation in the next chapter.

Managers with a high need for power who do not exercise it with self-control can be very disruptive: "They are rude to other people, they drink too much, they try to exploit others sexually, and they collect symbols of personal prestige such as fancy cars or big offices."[42] People with a high need for affiliation are better liked by their subordinates and have a higher level of job performance. The scholar we will examine next had many years of experience in business.

Work Is Natural

Douglas McGregor was a business executive for several decades and later taught at MIT. He contrasts two sets of *assumptions* about individuals and their desire to work.[43] The first has heavily influenced management styles; he calls it *Theory X*:

1. People do not like to work and will avoid it if they can do so.
2. People have little ambition, wish to avoid responsibility, prefer to be directed, and want security.
3. Therefore, in order to get them to do their work, they must be coerced, controlled, directed, and threatened with punishment.

Contrasting with this traditional view, McGregor presents another view favored by him, which he calls *Theory Y*:

1. Work is as natural to people as play or rest.
2. Individuals will exercise self-direction and self-control in the service of objectives to which they are committed.
3. Commitment to objectives is a function of the rewards associated with their achievement (especially satisfaction of ego and self-actualization).
4. People learn, under proper conditions, to accept and even ask for responsibility.

Each of these divergent views of the values and goals of people has a profound influence on the organizational climate and management style of any organization in which it predominates. Theory X provides the foundation for a formal, highly structured, control-oriented organization. One disadvantage that characterizes such organizations is goal displacement. This takes place in bureaucratic organizations when members turn procedures into goals. Mid-level

---

[41] David C. McClelland and David H. Burnham, "Power Is the Great Motivator," *Harvard Business Review* 54, no. 2 (1976): 101.

[42] *Ibid.*, p. 103. Also, Edwin Cornelius and Frank Lane, "The Power Motive and Managerial Success in a Professionally Oriented Service Industry Organization," *Journal of Organizational Psychology* (February 1984): 32–39.

[43] Douglas McGregor, *Human Side of Enterprise* (New York: McGraw-Hill, 1960), p. 33.

managers tend to make adherence to the rules and preservation of their office the purpose of their work, and this is most often at the expense of the persons or processes they are serving. For example, an official is asked to process 10 people per hour, and dutifully does so—even on a day when the line is five times longer than normal. Recent strategies to increase motivation are based more on Theory Y.

The above motivation models continue to influence managers and organizations. Meanwhile, other theories of motivation have been developed that take into account a wider variety of personality traits, attitudes, and needs. Equity Theory holds that a worker compares her tasks and compensation with peers. Negative equity comes when a worker perceives that she is receiving proportionately less than others. Positive equity comes when she perceives that she is receiving more than peers. Expectancy theory holds that peoples' motivation will be determined when they perceive themselves to be receiving either positive or negative equity for their efforts.[44] Lists of salaries, whether of CEOs, entertainment or sports figures, enable most to decide that they are not paid enough. This of course results in negative equity, along with greater envy, for all.

It is noteworthy that an person's attitudes and values are acknowledged in these theories of motivation. The theories build upon the values of the individual. On the other hand, the values and goals of the organization in which the individual works are not overtly considered. Psychologists respond that the goals of the firm are beyond their concern and competence. This may be true, yet an organizations' goals and values dramatically affect each participant's motivations. If the goals of the organization and the individual are in conflict, it will lead to frustration for the person and inefficiencies for the organization. In addition, neglect of values and goals leaves the impression that they are unimportant. Previous generations took organizational goals for granted; now we need to state and communicate these goals, yet we have few tools and little expertise for doing so.

Moving Blindly with Unexamined Assumptions

After his executive experience and working with Maslow, Douglas McGregor dug into the accepted ideology and the conventional assumptions that lie beneath thinking and literature on management and motivation. He was incisive in penetrating the "let's be practical, theorizing has no place in management" mentality, and he shows that "it is not possible to reach a managerial decision or take a managerial action uninfluenced by assumptions, whether adequate or not." Any decision maker makes assumptions and has implicit goals and values. The relevant question is whether these assumptions and implicit goals and val-

---

[44] For a summary of these theories, see Henry L. Tosi, John R. Rizzo, and John Schermerhorn, James Hunt and Richard Osborn, *Managing Organizational Behavior,* 5th ed. (New York: Wiley, 1994), pp. 179–85.

ues are adequate. McGregor notes a glaring deficiency of such self-imposed managerial blindness: "The common practice of proceeding without explicit examination of theoretical assumptions, leads, at times, to remarkable inconsistencies in managerial behavior."[45]

Management training and popular literature now emphasize the importance of reflection on our actions and goals.[46] It is not easy to cast a cool, clear eye on our own assumptions and values. We all engage in various shortcuts in considering our own and others' values. Rationalization, stereotyping, and other mechanisms block our ability to perceive what exactly these values are.[47] Sometimes these barriers also block our ability to reflect on the goals and the values of the organization. Some convince themselves, for example, that the growth of the organization benefits some people and thus automatically compensates for damage done to others. Some think that businesspeople waste time when they speculate on abstract values and goals.

On the other hand, it is clear that there is no such thing as value-free management. Carrying out the goals of an organization without knowing what presuppositions undergird those goals is itself choosing to make decisions on the basis of a value. That value is the unquestioning faith that the goals of the organization are justifiable, and that in a conflict with another organization or with the community, one should pursue the goals of one's own organization. The training program for traders at Wall Street's Solomon Brothers taught bullying, deception, and male chauvinist behavior toward customers. General Electric falsified overcharges to the government. Archer Daniels Midland conspired to fix artificially high prices for their products. Each of these actions encourage a lack of trust in management.

SOURCES OF SATISFACTION AND PRESSURE TO PERFORM

We have examined how the structure and climate of the organization affect the values of the manager. In this section, we will focus on the business manager and her or his personal values. In a classic empirical study of the backgrounds, education, and attitudes of business executives, the executive is characterized as a mobile person, able to leave and take up a new job in a new community rather easily:

> The mobile [manager] must be able to depart: that is, to maintain a substantial emotional distance from people, and not become deeply involved with them or

---

[45] McGregor, *Human Side of Enterprise*, p. 7; see also Bruce H. Drake and Eileen Drake, "Ethical and Legal Aspects of Managing Corporate Cultures," *California Management Review* 30 (Winter 1988): 107–23.

[46] See, for example, Stephen R. Covey, *Seven Habits of Highly Effective People* (New York: Fireside, 1990), and Peter Senge, *The Fifth Discipline* (New York: Currency, 1995).

[47] Steers, *Introduction to Organizational Behavior*, pp. 115–23.

committed to them; and [the manager] must be an energetic person and one who can focus energy on a single goal.[48]

These top managers are not always sensitive to the needs of other people. Even though their own success is often built on decisions that result in considerable loss to others, this does not seem to bother them. They are not "distracted into personal duels, for they do not allow themselves to become so involved with others." When Chevron eliminated 56,000 jobs and AT&T eliminated 100,000, executives could not allow that to overly affect them, even though more than a hundred thousand families were severely hurt. Yet evidence shows that if surviving managers do not understand the downsizing effort, it is impossible to do it effectively. It is an emotionally wrenching work, and such managers are ". . . often ill-prepared to make a full commitment, especially if they are confused about the reasons for the downsizing and their role in its implementation."[49]

Mobility and lack of concern for others enable these executives to approach managerial decisions dispassionately. This objectivity contributes to making them successful. But their success does not allow them the satisfaction one might expect. There is rarely time to relax or to look back on their successes, "for an essential part of the system is the need for constant demonstration of one's adequacy, for reiterated proof of one's independence."[50]

What sort of an upbringing gives a person the qualities of mobility and emotional distance from others and the need to constantly demonstrate personal adequacy? Researchers found that these executives tended to have strong, demanding mothers and weak or even absent fathers. Although the mothers of these successful executives are even-tempered and hard-working, they are also stern, rigid, moralistic, and controlling. They hold out high standards of achievement and parcel out their love as a reward for success. At the same time, the fathers are distant from their children; they do not provide support or reinforcement. These executives see their fathers as rather unreliable figures and could not identify with them. If they were to win their mothers' love and respect, they must prove themselves; they must be successful at what they are doing. They can never be fully sure that they have achieved enough. The overwhelming majority of the families of these executives are upper or middle class: 76 percent of the fathers were owners, executives, professionals, or white-collar workers. The executives are conservative in their politics. Moreover, when they have any involvement with community activities, it tends to be with conservative movements, such as the Chamber of Commerce and conservative charities.

The chief executive is still typically white, male, married, and politically conservative. Noteworthy is that most chief executives had a master's degree in

[48] W. Lloyd Warner and James Abegglen, *Big Business Leaders in America* (New York: Atheneum, 1963), pp. 81–82.

[49] Hugh M. O'Neill and D. Jeffery Lenn, "Voices of Survivors: Words that Downsizing CEOs Should Hear," *Academy of Management Executive* 9 (August 1995): 23–34.

[50] Warner and Abegglen, *op. cit.*, p. 83.

business administration, and 60 percent did not have a specific career goal in mind when they began with the firm.[51]

When the chief executives were asked what they would look for in their successors, they did not give high priority to such attributes as the ability to get along well with people of different races and classes. They would generally look for people who were much like themselves in background and attitudes. Organizations and their attitudes tend to be self-perpetuating. The ordinary struggle for survival and growth urges people and organizations to seek "their own kind." Although there are now some large black-owned and managed firms and some women in executive positions, both blacks and women are still severely underrepresented in chief executive positions.

There is new evidence that some people, who can afford to do so, are retiring early. Eugene Bernosky, 38, sold the semiconductor equipment firm he cofounded, Applied Chemical Solutions Inc. After putting in 80-hour weeks, he asked himself, "Is this what I really want to be doing?" He says that there are only two things that you can't buy with money—time and friends. Lonnie Fogel, 41, worked as public relations director at Home Depot and had thousands of shares of company stock. He realized he had enough money to quit, if he lived frugally. He is now writing a screenplay, bicycling, and doing volunteer work.[52] Another new social phenomena is spouses who elect to remain behind when the working partner is transferred to another city. The home spouse decides that the move is too disruptive to children's schooling, friends, and so on. The working spouse then commutes home on weekends to see the family. One survey indicated that as many as 5 percent remain behind when the transfer is overseas and 7 percent stay behind when the transfer is within the United States.[53]

The surveys discussed above remain some of the best sources of information on the characteristics of chief executive officers of American firms. A new survey may show changes. What changes would you expect?

Following Orders

Following orders within an organization is essential to any organization's success. To what lengths will a person go in following orders when those orders seriously conflict with his or her own moral values? Evidence of a person's willingness actually to do harm to another individual when instructed by authority to do so was provided by a series of controversial laboratory experiments.[54]

---

[51] "Profile of Leadership Emerges in Study of Top Corporate Executives," *Journal of Accountancy* (March 1987): 36–38.

[52] "Retire at 40—Some Do, with a Small Fortune and a Dose of Frugality," *Wall Street Journal*, August 21, 1996, pp. 1, 4.

[53] "To Some Commuters, Going Home Means A Long Plane Ride," *Wall Street Journal*, March 7, 1996, p. 1.

[54] Stanley Milgram, *Obedience to Authority* (New York: Harper & Row, 1974).

Subjects were told by an academic authority figure dressed in a white coat that they were to engage in experiments in memory and learning. Each subject was placed at a shock generator with thirty intervals marked, starting with 15 volts (labeled: slight shock) and going up to 450 volts (labeled: danger—severe shock). Another person (the learner), who was strapped in a chair with electrodes on his or her wrists, could be seen in an adjoining room through a glass partition. The learners were in on the experiment and were not really subjected to shocks. The subject was then instructed to shock the learner, increasing the intensity for every wrong answer the learner gave. As the shock level rose, the learner cried out in increasing pain, yet almost two-thirds of the subjects administered the highest level of shock.

Each subject would become nervous, agonize, and rationalize, but most nevertheless administered the highest level of shock under the auspices of authority. The experiment has been criticized as being unethical. Indeed, it did play with people's consciences. However, it also gave us frightening evidence of what one human being is willing to inflict on another when it seems to be legitimized by some authority.

Obedience in this experiment declines if the subject is in the same room as the learner or if the subject must actually touch the learner to administer the shock. The more impersonal the situation, the more willing the subject is to do harm to another. Ancient warfare involved face-to-face contact; modern warfare is closer to the above experimental situation and easier to wage. A person can push a button and never have to witness the destruction and death caused by the exploding missile.

Sometimes lower-level managers are instructed to do something that violates their ethics. The above experiment shows that about 60 percent of us will perform actions at serious variance with what we know is right if someone in authority instructs us. Yet this sort of obedience has its costs in tension, anxiety, stress, and the attendant physical ailments.

Modern organizations are designed to produce results in an impersonal fashion. Firings, exploitative advertising, and pollution are the result of decisions and policies made by executives. Such stressful and often unethical actions occur more often when executives do not view the victims of their actions. On the one hand the manager does not have to face his victims, and also, it was financial return on investment and preserving the jobs of others that demanded the downsizing. In the minds of some executives, the system demands that they act impersonally if their firm is to survive and grow.

Selling of Self: Careerism

Although the goals and values of a businessperson are influenced by background, education, and age, they are also influenced by the person's estimate of what sort of personal values will "sell" in the marketplace. The market concept of value, how much a person can obtain through entering the employment market, has a considerable influence on notions of self-worth.[55] We call selling one-self *careerism*.

For example, imagine the case of a businesswoman looking for a new position. She will be concerned about how she appears to prospective employers. Dressing for success and using proper grammar and terminology will be important. She might be less concerned about her own goals of achievement, satisfaction, and happiness. In short, her attention will focus on pleasing someone else rather than on her own values and goals. The more her self-esteem depends on how much she is worth in the market, the less control she will have over her own life. She may think that she is not valued for the person she is and that her adequacy is determined by unpredictable and insensitive market forces—the price others put on her in the marketplace. When she receives an increase in salary, it will be less the money itself that delights her than the fact that some-one has recognized that she has done a good job. Without a large salary increase, she might sink into depths of low self-esteem and even self-pity.

Furthermore, since the market is often the principal determinate of self-worth and since value in the market is subject to many changing, unpredictable forces and fads, she must remain flexible. Her present value may collapse, simply because there are too many with the same talents on the market. She must then be able to shift to a new career. The phenomenon of glutted labor markets demands that businesspeople maintain flexibility and maximum exposure. No matter how much she may like her present work or locale, it is not to her advantage to sink deep roots. If she becomes known as a one-talent person, her value, and hence her self-esteem, will be severely limited. This situation does not encourage developing loyalty to a firm or becoming involved in a community.

This notion of self-worth makes a businessperson dependent on others for his or her own self-esteem. Self-worth stems not from accomplishments or the affection of others but rather from the impersonal forces of the employment market, in this case, from company superiors. Someone who accepts this view is called "other-directed." The heavy influence of a changing external environment on personal values contributes to making Americans practical and pragmatic. They will rarely dispute principles for their own sake and consider martyrdom to be folly. Thomas More's beheading by Henry VIII because he would not turn his back on a principle makes superb drama in *Man for All Seasons*. Americans find the episode quaint but difficult to fully understand and smacking of fanaticism. Indeed, businesspeople find disputes over principles to be unproductive and time-consuming and will rarely allow themselves to be caught up in what seems to them to be impractical battles.

---

[55] Erich Fromm, "Personality and the Market Place," in *Man, Work, and Society: A Reader in the Sociology of Occupations*, ed. Sigmund Nosow and William Form (New York: Basic Books, 1962), pp. 446–52.

Loving, Caring, and Decisiveness

Another aspect of the tension that businesspeople experience is the conflict between the personal characteristics that are rewarded on the job and those that
make for a good spouse and parent. Consider an example. Imagine a typical
manager—aggressive, decisive, and fact-oriented. The manager makes decisions,
not on the basis of intuition or feelings, but on the basis of facts and defensible
reasoning. However, this talent of examining only the facts and then reasoning
from them does not work so well when the manager is at home with spouse and
children. For example, when one's spouse asks to go to a movie, it is not necessarily because she wants to see a particular film; she may simply desire to be
alone with her husband for a few hours away from the house and children.

The fact-oriented manager may also have difficulty determining what his
son or daughter is saying beneath either the quiet or the flurry of words. He has
trained himself to look for the facts and so he takes the situation at face value.
Furthermore, he might often be impatient with his wife and children for not
saying what they mean. For him, it is impossible to sift through the words to determine what his wife, son, or daughter is really saying—often nonverbally.
Moreover, in his impatience he is often unable to be open enough to encourage
them to communicate what they really are thinking and feeling. He is sometimes aware of this inability and the resulting conflict, and this causes additional tension and anxiety.

A person like the manager above has what is called a *Type A personality*,
which is characterized by impatience, restlessness, aggressiveness, and competitiveness. Type A people also tend to have many irons in the fire and to be under
considerable time pressure. Sixty percent of managers in the average organization are Type A. The Type A manager who is angry and cynical is two to five
times more likely to have heart disease or a fatal heart attack than other managers. It is the quickness to anger and a habitual hostile outlook that causes
heart problems. Children who do not get unconditional love from parents and
considerable physical contact are more likely to become untrusting, easy-to-
anger adults. Interestingly enough, it has been shown that although Type A
managers have the talents and attitudes that enable them to rise in the organization, chief executive officers are generally not Type A; they are more patient and
willing to examine the long-term ramifications of a decision.[56]

Chief Executives as Leaders

Some organizations provide environments that bring accomplishment and satisfaction, not stress, to their members. James Autry was a senior vice president of
a Fortune 500 firm, and has written the book *Love and Profit: The Art of Caring*

---

[56] Interview with Redford Williams, M.D., "Getting to the Heart of Type A's," *U.S. News & World
Report*, May 15, 1989, p. 68. See also Steers, *Introduction to Organizational Behavior*, pp. 507–8.

Leadership. He offers five guidelines for successful management. Three of these are: "Be honest," "Trust your employees," and "If you don't care about people, get out of management before it is too late." He emphasizes his last point by saying "Save yourself a heart attack and save many other people a lot of daily grief." This confirms what we have said above. Autry points out that in the work setting, "friends and co-workers are the new extended family." As a publisher he notes that younger workers are looking for good values in the workplace:

> This value-quest has produced, for the first time in the history of American publishing, a decade in which business books consistently have been on the bestseller list. And most of those books are dealing with values and relationships, not high finance.[57]

Autry then asks what kind of a CEO Jesus would be.

Autry finds that using the sports metaphor to describe business is not helpful:

> By invoking the metaphor of sports teams these days, we imply that we in business are involved in a game in which there must be winners and losers, in which there are stars who play and benchwarmers who watch, in which our personal success is measured only by the numbers on the scoreboard and not by how well we played, and in which our value to society is transitory at best.[58]

Max DePree, CEO of Herman Miller, Inc., underscores the same points and adds a religious viewpoint. For example, he talks about a business leader forming a "covenant" for the people in the firm. He says, "Covenants bind people together and enable them to meet their corporate needs by meeting the needs of one another." DePree emphasizes that leaders must take a role in developing, expressing and defending civility and values. As examples, he lists some actions to be avoided:

> To be a part of a throwaway mentality that discards goods and ideas, that discards principles and law, that discards persons and families, is to be at the dying edge. To be at the leading edge of consumption, affluence, and instant gratification is to be at the dying edge. To ignore the dignity of work and the elegance of simplicity, and the essential responsibility of serving each other, is to be at the dying edge.[59]

Founder and CEO of Amway Corporation, Richard DeVos, writes in a similar vein in his book, *Compassionate Capitalism.* He supports the free market system, but calls upon all to be sensitive to the needs of others, including the poor.[60]

---

[57] James A. Autry, *Love and Profit: The Art of Caring Leadership* (New York: Avon Books, 1991), p. 156.

[58] *Ibid.,* p. 46.

[59] Max DePree, *Leadership Is an Art* (New York: Bantam Doubleday, 1989), pp. 15, 21.

[60] Richard DeVos, *Compassionate Capitalism* (New York: Dutton, 1993).

Organizations can be changed to be better workplaces. Open communications, training and development, and clearly indicating the goals of the organization enables members to understand their job better, and thus to enjoy their work more. Moreover, in this way such organizations lower turnover, increase productivity, and generally are better financial performers in both the short- and long-term. For example, national Baldrige Winners, such as Federal Express, Cadillac, Xerox, and IBM Rochester provide a clear mission for all, ask employee involvement in planning, emphasize teams in employee development and compensation, and communicate constantly with employees via face-to-face meetings, live in-house television, and a variety of other techniques.

Motorola, Eli Lilly, Eddie Bauer, Unum Life Insurance, and DuPont get good marks from their employees for being family friendly firms. While workers at most firms feel that their work has a negative impact on their home life, this is not true in an increasing number of firms. Among other firms listed are American Home Products for child care programs; First Chicago for expanded sick leave, adoption aid, and retirement savings plans; and Procter & Gamble for new training and internal communication plans for women. These firms and an increasing number of others recognize that work has a profound impact on home and family. As a result, they encourage supervisors to be sensitive and they allow flexible hours to care for children and elder family needs. To make the list the jury had to answer yes to the question: "Can you have a good family life and still get ahead in your company?"[61]

Other firms, such as PepsiCo, Silicon Graphics, and AT&T encourage their people to become more reflective and prayerful. Executives in these firms judge that managers and workers alike will be more effective if they take time to reflect on and balance their own goals and activities.[62] Such firm initiatives come from ethical leaders and thus support the moral development of the members of the organization. We examined moral development in Chapter 2.

Summary and Conclusions

People's values are heavily influenced by business and the firm. During the working day, the expectations and behavior of supervisors influence the behavior of employees. In the evening and on weekends, products, corporations, and their values are sold through television programming and advertising.

---

[61] "Balancing Work and Family: Big Returns for Companies Willing to Give Family Strategies a Chance," *Business Week*, September 16, 1996, pp. 74–80; and "More Firms Compete to be Named on Lists as 'Family Friendly,'" *Wall Street Journal*, August 21, 1996, p. B1.

[62] Mark A. Huselid, "The Impact of Human Resource Management Practices on Turnover, Productivity, and Corporate Financial Performance," *Academy of Management Journal* (June 1995): 635–72; Richard Blackburn and Benson Rosen, "Total Quality and Human Resources Management: Lessons Learned from Baldrige Award-Winning Companies," *Academy of Management Executive* 3 (1993): 49–66; Stratford Sherman, "Leaders Learn to Heed the Voice From Within," *Fortune*, August 22, 1994, pp. 92–100.

Successful businesspeople generally are ambitious, achievement- and power-oriented, disciplined, and adaptable. Younger managers are intent on being "winners" and "self-developers," often at the expense of empathy for others. The business manager ingests many of these values when he or she joins the firm. The prevailing values of free market, competition, and opposition to government intervention are learned early, along with the specific values of the particular firm. Hence the goals of managers are largely determined for them—whatever goals must be accomplished for success within the firm. Moreover, when managers contribute to policy making, their goals come to include what must be accomplished to insure success for the firm. Just as early in life the rules of the game were set by others, so now the economic rules of the game come from outside the firm.

People's personal goals are changing. Individuals now desire more than salary and status. They desire challenging work, participation in decision making, the respect and approval of friends, the ability to identify with their community, and a stimulating and fulfilling life. A business firm can help in the achievement of many of these goals if its senior executives are wise in directing it.

Discussion Questions

1. Does rational decision making rest on values and ideological assumptions? What might those assumptions be?
2. Since business managers often claim their actions are "value-free," why inquire about values?
3. Is it acceptable for a firm to attempt to socialize its members? How does it do so? What are the unexpected costs of socialization?
4. Do business managers tend to be more interested in people, power, or tasks? Are executives more conformist or more innovative?
5. What do Solomon Asch's experiments on the influence of groups tell us?
6. What values develop as a person matures and becomes self-actualized? What role does concern for other people play in the set of values of a self-actualized person?
7. How does Maslow's description of the ethical values of the self-actualized person relate to Kolberg's Level III moral reasoning?
8. What sort of upbringing do people with a high need for achievement tend to have? What in a culture encourages a high need for achievement? Are those elements present in your own culture?
9. If business is the major outlet for a contemporary need for achievement, as opposed to religion and art, does this indicate an impoverishment of spirit?
10. What special problems in achieving do many women have?
11. Is a high need for power a help or a hindrance to effective leadership? Explain.
12. Describe the family life and values of the mobile manager.
13. Outline the pros and cons to the individual of having salary and status as goals. Do managers "sell" themselves?

14. Are you concerned with making yourself more "marketable"? What sort of values does this engender in a person?
15. How do published lists of salaries affect your sense of equity?
16. Describe the values that are most valuable to someone in organizational life and the values that are developed in family life. Is there a conflict here? How can it be resolved?
17. What is the effect of authority on a person's willingness to inflict pain, or even the danger of death, on another? Describe an experiment regarding this subject. Do parallel situations occur in your organization? In your country? Explain.

Exercise:
Write Your Own Obituary

Write your own obituary that will appear in your city newspaper. Assume that it is written by your best friend who knows the real you in addition to your accomplishments. After you do a first draft, show it to a good friend for their comments. Write this in a maximum of 300 words.

The Purchasing Manager's Car

Jim Angot is the purchasing manager for Nihco, Inc. He is responsible for buying two $1 million computer workstations. Nihco has a written policy prohibiting any company buyer from receiving a gift in excess of $50 and requiring that all gratuities be reported. A salesperson for a computer manufacturer offers to arrange it so that Angot can purchase a $20,000 auto for $6,000. The auto would be bought through a third party. Should Jim decline the offer? Should he notify his superior? Should he notify the salesperson's superior?

Local Manager in Trouble

You are the U.S.-based head of overseas operations for Star Electronics. You learn that one of your plant managers has been arrested in a distant country. His alleged "crime" is that goods found in your warehouse lack the proper customs stamps and papers.

But you learn that the truth is much more complicated. For years, "grease" has been a way of life in this country's bureaucracy, and your plant manager has been paying gratuities to the customs officers. But he knows that it is against home office policy, so he stops doing so. The price for dropping all charges is $40,000. What would you do? Would you pay the "fine?" Or would your let the plant manager be put in jail?

CHAPTER

Ethics and Performance Measures

Practical men, who believe themselves to be quite exempt from any intellectual influences, are usually the slaves of some defunct economist.
—John Maynard Keynes

Sustainability can be expressed as the economic golden rule: Leave the world better than you found it, take no more than you need, try not to harm life or the environment, and make amends if you do.
—Paul Hawken, *The Ecology of Commerce*

We understand much about a person by watching what that person does and how they act. This is also true of a firm; the activities and policies of a business firm are the clearest demonstration of its values and ethics. Actions tell us more about business values than do eloquent executive speeches or self-promoting advertising. Smart managers seek to reward good performance, both as a just reward to the individual and also to encourage similar behavior in others.

Let us examine some examples of performance and how that performance is rewarded:

Robert Allen, CEO of AT&T, received $5.83 million in personal basic pay and another $11 million in stock options in 1995. In that year Allen announced elimination of 40,000 jobs and AT&T's stock surged.[1]

In 1994 Steven Spielberg received $165 million personal compensation, Oprah Winfrey $72 million, Michael Jordan $30 million. Michael Douglas, Demi

---

[1] "Gross Compensation? New CEO Pay Figures Make Top Brass Look Positively Piggy," *Business Week*, March 18, 1996, pp. 32–34.

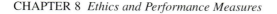

Moore, Arnold Schwarzenegger, Eddie Murphy and Bruce Willis each received $15 million per film; meanwhile, 90% of the 150,000 members of the Screen Actors Guild earned less than $5,000 that year for their acting work.[2]

Ford reported higher earnings than General Motors in 1988. Ford provided all its workers with a $2,100 profit-sharing bonus. GM allocated $169 million for profit sharing for executives, despite the fact that profits dropped by 26 percent. GM hourly and salaried workers received no bonus.[3]

Investment banking firm Lazard Freres announced that it was raising a $2 billion fund to make investments to aid companies that might be targets of hostile takeovers. Said the firm, "We think there is a major investment opportunity to work cooperatively with managements to bring about change in an orderly fashion and not when forced by a raider."[4]

The first two cases are examples of very high compensation for those few people that are judged to be the very best performers. As classic "pay for performance," they show how the free market system is able to attract the very best talent to do work that is judged to be extremely important.

On the other hand, critics maintain that these high salaries are a social ratification of greed, and exemplify a "winner-take-all" attitude in which a few receive very high compensation while many others find it hard to obtain enough salary on which to live. If there is but one winner, does this mean that all the rest of us are "losers"? This can result in cynicism and lost motivation for many. In addition, it tends to drain talent from important but underpaid occupations such as school teaching and public service. In any case, all of these actions and policies stem from the goals, priorities, and values of the firms involved. They will be discussed in this chapter.

In this chapter we will examine the effect of values and ethics on a firm's performance. We will go on to note some executives and firms who are excellent examples of concern for people and good ethics, along with others who seem to show little concern. We will then explore business strategies for encouraging better performance among managers and firms.

MANAGING FOR SELF OR TEAM

We will consider here different kinds of managers, management styles, and management actions. The intention is to present good and effective behavior that can be imitated and ineffective management styles that can be avoided.

[2] The figures are from "When Winners Take All: Is the Distribution of Income Throughout Society Becoming More Like That in Hollywood?" *The Economist*, November 25, 1995; also Robert Frank and Philip Cook, *The Winner Take All Society* (New York: Martin Kessler, 1995), p. 101.

[3] "GM's Bonus Babies," *U.S. News & World Report*, March 2, 1987, p. 42.

[4] Leslie Wayne, "Lazard Seeks To Build an Anti-Takeover Fund," *New York Times*, August 28, 1987, p. 27.

TABLE 8–1   Change of Values That Undergird the Business System

Protestant Ethic · · · *Has Shifted to* · · ·	Pluralism and Self-Fulfillment
1. Hard work	1. Salary and status
2. Self-control and sobriety	2. Self-fulfillment
3. Self-reliance	3. Entitlement
4. Perseverance	4. Short-term perspective (if not successful here, move on)
5. Saving and planning ahead	5. Immediate satisfaction (buy on time, little savings)
6. Honesty and observing the "rules of the game"	6. Obey the law (in any case, don't get caught)

To place this discussion in context, recall from Chapters 4 and 5 the traditional values that prevailed in the United States. The Protestant ethic urges hard work, self-control, self-reliance, perseverance, saving and planning ahead, honesty, and observing the "rules of the game." Note that most of these same values also characterize the entrepreneurial middle class in rapidly developing countries, for example, nations of the Pacific Rim. The global marketplace and treaties, such as the North Atlantic Free Trade Agreement (NAFTA), may shake us from our lethargy and bring us back to some of these early values. The market system itself encourages and rewards these values.

From what we have seen in earlier chapters, the values of Americans may have shifted toward short-term goals, such as a high salary, high status, self-fulfillment, entitlement, and immediate satisfaction (see Table 8–1). Do you think these traditional values are still predominant, or have a new set of self-fulfillment values been embraced by Americans? We will raise this question later in this chapter and again in Chapter 9.

Executive Compensation and Trust

The issue of the extremely high pay of chief executive officers is coming under increasing criticism in the business press.[5] CEO compensation is a classic case of the conflict between the free market system that rewards the very best with high pay, and a more subtle lack of fairness that such practices engender. Let us examine the current situation within larger U.S. firms.

Average compensation for American CEOs in 1995 rose 30 percent to $3,746,392. In that same year the pay of white-collar professionals rose 4.2 per-

---

[5] See, for example, "Executive Pay: CEO Pay Keeps Soaring—Leaving Everybody Else Further and Further Behind," *Wall Street Journal*, April 11, 1996, pp. R1–R18. A management consultant who helped create the CEO pay system is now critical of it; see Graef S. Crystal, *In Search of Excess: The Over Compensation of American Executives* (New York: Norton, 1991).

cent, factory worker pay rose 1.0 percent, and the inflation rate was 2.8 percent. Examining a longer trend, from 1990 to 1995, CEO pay rose 92 percent, while worker pay rose 16 percent, and worker layoffs increased 39 percent to 439,882 in 1995. In this same period, corporate profits were up 75 percent.[6] Much of the executive compensation is deferred, so as to shelter it from taxes. Moreover, when such a firm has financial troubles and its blue and white collar retirement payments are cut or eliminated, executive compensation is protected.[7]

An ethical dilemma is captured at United Technologies where Chairman Robert Daniel received $11,200,000 in compensation in 1995 and CEO George David received $6,700,000 in stock options in addition to his regular pay of $1,966,000. At the same time factory and office workers have lived with stagnant wages, the loss of 30,000 of their colleagues to downsizing, and the resulting increased workload to pick up the slack.

Many United Technologies people feel discouraged, disenfranchised, and angry. A middle manager who has been with the firm for almost 20 years, has received consistently good performance reviews, and is currently paid $64,000, says: "I used to go to work enthusiastically. Now, I go in to do what I have to do. I feel overloaded to the point of burnout. Most of my colleagues are actively looking for other jobs or are just resigned to do the minimum." He complains about his CEO's pay increase, while there are large layoffs and everyone else receives little salary increase.[8]

American top management and CEO salaries are higher than those of any other nation. Moreover, they are still rising dramatically compared to the wages of other workers. In 1980 the CEO's salary was 42 times that of the ordinary factory worker. By 1995 it had risen to 120 times that same factory worker. Given that self-esteem is often measured by salary, that CEOs help decide their own salaries and that they are often greedy, it is not surprising that U.S. CEO salaries are so high. The ratio of the pay of the average worker in the United States to that of the CEO is 1:120; in Japan this ratio is 1:16; in Germany it is 1:21; in the United Kingdom it is 1:33.[9] Boards of directors seem to be treating CEOs as superstars, much like Demi Moore and Eddie Murphy. What boards and CEOs are missing is that they are leading an organization of other people. And the success of that organization demands the energy and commitment of other people, too.

Efforts to encourage better communication, trust and cooperation are undermined by compensating executives at such a high rate. When trying to cut costs, top managers urge hourly and salaried workers to settle for little addi-

---

[6] "How High Can CEO Pay Go?" *Business Week*, April 22, 1996, pp. 100–122.

[7] See the two part series, "Special Tax Breaks Enrich Savings of Many in the Ranks of Management," *New York Times*, October 13, 1996, pp. 1, 14; and "Managers Staying Dry as Corporations Sink: Rushing Away from Taxes," *New York Times*, October 14, 1996, pp. 1, 8.

[8] *Ibid.*, p. 100.

[9] "Does America Still Work?" *Harper's Magazine*, May 1996, pp. 35–47.

tional compensation. Many CEOs have cut wages, closed plants, and urged early retirement. Some of this is necessary, but excessive executive compensation does not help to convince colleagues of the need to cut costs. Since CEO compensation is often public knowledge and is so clearly self-serving, it supports an attitude of "everyone for himself" and "get what you can, while you can." Comparing compensation of chief executives in American firms with other countries, Japanese management consultant Kenichi Ohmae says that in the United States, a "stockholder-oriented capitalism . . . places a disproportionate amount of personal wealth in the hands of top-level managers." Thus, according to Ohmae, workers do not share the benefits of success in a just fashion, and this brings less company loyalty.[10]

Huge pay packages disturb Donald Frey, who was chief executive of Bell & Howell. He says that nobody is worth the multimillion-dollar pay packages that most are getting, and he points to a problem. "More in executive suites than elsewhere, pay means status. A lot of CEOs rate themselves—their sense of self-worth—by how much money they're paid. Being on the list of the top 10 salaries is an ego trip."[11]

High executive compensation has several justifications. It can be (1) a reward for superior performance, (2) the sum required to attract the talent, (3) a just return for contributions, and (4) a signal to others in the firm about relative worth. Executive compensation packages are generally decided on the basis of the first two purposes, with the second two largely ignored. Therein lies the problem. Some of the extremely high CEO pay is tied to performance and the recent rise in the stock market, but there is little justification in the CEO being the only employee receiving a salary tied to performance or stock price.[12] Some firms now share the benefits with all of those in the firm who made them possible.

Derek Bok, recently retired president of Harvard University, has often spoken, written, and acted on behalf of ethical issues. Bok says that immense compensation in the private sector drains talented people away from teaching and public service at precisely the time when the public is asking for better education and better government. Bok takes issue with the very high pay of trial and corporate lawyers and specialized physicians, as well as business CEOs.

He notes that in the period since World War I, the only decades in which CEO salaries increased so dramatically, the 1920s and since the 1980s, were "two periods in which America's values moved sharply toward the celebration of material rewards." He also says that this is not inevitable, as in the period from 1940 to 1965 CEO salaries moved up less rapidly than salaries of average

---

[10] Kenichi Ohmae, *The Borderless World* (New York: Harper, 1990), p. 55. See also Kenneth Mason, "Four Ways to Overpay Yourself Enough," *Harvard Business Review* 88 (July–August 1988): 69–74.

[11] "How Four Chief Executives View Issue of Compensation at the Top," *Wall Street Journal*, March 28, 1988, p. 6.

[12] On the relationship between compensation and ethical behavior, see Nancy B. Kurland, "The Unexplored Territory Linking Rewards and Ethical Behavior," *Business and Society* 34 (April 1995): 34–50.

blue collar workers even though the economy was doing well. Bok's solution is twofold: He urges a change in values away from blatant materialism, and he also supports a more graduated income tax on those receiving such large pay.[13]

CEO compensation will continue to receive attention, both as a symbol of the appropriate rewards of the free market reward system and also as an example of inequity and greed. Many predict that negative reactions will cause American business increasing trouble in future years. But let us now examine other management and ethical issues.

American Supremacy Challenged

The United States has lost dominance in many product lines to Asian nations: cameras, watches, radios, televisions, and video cassette recorders. The United States has also lost the security of many middle management positions, along with high wages for factory workers, and huge domestic markets that were virtually captive. With global business, nations with low wages are doing work that has a high proportion of labor, such as sewing clothing and shoes.

Managers are vital to the success of any enterprise. Managers provide the vision, plans and motivation for the organization. However, managers can often be short-sighted. Many American managers invest too little in worker training and research and development, and spend too much on acquisitions. A group of chief executives and strategy scholars met under the auspices of the Harvard Business School and the Council on Competitiveness to determine why this is the case. Chair of the panel and business strategy scholar Michael Porter lays the blame on the way America's financial system allocates capital. In Porter's words, "the money doesn't go to the right companies for the right investments." In the external markets, the system underfunds firms that can deploy capital most productively. Internally, it directs funds to wasteful projects instead of toward research, training, and other initiatives that would aid a company's long-term prospects. Exacerbating the problem in large firms, since managers do not know the details of operations, they "manage by the numbers," using as indicators of success short term markers, such as earnings, return on investment, return on equity, or market share. Hence, the panel recommends a series of changes that would allow more productive use of capital.[14]

Bonus plans are generally based on last year's performance. However, managers often expect to be in their current job just a few years and then to move to a better position elsewhere. A newcomer who takes a manager's place would reap the reward of better long-term performance. Thus there is less incentive to plan and budget for several years out. Performance could be mea-

---

[13] Derek Bok, *The Cost of Talent: How Executives and Professionals are Paid and How It Affects America* (New York: The Free Press, 1993); also his "It's Time to Trim Hefty Paychecks," *New York Times*, December 5, 1993, p. F13.

[14] Judith H. Dobrzynski, "A Sweeping Prescription for Corporate Myopia," *Business Week*, July 6, 1992, pp. 36–37.

sured over a longer term, perhaps 5 or 10 years. Substantial growth is best accomplished when managers plan for the long term.

The larger and more diversified a firm is, the less top management is able to know specific products, markets, and employees. Because of its distance from customers, production, new product ideas, and the public, management is tempted to turn to what it can understand—the only control mechanism that is then available—"the numbers." Not only does this short-term thinking tend to reduce research, risk taking and productivity, but it also makes managers less likely to examine the ethics of management decisions. That is, the same pressure to achieve short-term results "in the numbers game" also short-circuits attempts to examine ethical issues.

Three examples from financial firms may help to clarify the issues. In the fall of 1994, Kevin Conway, 36, a partner at Goldman Sachs with annual compensation probably reaching $5,000,000, left for a more lucrative offer with a leveraged buyout firm. At Solomon Brothers, when management tried to rein in immense bonuses, Hans Hufschmidt who made $20 million left for a money managing firm, and Dennis Keegan who earned $30 million also left for greener pastures. Each case illustrates the immense sums going to people and firms who create no new products and no new jobs. They merely rearrange already existing assets, and provide huge rewards for very few.[15] The fact that their actions and values are dysfunctional is underscored by a 1996 report sponsored by the Securities and Exchange Commission, the New York Stock Exchange, and the National Association of Securities Dealers that charges that securities firms are not doing enough to police their own brokers.[16]

Perhaps compensation would be more reasonable if more firms asked employees to rate their own executives. Many of America's most admired companies do just that; they call it "upward evaluation" or "360 degree feedback." Among the firms that ask subordinates to rate their superiors, including the CEO, are: Alcoa, BellSouth, DuPont, Eaton, General Mills, Hewlett-Packard, Merck, Herman Miller, Morgan Stanley, Motorola, Procter & Gamble, and 3M.

To summarize: the principal cause of a lack of long-term planning is the shortsightedness of managers. Managers often prefer measurable, short-term results so that they may appear to be doing their job well. The same sort of motivation leads to unethical behavior. However, other executives, noted for their good ethics, run very profitable firms. Let us look at some of them.

LEADERSHIP DETERMINES ETHICS AND VALUES

Gun Denhart was born in Sweden and married her American husband, Tom, in Paris. Two years later they moved to Connecticut. Both worked, but Tom's job

---

[15] "Getting By on $2 Million a Year," *Fortune*, July 24, 1995, p. 17.
[16] "Brokerages Still Broken," *Business Ethics* (May 1996): 16.

was in New York City, and neither liked his one and one-half-hour commute. When their son was born in 1980, Gun noted the lack of and the expense of high-quality, cotton children's clothes.

A few years later, they sold their home and used the proceeds to purchase a similar home in Portland, Oregon, and with the remainder began a new mail order firm, Hanna Andersson's children's clothes. The firm was named for Gun's grandmother, since "Gun" did not sound appropriate for a children's clothing firm! Gun as CEO and Tom as marketing director were the sole employees in 1984. They were also concerned with the excessive waste they noticed in the United States, far more than Gun had experienced in Europe. To emphasize the high quality of their clothes, and also to discourage throwing clothes away when they were outgrown, they began the "Hannadowns" program. A customer could return a used Hanna piece of clothing and receive a credit of 20 percent of the cost of the original product toward a new purchase. Hanna Andersson in turn donates the used clothing to charities for women and children.

Gun Denhart calls the Hannadowns program a win-win-win-win program. As she describes it, all parties benefit from the program:

> It is good for Hanna as a company because it is a way, marketing-wise, to show our customers that these are great products and can be used for more than one baby. It makes the customer feel good because they have all these clothes in their closets and the kids have outgrown them. They don't know what to do with them, and they feel good that they will be used again by someone who really needs them. Employees love it, and finally, but not least, it is just wonderful for the kids who get the clothes because, normally, they wouldn't have this kind of quality clothing.[17]

These quality clothes were so attractive to customers that the firm grew to $35 million annual sales within 10 years, and it is still growing. Hanna Andersson has a management team that is 80 percent female and a participative management style. Working mothers appreciate the flexible work schedules. The firm also funds one-half of day-care expense. Hanna Andersson subsidizes fitness classes, has formal wellness programs, and provides exercise equipment and showers on the premises. The firm also provides jobs to some who had received Hannadowns as homeless or battered women. Hanna Andersson received the Business Enterprise Trust Award in 1992 for "exemplary acts of courage, integrity and social vision in business." Denhart also received one of *Forbes* magazine's first business ethics awards.[18]

Gun Denhart is concerned with many problems in contemporary society: waste, poverty, homelessness, and that many women and children are victims.

---

[17] "Recycling Clothes While Building Customer Loyalty," in David Bollier, *Aiming Higher* (New York: Amacom, 1996), pp. 23–36; the original quote is from *Social Entrepreneurship: The Story of Gun Denhart and Hanna Andersson* (Stanford: Business Enterprise Trust, 1992), p. 6.
[18] "Interview with Gun Denhart," *Business Ethics* (July–August 1994): 19–21.

She thinks that business has a responsibility, "I think you can't put all that burden on the government. I think individuals and corporations have to take some responsibility to help for a better world."[19]

Executives As Moral Leaders

We will now spotlight a few additional business leaders because of their contributions to business, business values, and business ethics. They have been selected because their values and actions serve as models for all businesspeople.

Ryuzaburo Kaku is chairman of Canon Inc., a firm based in Japan that has annual global sales of more than $16 billion on Canon copiers, computers, and computer printers. Kaku's interests go well beyond copiers and Japan. He is convinced that humankind may not survive its current problems of lack of food, environmental difficulties, and the imbalance of wealth between the nations. As a result of these concerns, Kaku began the use of solar energy at Canon. He has also initiated an extensive recycling program of both copier ink cartridges and of the copiers themselves.[20] Such recycling saves manufacturing costs, and perhaps more importantly, dumps less waste into the environment.

Kaku has attained international stature as an active member of the Caux Round Table of business leaders from Europe, Japan, and the United States. When the Caux Round Table developed their *Principles for Business*, a global code of business conduct,[21] the value of "human dignity," from the Western tradition, was agreed upon as one of the bedrock basic principles. Just as important, Kaku insisted that another of those basic values be "Kyosei" from the Eastern traditions. Kyosei means "living and working together for the common good." We will discuss the Caux *Principles for Business* again later in this chapter.

Kaku acknowledges that Kyosei as a basic principle has a low priority in Japan. Nevertheless, managers at Canon have already made the shift and Kaku himself is spending much of his own time trying to change general attitudes in Japan. Kaku is convinced that we must work for the common good, if our peoples, and indeed the planet itself, are to survive.

Physician and biochemist *Roy Vagelos* was CEO of Merck & Co., a very successful pharmaceutical company. Merck spends more money on research and development than any of its competitors (11% of sales, or $530 million). Among Merck's winning products is the drug Mevacor, an anticholesterol drug. Of Merck's business successes, *Business Week* had this to say:

> Merck's management has done a better job of managing its business than anyone we can think of in its industry or, for that matter, in U.S. business. Merck manage-

---

[19] *Social Entrepreneurship: The Story of Gun Denhart, op. cit.,* p. 16.

[20] "Interview with Ryuzaburo Kaku," *Business Ethics* (March–April 1995): 30–33.

[21] The Caux *Principals for Business* are in the Appendix.

ment has not been pressured into quick-fix strategies by Wall Street the way so many others have. Its reward: Investors now can't seem to get enough of Merck.[22]

Merck developed a drug called ivermectin for treating parasites and ticks common in dogs and farm animals. After years of testing by the World Health Organization (WHO), a version of the drug was found to be effective in combating river blindness disease, which is common in some poor countries. River blindness results from the bite of a fly, which deposits a parasite under the skin. That parasite can grow to two feet long and can generate millions more parasites; when it gets to the eye, it causes blindness. The disease afflicts an estimated 18–40 million people in Africa, the Middle East, and Latin America; roughly 340,000 have gone blind. The disease had been untreatable. But now a dose of Merck's tablets every 6 months can prevent the ravages of the disease. The problem: Most people who need it are so poor that they cannot pay for it. There is no market for the drug.

Merck decided to donate the drug as long as legitimate local medical personnel administered it. Both Merck and the World Health Organization monitor its use. The cost to Merck is substantial, and the firm does not want to set a precedent so that poor nations will expect drug companies to donate drugs. This would discourage the always expensive research into similar drugs. Yet Vagelos describes what gives such zeal to Merck employees:

> It's understanding that the most important thing you can contribute as a human being is improving the lives of millions of people. We do that every year, introducing drugs and vaccines that will change the course of diseases or prevent diseases. And what could be better than that?[23]

It is this vision that led Vagelos and Merck to donate the drug to millions of poor to prevent river blindness. Merck and Vagelos have received much favorable attention for their generosity.

Harold Nielson is founder of Foldcraft, a firm with $20 million annual sales and 300 employees in Kenyon, Minnesota. Foldcraft makes tables and benches used in fast-food restaurants, schools, and other public facilities. This successful firm contributes 10 percent of pretax profits to charity. In 1981 Nielson began a wellness program for employees which was so successful that it reduced health insurance costs for both employees and Foldcraft itself.

In 1983 Nielson and his wife traveled to poor parts of Honduras, Mexico, and Nicaragua. He was so touched by the poverty of the people that he set out to help in some way. Nielson and his wife, Louise, founded Miracle Ranch

---

[22] "The Miracle Company," and "Merck's Miracle Was Hard-Earned," *Business Week*, October 19, 1987, pp. 84, 90, 154; see also the updated account, "Quandry in Developing a Wonder Drug for the Third World," in Bollier, *Aiming Higher* (New York: Amacom, 1996), pp. 280–94.

[23] "Let's Hear It from the Winner," *Fortune*, January 19, 1988, p. 38; and Michael Waldholz, "Merck to Donate Drug for 'River Blindness,'" *Wall Street Journal*, October 22, 1987, p. 38.

Children's Home in Valle Las Palmas, Mexico as a shelter for poor, orphaned, and abused boys. They support the home with the entire earnings of the Third World Friends Thrift Shop in Kenyon, which they also founded. In order to enable employees of Foldcraft to learn firsthand the problems of Third World peoples, the firm sponsors up to 25 annual fully paid trips to visit firsthand the poor peoples of Mexico. Their only obligation upon return is to share their experiences with fellow workers at Foldcraft.[24]

Ralph S. Larsen followed *James E. Burke* as CEO of Johnson & Johnson (J&J), the biggest health care product company in the world, and its profits are among the best in the industry. J&J's products include Band-Aids, baby oil, and Tylenol. Burke was forced to center stage when someone placed cyanide in Tylenol capsules, replaced the bottles on store shelves, and waited for a customer to consume the poison. When seven people died, Burke and J&J were faced with how to respond. J&J could recall all unused Tylenol (at a cost of $100 million), be honest with customers, and try to win them back with a safer redesigned packaging. The FBI recommended not recalling the unused Tylenol, since that would encourage future poisoners. In making their decision, James Burke and other managers relied on J&J's much valued Credo (see Fig. 8–1).

Most company ethical codes state a set of rules, but the J&J Credo states the moral obligations the company has to its stakeholders. The Credo places customers as the first responsibility and profits and stockholders last. The Credo outlines these obligations in a practical, ethical fashion. According to Larsen, the Credo enables J&J to be decentralized, even operating redundant divisions. Because of the Credo each manager knows the goals of the firm. Regarding the Credo, Burke says, "The Credo is our common denominator. It guides us in everything we do. It represents an attempt to codify what we can all agree upon since we have highly independent managers."[25]

Given its credo, J&J had but one real option in the Tylenol poisoning case. They believed that their first obligation was to people who use their products, so they recalled the Tylenol. They took a $100 million loss but were able to retain the Tylenol brand name. According to Burke, the reason the Tylenol rescue succeeded was "not that we did anything dazzling or clever, but just that we are a company that tries to do the right thing."[26] Because of their honesty in this crisis, J&J gained even greater stature. Ralph Larsen, like Burke, is a man of integrity, and he builds on a company tradition of respect for family values and the dignity of all women and men.

---

[24] Kari Larson, "Not Business As Usual: Capitalists Experience Poverty," *Business Ethics* (March–April 1995): 36–37.

[25] "J&J Is on a Roll: The World's Largest Health Care Company Says It Puts Profits Last," *Fortune,* December 26, 1994, pp. 178–192; also, Laura L. Nash, "Johnson & Johnson's Credo," in *Corporate Ethics: A Prime Business Asset* (New York: The Business Roundtable, 1988), pp. 80–82.

[26] Laurence Shames, *The Big Time: The Harvard Business School's Most Successful Class and How It Shaped America* (New York: Mentor, 1986), p. 159.

Our Credo

We believe our first responsibility is to the doctors, nurses and patients,
to mothers and all others who use our products and services.
In meeting their needs everything we do must be of high quality.
We must constantly strive to reduce our costs
in order to maintain reasonable prices.
Customers' orders must be serviced promptly and accurately.
Our suppliers and distributors must have an opportunity
to make a fair profit.

We are responsible to our employees,
the men and women who work with us throughout the world.
Everyone must be considered as an individual.
We must respect their dignity and recognize their merit.
They must have a sense of security in their jobs.
Compensation must be fair and adequate,
and working conditions clean, orderly and safe.
Employees must feel free to make suggestions and complaints.
There must be equal opportunity for employment, development
and advancement for those qualified.
We must provide competent management,
and their actions must be just and ethical.

We are responsible to the communities in which we live and work
and to the world community as well.
We must be good citizens — support good works and charities
and bear our fair share of taxes.
We must encourage civic improvements and better health and education.
We must maintain in good order
the property we are privileged to use,
protecting the environment and natural resources.

Our final responsibility is to our stockholders.
Business must make a sound profit.
We must experiment with new ideas.
Research must be carried on, innovative programs developed
and mistakes paid for.
New equipment must be purchased, new facilities provided
and new products launched.
Reserves must be created to provide for adverse times.
When we operate according to these principles,
the stockholders should realize a fair return.

Johnson & Johnson

Reproduced with permission.

FIGURE 8–1 Johnson & Johnson's Corporate Credo.

Felix Rohatyn may be the best-known and best-connected investment banker in America; he is senior partner at Lazard Freres & Co. Rohatyn is a "soft-spoken man, polite without being warm, who doodles with geometric precision on unlined white paper." He was born in Austria and came to the United States in 1942 to escape the Nazi persecution of Jews. For 30 years he has been the principal deal maker at Lazard. In 1975, Rohatyn engineered a deal that made New York City, which faced bankruptcy, solvent again. Lazard Freres reports three times the profit per employee as its closest rival, Morgan Stanley, and it leaves other competitors such as Solomon Brothers, First Boston, and Merrill Lynch even further behind.[27] Rohatyn was one of the earliest and most skillful consultants to firms involved in giant mergers, yet he feels that the merger mania has gone too far.

He is sharply critical of many of his peers in investment banking. He says that the United States has done practically nothing to prevent a recurrence of the 1987 stock market crash. He notes that the primary purpose of the stock and bond markets is to provide investment funds for organizations that need capital. Yet the markets do not accomplish that well:

> The fundamental weakness in the securities markets, world-wide, is the result of excessive speculation, excessive use of credit, and inadequate regulation. This speculative behavior is not driven by individuals, as was the case in the 1920s, but by such institutions as pension funds, banks, savings and loans, and insurance companies. In many cases, these institutions are backed by federal government guarantees. Curbing speculation and promoting investment must be the objective of reform.[28]

He points out it is in the self-interest of investment bankers to complete "deals" (mergers or acquisitions), because their fees depend on such deals. The rewards of completing a deal occur even in the case where the merger is not in the best interest of the client. Rohatyn also thinks that investment bankers' fees are much too large. Rohatyn feels, according to one biographer, that he has a "responsibility to save capitalism from itself—that greed, ideological rigidity, or the simple lack of competence outside their narrow arenas of expertise can blind the movers and shakers of the business world to the risks of financial instability they are promoting."

The following are among Rohatyn's suggestions for encouraging investment and cooling speculation:

> Impose a 50 percent tax on the profit of securities held for less than a year. This tax would apply to individuals, corporations, partnerships, and currently tax-free institutions. At the same time, reduce capital gains taxes on securities held for more than five years to 15 percent.

---

[27] "The Last Emperor of Wall Street," *Business Week*, May 30, 1988, pp. 65, 67.

[28] Felix G. Rohatyn, "Institutional 'Investor' or 'Speculator'?" *Wall Street Journal*, June 24, 1988, pp. 14, 24.

Sharply limit the type and proportion of speculative investments held by federally insured institutions.[29]

Rohatyn's firm built up a fund to help companies faced with hostile takeovers, as was mentioned at the beginning of the chapter. Rohatyn has had considerable influence on the firm's policies. He takes into account the public interest, even in cases where it would mean limiting his own and his firm's fees. That is the mark of good leadership. In addition, Rohatyn encourages purchasers of securities to exercise conscientious management.

With regard to firms in general, being ethical may benefit a firm's sales. Recent surveys indicate that consumers prefer to purchase from a firm which has a good reputation. In one survey, 55 percent of consumers say that "they always take a company's ethics and values into account when purchasing a product or service." Forty percent always consider "treatment of employees" and 23 percent always look at the company's environmental record. In a second survey of 1,981 adults, 78 percent of the respondents said that they would buy a product made by a firm that contributes to education, medical research, and the like. Two-thirds said they would switch brands to a manufacturer that supported a cause they deemed worthy. One-third said they were influenced more by a firm's social activism than by its advertising.[30]

In a third survey of 1,000 heads of households, 39 percent of investors said they always or frequently check on business practices, values, and ethics before investing. Nearly 90 percent of consumers said that when price, quality, and service were equal, they are more likely to purchase from the firm with the best reputation for social responsibility. Perhaps most surprising is that nearly three-fourths are boycotting certain products, and 48 percent of this group were doing so because of business practices.[31]

More than 800 firms who are attempting to be socially responsible belong to a group called *Business for Social Responsibility*. The group meets annually, partially to support one another in their efforts to be socially responsible. Among these firms are Ben and Jerry's Ice Cream, Newman's Own Inc., Shorebank of Chicago, Tom's of Maine, and Glen Ellen Winery. A detailed account of 12 of these firms and briefer accounts of 27 others are contained in the book, *Companies with a Conscience*.[32]

Johnson & Johnson's *Credo*, and Rohatyn's suggestions for encouraging long-term investments, provide a good foundation for the section later in this

---

[29] Ralph Nader and William Taylor, "Felix Rohatyn: The Interstitial Man," in *The Big Boys* (New York: Pantheon, 1986), p. 210; and Rohatyn, "Institutional 'Investor' or 'Speculator?' " p. 14.

[30] The first study is cited in John Adams, "Dissecting Corporate Goodness," *American Advertising* (Spring 1996): 10–15. The second by Roper Starch Worldwide is quoted in "Good Stewardship is Good Business," *Fortune*, March 21, 1994, p. 16.

[31] "Good Guys Finish First," *Business Ethics* (March 1995): 13.

[32] Mary Scott and Howard Rothman, *Companies with a Conscience* (New York: Citadel, 1994); for additional information on Business for Social Responsibility, as well as a list of members, see Joel Makower, *Beyond the Bottom Line* (New York: Simon & Schuster, 1994), pp. 311–21.

chapter when we identify business strategies to make ethics a part of the fabric of the firm. But in spite of the rewards that integrity and cooperation bring, there are some businesspeople who look only to their own self-interest. Let us examine some cases.

Executives and Firms That Pursue Self-Interest

Most executives take their responsibilities very seriously and are concerned about the various stakeholders of their firm. On the other hand, there are other executives who focus exclusively on dollar return or personal gain—and that often hurts society and ultimately hinders the efficient operation of the firm. Some firms such as Lockheed, Philip Morris, Solomon Brothers, RJR, and General Dynamics have a long-standing reputation for self-interested behavior. Whether you are a customer, employee, or supplier of these firms, it is wise to check your contract closely and leave little to a handshake.

Houston financier *Charles Hurwitz* controls Maxxam and through it Pacific Lumber, Kaiser Aluminum, and several other firms; he is a veteran of the 1980s takeover years. Maxxam was cited in 1995 as one of the worst 10 polluters in the United States by the Council on Economic Priorities. Hurwitz's hostile takeover of Pacific Lumber in 1985 has brought him considerable attention.[33] Pacific Lumber had been a family operated firm, and possesses 189,000 acres of redwood forests in northern California. For 100 years the firm provided steady work for generations of lumber workers in the area around Scotia, California. Moreover, unlike its competitors, it had selectively cut its timber, that is, cut no more than naturally was replaced. Pacific Lumber also worked with conservation people to preserve its old growth redwoods as a state park. Until funds were available, Pacific Lumber had set aside much of its own property as a preserve.[34]

Hurwitz's takeover was financed by $800 million in junk bonds. The junk bonds were floated by his friend, Michael Milken at Drexel Burnham Lambert. Milken later pleaded guilty to six felonies, served time in jail, and agreed to pay a total of $1.2 billion in penalties and to settle all claims against him. Drexel Burnham paid $650 million in fines and restitution, and is now bankrupt.[35] Milken's friends Boyd Jefferies and Ivan Boesky both secretly and illegally parked large investments in Pacific Lumber stock until Hurwitz was ready to at-

---

[33] See David Harris, *The Last Stand: The War Between Wall Street and Main Street Over California's Ancient Redwoods.* (New York: Times Books, 1996), and "The Worst Polluters of 1995," *Business Ethics* (January 1996): 15.

[34] Lisa H. Newton, "Chainsaws of Greed: The Case of Pacific Lumber," in Thomas Donaldson and Al Gini, eds., *Case Studies in Business Ethics* (Upper Saddle River, N.J.: Prentice-Hall, 1996), pp. 86–106.

[35] John M. Holcomb and S. Prakash Sethi, "Corporate and Executive Criminal Liability: Appropriate Standards, Remedies and Managerial Responses," *Business and the Contemporary World* 4 (Summer 1992): 81–105.

tack. Both Jefferies and Boesky were also later convicted and served jail terms for their fraudulent raider tactics.

Once in control of Pacific Lumber, Hurwitz had to generate income to finance that debt. So he took $50 million of the $90 million Pacific Lumber employees' retirement fund, and placed the remaining $40 million in annuities with a firm that had helped finance the takeover. He also tripled the rate of cutting the redwoods, and began to clear-cut the forests. The problems with clear-cutting are: depletion of the 1,000-year-old redwood trees and erosion of the barren hillsides, causing increased sediment in streams, thus endangering fish and species that depend upon fish. Hurwitz also began to cut the old growth redwoods that had been set aside as a preserve.

The actions of Hurwitz brought retaliation from environmental groups, including public protests and legal actions. In order to stop the clear-cutting of redwoods, a radical group, Earth First!, began to drive spikes into the trees. The spikes would ruin chainsaws, and made cutting those trees dangerous and unprofitable.

Hurwitz is being sued in federal court for the 1988 failure of a Texas thrift that cost taxpayers $1.6 billion. The Federal Deposit Insurance Corp. wants Hurwitz to repay $250 million to the U.S. government. His corporate raider tactics are not new. Among dozens of other lawsuits against him was a suit in 1971 by the SEC for stock manipulation, and he paid $400,000 to settle the case.[36]

J. Ignacio Lopez de Arriortua had been group vice president at General Motors. In March, 1993, Volkswagen hired him away, along with seven of his former GM aids; VW quadrupled his GM salary to $1.6 million annually. Volkswagen had the highest costs of the major global automobile manufacturers, and was desperate to lower those costs. Volkswagen's chair, Ferdinand Piech, first contacted Lopez with the offer in October 1992—6 months before Lopez's official resignation. On the same day that he signed at Volkswagen, Lopez urged GM's public relations department to issue a news release saying he had no plans to leave GM. His tactics gave him continued access to GM's documents. He did resign GM one week later—on the same day he had agreed to appear at a press conference with the GM chairman to be named GM's number 2 executive. He kept his ruse alive to the last minute.

GM has evidence that Lopez stole cartons of documents containing inside information on plans for new plants and new cars, along with specifications, prices, and delivery schedules for thousands of GM parts and suppliers. GM contends that it took Volkswagen the use of 15 computer technicians 1 month to load the thousands of files into VW's computer system, and then to shred the GM paper documents.

---

[36] "Charles Hurwitz's Tough Raider Image Looms Large in Alumax Takeover Battle," *Wall Street Journal*, Febuary 26, 1996, p. B8; "The Raiders Return," *The Economist*, March 2, 1996, p. 68.

Lopez had been placed in charge of GM's purchasing a decade earlier. He was able to cut costs for parts by dictating low prices to suppliers. Suppliers had no choice but to sell to their largest customer at the designated price. Lopez sewed distrust in the relationships that GM had spent generations building with their suppliers. Ford and Chrysler were able to cut costs for parts by working with their suppliers. When Lopez left, GM vice president Thomas Gottschalk said:

> There are important principles here. One is that disloyalty and breach of trust by a senior officer cannot be allowed to occur without consequences. . . . By their actions they hurt not only General Motors as a company, but every employee, retiree, shareholder, dealer and supplier whose own interest is aligned with GM's interest.

GM is suing Volkswagen, Piech, and Lopez; and Lopez has resigned from VW. However, GM should not have been surprised at the ethics displayed by Lopez. It was the same selfish lack of concern for other people that Lopez displayed during his years as GM's high-handed director of purchasing.[37]

Gerald M. Levin presides over a Time Warner empire with $7.4 billion in annual sales that includes many old and valuable enterprises. Nevertheless, the firm's books, films, and music have also contributed to disrespect for people and a lack of morals in American culture. Time Warner signed Geto Boys "who sing lyrically about slitting women's throats and cutting off their breasts."[38] Sony and BMG refused to sign Dr. Dre, but Time Warner did sign him. He is author of the line, "Rat-a-tat and tat like that/Never hesitate to put a nigga on his back," which is a musical call for black men to kill each other. C. DeLores Tucker, chair of the National Political Congress of Black Women, says that Time Warner is "one of the greatest perpetrators of this cultural garbage."

In books Time Warner published a book of porn by Madonna which sold for $49.95, and then had its own Book of the Month Club declare it an alternate selection. In films, Warner produced the deceitful and cynical Oliver Stone film, *JFK*, and also wholesale killing graphically presented as fun in Stone's *Natural Born Killers*. All of these ventures are profitable for Time Warner, of course. Gerald Levin defends them by citing the First Amendment and the freedom of artistic expression. Under public pressure, Time Warner sold the worst offending record company. Does the fact that these businesses are legal, cater to some people's interests, and make money make them ethical? Gerald Levin has ultimate responsibility for both the money that is made by Time Warner and also for the firm's contribution to the degradation of American culture.

---

[37] "GM Goes After Lopez, VW," *The Detroit News and Free Press*, March 9, 1996, pp. 1, 7A; "The Lopez Case: Has Germany Been Dragging Its Feet?," *Business Week*, March 25, 1996, pp. 58–60; "VW President Resigns Under GM Pressure," *The New York Times*, November 30, 1996, pp. 21–22.

[38] John Leo, "The Leading Cultural Polluter," *U.S. News and World Report*, March 27, 1995, p. 16.

Paul A. Bilzerian was 38 years old when he named himself chairman (CEO) of the Singer Company after a successful $1.8 billion hostile takeover. Since then he has actively sought buyers for his firm so that he could parlay his money into additional millions. He had never run a successful company and said, "I don't think I want to be a manager."[39]

Bilzerian, a "high-school dropout, Vietnam veteran, Harvard Business School misfit, real-estate speculator, multimillionaire raider," has also "ridden roughshod over the securities laws of the U.S."[40] The United States Securities and Exchange Commission (SEC) is investigating Bilzerian for insider trading, "parking" of stock in accounts to conceal its true ownership, false public disclosure documents filed with the SEC, aiding and abetting the keeping of false books and records, conspiracy to violate the securities laws, and tax fraud. For example, he secretly purchased and parked 58,000 shares of H. H. Robertson Company stock with Jefferies & Company. Boyd Jefferies, the chairman of that firm, pleaded guilty to two felony securities law violations.

Bilzerian made his money early in real estate speculation. He "often voiced contempt for the Eastern establishment he encountered at Harvard" but felt comfortable with the "wealthy veterans of the rough and tumble real-estate world." He built a $3,000,000 house which features two pools, basketball and tennis courts, and a 2,000-square-foot game room; the grounds feature a lake for water skiing.

Bilzerian garnered $82 million in a failed bid for Cluet Peabody. He drove the price of the stock up and then sold his shares. In this raid and subsequent raids on Hammermill, Armco Steel, and other firms, Bilzerian concealed the amount of stock he had purchased, "parked" stock with Jefferies & Company and others, even though SEC securities regulations demand full disclosure of who owns that stock.

In 1989 Bilzerian was sentenced to 4 years in jail (later reduced to 20 months) and fined $1.5 million for nine counts of violating securities laws, conspiracy, and other crimes. He did 2 years of probation and 250 hours of community service when he finished his jail sentence.[41] In 1991 he filed for personal bankruptcy, but Florida law allowed him to keep his $3,000,000 home that he fondly calls the "Taj Mahal."[42]

Steven O'Neil was president and part owner of Film Recovery Systems, a small company in the Chicago metropolitan area that specialized in recovering silver from used film. Most of the workers were Polish or Mexican immigrants

[39] "Can Paul Bilzerian Fatten Singer for the Kill? " *Business Week*, May 16, 1988, p. 43; and "Boone's New Partner," *Fortune*, March 28, 1988, p. 92.

[40] "Secret Dealing Helped Paul Bilzerian Make Takeover Bids Work," *Wall Street Journal*, May 10, 1988, p. 1.

[41] "Paul Bilzerian Still Don't Get No Respect," *Business Week*, November, 23, 1987, pp. 14, 62; "Bilzerian Gets 4 Years in Jail, Stiffest in Stock Crackdown," *New York Times*, Sept. 28, 1989, p. C1.

[42] Paul A. Bilzerian in "Where Have All the Raiders Gone," *New York Times*, June 30, 1996, p. F10.

who spoke little or no English. Stefan Golab, a 61-year-old Polish immigrant who worked at Film Recovery, died in 1983. The Cook County medical examiner determined that his death was due to cyanide poisoning.

In order to recover the silver, Film Recovery mixed the used film with cyanide and water in large open vats. The vats released cyanide into the open air where it was breathed by the workers. Management was aware of the danger but failed to warn workers or equip them with protection from the toxic chemicals. Moreover, some company personnel had defaced the pictorial poison warnings on the chemical drums.[43]

O'Neil, plant manager Charles Kirchbaum, and plant foreman Daniel Rodrigues were all found guilty of murder in the death of Stefan Golab. The court decided that they had responsibility for the safety and lives of their workers. Their responsibility was even greater than normal, since the workers did not understand English. They were sentenced to 25 years in prison and fined $10,000 each. The conviction is for murder, so they will not be eligible for parole for twelve-and-a-half years.[44] This is the first time managers have been held responsible for the death of a plant worker.

Each of the above managers had a profound impact on the ethics and the values of the firm he or she led. A manager has an impact on peers and subordinates that is proportionate to his or her role in the firm. Let us now consider how a climate of responsible behavior is built and maintained in a firm.

ETHICS FOR STRATEGIC PLANNING

The moral responsibilities of management can be built into effective strategic planning. Planning which explicitly includes ethical considerations will build trust and commitment with employees, customers, investors, suppliers, and the community. This, in turn, fosters cooperation and innovation, essential elements of any organization. Strategic management and ethics scholar LaRue Tone Hosmer points out that the original gurus of strategy, Chester Bernard, Harold Simon, and Kenneth Andrews, see ethics as integral to strategic planning. Hosmer summarizes:

> Strategic planning must be both analytical and ethical. . . . Selection of a posture and the leveraging of resources are not enough in a global economy. Trust, commitment, and effort must be added to ensure cooperative and innovative acts on the part of all the stakeholders.[45]

Hosmer argues, "Ethics do pay . . . but in a much longer time frame and with a much wider organizational impact than previously considered."

---

[43] "Job Safety Becomes a Murder Issue," *Business Week*, August 6, 1984, p. 23.

[44] "Ex-Officials Get 25-Year Sentences in Worker's Death," *Wall Street Journal*, July 2, 1985, p. 14.

[45] Thanks to LaRue Hosmer for these insights. See especially, LaRue Tone Hosmer, "Strategic Planning As If Ethics Mattered," *Strategic Planning Journal* 15 (1994): 17–34.

A business executive cannot develop a strategic plan without a clearly conceived purpose; purpose is fundamental to any coherent strategy. Management ethics scholars Freeman and Gilbert show how strategic planning and ethics are intimately linked; they demonstrate that the key to understanding the revolution in management is values and ethics, and the role that they play in organizations.[46] Moreover, there is a new, strong external argument for encouraging the good behavior of members of a business firm.

In 1991 the United States Sentencing Commission's guidelines for the sentencing of organizations found guilty of violating federal laws became effective. Under these guidelines much greater financial penalties are imposed for violations. The penalties will be greater if a firm has experienced previous violations, or if high-level company personnel were aware of the violations. On the other hand, efforts on the part of the company to avoid illegal and unethical acts will greatly reduce penalties. This then is a powerful incentive for every business firm to, for example, develop an ethical code of conduct, educate members of the organization on the importance of ethics, and regularly audit the ethical record of the firm.[47]

Effective and successful firms such as 3M, J&J, Ford, Sony, HP, and McDonald's have a strong set of values, a clear core mission, and employees dedicated to achieving that mission.[48] Values and ethics are important to these firms. It is essential that CEOs and managers deal responsibly with ethical issues (e.g., respect for colleagues, honesty in advertising, pollution, relations with the local community). Many firms have a high-level committee or a staff that plans for and monitors these issues.[49]

Firms have integrated ethical and social responsibility issues into planning and strategy. Most financially successful firms are also more ethical. Investigations of corporate social responsibility and good financial performance have shown that most often the two go together.[50] Strategic planning is only the

---

[46] Daniel R. Gilbert, *The Twilight of Corporate Strategy: Comparative Ethical Critique* (New York: Oxford University Press, 1992); and R. Edward Freeman and Daniel R. Gilbert, Jr., *Corporate Strategy and the Search for Ethics* (Englewood Cliffs, N.J.: Prentice-Hall, 1988).

[47] For an overview of the guidelines and their significance for U.S. business, see Mark A. Cohen, "Sentencing Guidelines and Corporate Criminal Liability in the United States," *Business and the Contemporary World* 4 (Summer 1992): 140–57; also U.S. Sentencing Commission, "Sentencing Guidelines for Organizational Defendants," *Federal Register*, 1991, pp. 22786–22797.

[48] James C. Collins and Jerry I. Porras, *Built to Last: Successful Habits of Visionary Companies* (New York: Harper Business, 1994); also Thomas Peters and Robert Waterman, *In Search of Excellence* (New York: Harper & Row, 1983).

[49] See, for example, Thomas G. Marx, "Integrating Public Affairs and Strategic Planning," *California Management Review* 29 (Fall 1986): 141–60.

[50] See Samuel B. Graves and Sandra A. Waddock, "Institutional Owners and Corporate Social Performance," *Academy of Management Journal* 37(August 1994): 1034–1046. For a comprehensive overview of studies, see Donna J. Wood, "Corporate Social Performance Revisited," *Academy of Management Review* 16 (August 1991): 691–718; Max Clarkson, "A Stakeholder Framework for Analyzing and Evaluating Corporate Social Performance," *Academy of Management Review* 20 (January 1995): 92–117.

beginning of the responsibilities of the CEO. Let us now turn to the board to which the CEO reports.

Role and Responsibilities of CEO and Board of Directors

The chief executive officer of a firm is ultimately responsible for the firm's success or failure. The CEO, albeit in consultation with others, sets policy, decides on new products or services, establishes budgets, and sets the mission and tone of the firm. The CEO is the person most responsible for the values, ethics, and climate of the firm. A generation ago, a CEO might not be overly concerned with the attitudes of employees or citizens. Today this is no longer true.

The responsibility of the *board of directors* is to (1) hire, evaluate the performance of, and, when necessary, fire the CEO, and (2) approve major policies and actions recommended by the CEO. The oversight role of the board is vital to the effective functioning of the corporation. It is also necessary if that firm is to act ethically.[51] Yet the current constitution of corporate boards presents problems. In 80 percent of the largest firms in the United States, the CEO is also the chairperson of the board. Harold M. Williams, a former CEO and chair of the SEC, says simply "the CEO should not be chairman of the board. Control of the agenda and pace of the meeting is a powerful control."[52] Another former CEO, Harold Geneen, who is a member of many boards, is sharply critical of boards: "Among the boards of directors of Fortune 500 companies, I estimate that 95 percent are not fully doing what they are legally, morally, and ethically supposed to do. And they couldn't, even if they wanted to."[53] Nevertheless, company board member compensation is now "soaring to record levels."[54]

Williams, Geneen, and others point out why board members are unable to discharge their responsibilities effectively. The principal reasons are these:

1. Many board members, sometimes a majority, are in the full-time employ of the same firm ("inside" board members).
2. The chief executive officer of the firm is also the chairperson of the board of directors of that same firm.

As a result, there are conflicts of interest. First, inside board members are full-time employees of the firm, and this makes it difficult for them objectively to criticize company plans and proposals at board meetings. The proposals

---

[51] E. Eugene Arthur, "The Ethics of Corporate Governance," *Journal of Business Ethics* 6 (January 1987): 59–70.

[52] "Chairman and CEO: One Hat Too Many," *Business Week*, November 18, 1991, p. 124.

[53] Harold S. Geneen, "Why Directors Can't Protect the Shareholders," *Fortune*, September 17, 1984, p. 28.

[54] "And You Thought CEOs Were Overpaid: Outside Directors Are Catching up Fast," *Business Week*, August 26, 1996.

come from the CEO, the very person responsible for their own performance appraisal. It is the CEO who will decide whether they get a promotion and an increase in compensation.[55] Outsiders, however, have a limitation: They often do not have the information they need to ask good questions. This is made worse when those directors sit on numerous boards. Thus they cannot give the time that is required to do the homework to ask intelligent questions. *Business Week* has even published a list of poor directors, because they sit on too many boards and their companies are not performing well.[56]

Second, a CEO who chairs the board thus directs the very body that is charged with evaluating his or her own performance. The chair of the board determines what is discussed at the meeting, what information is sent to the members, and the order and pace of the board's discussions. The chair thus controls the agenda of the board meeting. The conflict: A primary role of the board is to assess the performance of the CEO, yet the CEO has vast influence over the very group that sits in judgment. In Japan, very few CEOs chair their own board.[57] Also note the contrast with university governance. In universities an outsider is the chair, whereas in 80 percent of American business firms the CEO is the chair. Yet, in firms where the profit motive is strong and large sums of money are involved, there is even greater danger of conflict of interest. Most outside experts argue that the CEO should not chair the board. Some go further and maintain that because of the conflict of interest the CEO should not even be a member of the board.[58] Now let us consider one means that a firm itself has for making explicit its own values and ethics: the code of ethics.

A Code of Ethical Conduct

Most managers want a code of ethics for their firm. This was shown more than three decades ago in a classic empirical study of business ethics. Raymond Baumhart's study, which included almost 2,000 business managers, revealed that more than two-thirds thought a code of ethics would raise the ethical level of business practice.[59] More than three-fourths thought that a code would be welcomed by businesspeople as a help in specifying the limits of acceptable

---

[55] Some researchers found that more outside directors do not result in better corporate ethics. See Frederick H. Gautschi and Thomas M. Jones, "Illegal Corporate Behavior and Corporate Board Structure," in *Research in Corporate Social Performance and Policy*, ed. William C. Frederick, vol. 9 (Greenwich, Conn.: JAI Press, 1987), pp. 93–106. Many defense firms were forced to add outside directors after being caught bribing and committing fraud. This may influence the findings.

[56] "Are These 10 Stretched Too Thin," *Business Week*, November 13, 1995, pp. 78–80.

[57] Dan R. Dalton and Idalene F. Kesner, "Composition and CEO Duality in Boards of Directors: An International Perspective," *Journal of International Business* (Fall 1987): 35, 40. The 75 percent figure is from Heidrick & Struggles, Inc., *Profile of a Chief Executive Officer*, 1980.

[58] Murray L. Weidenbaum, "Battle of the Boardroom: Controlling the Future Corporation," *Business and Society* (Summer 1986): 12; Geneen, "Why Directors Can't Protect the Shareholders," p. 29.

[59] Raymond C. Baumhart, S.J., "How Ethical Are Businessmen?" *Harvard Business Review* 39 (July–August 1961): 166–71; see also *idem., Ethics in Business* (New York: Holt, Rinehart and Winston, 1968).

conduct, and most wanted a code of ethics to help clarify their own ethical standards and decisions. In many instances, they did not know what was ethical and so felt they needed help. Cases of overseas bribery (Exxon, Lockheed, ITT, Northrop), of using privileged information for private gain (Solomon Brothers, Michael Milken), as well as other transgressions, have since underscored the problem.

When an ethical code is designed for a firm, the CEO is most often the initiator. More than 75 percent of all firms have a code; among the largest firms, the percentage jumps to 90 percent. Firms that have model ethical codes and systems for monitoring them are Johnson & Johnson (see Fig. 8–1), Cray, Caterpillar and Weyerhaeuser.[60] Caterpillar's code is distributed to all managers worldwide, and these managers must report annually to the home office on "any events or activities that might cause an impartial observer to conclude that the code hasn't been fully followed." The code's provisions recognize the difference between what is legal and what is ethical: "The company's most valuable asset is a reputation for integrity. If that becomes tarnished, customers, investors, suppliers, employees, and those who sell our products and services will seek affiliation with other, more attractive companies. We intend to hold to a single standard of integrity everywhere. We will keep our word. We won't promise more than we can reasonably expect to deliver; nor will we make commitments we don't intend to keep."[61] Weyerhaeuser not only established a code of ethics but also set up a Business Conduct Committee (BCC). The BCC, which consists of a small representative group of managers and workers, is charged with promulgating the code, answering questions on borderline cases, and helping to develop and update the code.[62]

For Japanese managers codes of conduct and company policy have a profound effect on their decisions. In Europe, also, research shows that the application of procedural justice increases compliance with firm policy, especially for managers of subsidiaries operating in global industries.[63] Within the United States, however, some codes have had less effect in bringing about more ethical conduct in corporations. Evidence shows that some firms with a code are not much more ethical than those without. This is partly explained by the fact that many corporate codes were felt to be necessary and thus designed to protect firms from their own employees. These codes generally cover relations with

[60] For additional information on J&J and Cray, see also Francis J. Aguilar, *Managing Corporate Ethics* (New York: Oxford University Press, 1994), pp. 61–71.

[61] Caterpillar Inc., *Caterpillar Code of Worldwide Business Conduct and Operating Principles* (Peoria, Ill.: Caterpillar, 1992), p. 1.

[62] Earl A. Molander, "Weyerhaeuser's Reputation—A Shared Responsibility," in *Responsive Capitalism* (New York: McGraw-Hill, 1980), pp. 224–37.

[63] Chiaki Nakano, "A Survey Study on Japanese Managers Views of Business Ethics," Paper given at the Society for Business Ethics annual meeting, Vancouver, B.C., August 4, 1995, p. 20. The European data is in W. Chan Kim and Renee Mauborgne, "Procedural Justice, Attitudes, and Subsidiary Top Management Compliance with Multinationals' Corporate Strategic Decisions," *Academy of Management Journal* 36 (June 1993): 502–526.

customers, keeping honest books and records, and potential conflicts of interest—issues of concern inside the firm. On the other hand, fewer than one-fourth of the codes deal with such items as product safety, product quality, environmental issues, matters of personal character, and civic and community affairs—issues of concern to customers and outside stakeholders.[64]

A Global Code of Ethical Conduct

The developing countries led economic growth in 1995 and have done so for several years. Their output of goods and services expanded by 6 percent, more than double the 2.5 percent increase of the industrial countries. Asia grew at an 8.7 percent rate with China leading those nations at 10.2 percent.[65]

The increasing influence of international business, which has been encouraged by the North Atlantic Free Trade Agreement (NAFTA), the European Union (EU), and the nations of the Pacific Rim, makes it apparent that individual company codes are not sufficient. Bribery of government leaders for permits and purchases is still common. In many countries workers are paid far less than it takes to live, and their government forbids them to organize to seek better pay and working conditions. Moreover, air, water, and solid waste pollution is devastating in many parts of the world. Global codes could set similar expectations among firms in different nations.

International bodies have attempted to state basic principles of just business transactions across national boundaries. The United Nations agreed in 1948 on the *Universal Declaration of Human Rights* and the International Labor Office (ILO) agreed in 1977 on the basic rights of working people in the *Tripartite Declaration.*[66] On a more specific product issue, because of widespread abuse, the World Health Organization (WHO) prodded major infant formula manufacturers, such as, Nestlé, American Home Products, and Abbott Laboratories, to agree on international guidelines for marketing infant formula.[67] With regard to pollution, 56 firms, including General Motors, Polaroid, and H.B. Fuller, have endorsed the Coalition for Environmentally Responsible Economies (CERES) Principles. These ten principles pledge endorsing firms to preserve and protect the environment at levels in some cases beyond what is required by U.S. law.

---

[64] For valuable additional insights, see Max B. E. Clarkson, "A Stakeholder Framework for Analyzing and Evaluating Corporate Social Performance," and Thomas Donaldson and Lee E. Preston, "The Stakeholder Theory of the Corporation: Concepts, Evidence, and Implications," *Academy of Management Review* 20 (January 1995): 65–91, 92–117.

[65] Lester R. Brown, "World Economy Expanding Steadily," in Lester Brown, Christopher Flavin and Hal Kane, *Vital Signs—1996: The Trends that Are Shaping Our Future* (New York: W. W. Norton, 1996), pp. 74–75.

[66] For an excellent overview of the content and impact of these and other international compacts, see William C. Frederick, "The Moral Authority of Transnational Corporate Codes," *Journal of Business Ethics* 10 (1991): 165–77. We should note that the U.S. stands alone in not ratifying the *Universal Declaration of Human Rights.*

[67] Again, the United States is the only nation that has never agreed to these international guidelines.

Some nations have attempted to make international business conduct more fair through domestic legislation. In the 1970s many U.S. firms bribed foreign leaders to obtain preference for doing business in their country or so they would purchase the company's products. Executives of Lockheed paid more than $22 million to leaders of Japan, Netherlands, Saudi Arabia, Korea, and other nations to purchase their aircraft. United Brand's executives paid $2 million to the president of Honduras to reduce taxes on bananas, and Gulf Oil paid the South Korean president $4 million to give it a permit to build an oil refinery. These bribes caused a government to fall in Japan and major embarrassment for the leaders of the other nations. In order to reduce this bribery of foreign leaders by U.S. executives, the U.S. Congress passed the Foreign Corrupt Practices Act in 1977.

The U.S. Foreign Corrupt Practices Act does not prohibit "expediting," "grease," or "tip" (to insure promptness) payments, for example, to customs or other minor officials to cut through the red tape. Payments are allowed if the official has no impact on the final decision, and the payment only makes the transaction move more quickly. What is prohibited is a major payment to an official to influence that official's judgment, for example, to obtain access or to purchase a product. The firm is also required to keep detailed records and accounts of all payments so that auditors may inspect and judge them. When Congress passed this legislation prohibiting major bribes, they presumed that other developed nations would follow with similar legislation to prevent bribery, so as to make international operations more fair. This has not happened. For example, German firms are still able to charge bribes off as a cost of doing business on their corporate income tax.

There has also been hesitation about doing business with Iraq, China, Burma, Sudan, and other countries with poor records in respecting human rights. In many other countries that manufacture consumer goods for U.S. customers, children sometimes work 60-hour weeks for 2 dollars a day, and are forbidden to organize to ask for better pay or working conditions. Understanding this, firms such as Levi Strauss, Reebok, and Wal-Mart have developed their own principles of how workers should be treated and they carefully monitor their suppliers. Other firms, such as Nike and Fruit of the Loom, continue to sell the products of sweatshops. In the United States, the Clinton administration has proposed a set of "Model Business Principles" for American companies to follow voluntarily when conducting international business. But these principles would affect only U.S. firms. Hence, many now call for international norms.

Recognizing the need for international standards of business conduct, a group of top executives from firms in Japan, Europe and the United States have developed a set of principles for business. This group, the Caux Roundtable, met in Caux, Switzerland, to formulate their *Principles for Business*. At that meeting were executives of Siemens, 3M, Canon, Chase Manhattan Bank, Matsushita, Dana, Nissan, Ciba Geigy, Ambrosetti Group, Philips Electronics, Sumitomo, and others. They took a set of principles for global business developed by Minneapolis-St. Paul executives, and added two major basic principles. The first, from the Eastern tradition, is the principle of "Kyosei," a Japanese word that means "living and working together for the common good—enabling cooperation and mutual prosperity to coexist with healthy and fair competition." The second principle, from the Western tradition, is "Human Dignity," which "refers to the sacredness or value of each person as an end, not simply as a means to the fulfillment of other's purposes."

The International Association of Jesuit Schools of Business, with representatives from 60 business schools in 20 countries, met in Recife, Brazil in 1994 and opted to seek an international code of business conduct. In their meeting at Sanata Dharma University in Yogyakarta, Indonesia in 1995, they agreed to encourage discussion and support for the Caux *Principles for Business*. The text of these *Principles for Business* is contained in the Appendix.

Planning for Ethics and Disclosure

A firm must develop a clear, motivating mission statement and must communicate that mission to members of the firm. The mission statement will be discussed in Chapter 9. Managers must then hire people who embody those values, and provide them rewards, including publicity and prizes, to encourage such activities. With the development of the mission statement and the code, top management's job is just beginning. The message must be reinforced within the corporation by: setting a good example, occasional ethical pep talks, and inspirational stories of real people within the firm.[68]

Firms that are open about their operations encourage ethical conduct and discourage ethical misconduct. Unethical business behavior thrives in secrecy. Disclosure requires: (1) communication of the mission, values, and models of behavior to members of the firm; and (2) communication of policies, successes, and yet-to-be-achieved goals to external stakeholders. We discussed internal communication earlier. We now focus on external disclosure.

The case for disclosure to external stakeholders (customers, employees, suppliers, and the community, as well as stockholders) is based on the fact that information enables free markets to operate more efficiently. Lacking accurate information, there are misallocations and inefficiencies. As Thomas Clausen, former CEO of Bank of America and the World Bank, put it, "a company's actions simply cannot be judged 'efficient,' 'responsive,' 'accountable,' or 'consistent with the public interest,' unless sufficient information about its activities is available." He adds that if government regulation becomes burdensome, it will be because business leaders were not sensitive to the needs of their stakeholders.[69]

---

[68] For examples of ethical behavior in the rank and file, especially among service workers, see Bill Fromm and Len Schlesinger, *The Real Heros of Business* (New York: Currency, 1993); see also Francis J. Aguilar, *Managing Corporate Ethics*, pp. 72–86.

[69] Thomas Clausen, "Voluntary Disclosure: An Idea Whose Time Has Come," in *Corporations and Their Critics*, Thornton Bradshaw and David Vogel, eds. (New York: McGraw-Hill, 1981), pp. 61–70.

A firm's internal auditor, the external auditor, and the audit committee of the board oversee finances to insure honest disclosure, and this information is reported in the annual financial report. The internal auditor sometimes must decide whether information that has been ignored by management should be brought to the attention of outside auditors. The willingness of the internal auditor to report fraudulent behavior depends on many variables, especially the total ethical climate of the firm.[70] Punishing a manager for violations of a code should be a last resort. Nevertheless, if it is perceived to be just, that punishment can have an impact on the behavior of both the person being punished and on others in the organization.[71]

As we indicated earlier, among the more important means of implementing socially responsible policies and adequate disclosure is oversight by the board of directors, which is often done with the aid of an ethics or social policy committee of the board. More than 100 large firms have ethics, social policy, or public policy board committees.[72] Among the firms with active ethics or social policy board committees are General Electric, Levi Strauss, Mead Corporation, General Motors, and Bank of America. These committees oversee the implementation of the corporate code of ethics. In addition, some firms have a public policy staff and a social issues planning group, whose purpose is to be alert to changes in community attitudes and values, follow government activities, contribute to planning, outline corporate policy options for management, and lobby government.

Social Audits, Ethics Officers, and Ethics Training

Social reporting requires a firm to state its goals and also to articulate its impact on society. About 40 percent of Fortune 500 firms report on social performance.[73] At least 32 firms publish separate reports. Others describe their social activities briefly in their annual financial report (Ford, IBM, Xerox) as well as in executive speeches and advertisements (Sears, Dow, DuPont, Mobil).

Corporate reports on public interest issues provide disclosure on social issues. These periodic reports contain descriptions of corporate activities that have a social impact (e.g., waste disposal, energy saving, equal employment op-

---

[70] Arthur Brief, et. al., "What's Wrong with the Treadway Commission Report? Experimental Analyses of the Effects of Personal Values and Codes of Conduct on Fraudulent Financial Reporting," *Journal of Business Ethics* 15 (1996): 183–98. See also "U.S. Congress Looks at Internal Auditors," *Internal Auditor* (October 1987): 4–7.

[71] Linda Klebe Trevino, "The Social Effects of Punishment in Organizations: A Justice Perspective," *Academy of Management Review* 17 (October 1992): 647–76. See also Gail Ball, Linda Trevino, and Henry Sims, "Just and Unjust Punishment: Influences on Subordinate Performance and Citizenship," *Academy of Management Journal* 37 (April 1994): 299–322.

[72] "The Ethics Committee: A Vehicle to Keep the Process Moving," *Ethicos* (September–October 1990), 6. Also U.S. Department of Commerce, "Business Strategies for the 1980's," in *Business and Society: Strategies for the 1980's* (Washington, D.C.: U.S. Department of Commerce, 1980), pp. 33–34.

[73] W. Michael Hoffman, et al., "Are Corporations Institutionalizing Ethics?" *Journal of Business Ethics* 5 (August 1986): 88–89.

portunity, contributions to community and education) and assessments of the success of these activities. Equal employment opportunity and pollution control can be quantitatively measured and reported. Clear targets and measurable results can be obtained in these two areas, since it is possible to count the numbers of people in various jobs and the parts per million of pollutants. Hence many firms have been measuring performance in these areas for decades. Reporting the other issues is generally in the form of a description of activities.

Among firms that produce a detailed report on their social activities are General Motors, Aetna Life and Casualty Company, Norton Company, and Atlantic-Richfield. The reports of the first three are prepared internally and go into some detail on what the firm is doing on socially important issues. For example, *General Motors Public Interest Report—1994* presented equal employment opportunity statistics for the corporation and described GM's efforts regarding global trade policy, clean air, alternative fuels, auto safety, and sustainable development. These social reports provide information to shareholders and other stakeholders.

A few firms have asked outside auditors to examine their social performance. Ben and Jerry's Homemade Ice Cream has published an outside audit of their firm for several years. In the wake of criticism of their "clean" claims, The Body Shop, a British-based cosmetics firm, published an outside audit of their social activities in 1995. Because of the U.S. sentencing guidelines and other reasons, some expect that external audits will become more common. Migros of Switzerland, a large food retailer, has published a candid social report. For example, Migros acknowledged exaggerations in advertising and admitted that it did not sufficiently promote healthier foods.[74] The Migros report was also done by an outside management consulting group. When a firm acknowledges its own failures and publishes assessments that are critical of its own activities, its reports gain credibility. They are thus more readily believed when they report positive accomplishments. A new group at KPMG Peat Marwick is gearing up for such audits, and they expect the other big six accounting firms to follow.[75]

---

[74] See "Migros of Switzerland Prepares a Social Audit," *Responsive Capitalism: Case Studies in Corporate Social Conduct*, ed. Earl A. Molander (New York: McGraw-Hill, 1980) pp. 250–63. For a view by the director of that audit, see Meinholf Dierkes, "Corporate Social Reporting and Performance in Germany," in *Research in Corporate Social Performance and Policy*, ed. Lee E. Preston, vol. 2 (Greenwich, Conn.: JAI Press, 1981). A good handbook to aid in preparing a social audit is American Institute of Certified Public Accountants, *The Measurement of Corporate Social Performance* (New York: American Institute of Certified Public Accountants, 1977); see also U.S. Department of Commerce, *Corporate Social Reporting in the United States and Western Europe* (Washington, D.C.: U.S. Department of Commerce, 1979).

[75] "This Auditing Team Wants You to Create a Moral Organization," *The Wall Street Journal*, January 19, 1996, p. B1; See the comprehensive overview, Michael Metzger, Dan Dalton and John Hill, "The Organization of Ethics and the Ethics of Organizations: The Case for Expanded Organizational Ethics Audits," *Business Ethics Quarterly* (January 1993): 27–43; also "Social Auditors: The New Breed of Expert," *Business Ethics* (March 1996): 27–32.

Kirk Hanson of Stanford Business School, who did The Body Shop audit, predicts that there will be 20 organizations doing such audits within 10 years.

An outside consulting firm reviewed the social performance of most of the largest 400 U.S. firms, and published their ratings. They rated the firms with explicit standards on several criteria: the community, employee relations, the environment, product, women, and minorities. Another agency, the Council on Economic Priorities, has for decades done regular comprehensive, objective reports on the social policies and actions of firms.[76] Considerable voluntary disclosure is involved in obtaining information for the book, *The 100 Best Companies to Work for in America*. The authors give background on each firm and also rate each on the following specific criteria: pay and benefits, opportunities for promotion, job security, pride in work and company, openness and fairness, and camaraderie and friendliness.[77]

Many large firms have a corporate ethics officer who is designated to oversee the firm's ethics initiatives. This person generally monitors and oversees the firm's legal, ethical, and social responsibility issues. The ethics officer is often asked by the CEO to help write and communicate the firm's ethics code of conduct. Therefore, this person must have intimate knowledge of the firm, and must have very good people skills.

In order to provide education and support for corporate ethics officers, the *Ethics Officer Association* began in 1991 and has grown to 247 members, including 98 firms who sponsor the organization. Sponsoring members include AlliedSignal, Bombardier, Eaton, General Electric, Hershey Foods, Honeywell, Hughes, Polaroid, Prudential, Sears, Siemens, Sony, Sun Life of Canada, Texas Instruments, and Westinghouse. The organization sponsors annual meetings to provide information to the ethics officers, and also publishes a regular newsletter to update them on current issues.[78]

Cummins Engine, Citibank, McDonnell Douglas, and General Dynamics sponsor ethics training for all managers. Top managers initially spend a day, and middle managers several hours, in ethics training, and there are periodic follow-up programs. About 44 percent of large firms have some sort of ethics training.[79] In addition, General Dynamics and some other firms have estab-

---

[76] Peter D. Kinder, Steven Lydenberg, and Amy Domini, *Social Investment Almanac: A Comprehensive Guide to Socially Responsible Investing* (New York: Henry Holt, 1992), pp. 745–88; the book is a comprehensive treatment of socially responsible investing. See also Steven Lydenberg, Alice Tepper Marlin, and Sean Strub, *Rating America's Corporate Conscience* (Reading, Mass.: Addison-Wesley, 1986).

[77] Robert Levering and Milton Moskowitz, *The 100 Best Companies To Work for in America* (New York: Penguin, 1994).

[78] Further information on the Ethics Officer Association can be obtained at its administrative office at the Center for Business Ethics, Bentley College, 175 Forest Street, Waltham, Mass., 02154.

[79] Many defense and some other firms have developed a code, provide ethics training, established a whistleblowing policy, and hired an ethics officer in order clean up after a scandal. See "Ethics for Hire: Laundering Images of Soiled Companies is Turning into Big Business," *Business Week*, July 15, 1996, pp. 26–28. For an overview of corporate ethics in ten leading American firms, see Business Roundtable, *Corporate Ethics: A Prime Business Asset* (New York: Business Roundtable, 1988).

lished an ethics hotline and/or an ombudsman who can be spoken to anonymously by any employee on ethical issues. Each of the above strategies depends on the initiatives of managers within the firm. But outside stakeholders, especially shareholders, can also have an influence on the values and ethical performance of those inside the firm.

The Influence of Institutional Investors

Institutional investors (pension funds, mutual funds, trust funds, university endowments, and banks) have a large and increasing influence on publicly held corporations in the United States. This was not true a generation ago. In 1955 pension funds and mutual funds owned less than 5 percent of corporate stock; by 1994 they owned 40 percent.[80] Earlier, they did not try to exercise control over the firms in which they invested. They were content to receive dividends and to watch capital gains. Institutional investors own in many cases well over 50 percent of the outstanding common stock of particular firms (see Table 8–2).

TABLE 8–2   Institutional Investors and Their Corporate Stock Holdings

Company	Value (in billions)	Percentage of Shares Held
Companies listed by dollar value of stock held by institutional investors		
IBM	$29.64	46.1%
Exxon	19.05	31.8
General Electric	16.27	44.0
Philip Morris	12.26	57.8
Ford Motor	12.01	53.1
Merck & Co.	10.79	50.2
Digital Equipment	8.83	55.0
Companies listed by percentage of stock held by institutional investors		
Allegis Corp.	$1.88	98.0%
CNA Financial	3.41	93.9
NWA Inc.	1.22	93.3
St. Paul Cos	1.71	84.8
AMR Corp.	2.13	83.7
Tele-Communications	2.60	82.4
Continental Corp.	1.86	80.4

A survey of the investments of institutions that manage $100 million or more in discretionary equity assets. Figures as of March 31, 1988.

Sources: New York Times, July 5, 1988, p. 29; and CDC Investment Technologies. Copyright © 1988 by the New York Times Company. Reprinted by permission.

---

[80] "Does America Still Work?" *Harper's Magazine,* May 1996, p. 43.

The influence of institutional investors on business managers is exercised in two ways: (1) by means of the actions of the institution's portfolio manager, who seeks short-term gains in its investments; and (2) by means of voting shares at the annual shareholder meeting on issues that have been placed on the ballot by various investors.

The actions of portfolio managers were treated earlier. These actions can include pressuring company management for short-term returns and supporting the attempts of corporate raiders when the likely result will be a quick increase in share value. Such actions often damage a firm that is trying to work for the long term, as was indicated in Chapter 1.

The second way of exercising influence is through voting their shares. Institutional investors began voting in the 1970s. Any shareholder, by following SEC rules, can place an issue on the ballot for vote at the shareholder meeting of any publicly held firm. In 1995, 38 affirmative action and 36 tobacco related resolutions were presented to companies to be placed on their ballots. Over 20 companies were challenged with resolutions to bring board member's compensation under control. The average board member of a large company received about $83,000 compensation in 1995. Other issues raised were: environmental responsibility, board diversity, CEO pay, pay and working conditions in developing countries, and Northern Ireland.[81] By placing these issues on the ballot, the initiating group is able to focus top management's attention, inform the general public, and often negotiate an agreement with management that will achieve its ends.

It is rare for a shareholder resolution opposed by management to obtain a majority vote. Nevertheless, even a small percentage can represent hundreds of thousands of shares belonging to individual and institutional owners who are questioning management policy. The embarrassment of having these shareholders vote against management is often pressure enough. The Interfaith Center for Corporate Responsibility (ICCR) is the most active agent for placing social issues on shareholder ballots. The ICCR is a division of the National Council of Churches. It represents 25 Protestant denominations and 230 Roman Catholic orders and dioceses.[82] In 1996, more than 300 resolutions were presented to 200 firms.

To help institutional investors reach a judgment on the merit of the various proposals, the Investor Responsibility Research Center (IRRC) was set up in 1972, with the assistance of the Ford, Carnegie, and Rockefeller Foundations.[83] The IRRC (not to be confused with the ICCR) presents the position of both

---

[81] For a complete discussion of these issues plus the figures quoted, see Archie B. Carroll, *Business and Society: Ethics and Stakeholder Management*, 3rd ed. (Cincinnati: South-Western, 1996), pp. 615–21.

[82] Timothy Smith, "Shareholder Activism," *Social Investment Almanac*, ed. by Peter Kinder, et al. (New York: Henry Holt, 1992). The *Almanac* is a comprehensive source of information on a wide variety of social investing issues and agencies.

[83] Theodore V. Purcell, "Management and the 'Ethical' Investors," *Harvard Business Review* (September–October 1979): 26.

management and the activist group that introduced the proposal. The IRRC then analyzes the proposal and poses critical questions that merit consideration. The IRRC does not recommend how to vote; that is the investor's decision. At the end of the proxy season, the IRRC publishes a summary of the season's voting. It lists the firms, the issues, and the percentage of shareholders supporting the proposal; it also often indicates which institutional investors supported or opposed individual proposals and why.

The shareholder resolution as an instrument for raising social policy issues is now accepted by most institutional investors. This change reflects the fact that ownership carries with it a responsibility to express judgment on major policy questions. The shareholder resolution can also be an aid to management. It brings to the attention of management many questions that could easily be overlooked. Moreover, it provides an early warning system that alerts management that certain issues may become more important in the future and more deserving of attention. The ethical investor movement can help stakeholders catch the attention of management. Management is thus less likely to be locked into a narrow mindset.

Going one step further, some investors place their money in funds that use a "social screen" for their investments. That is, they invest only in firms which have a good social record. This movement has grown from investments of $40 billion in 1984 to more than $625 billion today.[84]

Growth and Narrow Interests

Economic indicators provide conflicting signals on the health of the American economy. Some suggest a healthy economy: total employment is higher than ever before, the unemployment rate is down, American firms are competing better in world markets, and freedom of choice still encourages initiative and innovation. Other economic indicators are not good: We have the largest foreign debt of any nation in the world, our federal budget deficit is still immense (most of it accumulated during the 1980s), and delayed gratification is no longer one of our values. Moreover, many of our cities are decaying, and crime is higher.

Moral indicators provide conflicting signals on the health of American society. On the positive side, we still value family, honesty, and integrity. Church attendance is higher in the United States than in other industrialized countries. Fraud, kickbacks, and unethical activities, whether in business or in government, still cause scandal and outrage. On the other hand, there is increasing evidence of a "me first" attitude among businesspeople, and our society suffers from bribery, alcoholism, drug addiction, street crime, murders, and white-collar crime.

People motivated by self-interest, when faced with such large problems, often focus on protecting themselves. In the political sphere, special interest lobbying groups have fractured society into competing camps. Witness, for ex-

---

[84] Kinder, et. al., *Social Investment Almanac*, p. 11.

ample, the success of gun owners, used car dealers, and trial lawyers in achieving their goals—even when the goals are contrary to the good of the community. Among world democracies, the United States has one of the lowest rates of voting. For example, Ronald Reagan and Bill Clinton were elected by less than one-third of the voters. More than half didn't even bother to vote.

Most of the changes required in American society (e.g., balancing the budget, dealing with crumbling cities, helping poor and underprivileged people, decreasing the hostility of labor-management relations, and limiting our voracious use of energy) will require careful planning and good leadership, but also an open mind, humility, and sacrifice. History tells us that little can be accomplished without sacrifice, but we now hear little mention of it. Yet faced with these problems, in order to create a better society, along with our strengths, few are willing to acknowledge our personal and national weaknesses. We will discuss what to expect in the future in the next chapter.

Summary and Conclusions

Business activities evidence an underlying set of goals and values. Values and ethics are communicated to members and to outside stakeholders by the CEO. Some CEOs are concerned for the long-term good of the firm and society, too. Humane, cooperative, and ethical values can create a more participative, attractive, and effective climate. In such a climate, employees are more likely to use their abilities to achieve the goals of the firm. Some executives, however, exclusively seek their own financial gain, which harms other people, the firm, and society. Individualism and the Protestant ethic have carried Americans fast and far, but now delayed gratification has given way to the consumer ethic of "buy now, pay later." Individualism encourages "get rich quick" schemes that are not always to the benefit of society.

Traditional American flexibility and some changes offer signs of hope. Social concerns are now a part of corporate strategic planning. Pension and mutual funds, endowments, and foundations now exercise more influence on owners, and often bring pressure on management through their voting on various social issues at shareholder meetings.

Boards of directors now take their responsibilities more seriously. Implementation of social policy and ethics brings a code of ethics. Moreover, most American firms also consider social issues in evaluating the performance of managers and inform their stakeholders about their social and ethical activities, whether in a social report or some other form.

Executives recognize that most stakeholders want more from a firm than merely return on investment. Quality products, planning for the long-term, and involvement with local communities are but a few of the expectations citizens have of firms. To the extent that firms do not respond willingly, government will legislate or regulate. The alternative is for management to voluntarily initiate policies to insure their obligations are met.

Discussion Questions

1. Is the salary of Robert Allen of AT&T rational? Is it just? What of Steven Spielberg's compensation? Use the norms developed in Chapter 3.

2. Evaluate the GM and Ford compensation schemes described at the beginning of the chapter. Are they good long-term strategies?

3. Do you think that American values have shifted as indicated in Table 8–1? How does this affect the values of managers?

4. Is CEO pay a problem in the United States now? Is it just? Is there a confidence problem for these CEOs? What does the data on the increase of executive salaries versus hourly worker salaries tell you?

5. Is there a lack of incentive for managers to plan for the long term? Explain.

6. How would you characterize the values, ethics, and management style of Gun Denhart (Hanna Andersson)? What of the values of Ryuzaburo Kaku (Canon)? The values of James Burke and Ralph Larsen of J&J? And those of Roy Vagelos (Merck)? Felix Rohatyn (Lazard Freres)?

7. Do people consider a firm's ethical reputation when they purchase a product? Do you do so?

8. How would you characterize the values, ethics, and management style of Charles Hurwitz (Maxxam)? Given Ignacio Lopez's tactics as a GM vice president, are you surprised if he took GM's trade secrets to Volkswagen?

9. Does Gerald M. Levin bear any responsibility for undermining American values? Identify the values and ethics of Paul Bilzerian. Likewise for Steven O'Neil of Film Recovery Systems.

10. What problems arise when a board is made up mostly of insiders? What problems arise when the CEO is the chair of the board?

11. How has the U.S. Sentencing Commission influenced how managers treat ethics within the firm?

12. Are the mission, goals, values, and ethics of a firm integral to corporate planning? Describe how to make ethics an effective part of planning.

13. Is there a need for a global code of business ethics? If so, do the Caux *Principles for Business* fulfill the need? Evaluate the strengths and weaknesses of these *Principles for Business*.

14. What is the argument for disclosure of financial information? What is the argument for social issue disclosure? Describe the ways in which social issue disclosures are made.

15. Describe the influence institutional investors have on firms in which they hold stock. What are the advantages and disadvantages of this involvement from the standpoint of the firm? From the standpoint of society?

Exercise:
Business for Social Responsibility

The following firms have a record of exemplary business behavior. They are all described in the book *Companies with a Conscience*.[85] For this exercise, compare one of these companies with one other in the same industry not on the list on such issues as: employment diversity, pollution, attitudes toward and programs for employees, and any other special issues that you note.

Firm	*Industry*
Ben & Jerry's	Ice cream
Shorebank	Banking
Patagonia	Clothing designer and distributor
America Works	Employment agency
Newman's Own	Food
Cultural Survival Enterprises	Help natives preserve rain forests
Glen Ellen Winery	Make and distribute wine
Sunrise Medical	Wheelchair manufacturer
Greystone Corp	Bakery, construction
Birkenstock Footprint Sandals	Manufacture, distribution

Ebola Virus and Entertainment CASES

The 1995 film *Outbreak* is based on a real-case outbreak of the Ebola virus in Zaire, Africa. The Atlanta Center for Disease Control (CDC) sent a team to a "hospital deserted save for a few patients dying the ugly, bloody death of Ebola . . . no running water, no telephones . . ."[86] and contained the disease.

Dustin Hoffman played the movie lead role. C. J. Peters, MD, is chief of Special Pathogens, CDC. Peters is fighting budget cuts for his unit. Note the comparative data.

CDC's Pathogens Branch		*Warner Brothers Outbreak*	
Salary: Dr. C. J. Peters:	$ 125,000	Dustin Hoffman:	$ 6,000,000
Budget: CDC FY 1995:	$7,200,000	Production:	$54,000,000
Spending on Ebola:	$1,800,000	Gross in 3 months:	$67,000,000

---

[85] Mary Scott and Howard Rothman, *Companies with a Conscience* (New York: Citadel Press, 1994).

[86] "The Point Man in Germ Warfare," *Business Week*, August 21, 1995, pp. 72–73.

1. What do these comparative expenditures tell us about our values and our priorities?
2. Is there an inequity in these figures? Why or why not?

Stock Purchase Deal

Through his banking work, Kenneth McGinty learns that Maco Corp. is about to purchase Digital Optics. Digital Optics is a small publicly held firm which has had an unprofitable year and its stock is undervalued. The price of the stock is sure to rise when the buyout is announced. Setting aside legality and looking only to the ethical issues, can Ken purchase some stock for himself? May he tell a good friend? Explain.

Company Controller

Carol Goudreau, company controller, is asked by the chief financial officer (CFO) to "manage earnings" in such a way as to present more favorable financial results for this quarter. The CFO does Carol's performance appraisal. What should Carol do? Why?

CHAPTER

Business Values
for the Future

We do not see the poor of the world's faces, we do not know their names, we cannot count their number. But they are there. And their lives have been touched by us. And ours by them. George Bernard Shaw put it perfectly: "You see things, and say why? But I see things that never were, and I say why not?"

—Robert S. McNamara, Conclusion of his last address as president of the World Bank

The purpose of business is to efficiently provide people with products, services, jobs, and family income. Business is a means of achieving these outcomes; it is not an end in itself. The focus of business, as with all human endeavors, is on the welfare of people. This is the foundation for successful business planning and a healthy society.

Planning for the future is essential to business success. Planning in turn is based on projections of what to expect in the coming decades, coupled with a clear sense of the organization's mission and capabilities. Markets for new products and expectations regarding the future work force are the center of corporate planning. These potentials depend on people's values. Thus, being alert to changing values enables a firm to formulate better business plans and to be a more effective corporate citizen. This chapter probes the current setting for planning, examines the importance of having a coherent business ideology, investigates future scanning for business, and charts the direction of changing values and ethics over the coming decades.

TODAY'S BUSINESS VALUES

How the values of businesspeople develop and how they influence current business practices has been examined in previous chapters. But business is not an isolated institution. It operates in society and is influenced by cultural values and government. The most visible relationship exists between business and government. Government regulates business in order to achieve the common good, and business lobbies government to obtain its goals.

How extensive government regulation should be—and how much the individual firm should work for the public good even when it is not regulated and it is costly to do so—is disputed. Some maintain that each firm should exclusively pursue its own profit. As we have seen in earlier chapters, these proponents of free enterprise say that people as a whole will automatically be better off as a result. On the other hand, most hold that the good corporate citizen will explicitly consider the well-being of others, even in cases where it will cost the firm. In spite of the disagreement, both agree on two points:

1. Free enterprise is the most efficient, productive, flexible, and innovative socioeconomic system yet devised.
2. Nonetheless, free markets do not in themselves always provide social goods that are costly to firms—for example, clean air, safe drugs, and truthful advertising.

There is significant agreement on the strengths, direction, and limitations of the U.S. economy. This consensus allows us to deal more effectively with the major business and global problems that face us.

Free Markets Triumph

Almost all of the countries of the world today have some version of a free market economy. Former Communist nations, such as Eastern Europe, Russia, and China now also have market systems that encourage market exchange, and hence also innovation and efficiencies.[1] The fact that markets are now global is both an opportunity and a challenge to people in every country. If a firm anywhere in the world is able to produce high quality goods at low cost, that firm has the opportunity to be a success and to create jobs. But we also know that empowerment, loyalty, and efficiencies come to firms in which people deal with each other honestly and openly.

People in every nation also know that government must provide vital services which the market system does not support. Free markets do not provide parks, libraries, street lighting, art museums, or clean air and water. For example, in the absence of government regulations, free markets encourage busi-

---

[1] For the rapid movement to a free market in Asia, see John Naisbitt, *Megatrends Asia* (New York: Simon & Schuster, 1996), especially Chapter 4, "From Government-Controlled to Market-Driven," pp. 121–56.

nesses to cut costs by dumping pollutants in local streams. Moreover, economic systems are not democratic; each person does not have one vote.

Aristocratic Markets

From the viewpoint of income and purchasing power, free market nations are aristocratic. Some people earn one hundred times the annual income of others, and as a result they possess one hundred times the economic "voting power." They may spend their discretionary personal income funding entrepreneurs in the inner city or education for the poor, or spend it on expensive clothes, lavish vacations, or huge houses.

Some who work as hard or harder than other very well paid fellow citizens find it difficult to pay the rent or the food bills. Although we say that wealth is the reward for hard work, we also know that good fortune—especially birth into an affluent family—is even more important. Those children born to college-educated parents in the United States have many advantages over those born, for example, to uneducated parents in Bangladesh.

Free enterprise can also encourage selfish activities. According to its ideology, free markets and competition—guided by Adam Smith's "invisible hand"—result in the most economic use of resources. Or, as the seventeenth-century British pamphleteer put it, "Private vices make public profit." In the short term, capitalism can reward those who are selfish. Furthermore, it provides a rationalization that can promote and bless self-seeking, self-centered behavior.

Consumer sovereignty places the consumer in the role of decision maker and policy maker. In the very act of purchasing goods, each consumer sets priorities for him or herself, for others, and for society. Making consumer sovereignty the basis for setting social goals is convenient, because it distributes responsibility. But then, who is responsible for the many problems that we have drifted into in the past generation, such as the trade and the federal deficit, the excessive use of petroleum, and air, water, and solid waste pollution? Consumer sovereignty leads to unplanned, promiscuous economic growth. It is also a convenient principle for those who claim to be value-free, for it enables them to dodge important questions about the common good. However, such blind adherence to consumer sovereignty values the individual over the community, encourages self-centered behavior, and leads to stalemates as special interest groups pull us in opposite directions. Exclusive reliance on consumer sovereignty and free enterprise thus enable us to avoid the vital questions of what kind of society we want—that is, avoid them until crises are upon us, flexibility is gone, and options have been narrowed.

Capitalism in the United States was built on self-interest and rugged individualism. In the nineteenth century, huge fortunes were amassed before social legislation was enacted. Workers and small businesspeople were often hurt by the actions of the robber barons. Nevertheless, many of these wealthy men later used that wealth to benefit the public. Indeed, Andrew Carnegie's defense of large fortunes was based on the claim that rich people better use the wealth created by industry for public purposes (see Chapter 5). John D. Rockefeller built the University of Chicago, Carnegie funded libraries across the United States, and Collis P. Huntington built a superb rail rapid transit system for Los Angeles (which was dismantled in the 1950s by a combine of GM, Firestone, Phillips Petroleum, and Standard Oil of California). Foundations were set up by wealthy men (e.g., Ford, Carnegie, and Rockefeller) to serve the public, and these foundations have continued to fund valuable new programs. Bill Hewlett and David Packard used their wealth to fund education, the arts, and other public institutions. Will Warren Buffet, Bill Gates, and others who make a fortune in this generation use their immense wealth to help other people?

Threat of Special Interests to Democracy

We know how essential planning is for business. However, in the public sector, there has not been much planning for the United States or for the world during the past three decades. Fewer libraries, museums, or parks have been built, and suburbs sprawl haphazardly, paving over farmland that a generation ago might have been set aside as parks or rapid transit right-of-ways. Most suburban housing tracts do not even have sidewalks for children, walking, and bicycles. Vision and planning are required to make cities and society liveable; both are in short supply today. Attention is focused on new plants, new offices, and new homes. Meanwhile, cities deteriorate, since so many of our roads, public transit facilities, libraries, and parks were built 50 or more years ago. As the infrastructure deteriorates, it comes as a shock. However, when individuals pursue their own self-interest, the community as a whole does not always benefit.

National priorities are agreed to slowly, primarily through the political process: voting and legislation. On public interest issues, Americans are generally committed to an open system and to consensus. However, it generally takes a catastrophe to alert us to inadequacies in our social or business goals. Millions of birds died from pesticides before we learned how we were poisoning them.[2] It took Three Mile Island and Chernobyl to alert us to the costs and dangers of nuclear power. Lake Erie died before we realized the dangers of water pollution. It took the Los Angeles riots and white supremacists to force us to face the continued extent of racial and job discrimination. Right wing militias and skinheads distrust government, and even would prefer no government at all. Blowing up the federal building in Oklahoma City with the loss of 140 lives demonstrated a hatred of government and society. Such widespread distrust makes it difficult to develop long-range national policies for the common good.

This discussion of the strengths and weaknesses of society and of business enterprise brings us to a core question: How does the business system adapt to change? How are internal and external inefficiencies and inequities addressed?

---

[2] Rachel Carson, *Silent Spring* (Boston: Houghton Mifflin, 1962).

What does business have at its disposal that enables it to face the future with confidence?

A democracy works slowly and often requires a crisis to awaken its citizens to new public needs. Men and women must personally feel that need. This makes long-range planning for a city, a nation, or the globe extremely difficult. Pressure is on legislators to vote on issues in such a way as to benefit constituents. There is little incentive to sacrifice present goods for future goods, and any investment policy is precisely such a tradeoff. On the contrary, special interests, short terms in office, and felt needs back home all militate against the kind of long-term investment of time and capital in research and planning that will pay off a generation from now. Moreover, many of the problems we now face are serious and long-term (e.g., broken families, poor education, urban decay, pollution, and dwindling resources). When a crisis occurs before we grasp the seriousness of these problems, there is little time left to find solutions. This may be the most serious flaw of democracy.

Nevertheless, human beings are amazingly imaginative and flexible. If we are able to take the long-term perspective, we will be able to acknowledge our needs. If we can marshal the talent and initiative that we possess, we can find solutions.

Lack of Clear Values

A few years ago a survey found young people critical of the beliefs of their parents and other elders. They were not critical of what they believed but of their seeming lack of beliefs and convictions. The values of their elders seemed to be largely inherited and absorbed passively from the surrounding culture. Their elders had few thought-out, internalized goals and values.

Young people are often the victims of homogenized mass education and passive entertainment. Not only does mass education directly influence thinking, but it also indirectly influences values through the clothes, food, and TV programs that are "acceptable." Mass education, in fact, has as much influence outside the classroom as inside. It substitutes tastes and fads for critical thinking and the development of personal goals and values. Often people escape thinking by turning on the TV. Thus the moral and intellectual fiber of our country has been softened by being pounded for decades by violence, sex, and quick solutions to every problem.

The confusion, apathy, and cynicism that is sometimes found in young people puts a greater burden on their elders to articulate their own values and ethics. If adults, with more experience, are unclear about their own life goals and aspirations, young people are left with no one giving leadership. It is especially important that individuals know their own values in a time of rapid change. Otherwise, men and women are left with no rudder and are pushed by events from one job or problem to another. Without values and goals, people are not in control of their own lives, careers, or destinies. Opportunities, challenges, and crises come rapidly, and individuals who have not reflected on why they live, what they do, and why they do it are unable to deal with them. Such people will be confused, frustrated, and hurt. By gaining ownership of their roots and goals, these people will be able to profit and grow.

Minds are like parachutes: They only work when they are open. Yet a critique of American society is entitled *The Closing of the American Mind.*[3] The author maintains that people of all great civilizations were steeped in knowledge of other times and other thinkers. But American universities have virtually stopped conveying a tradition. Since we so rarely examine the most important questions (e.g., What kind of person do I want to be? What is my goal in life?), we have become a pragmatic, shallow civilization.

A major purpose of education is to encourage students to reflect on their own values and make them explicit so that they may then be able to grow and make clear life choices. Alvin Toffler, in analyzing this problem, is critical of the schools:

> Students are seldom encouraged to analyze their own values and those of their teachers and peers. Millions pass through the education system without once having been forced to search out the contradictions in their own value systems, to probe their own life goals deeply, or even to discuss these matters candidly with adults and peers. . . .
>
>   Nothing could be better calculated to produce people uncertain of their goals, people incapable of effective decision-making under conditions of over-choice.[4]

Toffler is speaking of the failure of schools a generation ago; it is even more true today. The need for individuals to make explicit their own values and goals is greater in a period of rapid change, and schools are primary vehicles for this sort of examination and evaluation—yet schools, from kindergartens to universities, have failed in this respect. Many educators still maintain that education should be "objective" and that values are too controversial for a public institution dealing with people of various backgrounds. What they fail to recognize is that such a position in itself embodies a value. People growing up without clear goals and values contribute to national confusion, apathy, and cynicism. The resulting individualism and inability to achieve a consensus on public goals create severe strains within all democratic societies.

An Aid to Core Beliefs and the Work Ethic

People whose personal values and goals are clear have greater self-esteem, and thus are more likely to be able to work with others. Hence both individuals and organizations benefit when people probe their basic values, and articulate answers to basic questions such as the following:

---

[3] Allan Bloom, *The Closing of the American Mind* (New York: Simon & Schuster, 1987).

[4] Alvin Toffler, *Future Shock* (New York: Random House, 1970), p. 370.

- What is my fundamental purpose in life?

- Are men and women basically self-seeking or are they basically good and generous?

- Do women and men have a spiritual end or is this present life, with its pleasures and material satisfactions, all there is?

- Are there moral goods and evils (e.g., murder), or is everything relative?

- Does society exist for people or do people exist for society? What is the purpose of the business firm? What is the purpose of the state?

- Are human beings moving toward long-term progress? Or toward decline and perhaps collapse?

The responses to such questions have an effect on the goals of organizations and also on government legislation and regulations.

If you reflect on the above questions and answer them, you will learn much about yourself. This will complement the *Personal Goals and Values Inventory* paper from Chapter 1 that you wrote. Your answers to these questions may show that you are focused on your own interests and that you see other people as instruments to attain your own goals. On the other hand, your responses may show that you have a concern for others and are often willing to sacrifice your own interests for their sake. To gain another perspective, what responses to these questions would you prefer from a future business partner? Or a potential spouse? If you were hiring new people, which attitudes of a potential employee would incline you to hire the person?

As for choosing a job, what sort of a firm you would like to work for—a firm whose employees are exclusively interested in their own careers, or a firm whose employees are also concerned about others? In which sort of firm would you be likely to do better work and enjoy that work more? In which would you be more successful?

When business firms provide ethics education for their people, they stress practical skills. This is helpful, but it does not go far enough. Ethics training programs at business firms less often stress critical thinking and self-assessment such as we have described here, which is essential to personal maturity and moral development.

A VIABLE BUSINESS CREED

The most salient and precious American business value is freedom: free markets, free competition, free movement of people and capital, and most especially freedom of the individual. Important as personal freedom is in American society, it is not unlimited. An individualism that is not conscious of other people leads to mistrust, frustration, and ultimately chaos. One does not have the freedom to shout "Fire!" in a crowded theater. Traffic lights are restrictions that were objected to by early libertarians. A business firm does not have the freedom to mislead in its product advertising or to dump its waste in a lake. As people live closer together and become more dependent on one another, freedom must be limited by both self-control and external checks. In fact, real freedom paradoxically emerges only when a people have formed internal constraints: "Freedom is endangered if a free society's shared values are no longer sufficiently vigorous to preserve the moral cohesion on which the discipline of free people rests."[5] Although it is hard to understand for an individualist, limitations based on a consideration for others (e.g., in the case of traffic lights or truth-in-advertising laws) introduce even greater freedom for all. People have less fear and greater trust in the safety of driving and in what is claimed in advertising, and thus they can act more freely.

One of the strengths of American business has been its pragmatism—getting the job done while avoiding theoretical and ideological issues. As Daniel Bell put it, "The ideology of American business became its ability to perform. The justification of the corporation no longer lay primarily in the natural right of private property, but in its role as an instrument for providing more and more goods to people."[6] Pragmatism thus leads us to accept values and goals simply because they work and often regardless of undesirable by-products and inequities.

Any valid defense of the values of business and the economic system cannot rest merely on the importance of freedom and efficiency, because the following questions then arise: Freedom for what? Efficiency for what? Freedom, efficiency, and the business system they support are not ultimate ends of their own, but are means that allow people to pursue more important goals. Greater freedom and productivity allows a society to provide more jobs, goods, and services with less effort. This allows its citizens to pursue other goals. In short, higher productivity is a major benefit but not the end of society.

Problems for Future Managers

Some of the problems that now hinder business in the United States have a potential for creating even more trouble in future years. The United States had a trade deficit of $641 billion in 1994, up from $545 billion the year before or 10 percent of gross domestic product. Compare this with Japan's trade surplus of $681 billion.[7] We purchase that many more goods and services from overseas than we are able to sell. Moreover, we must borrow from overseas to buy these additional goods and services. The largest single commodity we purchase from other countries is petroleum. Even though the United States remains one of the largest petroleum producers in the world, that still is not enough to satisfy us; we spend an additional $53 billion each year to purchase more petroleum from

---

[5] Peter Viereck, *Shame and Glory of the Intellectuals* (Boston: Beacon, 1953), p. 196.

[6] Daniel Bell, *The Coming of the Post-Industrial Society* (New York: Basic Books, 1973), p. 272.

[7] "America Owes, Japan Owns," *The Economist* (November 1995): 76.

other countries.[8] Thus, we are on the slippery slope of borrowing foreign money to purchase foreign goods, all the while increasing our outstanding foreign debt. The United States was the largest creditor nation in the world until 1985. We financed many activities beyond our borders and received interest on those loans. Currently we are the largest debtor nation in the world, and we now borrow more capital from other nations than any other country in the world. This increases the cost of investment capital for entrepreneurs in the United States. Having a large foreign debt is generally characteristic of poor nations, who need to borrow capital from wealthier nations to finance their own development programs.

In addition to the balance of trade deficit, the United States has an accumulated federal budget deficit of $5 *trillion*.[9] To get some sense of the size of what is owed, consider that it comes to $20,000 for every man, woman, and child in the United States and that to pay the interest on it annually costs each person $1,600. That is $1,600, or $6,400 for a family of four, that we spend for which we have nothing to show.

Much of the debt is owed to Japanese, Europeans, and petroleum producers. Japan has moved past Britain and the United States into the top spot among international investors. A list of the world's largest banks by assets demonstrates this. Of the largest ten, six are Japanese; the first American bank on the list, Citicorp, is number 6.[10] The second largest American bank, Bank of America, is number 23. The Japanese remain prodigious savers, and they thus still have the capital to invest around the world.

How will this affect business in the future? It will require increased taxes, which add to the cost of production, to pay for the spending of previous generations. It thus adds additional costs when we are attempting to be competitive in world markets. In addition, the trade and federal deficits also illustrate a new American value: If you can obtain goods today without paying full price, do so, even if your children must pay later. Ted Turner illustrates our spending habits by the following fact: "In the United States we have 2.5 percent of the children of the world, but we spend 60 percent of all that is spent in the world on toys."[11]

Mission Statement and Core Ideology

Firms that have a clear and strong vision or mission statement tend to outperform their rivals in the marketplace. Put another way, the most successful and profitable firms have a much stronger vision than their competitors. A recent book length study establishes that the best companies in a field have a very

---

[8] Calculated from *Statistical Abstract of the United States—1994.* (Washington, D.C.: U.S. Department of Commerce, 1994), p. 582, and *The Economist*, June 29, 1996, p. 104.

[9] *Ibid.*, pp. 329–330.

[10] "500 Ranked Within Industries: Commercial Banks," *Fortune*, August 5, 1996, pp. F-16–F-18.

[11] Ted Turner's address at the University of Detroit, November 25, 1985.

strong vision, which is expressed in their mission statement and acted out by the people in the organization.[12]

The firms that were studied were well established and highly successful. These visionary companies include: 3M, American Express, Boeing, Citicorp, Ford, General Electric, Hewlett-Packard, IBM, Johnson & Johnson, Marriott, Merck, Motorola, Nordstrom, Procter & Gamble, Sony, Wal-Mart and Walt Disney. Each of these firms is premier in its industry, is widely admired by businesspeople, has made an indelible imprint on the world in which we live, and was founded before 1950. Their stock has outperformed the market by a factor of more than 12. Moreover, from the standpoint of people who work there, they find more satisfaction with their jobs, *if* they agree with the vision.

Each of the visionary companies "more thoroughly indoctrinate employees into a core ideology than do comparison companies." The visionary companies more carefully nurture and select senior management. Visionary companies selected their chief executives from inside the company in 96.5 percent of the cases, while comparison companies selected their chief executives from inside in only 78 percent of the cases.

An organization's mission statement and goals reflect the core values of those who formulate the statement. The J&J Credo (see Fig. 8–1) reflects the core values of the firm over the past 50 years. It is "the glue that holds the organization together," in the CEO's words.

The mission statements of the above firms stress elements like the importance of integrity, respect for the individual employee, service to the customer, and responsibility to the community. However, not surprisingly, each mission is unique and there is no one element that is explicitly contained in every statement. What is common is authenticity of the ideology, that is, the extent to which the firm's actions are consistent with what it claims in its mission statement. The authors choose their visionary companies *regardless of the content of the vision*. Philip Morris was included in spite of the fact that its principal product, tobacco, seriously injures and kills people.[13]

These businesses, with the exception of Philip Morris, have higher ethical and spiritual ideals. The resulting climate then attracts like-spirited people to the organization. A test for such an organization is to institutionalize those values so they remain after the retirement of those who created the statement of ideals. It is essential that all members of the organization have ownership of the mission.[14] Each of the above firms has already passed this test.

Collections of some of the best business mission statements have been gathered and analyzed. Moreover, the collectors also provide historical back-

---

[12] James C. Collins and Jerry I. Porras, *Built to Last: Successful Habits of Visionary Companies* (New York: Harper Business, 1994).

[13] *Ibid.*, p. 87.

[14] Burt Nanus stresses the importance of discussing the mission statement with the entire group in his "Leading the Vision Team," *The Futurist* (May–June 1996): 21–23.

ground on the firm and how the statement was developed. The firms that are discussed include: Dayton Hudson, Delta Airlines, General Mills, Georgia-Pacific, Gillette, Hallmark, Honda, IBM, Johnson & Johnson, Kellogg, Merck, Motorola, Saturn, Southwest Airlines, and many more. These statements always speak of values, a credo, and that customers and employees are treated with respect. They attempt to articulate a vision for the firm.[15]

A Spiritual Business Vision

Technology and rational systems have contributed much to our contemporary standards of living and our life-styles. We expect to apply our rational skills to problems and that we will be able to solve them. However, in recent years, we have become aware that the most serious problems that we face in the world are not able to be solved by rational solutions alone. Consider, for example, the dangers of famine, terrorism, the widening gap between the rich and the poor, AIDS, depletion of nonrenewable resources, and the shallowness and crassness of news and entertainment media.

Vaclav Havel, the president of the Czech Republic, maintains that we are at the "end of the modern era," and that we need a new approach to deal with these problems. He maintains that we need:

> . . . an elementary sense of justice, the ability to see things as others do, a sense of transcendental responsibility, archetypal wisdom, good taste, courage, compassion. . . . Such forces must be rehabilitated.
>
> We must try harder to understand than to explain. The way forward is not in the mere construction of universal systemic solutions, to be applied to reality from outside; it is also in seeking to get to the heart of reality through personal experience.[16]

For the same purpose leaders in business ethics have reintroduced the insights of various religious traditions to enable us to better understand the problems that face us. Religion historically was central to the marketplace in the West and remains central for many cultures today. Medieval European citizens planned their cities with their cathedral at the center of the city. They regularly expected the church to set standards for trade and norms of fairness, bring disputants together to adjudicate those disagreements, and finally to insure that the interests of the poor and the disadvantaged were not forgotten. Such an active role of religion was not limited to medieval Europe. For Native Americans, religion was generally central. For both Mayan and Aztec peoples, religion was a principal integrating force in their lives, and they designed their religious tem-

---

[15] Jeffrey Abrahams, *The Mission Statement Book: 301 Corporate Mission Statements from America's Top Companies* (Berkeley, Calif.: Ten Speed Press, 1996); also Patricia Jones and Larry Kahaner, *Say It and Live It: The 50 Corporate Mission Statements that Hit the Mark* (New York: Currency Doubleday, 1995).

[16] Vaclav Havel, "The End of the Modern Era," *New York Times*, March 1, 1992, p. 11.

ples as the largest and most central buildings in their cities. The medieval Europeans and Native Americans are not exceptions. The role that they had for religion is typical of societies. Note the major role of religion in the Middle East, Africa, Latin America, and in many Asian countries.

What happened that severed this connection for the Western world? The Enlightenment at the beginning of the last century greatly influenced modern Western states. "The legitimacy of the state and all other social structures was reformulated on so-called nonreligious grounds or principles to which all rational thinking individuals could subscribe."[17] Although the immediate effect of this was negligible; over time this separating of religion from business and public life had a profound effect. Thus the U.S. Constitution separated church and state. Religion became a private matter. The irony of the separation is underscored when we consider the great influence theologian John Calvin had on the Protestant ethic, and the fact that the first economist, Adam Smith, was a professor of *moral philosophy* (see Chapter 4).

Steven Carter, professor of law at Yale University, points out how Western peoples seldom have outright hostility to religion. Nevertheless, we do have a tendency to trivialize religion, to treat it as a hobby, or a "mystical irrationality." Carter finds this tendency especially in liberals. For the liberal, it is alright to make polite references to God at public events. But this reference to God should not be substantive; it should not be a foundation for public policy. Yet Carter is convinced that religion is much more likely to survive as a major influence on people and policy than is liberalism. Carter does not opt for prayer in public schools and he is in favor of a wall separating church and state, although he does feel that the wall should have some doors of influence in it.[18]

While the European Enlightenment had a profound influence on Western values, there is now a new interest in spirituality in the workplace. In the wake of downsizing, employees feel more pressed and ask themselves "Why do I feel so unfulfilled?" Firms like AT&T, Boeing, Lotus, and Medtronic have programs of prayer and reflection within the firm. Other firms hire "spiritual" consultants who include poet David Whyte, Tom's of Maine founder Thomas M. Chappell, former senior vice president of Meredith Magazine Group and author James A. Autry, and corporate culture scholar Terrance Deal. Many Christian entrepreneurs are conservative. They may support programs for the needy, while many also support Republican causes and political candidates.[19]

A best-selling business book in 1996 was *Jesus, CEO: Using Ancient Wisdom for Visionary Leadership* by Laurie Beth Jones. Jones is president and

---

[17] Gedeon Josua Rossouw, "Business Ethics: Where Have All the Christians Gone?" *Journal of Business Ethics* 13 (1994): 557–70.

[18] Stephen L. Carter, *The Culture of Disbelief* (New York: Basic Books, 1993). Carter has followed this by another book, *Integrity* (New York: Basic Books, 1996), and he intends two more, *Civility* and *Compassion.*

[19] "Companies Hit the Road Less Traveled," *Business Week*, June 5, 1995, pp. 82–86. See also "The Christian Capitalists," March 13, 1995, pp. 52–63.

founder of a management consulting firm specializing in health care marketing. She uses Jesus as a model of excellent leadership with Gospel citations. Jones shows how Jesus "kept in constant contact with his boss" (the Father), "stuck to his mission," "held them accountable," "looked out for the little guy," and much more. She cites Jesus as a model in a prayerful and respectful fashion.[20]

In another recent book on spirituality in the workplace, Jay Conger says that spirituality builds upon St. Augustine and Thomas Merton, but it also includes finding God everywhere and giving "expression to the being that is in us; it has to do with the feelings, with the power from within, with knowing our deepest selves and what is sacred to us."[21]

From the grass roots, groups of businesspeople in most cities of the United States gather weekly or monthly at prayer breakfasts, and discuss and pray over their faith, families, and firms. Several of these groups, such as the *Woodstock Business Conference* and *Legatus*, are organized nationally.[22] Santa Fe hosted a conference on spirituality in business in April 1996.

The Protestant ethic has had a profound effect on business values. As discussed in Chapter 4, the Protestant ethic emphasizes self-interest and achievement. Some are rediscovering a spirituality that has deeper roots and provides a balance to the Protestant ethic. They call it the Catholic ethic:

> The Catholic ethic views the world through the lenses of family and forgiveness. The Protestant ethic views it through lenses of individualism and immutability. In the Catholic ethic, life in this world is a process, a journey, in which forgiveness is always possible. In the Protestant ethic, one's efforts to "succeed" may help in this world but have less influence in the next. . . .
>
> The merciful culture of the Catholic ethic has many elements that make the sharing of resources natural and ordinary and that temper hostility toward the needy, and these elements guide the daily decisions of those who are influenced by this ethic.[23]

Southern Baptist President Bill Clinton commented on the influence of the "Catholic ethic" on him during his days at Catholic Jesuit Georgetown University:

> The Catholic influence on me is manifested in two ways. First of all, a real sense that we are morally obliged to try to live out our religious convictions in the world, that our obligations to social mission is connected to religious life. . . .

[20] Laurie Beth Jones, *Jesus, CEO: Using Ancient Wisdom for Visionary Leadership* (New York: Hyperion, 1995). For other excellent books by Christian business executives, see James A. Autry, *Love and Profit: The Art of Caring Leadership* (New York: Avon Books, 1991); also Max DePree, *Leadership Is an Art* (New York: Dell, 1989).

[21] Jay A. Conger, *Spirit at Work: Discovering the Spirituality in Leadership* (San Francisco: Jossey-Bass, 1994), p. 9.

[22] The national offices are: Woodstock Business Conference, Woodstock Theological Center, Georgetown University, Washington, D.C., 20057-1097, Phone: (202) 687-6565. Legatus is c/o Domino Farms, 30 Frank Lloyd Wright Dr., P.O. Box 997, Ann Arbor, Mich., 48106-997, Phone: (313) 930-3854.

[23] John E. Tropman, *The Catholic Ethic in American Society* (San Francisco: Jossey-Bass, 1995), p. 99.

And the other thing I got out of my Catholic tradition is the real respect for the obligation to develop one's mind. . . .[24]

In sum, those who bring spirituality, prayer, and reflection into the workplace range from conservative Christians to New Age people. But the majority are ordinary people who are trying to better understand themselves and their work lives. They would like to break down the compartments in their lives, and better integrate their work life, their family life, and their religious faith.

PLANNING AND FORECASTING

Most CEOs say that they would like to spend more time on strategic planning. But strategic planning can be done only when one has some notion of what to expect in the future.[25] Much information is available from public sources: demographics, availability and price of resources, employment skills, and economic forecasts. Also needed are forecasts of what public policy issues will emerge in the future. Most of the issues discussed in Chapter 8 concern public policy.

Organizing for the Future

The advantages of having the information that is required for forecasting and using it within the firm are that it (1) enables the firm to plan, (2) reduces the possibility of unpleasant surprises, (3) enables the firm to focus on opportunities and get ahead of issues, and (4) enables the firm to engage in consensus building.[26] A firm may ask in-house staff, a trade association, or a consulting group to prepare materials for strategic planning. They obtain, analyze, and report information on future trends.

Various sources of information and techniques for gathering information are available. For example, considerable information is readily available on population, economic trends, production, and use of food and energy, transportation, and perceptions with regard to what constitutes quality of life.[27]

Capital-intensive firms in stable industries have more need of advance warning of future developments because of their large investment and lessened flexibility.[28] Firms that are flexible with respect to resource deployment have

---

[24] "President-elect Bill Clinton: 'My Catholic Training,' " *National Jesuit News*, January, 1993, p. 7.

[25] See, for example, John Naisbitt, *Megatrends* (New York: Warner, 1988), also Naisbitt's *Megatrends Asia*.

[26] Burt Naus, "Visionary Leadership," The Futurist (September–October, 1992): 20–25. For an excellent presentation of corporate planning in an ethical context, see LaRue T. Hosmer, *Strategic Management* (Englewood Cliffs, N.J.: Prentice-Hall, 1982).

[27] See the excellent sources, Lester R. Brown, Christopher Flaven, and Hal Kane, *Vital Signs—1996* (New York: W. W. Norton & Co., 1996), also L. R. Brown et al., *State of the World—1996* (New York: W. W. Norton & Co., 1996). These two reports are issued annually.

[28] John E. Fleming, "Public Issues Scanning," in *Research in Corporate Social Performance: A Research Annual*, ed. Lee E. Preston, vol. 3 (Greenwich, Conn.: JAI Press, 1981), pp. 155–73.

more opportunity to quickly respond to new trends. One way of obtaining "best guesses" on forthcoming sociopolitical issues is to use the Delphi technique, which is a structured method for arriving at a consensus of opinion among a panel of experts.

Trend Analysis

A second technique used by many firms is called *trend analysis*. Using this technique, certain critical issues are followed in an effort to determine the direction and speed of their future development. Sometimes the CEO or a group of top managers initially determine which issues will be followed. At other times, corporate staff poll managers or scan media sources to determine which issues are emerging.

Print media can often provide early indications of new trends. Firms can obtain the results of periodic surveys of selected "opinion leaders" from, for example, *The Wall Street Journal, New York Times*, or *Washington Post*. Either corporate staff or a consultant can do a brief summary of articles on the specified public policy issues. Over time, interest in a certain issue may increase, as measured by the number of column inches devoted to it in particular print media. This may indicate emerging new products, services, or strategies for the firm, new pressures on the firm, or potential government oversight. Public issues scanning provides an early warning system for discovering future developments. The life insurance industry has engaged in trend analysis since 1970 and finds it essential for planning. General Electric (GE) has been a leader in such forecasting for decades.[29]

Careers with a Future

The global marketplace, electronic communication, and the new importance of knowledge and information is having a profound effect on current jobs and new employment needs.[30] Workers will be able to do more work from a computer workstation at home or other locations. Firms will more often hire people to do specific jobs on contract; and more people will be hired part-time to help with specific tasks.[31]

There are fewer jobs in manufacturing. However, contrary to popular belief, manufacturing output has constituted roughly the same percentage of U.S. gross national product over the last 50 years, and this percentage will probably be maintained. Hence increasing manufacturing productivity and innovation will continue to be important.

---

[29] John Stoffels, *Strategic Issues Management: A Comprehensive Guide to Environmental Scanning* (Elmsford, N.Y.: Pergamon, 1994), and Sheila Moorcroft, ed., *Visions for the 21st Century* (England: Adamantine Press, 1992).

[30] Robert Barner, "The New Millennium Workplace," *The Futurist* (March–April, 1996): 14–18.

[31] See Charles Handy, *The Age of Paradox* (Boston: Harvard Business School Press, 1994), also Handy's *The Age of Unreason* (Boston: Harvard Business School Press, 1989).

More jobs are in the service sector: hospitality, banking, insurance, transportation, and a wide variety of other services. However, most of these jobs are not as high-paying as those lost in manufacturing.

With more electronic equipment being used in manufacturing and services, there is a need for people to design, manufacture, and maintain this equipment. Biotechnology requires people with skills in biochemistry, microbiology, and molecular biology.

Hazardous waste disposal skills are also in great demand, along with skills in energy conservation, solar energy, and laser technology. Engineering and business skills will continue to be important as society becomes even more complex. There will continue to be a demand for people in information processing, including those who can design hardware, write software, and operate and maintain systems.

The dramatic increase in the importance of knowledge and innovation skills will affect education and training. There will be less emphasis on rote learning in large groups and more emphasis on encouraging new ideas, understanding, and creativity among individuals and small groups of learners. Institutions of higher learning serving college-age students will be smaller and more individually oriented, so as to better meet students' needs. Business will sponsor a wide variety of education and training programs for its own people, both in-house and off-site.

FUTURE BUSINESS VALUES

American business and its values have shifted over the last decade; earlier chapters of this book charted these shifts. Because changes continue at a rapid rate, it is imperative that we understand the direction and the substance of current changes.

In this final section we will review the changes that are taking place and try to assess their potential impact on American business. We will identify emerging values that will significantly affect people, firms, and American business ideology. Note that these emerging values are extensions of traditional American values; there are few sharp breaks (see Table 9–1). We will attempt to make projections by using data and expert opinion.

Central Role of the Person

The importance of the individual person pervades American life, literature, and thought. Individualism is increasingly important also in China, Singapore, South Korea, Japan, and other Asian countries.[32] Individualism, democracy, human rights, the free market, and the courts build on the centrality of the dignity

---

[32] For a comparison of and demonstration of the similarity of basic Asian and American values, see John Naisbitt, *Megatrends Asia, op. cit.,* pp. 53–55.

TABLE 9–1 Traditional American Values Lead to Future Business Values

Traditional American Values . . . *Lead to* . . .	*Future Business Values*
Dignity of the individual	Central role of the person
Entrepreneurship and democratic spirit	Participation in management decisions
Self-reliance	Sustainable development
Planning ahead	Long-range perspective
Business as a provider of goods and services	Business as a servant of society
Growth and progress	Technology and innovation
Democratic nation	A nation among nations
Respect for the land	Harmony with the environment
Frontier and self-sufficiency	Local control: small is beautiful
Influence of religion and churches on American life	Spiritual roots of the new business mission
Helping neighbors (building barns, labor unions, charitable organizations)	Concern for others
Centrality of the individual, the family, and the local community	New measures of success
Optimism and openness	Vision and hope

of the individual person. Demands for greater productivity, coupled with the central role of the person, will bring more upgrading of skills and management development, along with flexibility in peoples' workday, workweek, and career. Most recognize that teams and loyalty bring success and satisfaction. The family will again be emphasized as the bedrock of America's social structure.

A firm in which the talents of each employee are challenged, in which coworkers communicate and supervisors provide feedback on work, is one in which each individual will grow in skills, satisfaction, and as a person. For a business firm to succeed, its workers must be committed to a quality product or service. The firm must enlist the efforts of all workers in pursuing its goals by communicating its mission statement, creating a cooperative climate, allowing time in the work week for group sessions on better quality, and rewarding groups and individuals that contribute to reaching the goals.

Firms recognize that the best way to succeed is to draw on the full talents of all workers. Workers feel that they are part of the team when they are asked their opinions of products and processes. Workers then develop a sense of ownership with respect to the job and the firm, and they work better, experience less fatigue, and enjoy greater satisfaction as a result.[33]

---

[33] See Gerald F. Cavanagh, "Evolution of Corporate Social Responsibility: Educating Stakeholders and Virtuous Entrepreneurs," in John W. Houck and Oliver F. Williams, eds., *Is the Good Corporation Dead?— Social Responsibility in a Global Economy* (Lanham, Md.: Rowman & Littlefield, 1996), pp. 169–99.

Participation in Management Decisions

Managers now also encourage participation in decisions. Various schemes have been developed in the United States, Sweden, Japan, and elsewhere to obtain worker input and to share the responsibility for decision making with workers. Decision making through consensus at the grass roots level among workers, as opposed to decision making only at the top, is now common. The American Catholic bishops devoted an entire section in their letter on the U.S. economy to participation.[34] However, Sar Levitan, veteran observer of work, cautions,

> In most cases . . . management preaches worker cooperation but ignores workers' priorities if they conflict with immediate profit-maximization efforts. Employees are encouraged to participate in corporate decision making only if it does not infringe on management prerogatives.[35]

Most people find that liking their coworkers is essential to job satisfaction. If coworkers are friendly, cooperative, and interested in each other, work can be something to look forward to. Firms that previously would transfer talented, high-potential managers every few years now recognize the needs people have for family, friendships, and some stability. Life on the job and in the suburbs can be impersonal, and friendships there can be superficial. If one might be transferred and thus forced to go through the pain of leaving friends, it can be too great a risk to get to know people well. It is easier and less painful not to get involved. Recognition of the need for stability for the sake of spouse and children has caused some firms not to demand that their achievement-oriented executives move as often. Thus, managers can become more involved with their family, neighborhood, and local community, and thereby increase their own confidence and self-esteem.

Most American firms now have programs designed to increase employee involvement and satisfaction. For example, Ford reduced the number of defects in its vehicles by 48 percent in a 2-year period by enlisting the efforts of workers. Where labor relations are not adversarial, management is able to ask employees to help improve quality by monitoring the product as it is made and by suggesting better manufacturing processes. Ford engineers took a prototype of a pickup truck to line workers and asked for their suggestions. Larry Graham, an assembly-line worker who had worked on a previous model pickup, suggested that the design be altered to allow assemblers to bolt the pickup cargo box from above rather than from below. When bolting from below, an assembler had to lift a heavy pneumatic wrench over his or her head from a pit beneath the truck.

---

[34] United States Catholic Bishops, *Catholic Teaching and the United States Economy* (Washington, D.C.: United States Catholic Conference, 1986), part 4, nos. 295–325. For a discussion of the development of the document, see Manuel Velasquez and Gerald F. Cavanagh, S.J., "Religion and Business: The Catholic Church and the American Economy," *California Management Review* 30 (Summer 1988): 124–41.

[35] Sar A. Levitan, "Beyond 'Trendy' Forecasts," *The Futurist* (November–December 1987): 30.

Bolts were not firmly tightened, and customer complaints came in. The engineers used Graham's suggestions to redesign the assembly process, resulting in easier assembly and far fewer consumer complaints.[36]

Sustainable Development

The last 2 decades have been sobering, not only to Americans but to all peoples. Citizens in Europe, Japan, and the United States now realize that they will never again attain the supremacy in world markets or the growth rate that they had in the 1950s and 1960s.[37] Rainforests are being destroyed in Latin America, Africa, Indonesia, and India.[38] No substantial housing for millions plagues Mexico City, Jakarta, Bombay, and hundreds of other cities. Moreover, we anticipate one billion people in China and India owning autos that use petroleum and add to pollution. Hence, we realize that development and growth must be such that the generation following us may enjoy both a decent standard of living and a liveable world.[39]

In the United States, data shows that 15 percent of citizens have family incomes below the poverty level. In the last chapter we cited the huge compensation of top executives. This gap between the rich and the poor is widening each year. During the last 25 years, while the gross domestic product has doubled, an index of social health has declined to about one-half its former level. Developed at Fordham University, this index includes 16 items such as infant mortality, drug abuse, high school dropouts, elderly poverty, child abuse, teen suicides, child poverty, health insurance coverage, unemployment, real wages, homicides and the gap between the incomes of the rich and the poor.[40]

The gap between the rich and the poor is larger and more apparent in many Asian, Latin, and African countries, also. It will be extremely difficult for business to prosper in the long term, given such problems, both because potential markets are thus limited, and also because of the danger of social instability.[41] Moreover, many of the new service and some high-tech jobs are not challenging. They do not provide the opportunity for expanding one's skills or for advancement, as we note at Burger King, McDonald's, and retailing.

---

[36] "A Better Idea: American Car Firms Stress Quality to Fend off Imports," *Wall Street Journal*, August 26, 1982, pp. 1, 14.

[37] Katherine S. Newman, *Declining Fortunes: The Withering of the American Dream* (New York: Basic Books, 1993).

[38] Anjali Acharya, "Tropical Rainforests Vanishing," in Lester R. Brown, Nicholas Lenssen, and Hal Kane, eds., *Vital Signs, 1995—The Trends That Are Shaping Our Future* (New York: W. W. Norton, 1994), pp. 116–17.

[39] Hal Kane, "Shifting to Sustainable Industries," and Lester R. Brown, "An Acceleration of History," in Lester R. Brown, et. al., *State of the World—1996* (New York: W. W. Norton, 1996); see also the special issue of *Academy of Management Review*, 20 (October 1995): 873–1089, which is dedicated to seven studies of ecologically sustainable organizations.

[40] "A Warning Sign," *U.S. News & World Report*, October 21, 1996, p. 30.

[41] Paul Krugman, *The Age of Diminished Expectations* (Cambridge: MIT Press and Washington Post, 1994).

In addition to the above, resources are now more expensive. Most manufacturing and services add to pollution, and the cost to clean it up increases our cost of living. Finally, all peoples must compete for markets with every other country. This was discussed in Chapters 1 and 8.

In contrast to the "cowboy economy" of the 1980s, in which gross production and consumption measured success, the newer "spaceship economy" of the twenty-first century recognizes that all men and women live together on a fragile planet. This planet has only finite resources and a limited ability to cleanse itself of pollution. Thus, if human needs and desires could be met with less use of resources, less production, and less consumption, that economy would be superior. To say this is economic heresy. However, if we can meet human needs with less resources, waste, and pollution, are we not better off? Consumption and production without limit harm all people and the environment, and they should hardly be considered as goals in themselves.

There is resistance to this reformulation of goals and to the new criteria of success that this demands. The reformulation requires that we make judgments on the type of growth and the products we want and on the tradeoffs and costs we are willing to accept. Such judgments require discussion, common understandings, and building consensus—an immense task in a fractured democracy. It is easier to allow the "free market" to decide all issues. However, giving such power to the market wastes resources, arable land, and human lives, and thus is not a responsible policy.

As for work and home life, many already opt for simplification. For example, note transportation. Much of the time that was saved in shortening the workday is lost in driving to and from work, schools, church, and stores. In older neighborhoods one could walk to each; many suburbs do not even have sidewalks upon which one could walk. This total reliance on the automobile wastes not only time but also petroleum and other natural resources. It constitutes not progress, but a loss of freedom. Similarly, time is lost in filling out income tax returns, insurance forms, and questionnaires and in listening to advertisements. Some urge: wherever there is a choice between making more money and simplifying life, the latter road should be taken.

From another point of view, a new series of cultural "thou shalt nots" may be required in the future. Humankind will not be able to survive if individual humans do not set limits to their appetites, do not develop an habitual willingness to conserve and preserve, and do not maintain a conscientious concern for others. Although these attitudes are difficult to achieve, they are essential if we are to prevent mass starvation, war, and chaos.[42] The development of spiritual, human values that are integrated into everyday life and institutional decision making is a priority. Developing countries, especially Asian nations, are also experiencing many of these dilemmas. Fortunately, most of these nations still have

---

[42] Daniel Callahan, *The Tyranny of Survival* (New York: Macmillan, 1974).

their traditional religions and respect for family to support concern for future generations. On this shrinking planet, economic and political planning must consider the larger issues.

Fortunately, many of the above attitudes are now taking hold in our society. They will have a significant impact on the firm and its activities. The successful leader is alert to changes in attitudes and will gear actions and policies to the new situation. Future sources of jobs, government policy, and personal values will all be heavily influenced by the coming era of entrepreneurship and sustainable development.[43]

Long-Range Perspective

Every business executive agrees that future business thinking must include planning that includes a long-range perspective. In a survey of CEOs, 89 percent said that they thought that American companies were too oriented toward the short term.[44] New business and new products depend on R & D, but cost-cutting and short-term thinking often results in too little time and money being devoted to it. In their study of effective business leaders, James Kouzes and Barry Posner summarize their findings:

> Traditional management teaching focuses our attention on the short term, the Wall Street analysts, the quarterly statements, and the annual report. Yet all the effective leaders we've seen have had a long-term, future orientation. They've looked beyond the horizon of the present.[45]

The survival and growth of American business demands an increased attention to long-term concerns. Pressure resulting from short-term financial interests makes long-term planning difficult but does not alter its importance for the future. This issue was also discussed in Chapters 1 and 8.

Business as a Servant of Society

The free market model views the business firm as independent, isolated, and competing with other firms to survive and grow. As long as a firm shows a profit, financial analysts and *Forbes* call it a success. The firm is thus judged successful whether it makes high-quality, energy-efficient necessities with less pollution (for example, Hewlett-Packard: computers; Merck: medications) or dangerous, trivial products (RJR Nabisco: cigarettes). The firm's "success"

---

[43] See Paul Hawken, *The Ecology of Commerce: A Declaration of Sustainability* (New York: Harper Collins, 1993). Excellent data for planning and for sustainable development are in Lester R. Brown, Christopher Flavin, and Hal Kane, *Vital Signs—1996: Trends that are Shaping Our Future* (New York: W. W. Norton, 1996), also Lester R. Brown, et al., *State of the World—1996* (New York: W. W. Norton, 1996).

[44] Ben J. Wattenberg, "Their Deepest Concerns," *Business Monthly* (January 1988): 27–36.

[45] James M. Kouzes and Barry Z. Posner, *The Leadership Challenge* (San Francisco: Jossey-Bass, 1995), p. 15.

might even be at the cost of unsafe working conditions (sweatshops in the United States and overseas) and the pollution of neighborhoods. The models and ideology of old-school economists and businesspeople urged profit making, production, and consumption. To many people even today, any increase in gross national product (GNP) indicates success. However, note that the manufacture of cigarettes and the hospital expenses for those with lung cancer or heart disease due to smoking add to GNP. A serious injury auto accident and the generation of pollution also leads to an increase in GNP—the cost of the work required to repair the damage to humans and the physical environment. What does it mean to consider unnecessary hospital bills, accidents, or pollution as success?

It is therefore apparent that these criteria of success are not complete. businesspeople and business firms are servants of society. Their purpose is to provide for the needs of citizens, to provide family incomes, and to make lives safer, healthier, and happier.[46]

An innovative and related perspective on leadership has been developed by the servant-leadership movement. The movement shows how a leader is most effective when the leader is able to elicit the best efforts from each member of the group. The leader empowers each worker to do their best and thus be a "servant of the group." This viewpoint is now popular and is aided by the writings of Robert Greenleaf, who had been an executive and management researcher at AT&T, and later at the Greenleaf Center.[47] The Center holds seminars and publishes books and a newsletter. Community volunteer work develops leadership skills and attitudes of service, and builds upon servant-leadership theory. Volunteer programs are now common among secondary and university students.

Conscientious corporate executives have long acted on the notion that the firm should serve society. CEOs have redirected their firms to ensure that social objectives are met.[48] Many new and developing industries that have high growth potential are geared to genuine human needs, such as robotics, solar power, office technology, energy conservation, cable TV, and genetic engineering.

A major criteria of the worth of any skill or work up to the time of the Industrial Revolution was the relative value of the good or service to society. As we have seen in earlier chapters, with the growth of industry and the division of

---

[46] For a plan to achieve a just economic order, see John Paul II, *Centesimus Annus* (*On the Hundreth Anniversary of Rerum Novarum*) (St. Paul: Media Books, 1991). For an assessment of the influence of the letter on business ethics, see S. Prakash Sethi and Paul Steidlmeier, "Religion's Moral Compass and a Just Economic Order: Reflections on Pope John Paul II's Encyclical *Centesimus Annus*," *Journal of Business Ethics* 12 (1993): 901–17.

[47] Robert K. Greenleaf, *The Servant as Leader* (Newton Center, Mass.: Greenleaf Center, 1970). Greenleaf also wrote *The Institution as Servant*, and several other essays. The newsletter is *The Servant Leader* and is published by the Greenleaf Center, now located at 1100 W. 42nd St., Suite 321, Indianapolis, Ind. 46208.

[48] See Business Roundtable, *Statement on Corporate Responsibility* (New York: Business Roundtable, 1981), pp. 1, 8, 12–14. The Business Roundtable is an organization composed of the CEOs of 170 large firms in the United States.

labor, an ideology developed that bestowed value on any work regardless of its outcome. The amount of financial return received became more important than what was accomplished. However, a growing number of men and women now question the value of some work no matter how well paid it may be. Some people will not work for a strip-mining firm, a hard-sell advertiser, a manufacturer of automatic weapons, or a junk bond firm with a shady reputation. On the other hand, individual transportation vehicles are important for society, and thus an auto worker's efforts take on value beyond the paycheck and benefits. Thus we reintroduce criteria that had been pushed aside. The value of a job or position is judged both by the contribution of the worker to a product or service *and* by the contribution the product or service makes to society.

Does it make any difference whether one is helping to produce electricity, tractors, cigarettes, throw-away bottles, nutritious foods, or Coca-Cola? All goods are not of equal value to society, and judgments can be made on the relative merits of these goods. In a small, primitive economy, these questions do not arise, since there are only enough resources and energy available to provide the necessities. Our society has many goods along with diminishing and more expensive resources, so questions about relative values are forced on us. It is necessary to determine which goods are more valuable to society. A principle might help in developing these criteria: Goods and services might be judged to be worthy insofar as they support life, families, neighborhoods, give freedom, and provide joy and happiness.

Technology and Innovation

Reliance on technology has been the principal means of increased business efficiency and productivity over the decades. In the future, technology will continue to be a generator of business "progress." However, what is seldom realized is that the sort of technology chosen reflects the values of the chooser, and, perhaps more importantly, that same technology has a profound influence on the values and life-styles of all who use it. The choice of electrical power generation grids and large manufacturing plants influence the hours that we work and the way we live, even outside of work. Asbestos insulation and chlorofluorocarbon aerosol propellants are examples of choices whose costs we later learned were greater than their benefits. The promotion of the automobile with a tax supported freeway system over rapid public transportation is a choice that reflects a "triumph of individualistic over communal values."[49]

In the future telecommuting, that is, doing work from a computer work station at home or at a substation, will increase flexibility and freedom, but will

---

[49] John M. Staudenmaier, S.J., "Technology," *A Companion to American Thought*, ed. Richard W. Fox and James T. Kloppenberg (Oxford: Blackwell, 1995). See also Staudenmaier's "Computerization" and "Technology" in *A New Dictionary of Catholic Thought*, ed. Judith A. Dwyer and Elizabeth L. Montgomery (Collegeville, Minn.: Michael Glazer, 1994).

decrease teamwork and the sense of community that is found at a central work site. Computers, and their ability to store data, also pose ethical questions of how this data is used. TRW holds credit records on each of us that can be obtained for a fee. Some of this record is personal and some of it is in error, yet people use this information to make decisions on hiring, making loans, and for many other purposes. The Internet with its extraordinary advantages for swift, global communications, also allows adolescent or less innocent hackers into the most sensitive and personal data that is available.

Emerging technologies will give firms and their employees access to data about individuals that many would prefer remain private. Are there any limits to using this information to sell products? It is essential that we use our moral and ethical skills in deciding how this information can be used.

The technology that one adopts and how one uses it depends upon the values of the one who chooses. The technological systems themselves are generally selected by elites—that is, leaders of business and government. Hence it is even more essential for justice and the stability of society to keep in mind the needs of *all people*, including those without a voice: the poor and disadvantaged.

A Nation Among Nations

In this world of increasing population, faster transportation and communication, and more choices in life-styles, people are becoming more interdependent. On the individual level, each of us depends on each other and requires interaction to develop as a person. For example, when people flee the problems of the city, their affluent children, without parks, libraries, and corner stores within walking distance, find little to do and become bored. Bus service is not readily available in most of these communities, leading to isolation for anyone who does not drive. Many children then use alcohol, drugs, drop out of school, and run away from home. On the international scene, a war or a revolution in the Middle East, Latin America, or Asia is brought to us by TV within hours. Starvation among refugees in Africa also comes into our living rooms, along with the fact that our use of dog food, lawn fertilizer, and red meat may play a role in depriving those Africans of life-giving grain. No nation can any longer assume that what is good for them is therefore good for all peoples.

Many problems that face the world cannot be solved by any single nation acting alone. Take, for example, acid rain, the greenhouse effect, malnutrition, toxic waste, dwindling finite resources, the threat of terrorism, and even a balance of trade deficit. Too often U.S. officials are insensitive to worldwide reaction to U.S. policies. This country's lone vote against the World Health Organization's code for marketing infant formula and its repudiation of the Law of the Sea Treaty lost the United States much international respect. Business managers know that nationalistic attitudes that might have served well a generation ago are no longer sufficient. They now operate in world markets and must be responsible citizens of more than one country. As the world gets smaller, all people depend more on each other. Yet, paradoxically, a new nationalism is afoot. Many nations are unwilling to limit their sovereignty or their self-interest. Hence we see individualism clash with the reality of interdependence.

Sociologist Robert Bellah thinks America's failure lies in its emphasis on the atomistic self and on rational self-interest and in its break with the basic understandings of the Founding Fathers. In early America, there was a strong social, collective emphasis: Citizens were together responsible for the state. Bellah demonstrates how this emphasis derived from the biblical covenant between God and God's people and from the gospel notion of a loving community based on membership in the common body of Christ. Bellah is convinced that the economic system of contemporary industrial America no longer is based on the early American view that economic interdependence is the foundation of the political order.[50] Perhaps our early ideals can be recaptured. The urgency and importance of the problems that face the peoples of the world demand that leaders work together for solutions.

Harmony with the Environment

In the course of meeting people's needs, business firms will operate with greater respect for the natural environment. Scarcity of resources, pollution, and undesirable by-products place constraints on the direction and pace of economic and business growth. These physical constraints will become more pressing, and citizens' expectations that firms will respect those constraints will become more pronounced. Hazardous industrial waste looms as an ever-increasing problem during the coming decade. The cost of its transportation and disposal, as well as the effort to determine liability, will increase; this, in turn, poses costly problems for business in the future.

Is it then surprising that West Africa is becoming the dumping ground for American and European toxic waste? As the costs of disposing of this waste go up, it becomes cheaper to pay Morocco, Congo, or Niger to bury it on their land. For example, in early 1988 American and European private waste disposal firms offered Guinea-Bissau $120 million annually to bury 15 million tons of toxic waste from tanneries and pharmaceutical companies. This is slightly less than the African country's gross national product of $150 million.[51] This practice has created a furor in West Africa, with many people in these nations demanding that the contracts be repudiated.

Local Control: Small Is Beautiful

The entrepreneur and the small firm has been respected, encouraged, and often preferred to the large firm in the United States. In a time when there are many

---

[50] Robert N. Bellah, *The Broken Covenant: American Civil Religion in Time of Trial* (New York: Seabury, 1975).

[51] "West Africa Attracts Toxic Waste Dumpers," *Cleveland Plain Dealer*, July 17, 1988, p. 19.

new and changing needs, the flexible entrepreneur has a very important role.[52] Small businesses are encouraged in the United States by lower tax rates. Large size is necessary, when economies of scale are required for the purpose of competing in large international markets, for example autos and computers. Nevertheless, encouraging entrepreneurs and keeping the government's role limited are traditional American values. Even in providing human services, such as education, health, and retirement, the independent sector can generally deliver better services at a lower cost than can the government. As long as these services are provided to the poor and disadvantaged, local control in both the public and private sectors has several advantages: (1) It gives people more control over their work and lives and thus provides increased personal involvement; (2) it more clearly locates responsibility; (3) it eliminates layers of organizational bureaucracy; (4) it is less costly; and (5) it is in the American tradition of self-reliance.

Spiritual Roots of the New Business Mission

Personal and national goals in the United States have been heavily influenced by religion, especially Christianity. We live on a foundation provided by the Judeo-Christian culture. Although our values and attitudes are currently not well anchored, the older roots continue to provide sustenance and life. As our society became more pluralistic (each person's values are deemed as good as any other person's) and atheistic (the existence of God is denied), our values became more free-floating. Although it soon became secular, the Protestant ethic stemmed from Christianity. Religious values have had a profound influence on business and economic life in the past, so it is appropriate to ask: will spiritual and religious ideals have an impact in the future?

There has always been a strong streak of moralism in American culture. Witness our condemnation of buying votes in government, the sexual infidelities of political leaders, and the selfish activities of corporate raiders like Ivan Boesky, Charles Hurwitz, and Sir James Goldsmith. This sort of reaction is not new; our history is replete with morally rooted reaction to issues. In the nineteenth century, the powerful antislavery (abolition) and antitrust (muckraking) movements were morally motivated and received their inspiration from the Gospels.

The civil rights movement in the United States was led by Martin Luther King, Jr., a Baptist minister. He preached "love for the oppressor" and espoused nonviolent techniques to gain social justice for blacks. The record shows how effective the movement and his leadership were. The role of the churches in political life is increasing, and polls indicate that most people want that. Many of the most committed social activists are inspired by the Gospels. Ralph Nader comes from a religious family with high ideals, and Common Cause appeals to

---

[52] Rosabeth Moss Kanter, *World Class: Thriving Locally in the Global Economy* (New York: Simon & Schuster, 1995), p. 26.

the generosity and moral qualities of Americans. Mahatma Gandhi was an inspiration to many of these people, and he was inspired by the life of Christ. Moreover, his nonviolent approach to gaining India's independence from England was successful.

In Poland and other Eastern European countries, religious convictions moved people to overthrow dictatorships. Many Catholic priests and sisters have defended the interests of the poor, and as a result have been murdered in Guatemala, El Salvador, Brazil, Bolivia, Chile, and other Latin American countries.[53] Their inspiration comes from Jesus, his love for the poor, and his commitment to bring justice to those at the bottom of the socioeconomic ladder (Matt. 5:3; Luke 6:20). The goal of these Gospel-inspired leaders is freedom. They want the poor, ordinary citizen to have the freedom to own land, to vote, and to be a self-respecting citizen, as well as the freedom to work and earn a fair day's pay. They want self-determination for peoples around the world. Thus they often find themselves in opposition to a global business firm or a military government. Hindu and Muslim fundamentalist groups are having a profound influence in Asia, Africa, and the Middle East. They reject the Western values of violence and free sex that they see on our films and exported TV. Westerners, who have been influenced by the Enlightenment, have difficulty in understanding the appeal of the fundamentalists.

It is no accident that 11 of the *100 Best Companies to Work for in America*[54] are located in two areas of the United States that are heavily influenced by religious values. The 100 firms are rated on: pay and benefits, opportunities, pride in work, job security, openness and fairness, and camaraderie and friendliness. Minneapolis-St. Paul is home to 3M, Dayton Hudson, General Mills, H.B. Fuller, and many other firms with outstanding records in social responsibility. The area is strongly Lutheran and Catholic and has long been a leader in the United States with regard to firms having a strong sense of social responsibility. Western Michigan is home to Donnelly, Herman Miller, Kellogg, Steelcase, and others and is much influenced by the Calvinist Dutch Reformed Church.

Religion views the manager or owner as a steward. Thus wealth and power constitute a trust that is held for others. Based on the understanding that the world and all its goods come from and ultimately belong to God, the individual businessperson holds all this in stewardship—in trust for others.[55] Numerous organizations and prayer groups now meet to enable businesspeople

---

[53] "Roman Catholic Priest Has Struggle Changing Lives in Rural Brazil: Father Ricardo Resende Faces Violence, Makes Enemies in Fight to Aid Landless," *Wall Street Journal*, August 28, 1986, pp. 1, 16. For additional examples, see Penny Lernoux, *Cry of the People* (New York: Penguin, 1980); Martin Lange and Reinhold Iblacker, *Witness of Hope: The Persecution of Christians in Latin America* (Maryknoll, N.Y.: Orbis, 1981).

[54] Robert Levering and Milton Moskowitz (New York: Penguin, 1994).

[55] See Oliver F. Williams, C.S.C., "Religion: The Spirit or Enemy of Capitalism," *Business Horizons* (November–December, 1983): 6–13; also Williams's, "Who Cast the First Stone?" *Harvard Business Review* (September–October 1984): 151–60.

to better understand: faith, family, and firm. Paradoxically, it is "old-fashioned" religion that has traditionally urged concern for others, especially poor people in other nations and future generations.

Concern for Others

People who are loved develop into more mature persons, are less turned in on themselves, and more concerned about others. Self-centeredness and insularity are vices of the immature, as we saw in Chapter 2. Love for others is a basic human virtue. Expressing such love is a matter of giving—often without hope of return. Altruistic love is possible for anyone, although it is more readily achieved by those who have been loved. It is essential for the development of persons, families, and society, yet it is sometimes difficult. Speaking of this sort of love, economist Kenneth Boulding says,

> It always builds up, it never tears down, and it does not merely establish islands of order in a society at the cost of disorder elsewhere. It is hard for us, however, to learn to love, and the teaching of love is something at which we are still very inept.[56]

Much of the energy of the poor is spent on obtaining the necessities of life. Once a person's basic needs are reasonably satisfied, that person is more inclined to consider the needs of others in society. Thus, material security is often a foundation for loving and giving. Having food and shelter enables people to reach beyond themselves and their own problems to other human beings and to realize the interdependence of people and institutions.

Concern for others is an important part of the organizational climate at Hewlett-Packard and IBM. The Ford worker-involvement program encourages all Ford employees to focus on quality. The Parts and Services Division has called itself "the loving and caring division of Ford." Aetna, L.L. Bean, Dow, Steelcase, and Johnson & Johnson have all established model programs to better the health of their employees. With less illness and injury, it also saves money for the firm.[57]

New Measures of Success

A goal of most people is to obtain happiness. If, however, happiness is measured by more compensation or more wealth, one can never achieve happiness. "People are prosperous as long as they can say, 'We have enough.' "[58] In a parallel fashion, to be successful a business firm must be efficient and profitable. However, corporate leaders no longer claim that profit maximization is the only goal of

---

[56] Kenneth E. Boulding, *The Meaning of the Twentieth Century* (New York: Harper & Row, 1964), p. 146. The importance of the manager's love and caring was reinforced in the 1995 study by Kouzes and Posner, *The Leadership Challenge, op. cit.*

[57] Shawn Tully, "America's Healthiest Companies," *Fortune*, June 12, 1995, pp. 98–106.

[58] Richard C. Haas, *We All Have a Share* (Chicago: ACTA Publications, 1995), p. 32.

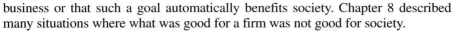

business or that such a goal automatically benefits society. Chapter 8 described many situations where what was good for a firm was not good for society.

New measures of success for business firms arise when we realize that such firms operate to benefit people.[59] They are essentially instruments of service to people—all kinds of people. Those who benefit include customers and shareholders but also employees, suppliers, and members of the local community. Benefits to one constituency are generally not at the expense of another group; business is not a zero-sum game. When J&J acts out its statement that its first obligation is to customers and its last to shareholders, the shareholders do better than they would otherwise.

Just as a financial audit sketches a firm's financial performance, a social audit outlines the impact of the firm's operations on its other constituents. Criteria for judging social performance are crucial if we are adequately to decide the degree of success achieved by a firm.[60]

Business firms are aware of the need for corporate social performance measures. The Business Roundtable, composed of the CEOs of the largest U.S. firms, described the importance of social goals and how to structure a firm so that these social goals are achieved.[61] These CEOs also sponsored a handbook that aids firms in the achievement of their social goals.[62] Government policy, too, both national and international, must be assessed using the same criteria: what is better for all people?

The new measures of success focus on the benefits that accrue to people— all the stakeholders of the firm. This focus constitutes a fundamental change in perspective for corporate managers. Because achievement of social goals is increasingly among the criteria for measuring the success of business managers, social goals have an impact on the values and perspective of managers.

Vision and Hope

The problems that we face—trade and budget deficits, pollution, refugees, unjust governments, lack of jobs, broken families—are so immense that many find it easier to deny them. These problems are often the result of trying to achieve other goods or, in some cases, of callously disregarding the welfare of people. We then must ask: are we motivated to seek a solution when the solution has a cost to me? And are we able to alter our actions to make more ethical tradeoffs? Can we build the values and institutions necessary for justice and peace throughout the world?

---

[59] See the alternate definition of productivity in Haas, *We all Have a Share, op cit.,* p. 12.

[60] Cetron, Rocha, and Luckins, "Into the 21st Century," p. 40.

[61] Business Roundtable, *Statement on Corporate Responsibility*; see also the earlier Roundtable statement, *The Role and Composition of the Board of Directors of the Large Publicly Held Corporation* (New York: Business Roundtable, 1978).

[62] Francis W. Steckmest, ed., *Corporate Performance: The Key to Public Trust* (New York: McGraw-Hill, 1982).

Vision and hope have always been American virtues. Ever since the days of the frontier, we have never been defeatists or fatalists. Nevertheless, it would be foolish to underestimate the enormous problems before us. Many people today are concerned mainly with their own personal lives and careers and care little about what they can do to help solve others' problems. Yet, as we have seen, a single individual or a small group of talented, generous people can have a profound impact on the lives of others and on the world as a whole.

Summary and Conclusions

The challenge of the future is to provide products, services, jobs, and a reasonable standard of living for all people, and yet not needlessly exploit finite natural resources or leave the world more polluted than we found it. Business firms have achieved unprecedented efficiency, productivity, and growth. Nevertheless, it is clear that the free market is not able to provide such goods as clean air and water, safe products, or even fair competition. A firm that provides jobs and goods sometimes also destroys natural beauty and harms people's health. Its operations may be demeaning or dangerous, use nonrenewable resources, or cause pollution.

Generating cooperation and providing benefits to people are appropriate goals for business and government. Pressure from special interest groups, coupled with apathy and lack of clear goals, has pushed American society into many unfruitful, expensive, and frustrating traps. Note, for example, defective and dangerous products, collapsing railroads and urban public transportation systems, disappearing farmlands, defective nuclear power plants, and expensive and wasteful defense systems. Exacerbating the problem is the fact that traditional business ideology justifies and rewards selfishness. More humane personal values and an acknowledgment of public goals helps to avoid these costly blunders. Most firms forecast future values so that they can initiate product planning, employee participation, and advertising to meet new needs.

Future business values require business efficiency and innovativeness. Moreover, citizens now demand that business decisions contribute to the overall goals of society. A business firm is not merely a *private* enterprise; its role is to serve the needs of society. If business firms do not choose to act responsibly, legislation or tax incentives will be required to encourage such behavior.

Americans want greater independence, even in the face of the dehumanizing factors of modern life. In spite of large corporations and big government, individuals still prefer autonomy, personal responsibility, and the ability to share decisions. Businesses will be structured to encourage such self-reliance and responsibility.

Religion has in the past, and will in the future, provide a foundation for business values. Religious values run counter to self-interest and what has come to be known as the consumer ethic. The Protestant ethic demanded moderation, planning, and self-sacrifice. Budget deficits, pollution, anxiety, crime, and substance abuse demonstrate the failure of current values. Americans now may be ready for some sacrifice for the sake of a larger purpose. Most would sacrifice a vacation in Cancún or a third automobile if it meant that they would have a more satisfying job, a happier life, and better relationships, and that their grand-children would not inherit a world ravaged by deforestation and cancer-causing chemicals. Religion directs people's attention beyond themselves. As we regain this perspective, we will share expertise and resources with poorer peoples of the world so that they, too, may enjoy some of the humane fruits of business. Religion urges self-discipline and generosity toward neighbors based on a rev-erence for God and a loving concern for others.

Clarifying and internalizing values and goals is necessary for any person as he or she grows to maturity. Especially during times of rapid change, inter-nalized values provide a firm foundation on which to build a stable, challeng-ing, and satisfying life. Furthermore, personal values and personal needs will be the building blocks of future business goals and policies. The process of articu-lating society's values and goals requires leadership. The problems are pressing and complex. Nevertheless, business, religious, government and educational leaders, as well as all citizens, have the opportunity to inspire confidence, and help set goals and meet the challenges of tomorrow.

Discussion Questions

1. What are the issues on which there is general agreement between business managers and business critics? What is the major issue on which they disagree?
2. Outline the current major domestic and international evidence on the success of free markets.
3. What does it mean to say that free markets are aristocratic? Do you think this is true? Why or why not?
4. What are the strengths and weaknesses of a democratic society in meeting new social needs (e.g., pollution control or energy conservation)?
5. How do special interests undermine the effective operation of democracy?
6. What are the limitations of personal freedom?
7. What are some of the problems we have created for managers in the coming decades?
8. How would you describe "visionary companies"?
9. What role has religion had in the formation of values? What influence are spiri-tual values now having on business values?
10. Outline the techniques of future forecasting.
11. Which of the "future business values" listed in Table 9–1 do you think is likely to become prevalent? If they do become operative, what significance would each have for your organization?
12. If these business values did become prevalent, would it increase or decrease the quality of life? Explain.
13. Is an increase in gross national product a mark of success for an economy? Why or why not?

14. Would people be better off if they could meet their needs with less consumption, less pollution, and less use of finite resources?

15. Americans need to save more to provide for investment and to reduce foreign borrowing. How much do you save of your take-home pay? How much does your family save? Why?

16. What is servant leadership? Does it make sense to you? Explain.

17. If we are becoming increasingly interdependent, what does this mean for a firm? For you as a citizen?

18. Upon what basic values might it be possible to build a public policy consensus for the future? Will spiritual values have a role in articulating this consensus?

America's Most Admired Corporations

A survey of executives and financial analysts to determine "America's most admired corporations" ranked Merck as number one and Philip Morris and RJR Nabisco among the top ten.[63] Criteria included quality of management, quality of products or services, financial soundness, and community and environmental responsibility. Manville was rated among the "least admired" because of its involvement with asbestos. The core business of both RJR Nabisco and Philip Morris is cigarettes. (1) Do you agree with ranking Merck as number one? (2) Do you agree with the rating of Manville? Of Philip Morris and RJR Nabisco? Explain why in each case.

Business Decisions and Religion

Briggs & Stratton, a manufacturer of small engines located in Milwaukee, sued a national weekly newspaper, *The National Catholic Reporter*, for $30 million for libel and invasion of privacy. Executives at Briggs & Stratton decided to move 2,000 unionized manufacturing jobs from Milwaukee to the nonunionized

---

[63] Ellen Schultz, "America's Most Admired Corporations," *Fortune*, January 18, 1988, pp. 32–39.

south in order to save labor costs. The *National Catholic Reporter* criticized the decision and the way it was made in a December 1994 front-page story, "Adios, American Dream." The story told the likely effect of the move on Briggs employees. In an editorial the *Reporter* said that the major decision makers President John Shiely, V.P. George Thompson, and labor lawyer Tom Krakowski are among "Catholics educated in Catholic institutions," and they lived "in either denial or moral blindness" when they took their job-reduction actions. Each of the three officers was educated in Catholic universities.

In the lawsuit filed 18 months later, the firm and the three executives claim that the newspaper defamed the officers and invaded their privacy by revealing their religion. Moreover, George Thompson said that "My religious upbringing" along with that of the other two officers, "has absolutely nothing to do with the basic economic decisions" made by the company.

1. Is it appropriate for a religious journal to critique business decisions from the standpoint of religious values?
2. Do you agree with Thompson's separation of religion and business decisions? Why or why not?

A P P E N D I X

Caux Round Table
Principles for Business[*]

These principles are rooted in two basic ethical ideals: *kyosei* and human dignity.

The Japanese concept of kyosei means living and working together for the common good—enabling cooperation and mutual prosperity to coexist with healthy and fair competition. "Human dignity" refers to the sacredness or value of each person as an end, not simply as a means to the fulfillment of other's purposes or even majority prescription.

The General Principles in Section 2 seek to clarify the spirit of kyosei and "human dignity," while the specific Stakeholder Principles in Section 3 are concerned with their practical application.

SECTION 1.   PREAMBLE

The mobility of employment, capital, products, and technology is making business increasingly global in its transactions and its effects.

Laws and market forces are necessary but insufficient guides for conduct.

Responsibility for the policies and actions of business and respect for the dignity and interests of its stakekholders are fundamental.

Shared values, including a commitment to shared prosperity, are as important for a global community as for communities of smaller scale.

For these reasons, and because business can be a powerful agent of positive social change, we offer the following principles as a foundation for dialogue and action by business leaders in search of business responsibility. In so doing, we affirm the necessity for moral values in business decision making. Without them, stable business relationships and a sustainable world community are impossible.

---

* Quoted with permission.

SECTION 2.   GENERAL PRINCIPLES

PRINCIPLE 1.   The Responsibilities of Businesses: Beyond Shareholders Toward Stakeholders

The value of a business to society is the wealth and employment it creates and the marketable products and services it provides to consumers at a reasonable price commensurate with quality. To create such value, a business must maintain its own economic health and viability, but survival is not a sufficient goal.

Businesses have a role to play in improving the lives of all their customers, employees, and shareholders by sharing with them the wealth they have created. Suppliers and competitors as well should expect businesses to honor their obligations in a spirit of honesty and fairness. As responsible citizens of the local, national, regional, and global communities in which they operate, businesses share a part in shaping the future of those communities.

PRINCIPLE 2.   The Economic and Social Impact of Business: Toward Innovation, Justice and World Community

Businesses established in foreign countries to develop, produce or sell should also contribute to the social advancement of those countries by creating productive employment and helping to raise the purchasing power of their citizens. Businesses also should contribute to human rights, education, welfare, and vitalization of the countries in which they operate.

Businesses should contribute to economic and social development not only in the countries in which they operate, but also in the world community at large, through effective and prudent use of resources, free and fair competition and emphasis upon innovation in technology, production methods, marketing, and communications.

PRINCIPLE 3.   Business Behavior: Beyond the Letter of Law Toward a Spirit of Trust

While accepting the legitimacy of trade secrets, businesses should recognize that sincerity, candor, truthfulness, the keeping of promises, and transparency contribute not only to their own credibility and stability but also to the smoothness and efficiency of business transactions, particularly on the international level.

PRINCIPLE 4.   Respect for the Rules

To avoid trade frictions and to promote freer trade, equal conditions for competition, and fair and equitable treatment for all participants, businesses should respect international and domestic rules. In addition, they should recognize that some behavior, although legal, may still have adverse consequences.

PRINCIPLE 5.   Support for Multilateral Trade

Businesses should support the multilateral trade systems of the GATT/World Trade Organization and similar international agreements. They should cooperate in efforts to promote the progressive and judicious liberalization of trade, and to relax those domestic measures that unreasonably hinder global commerce, while giving due respect to national policy objectives.

PRINCIPLE 6.   Respect for the Environment

A business should protect and, where possible, improve the environment, promote sustainable development, and prevent the wasteful use of natural resources.

PRINCIPLE 7.   Avoidance of Illicit Operations

A business should not participate in or condone bribery, money laundering, or other corrupt practices: indeed, it should seek cooperation with others to eliminate them. It should not trade in arms or other materials used for terrorist activities, drug traffic, or other organized crime.

SECTION 3.   STAKEHOLDER PRINCIPLES

Customers

We believe in treating all customers with dignity, irrespective of whether they purchase our products and services directly from us or otherwise acquire them in the market. We therefore have a responsibility to:

+ provide our customers with the highest quality products and services consistent with their requirements;
+ treat our customers fairly in all aspects of our business transactions including a high level of service and remedies for their dissatisfaction;
+ make every effort to ensure that the health and safety of our customers, as well as the quality of their environment, will be sustained or enhanced by our products and services;
+ assure respect for human dignity in products offered, marketing, and advertising; and
+ respect the integrity of the culture of our customers.

Employees

We believe in the dignity of every employee and in taking employee interests seriously. We therefore have a responsibility to:

+ provide jobs and compensation that improve workers' living conditions;
+ provide working conditions that respect each employee's health and dignity;
+ be honest in communications with employees and open in sharing information, limited only by legal and competitive restraints;
+ listen to and, where possible, act on employee suggestions, ideas, requests, and complaints;
+ engage in good faith negotiations when conflict arises;
+ avoid discriminatory practices and guarantee equal treatment and opportunity in areas such as gender, age, race, and religion;
+ promote in the business itself the employment of differently abled people in places of work where they can be genuinely useful;
+ protect employees from avoidable injury and illness in the workplace;
+ encourage and assist employees in developing relevant and transferable skills and knowledge; and
+ be sensitive to serious unemployment problems frequently associated with business decisions and work with governments, employee groups, other agencies and each other in addressing these dislocations.

Owners/Investors

We believe in honoring the trust our investors place in us. We therefore have a responsibility to:

+ apply professional and diligent management in order to secure a fair and competitive return on our owners' investment;
+ disclose relevant information to owners/investors subject only to legal requirements and competitive constraints;
+ conserve, protect, and increase the owners/investors' assets; and
+ respect owners/investors' requests, suggestions, complaints, and formal resolutions.

Suppliers

Our relationship with suppliers and subcontractors must be based on mutual respect. We therefore have a responsibility to:

+ seek fairness and truthfulness in all of our activities, including pricing, licensing, and rights to sell;
+ ensure that our business activities are free from coercion and unnecessary litigation;
+ foster long-term stability in the supplier relationship in return for value, quality, competitiveness, and reliability;
+ share information with suppliers and integrate them into our planning processes;
+ pay suppliers on time and in accordance with agreed terms of trade;
+ seek, encourage, and prefer suppliers and subcontractors whose employment practices respect human dignity.

Competitors

We believe that fair economic competition is one of the basic requirements for increasing the wealth of nations and, ultimately, for making possible the just distribution of goods and services. We therefore have a responsibility to:

+ foster open markets for trade and investment;
+ promote competitive behavior that is socially and environmentally beneficial and demonstrates mutual respect among competitors;
+ refrain from either seeking or participating in questionable payments or favors to secure competitive advantages;
+ respect both tangible and intellectual property rights; and
+ refuse to acquire commercial information by dishonest or unethical means, such as industrial espionage.

Communities

We believe that as global corporate citizens, we can contribute to such forces of reform and human rights as are at work in the communities in which we operate. We therefore have a responsibility in those communities to:

+ respect human rights and democratic institutions, and promote them wherever practicable;
+ recognize government's legitimate obligation to the society at large and support public policies and practices that promote human development through harmonious relations between business and other segments of society;
+ collaborate with those forces in the community dedicated to raising standards of health, education, workplace safety, and economic well-being;
+ promote and stimulate sustainable development and play a leading role in preserving and enhancing the physical environment and conserving the earth's resources;
+ support peace, security, diversity, and social integration;
+ respect the integrity of local cultures; and
+ be a good corporate citizen through charitable donations, educational and cultural contributions and employee participation in community and civic affairs.

Support for Caux (Switzerland) *Principles for Business* from International Association of Jesuit Business Schools

The International Association of Jesuit Business Schools, at both its 1993 meeting in Barcelona, Spain and 1994 meeting in Recife, Brazil, decided to support a global code of business conduct. At its 1995 meeting in Yogyakarta, Indonesia, the group elected to present to member schools, their alumni, and their local business leaders the Caux *Principles for Business* for consideration.

A Statement of Support[*]

The International Association of Jesuit Business Schools (IAJBS) welcomes this opportunity to provide a statement of support, in the form of a rationale reflective of the values of our own Jesuit institutions, for the *Principles for Business* issued by the Caux Round Table in 1994. The Caux Principles are intended to serve as a framework within which individual organizations operating in foreign countries can draft their own freely-chosen codes of business conduct.

The Caux Round Table (CRT) is an international group of business leaders formed in 1986. Participants from Japan, Western Europe, and the United States meet at regular intervals in Caux, Switzerland for discussions aimed at reduction of international trade tensions and fostering development of an improved international business climate. The Caux Principles, appended to this statement, are, in our judgment, worthy of favorable and widespread consideration, especially in Jesuit-sponsored programs of education for business. We take this position for the following reasons:

1. Collaborative economic activity is not only compatible with, but essential to the protection of individual human dignity in economic affairs. Responsible cooperation is preferable to destructive competition in both the workplace and the marketplace, domestic and international.
2. Respect for human dignity is an inviolable principle of socially responsible business activity.
3. Communitarian concerns are characteristic of the socially responsible person or organization in business.
4. A "stakeholder" outlook—i.e., a point of view with a focus wider than shareholders or owner interests—is appropriate for any management at any time, if management is to be at all times ethical and socially responsible in business decision making. The Caux Principles explicitly and individually address the interests of customers, employees, suppliers, owners/investors, competitors, and communities (understood in sufficiently broad terms to include the physical environment and the local culture). All of these are "stakeholders" in the organizations that managers manage.
5. Other Caux principles direct managerial attention to an organization's responsibility to (a) advance social development and protect human rights in foreign lands where the organization produces or markets its products and services; (b) go beyond the letter of the law to what is ethically required, although not legally prescribed; (c) respect both international and domestic rules; (d) support multilateral trade; (e) protect and improve the environment; (f) avoid all corrupt practices while refusing to trade in armaments or other materials that assist terrorism, drug traffic, or organized crime.

---

[*] By William J. Byron, S.J., Rector, Georgetown University, former President, Catholic University of America.

Underlying these principles is an understanding of and commitment to the common good.

IAJBS welcomes the Caux initiative. We support the Caux Principles because they succeed in extending to the context of international trade the following general principles to which we, as business educators in the Jesuit tradition, freely subscribe: (1) the principle of human dignity; (2) the principle of participation and association; (3) the principle of subsidiarity; (4) the principle of preference for the poor (expressed, in the present instance, by means of trade-based economic development in less developed areas of the world).

The principle of human dignity is the bedrock of all the principles we promote under the twin rubric of business ethics and social responsibility. Human dignity is the natural endowment of every human person. But human dignity does not exist in a disembodied, abstract state. It requires association and participation with others in many ways, including trade. It also requires protection by the principle of subsidiarity, which assigns to a higher level of organization only those tasks that cannot be reasonably and effectively met at lower levels. It is in the spirit of subsidiarity that the Caux Principles are offered as a framework within which any economic participant in international trade can compose and adopt its own code of conduct.

Origin of Caux *Principles for Business*

The Caux Round Table is composed of business executives from Europe, Japan and the United States. Several years ago they recognized the need for some common understandings to provide the basis for the conduct of global business. For two years they worked on the formation of global principles of business conduct with other executives, especially with a group in Minneapolis, Minnesota, U.S.A, which had already developed a set of principles of conduct for global business. By 1994 they together developed the Caux *Principles for Business* to outline conduct for international business. The Caux *Principles* have so far been translated into seven languages.

Executives from the following firms serve or have served on the Steering Committee of the Caux Round Table: Siemens, Chase Manhattan Bank, ABC Telecommunications, Canon, Matsushita, Ambrosetti Group, Timken, Prudential, 3M, Dana, Nissan, Ciba Geigy, Philips Electronics, Sumitomo, and others. The Caux Round Table plans a dialogue with businesspeople from other countries and other continents in regard to the Caux *Principles for Business*.

For copies of the Caux Round Table *Principles for Business* or further information, you may contact the **Caux Round Table Secretariat:**

Europe:
Amaliastraat 10
2514 JC The Hague
The Netherlands
  Phone   (070) 360-5260
  Fax   (070) 361-7209

Japan:
Vega House, Mitake Bldg. 102
5 - 49 - 2 Sendagi, Bunkyo-ku
Tokyo 113
Japan
  Phone   (03) 3821-3737
  Fax   (03) 3821-6479

The United States:
4626 France Avenue South
Minneapolis, Minnesota 55410
  Phone   (612) 924-9234
  Fax   (612) 924-0068

•   •   •

Questions on the Caux *Principles for Business*:

1. Do you think that a code of international ethics would be good for business?
2. Would a code of global ethics also benefit individual workers, families, and people in general?
3. Would such a code benefit developing countries? Why?
4. The Caux *Principles for Business* were developed by business executives from Europe, Japan, and the United States. What do you think of these principles?
5. What advantage would there be if firms used the Caux *Principles* as the basis for their own firm's code of ethics?
6. How would you use the Caux *Principles* in designing a code of conduct for your firm?
7. Is there any way in which you would like to qualify or change any of the principles for the purposes of your firm?
8. Would you like to support the promulgation and implementation of the *Principles*?

Index

7/21/03